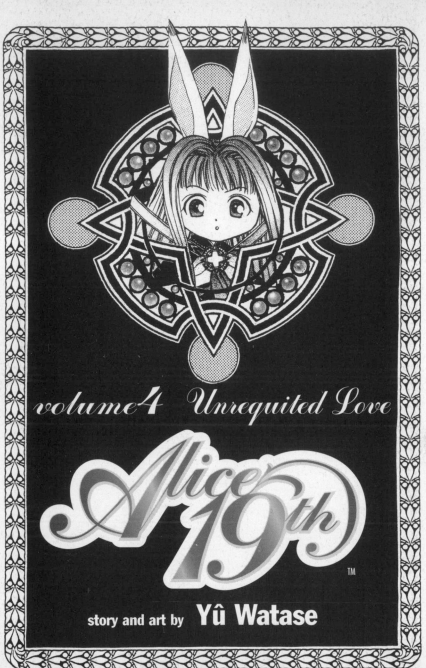

volume 4 Unrequited Love

Alice 19th

story and art by Yû Watase

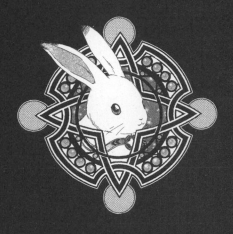

Story thus far

Kyô and Alice have come face to face with the evil spirit of Mara, and Frey realizes that they are well on their way to becoming true Lotis Masters.

Although Mayura is finally safe and sound, returning from the dark world of Mara through the heroism of Alice, Kyô, Nyozeka and Frey, things aren't returning back to normal. When Alice confesses her true feelings about Kyô to her sister, things go terribly wrong. Mayura is still clouded by the powers of the Mara and has placed a Mudoru curse upon Kyô. The curse is deadly, burning a symbol for hatred into Kyô's body, if Kyô were to ever hear the word "love" from anyone other than Mayura the curse would activate and the flames of hatred would surely consume him. Alice will never be able to tell Kyô that she is in love with him, even though she has finally found the courage; if she does, Kyô's life would be in serious danger and he could die.

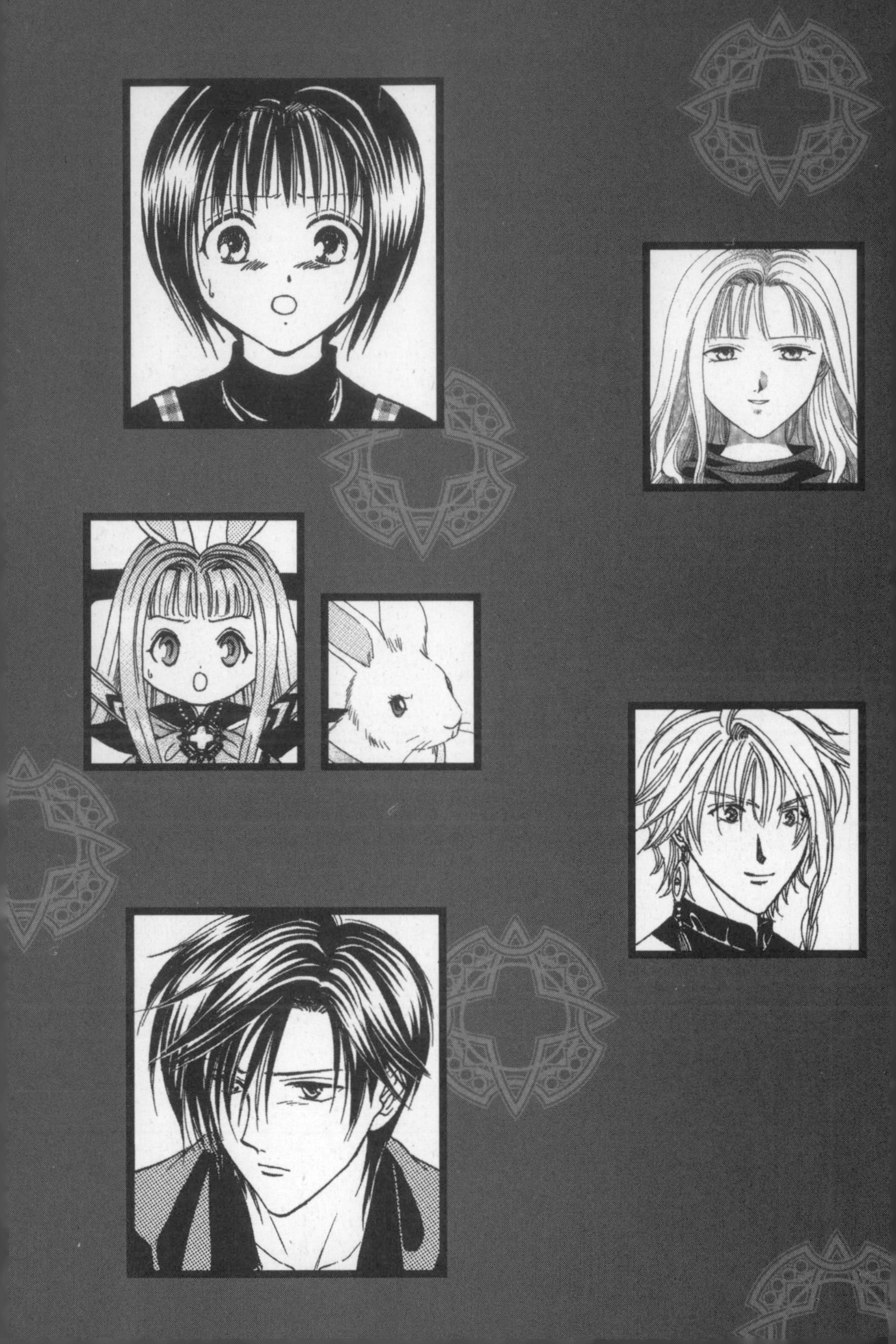

CHAPTER 4 ONE-SIDED LOVE

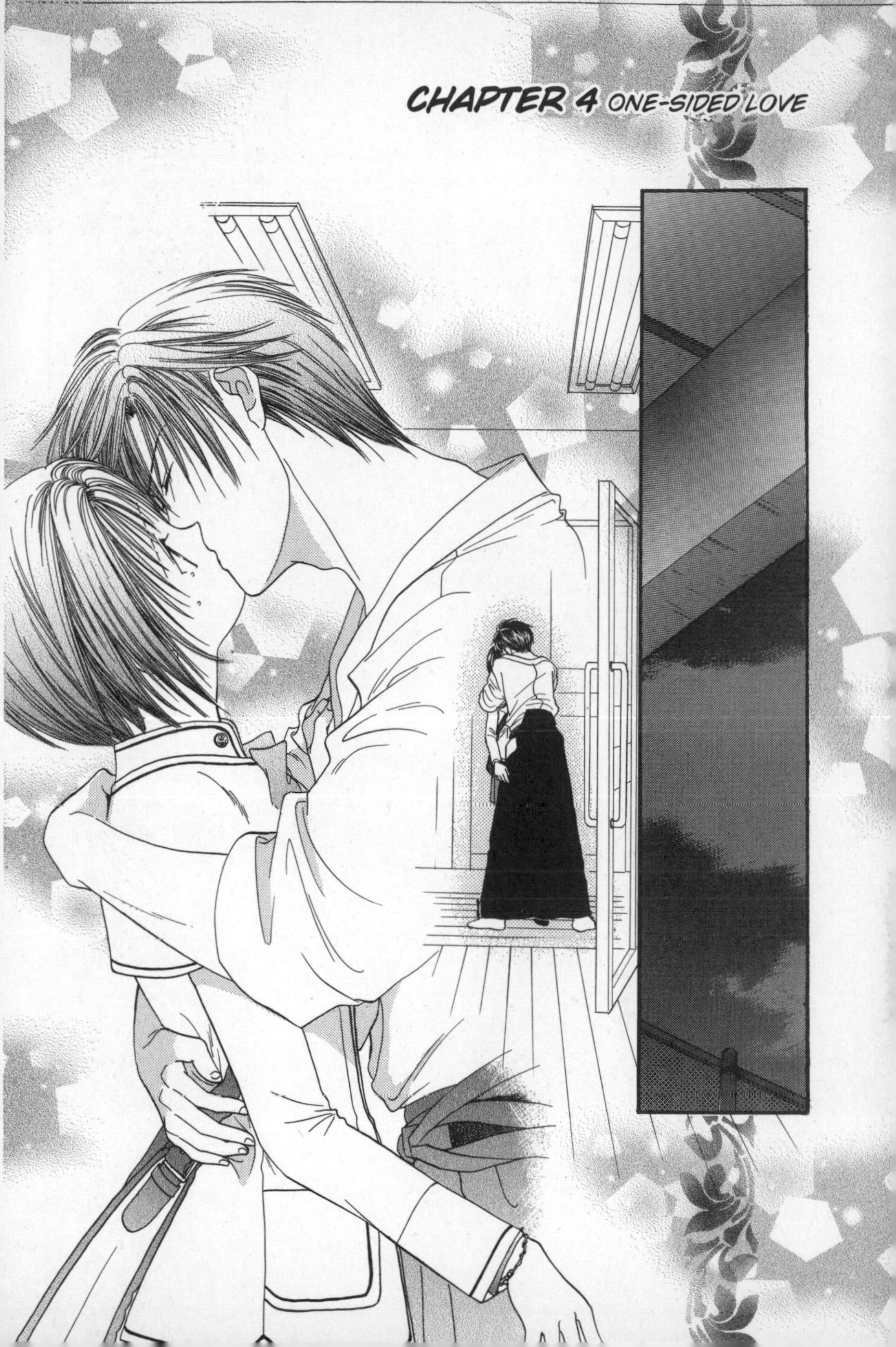

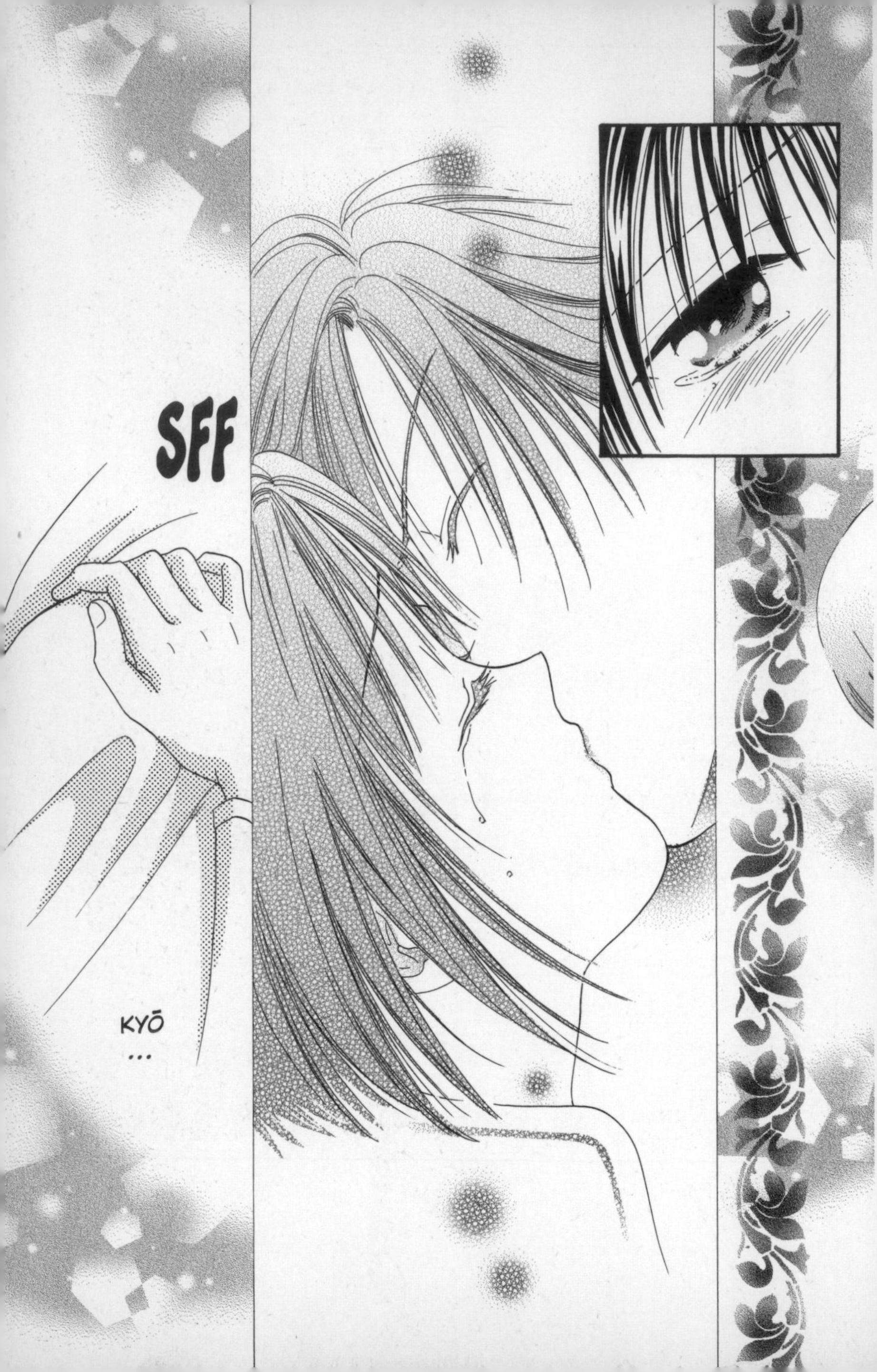
SFF
KYŌ
...

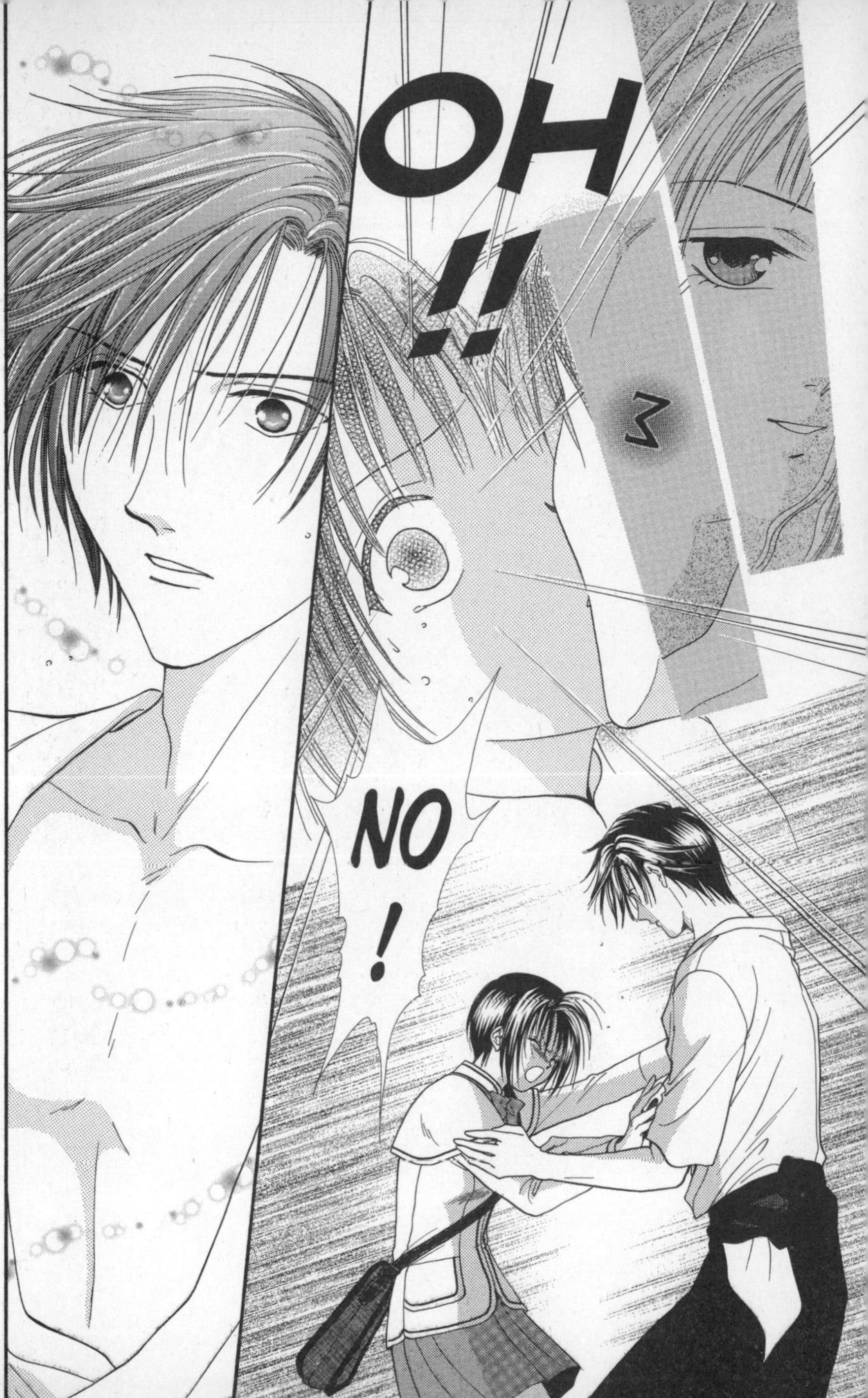
OH!!
NO!

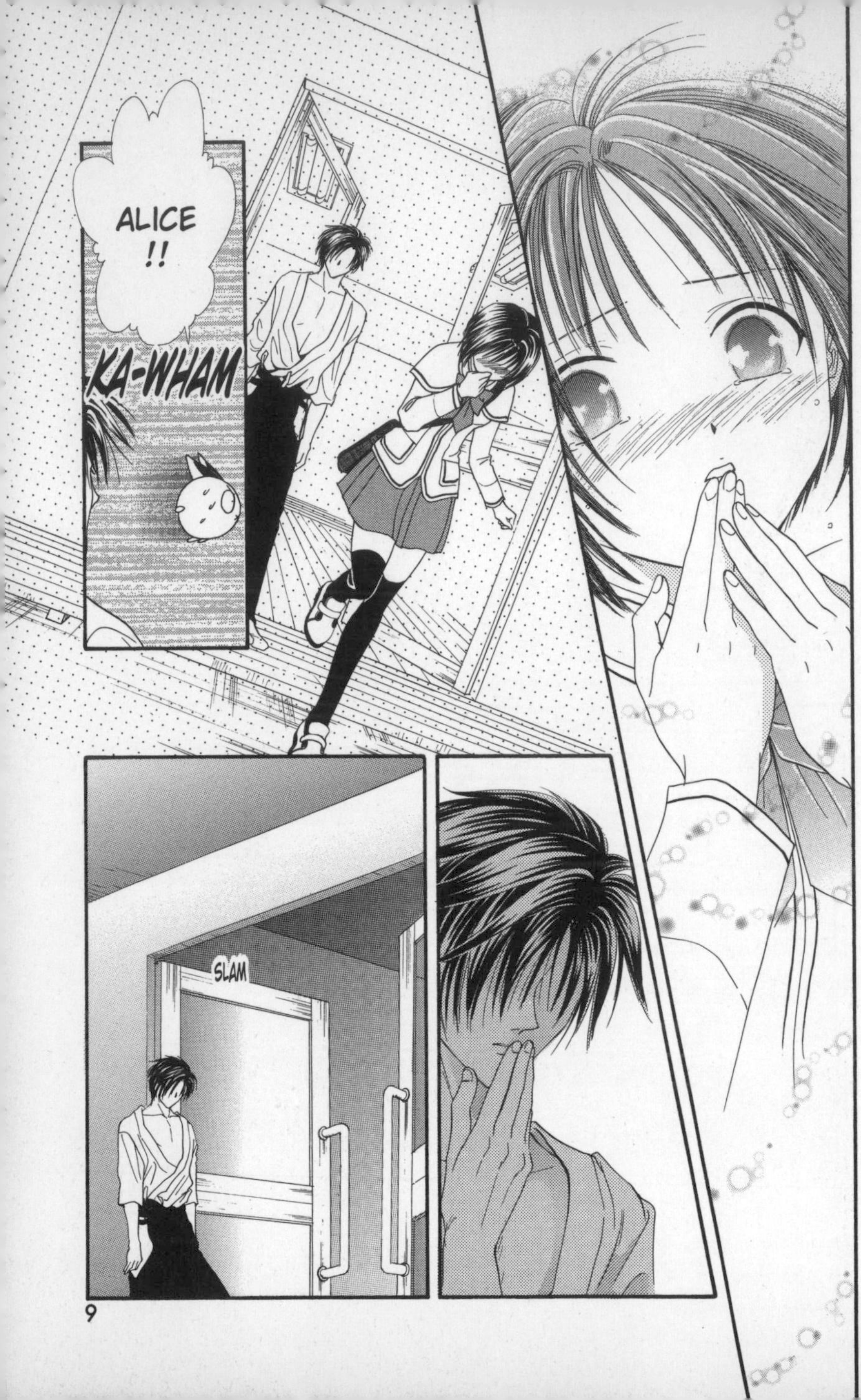
ALICE !!
KA-WHAM
SLAM

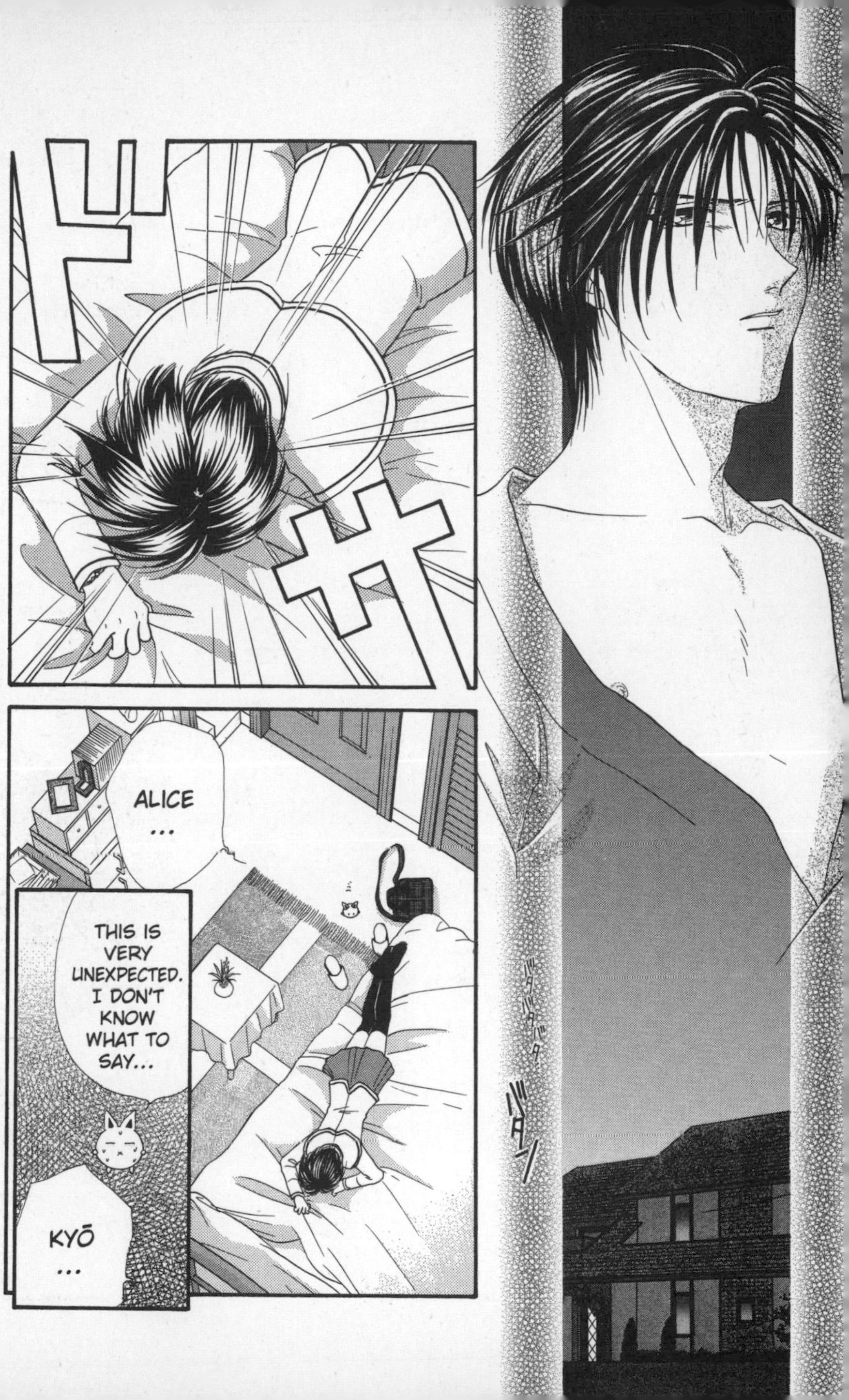

バタバタバタ
バタン
ドサ
ALICE ...
THIS IS VERY UNEXPECTED. I DON'T KNOW WHAT TO SAY...
KYŌ ...

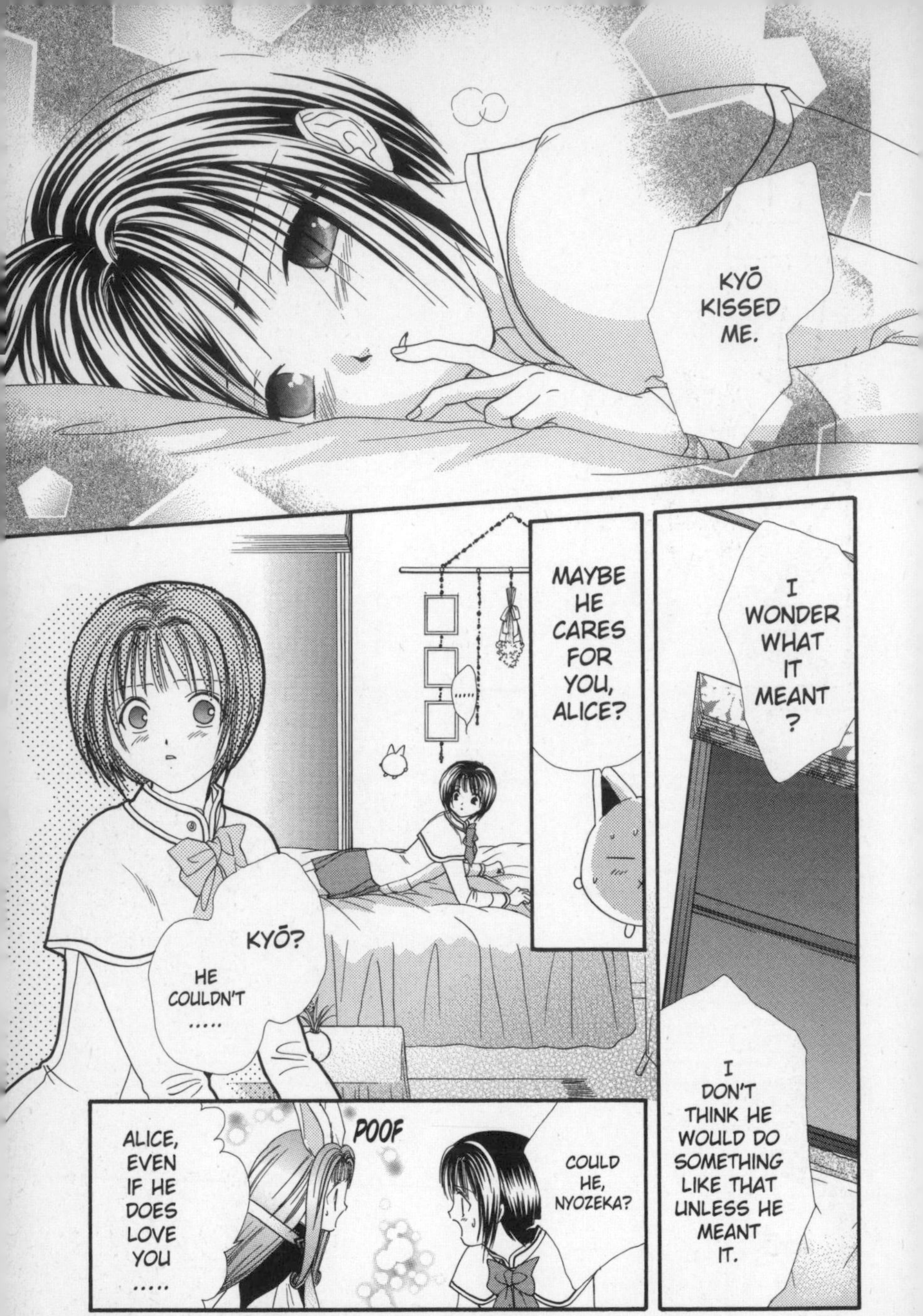
KYŌ KISSED ME.
I WONDER WHAT IT MEANT?
I DON'T THINK HE WOULD DO SOMETHING LIKE THAT UNLESS HE MEANT IT.
MAYBE HE CARES FOR YOU, ALICE?
......
KYŌ?
HE COULDN'T ......
COULD HE, NYOZEKA?
POOF
ALICE, EVEN IF HE DOES LOVE YOU ......

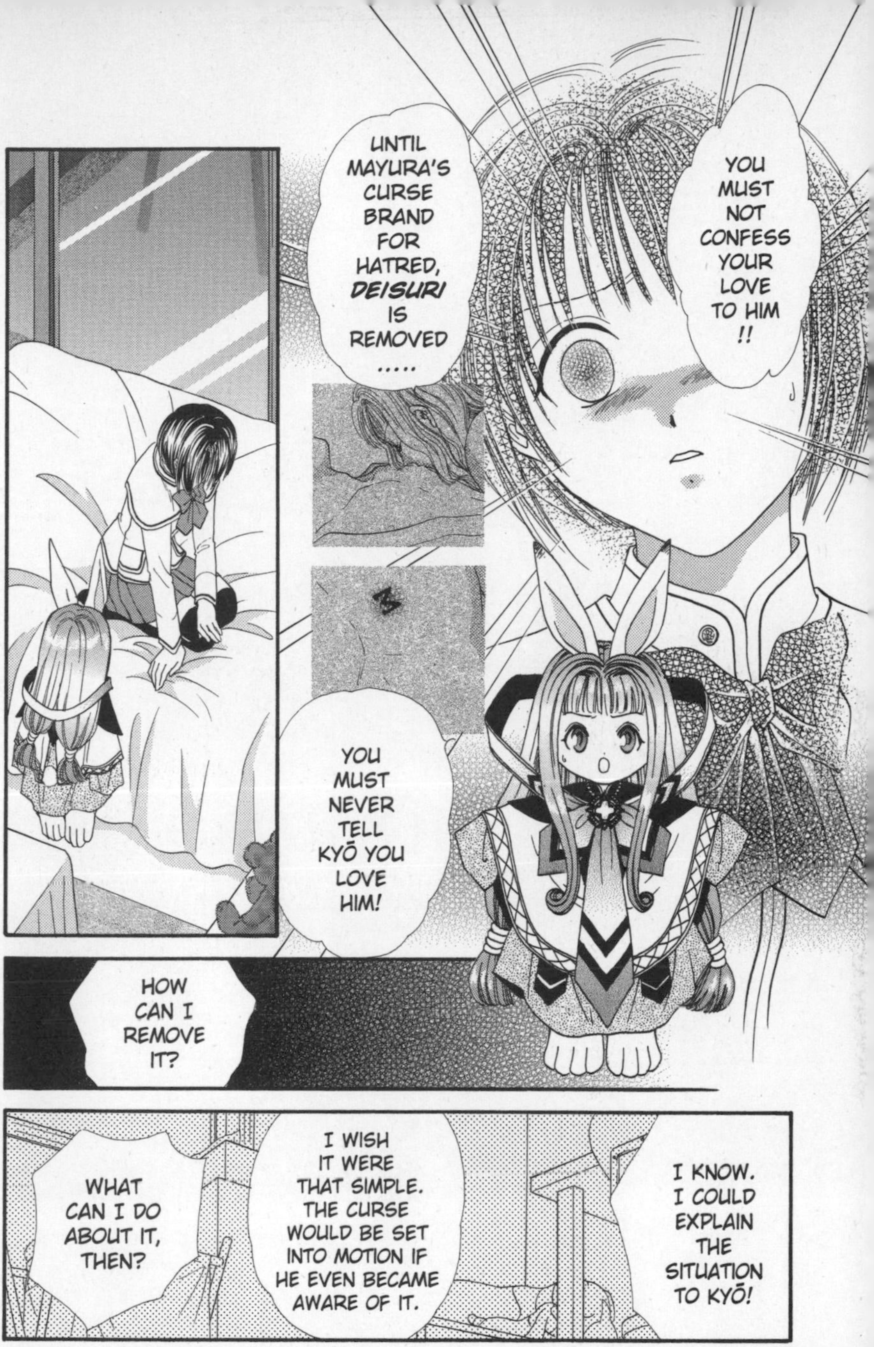
YOU MUST NOT CONFESS YOUR LOVE TO HIM !!
UNTIL MAYURA'S CURSE BRAND FOR HATRED, *DEISURI* IS REMOVED .....
YOU MUST NEVER TELL KYŌ YOU LOVE HIM!
HOW CAN I REMOVE IT?
I KNOW. I COULD EXPLAIN THE SITUATION TO KYŌ!
I WISH IT WERE THAT SIMPLE. THE CURSE WOULD BE SET INTO MOTION IF HE EVEN BECAME AWARE OF IT.
WHAT CAN I DO ABOUT IT, THEN?

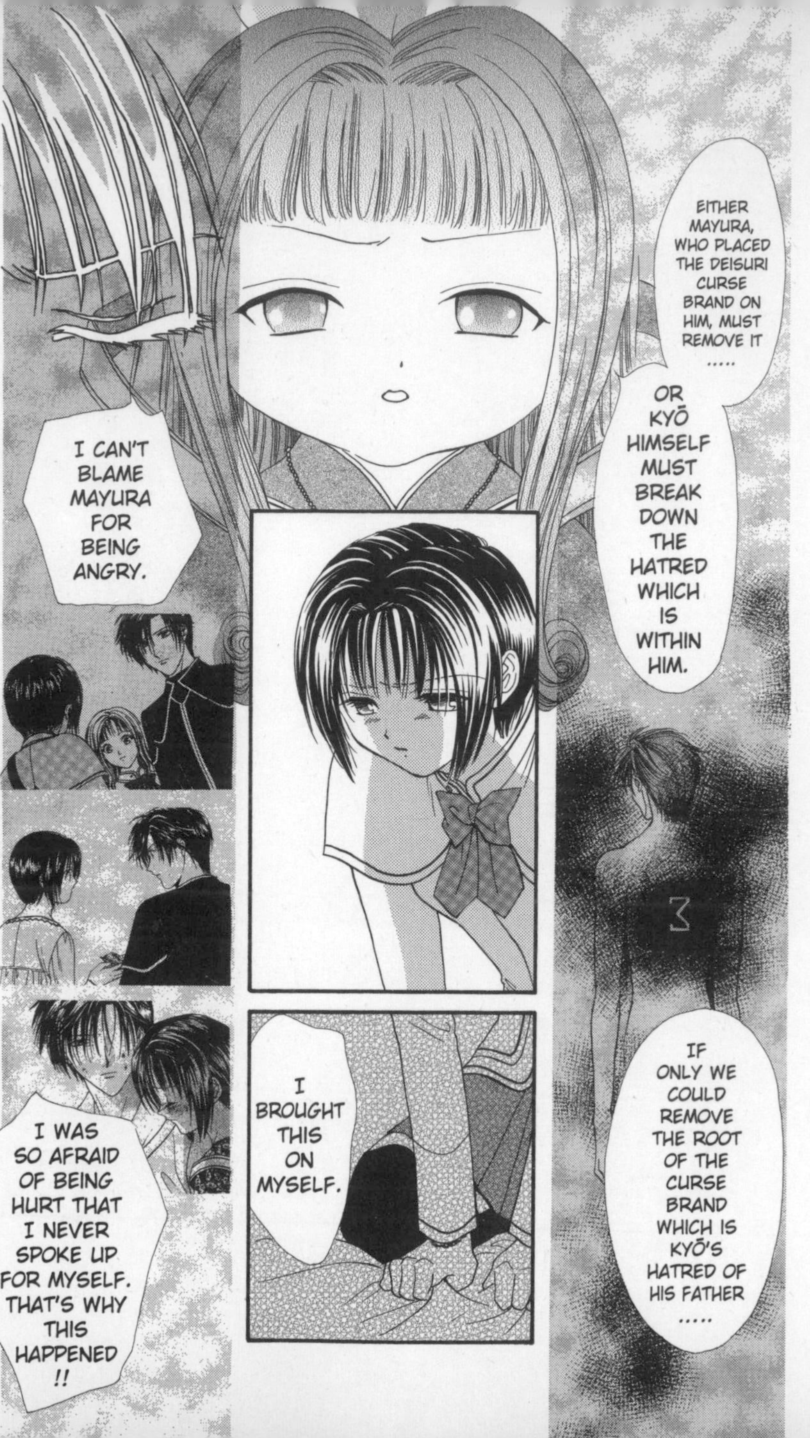
EITHER MAYURA, WHO PLACED THE DEISURI CURSE BRAND ON HIM, MUST REMOVE IT .....
OR KYŌ HIMSELF MUST BREAK DOWN THE HATRED WHICH IS WITHIN HIM.
IF ONLY WE COULD REMOVE THE ROOT OF THE CURSE BRAND WHICH IS KYŌ'S HATRED OF HIS FATHER .....
I CAN'T BLAME MAYURA FOR BEING ANGRY.
I BROUGHT THIS ON MYSELF.
I WAS SO AFRAID OF BEING HURT THAT I NEVER SPOKE UP FOR MYSELF. THAT'S WHY THIS HAPPENED !!

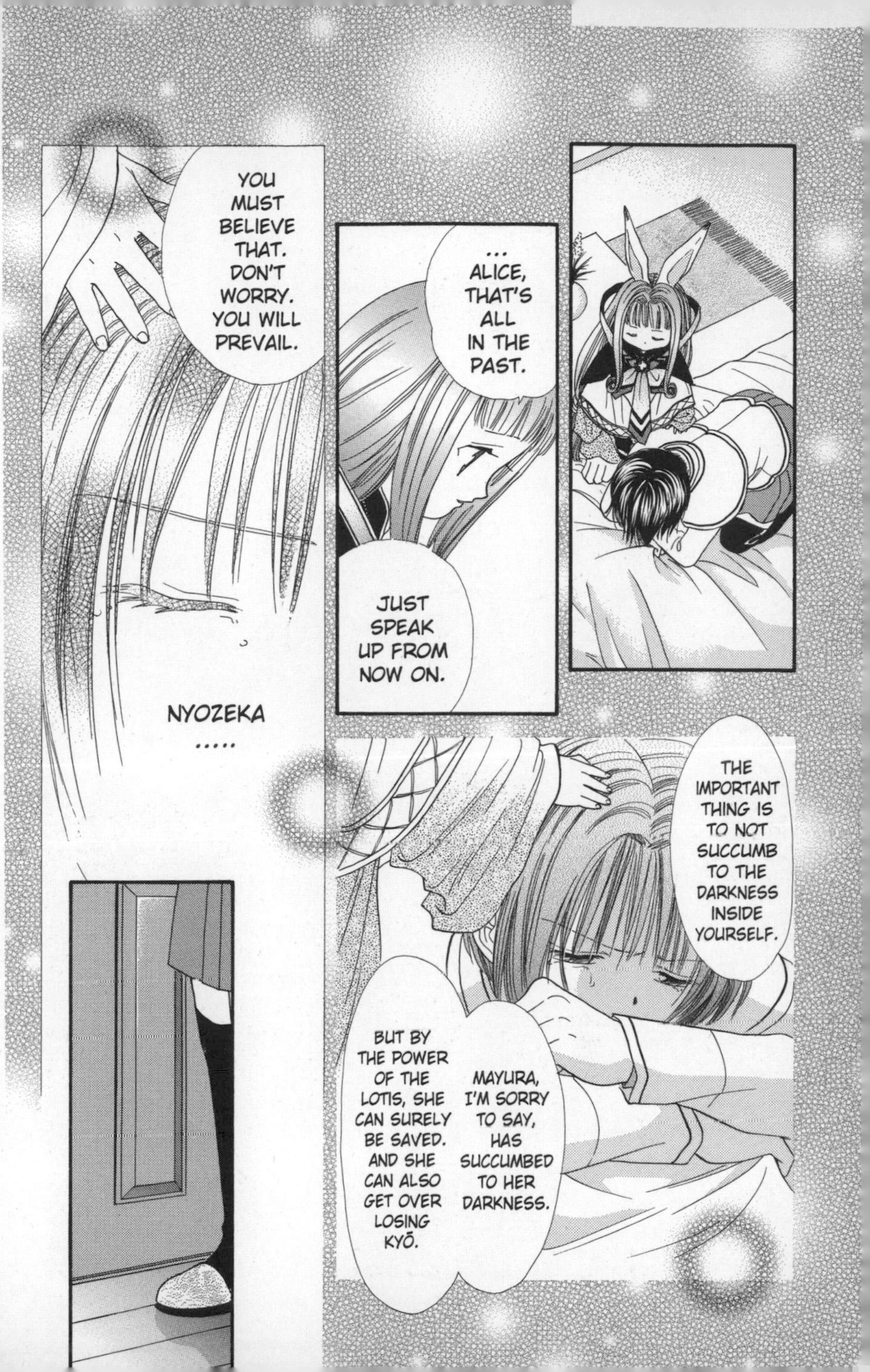

... ALICE, THAT'S ALL IN THE PAST.
JUST SPEAK UP FROM NOW ON.
YOU MUST BELIEVE THAT. DON'T WORRY. YOU WILL PREVAIL.
NYOZEKA .....
THE IMPORTANT THING IS TO NOT SUCCUMB TO THE DARKNESS INSIDE YOURSELF.
MAYURA, I'M SORRY TO SAY, HAS SUCCUMBED TO HER DARKNESS.
BUT BY THE POWER OF THE LOTIS, SHE CAN SURELY BE SAVED. AND SHE CAN ALSO GET OVER LOSING KYŌ.

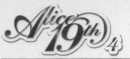

And so Volume 4 is out. (I hope everyone will enjoy it.) I've been writing it up until a week ago, I was in Raleigh, North Carolina participating as a guest at Animazement, which is my custom every year. The second half of the event was in San Francisco. (It was so cold, I wore fleece.) During the autograph session of the event, I saw a Nyozeka cosplayer!! I was so shocked! She even had bunny feet! Some of the best cosplays I've seen were the God, Suzaku, (He even had red eyes...contact lenses) and Tama (cat)! They are both characters from Fushigi Yûgi, and their looks were so exact that I was blown away. I reported this in Volume 1 of Imadoki, too.
Inside was a cute girl. Oh, yes! I had my picture taken with her, and almost got stabbed by her whiskers.

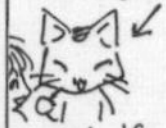

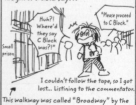

Also, the cosplayer Ceres from Ceres was half-naked and amazing.
(I didn't mean it that way.)
So while writing this and traveling for ten days, there were a lot of people saying, "Is there going to be a terrorist attack again? Is there going to be a terrorist attack again?" But, I spent my time not worrying too much about it.
In San Francisco, I went to Alcatraz, but I was surprised that the tour ended so soon. ☺
It's where they filmed "The Rock." I wandered around the prison listening to a tape of a guide explaining everything in Japanese. The Japanese voice actors doing the parts of the convicts sounded like "amateurs who only reside in America!" It was very documentary style and it made me laugh. It would say...

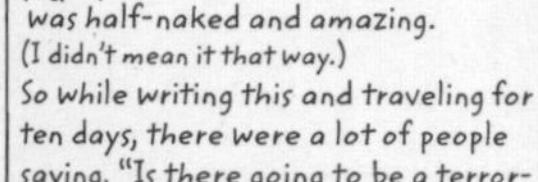
Huh?! Where'd they say C Block was?!"
"Please proceed to C Block."
Small prison

I couldn't follow the tape, so I got lost... Listining to the commentator.
This walkway was called "Broadway" by the prisoners.
Long ago these Brothers plotted to escape by digging out the wall with a spoon and left dummies in their beds. It looked so real.

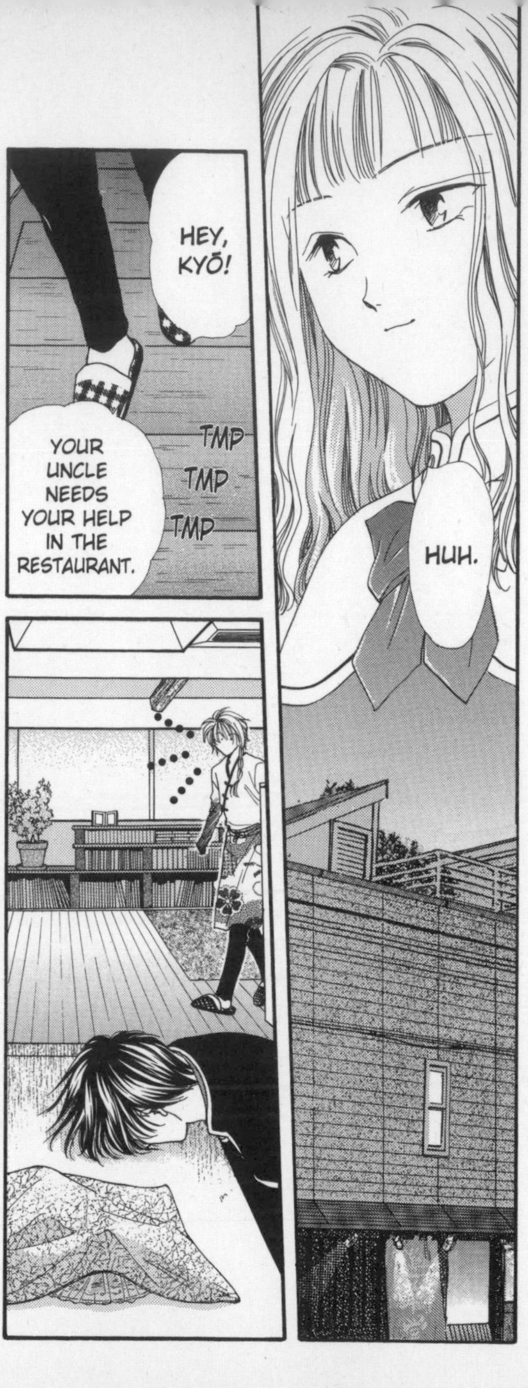
HEY, KYŌ!
YOUR UNCLE NEEDS YOUR HELP IN THE RESTAURANT.
TMP
TMP
TMP
HUH.

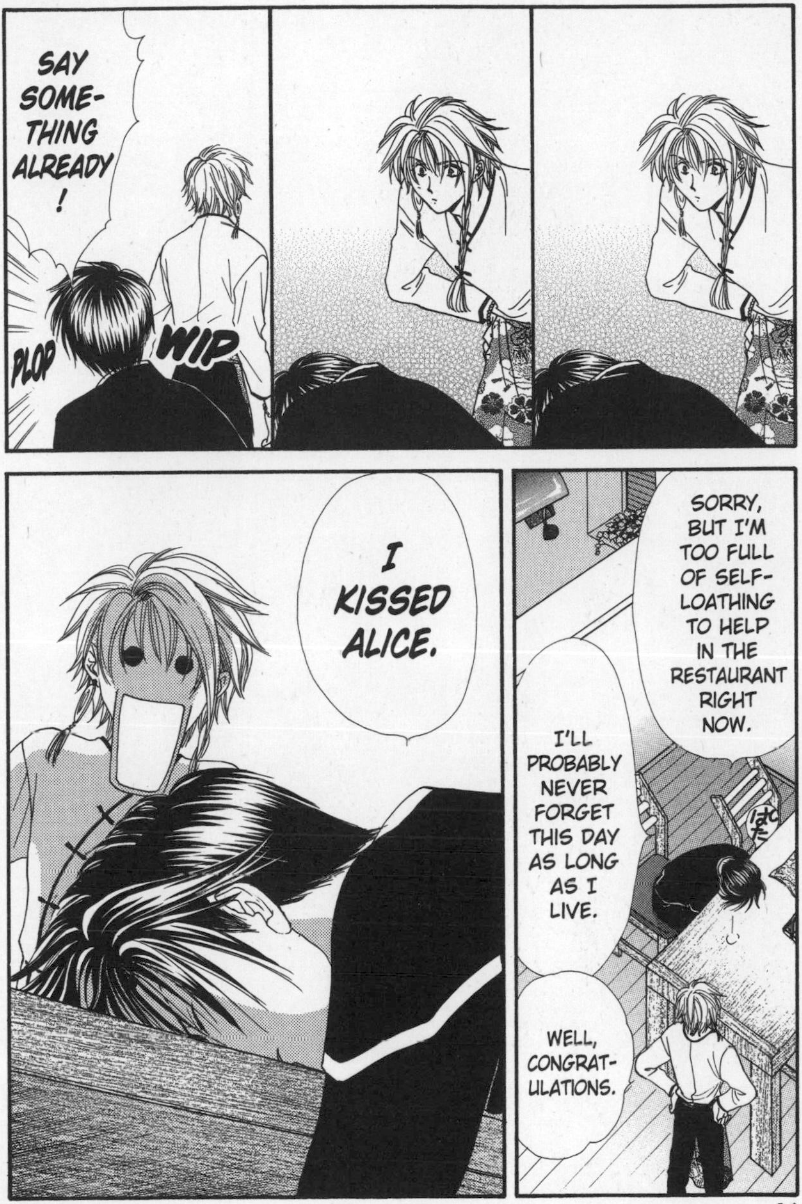
SAY SOME-THING ALREADY!
PLOP
WIP
I KISSED ALICE.
SORRY, BUT I'M TOO FULL OF SELF-LOATHING TO HELP IN THE RESTAURANT RIGHT NOW.
I'LL PROBABLY NEVER FORGET THIS DAY AS LONG AS I LIVE.
WELL, CONGRAT-ULATIONS.

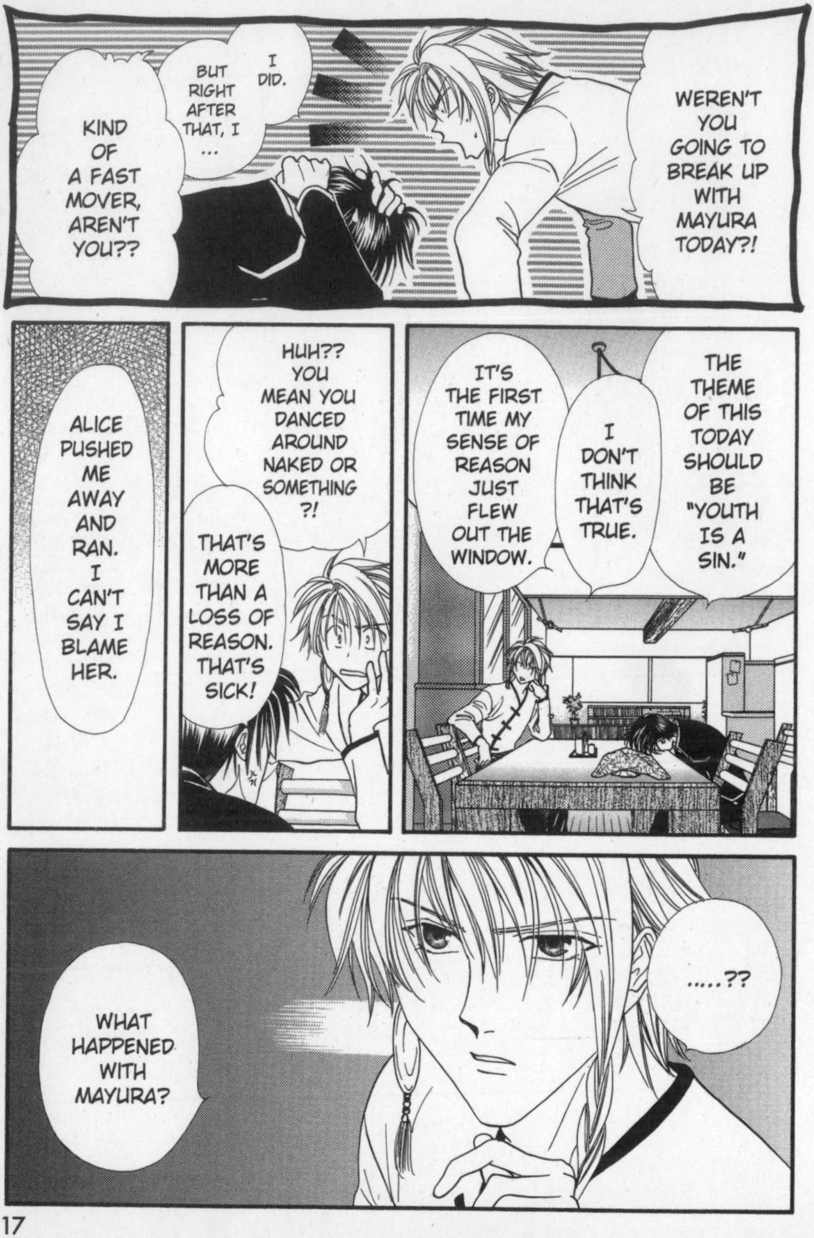
WEREN'T YOU GOING TO BREAK UP WITH MAYURA TODAY?!
I DID.
BUT RIGHT AFTER THAT, I ...
KIND OF A FAST MOVER, AREN'T YOU??
THE THEME OF THIS TODAY SHOULD BE "YOUTH IS A SIN."
I DON'T THINK THAT'S TRUE.
IT'S THE FIRST TIME MY SENSE OF REASON JUST FLEW OUT THE WINDOW.
HUH?? YOU MEAN YOU DANCED AROUND NAKED OR SOMETHING?!
THAT'S MORE THAN A LOSS OF REASON. THAT'S SICK!
ALICE PUSHED ME AWAY AND RAN. I CAN'T SAY I BLAME HER.
.....??
WHAT HAPPENED WITH MAYURA?

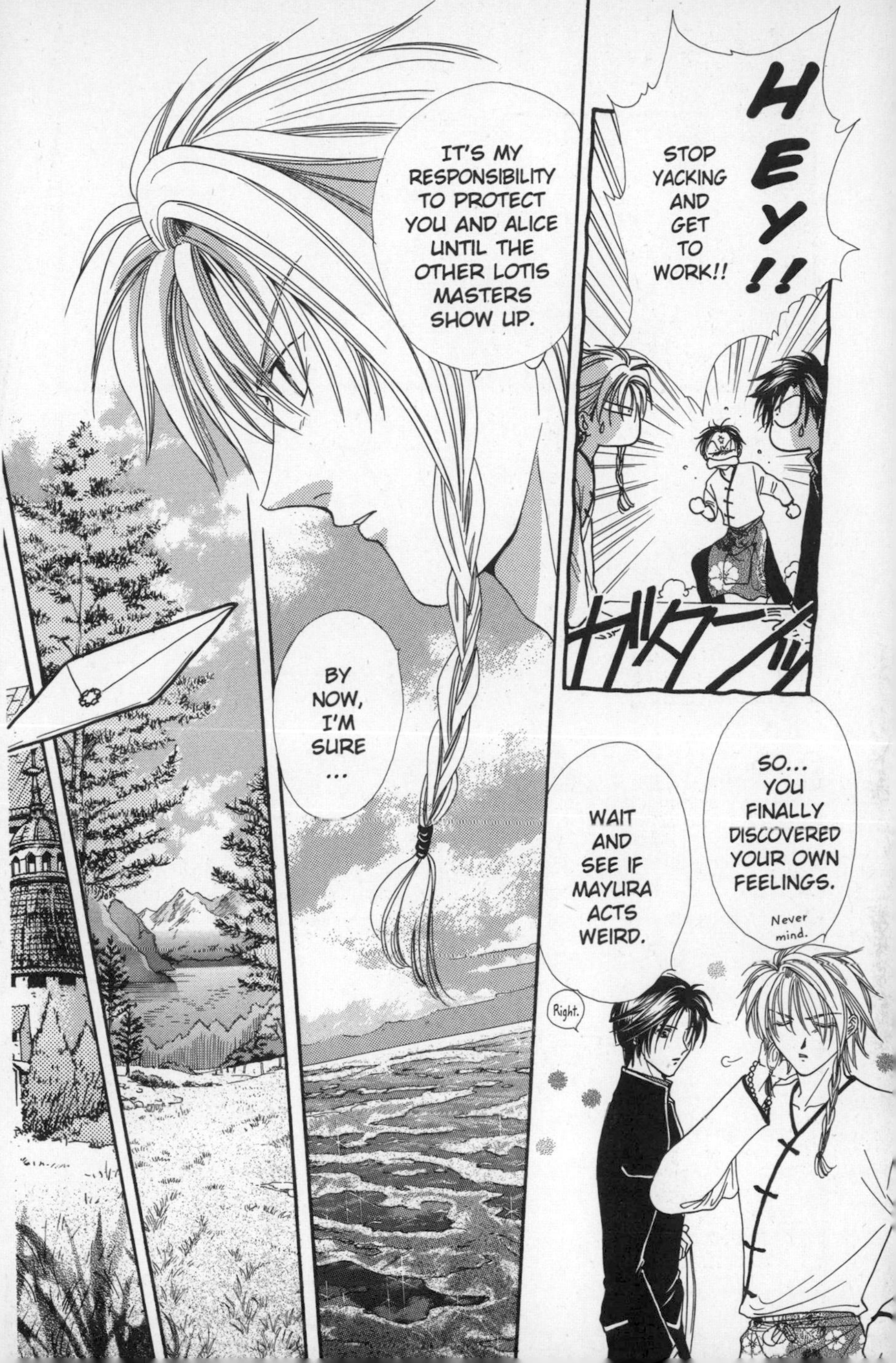
HEY!!
STOP YACKING AND GET TO WORK!!
SO... YOU FINALLY DISCOVERED YOUR OWN FEELINGS.
Never mind.
WAIT AND SEE IF MAYURA ACTS WEIRD.
Right.
IT'S MY RESPONSIBILITY TO PROTECT YOU AND ALICE UNTIL THE OTHER LOTIS MASTERS SHOW UP.
BY NOW, I'M SURE ...

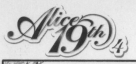

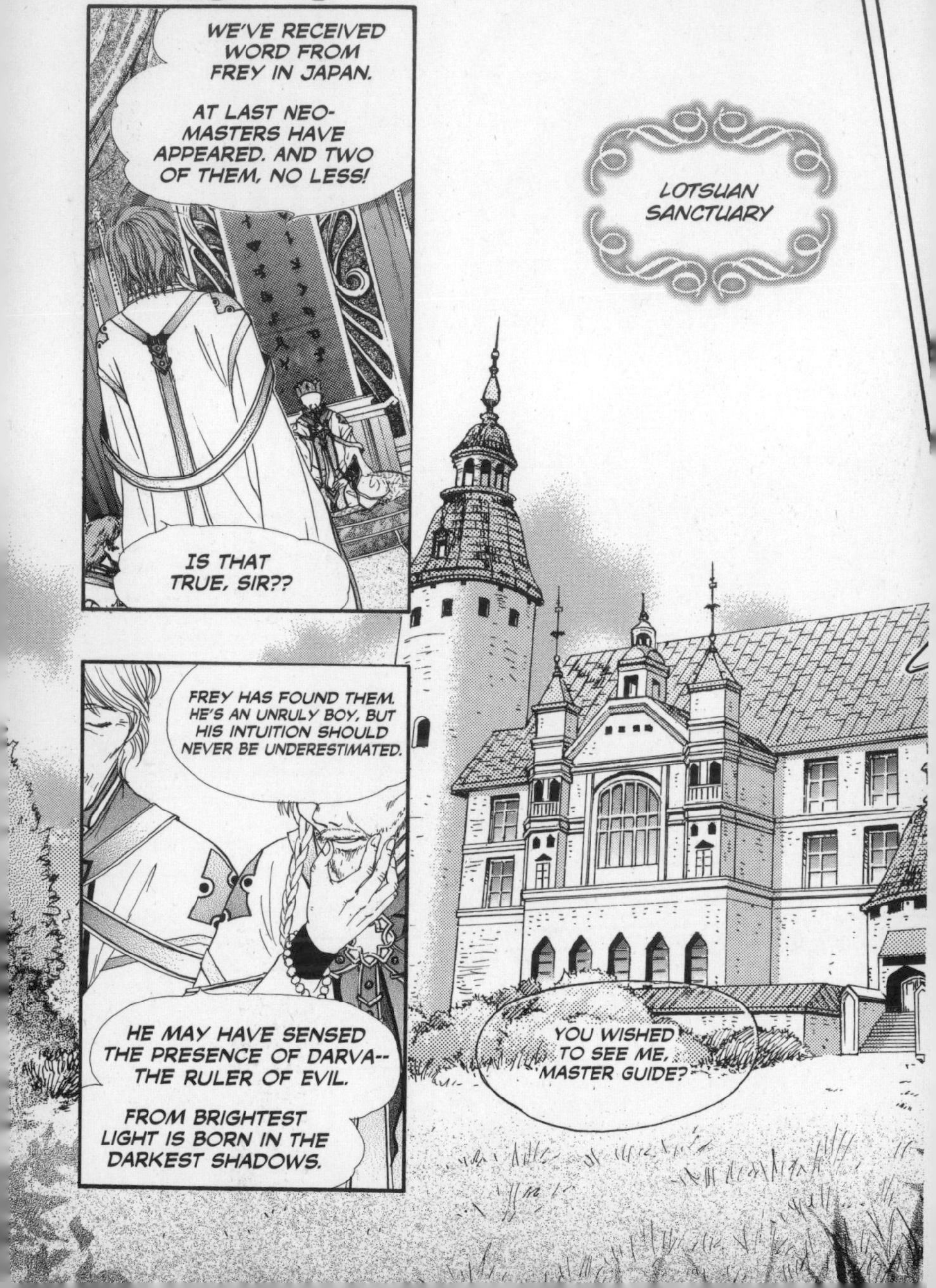
LOTSUAN SANCTUARY
YOU WISHED TO SEE ME, MASTER GUIDE?
WE'VE RECEIVED WORD FROM FREY IN JAPAN.
AT LAST NEO-MASTERS HAVE APPEARED. AND TWO OF THEM, NO LESS!
IS THAT TRUE, SIR??
FREY HAS FOUND THEM. HE'S AN UNRULY BOY, BUT HIS INTUITION SHOULD NEVER BE UNDERESTIMATED.
HE MAY HAVE SENSED THE PRESENCE OF DARVA-- THE RULER OF EVIL.
FROM BRIGHTEST LIGHT IS BORN IN THE DARKEST SHADOWS.

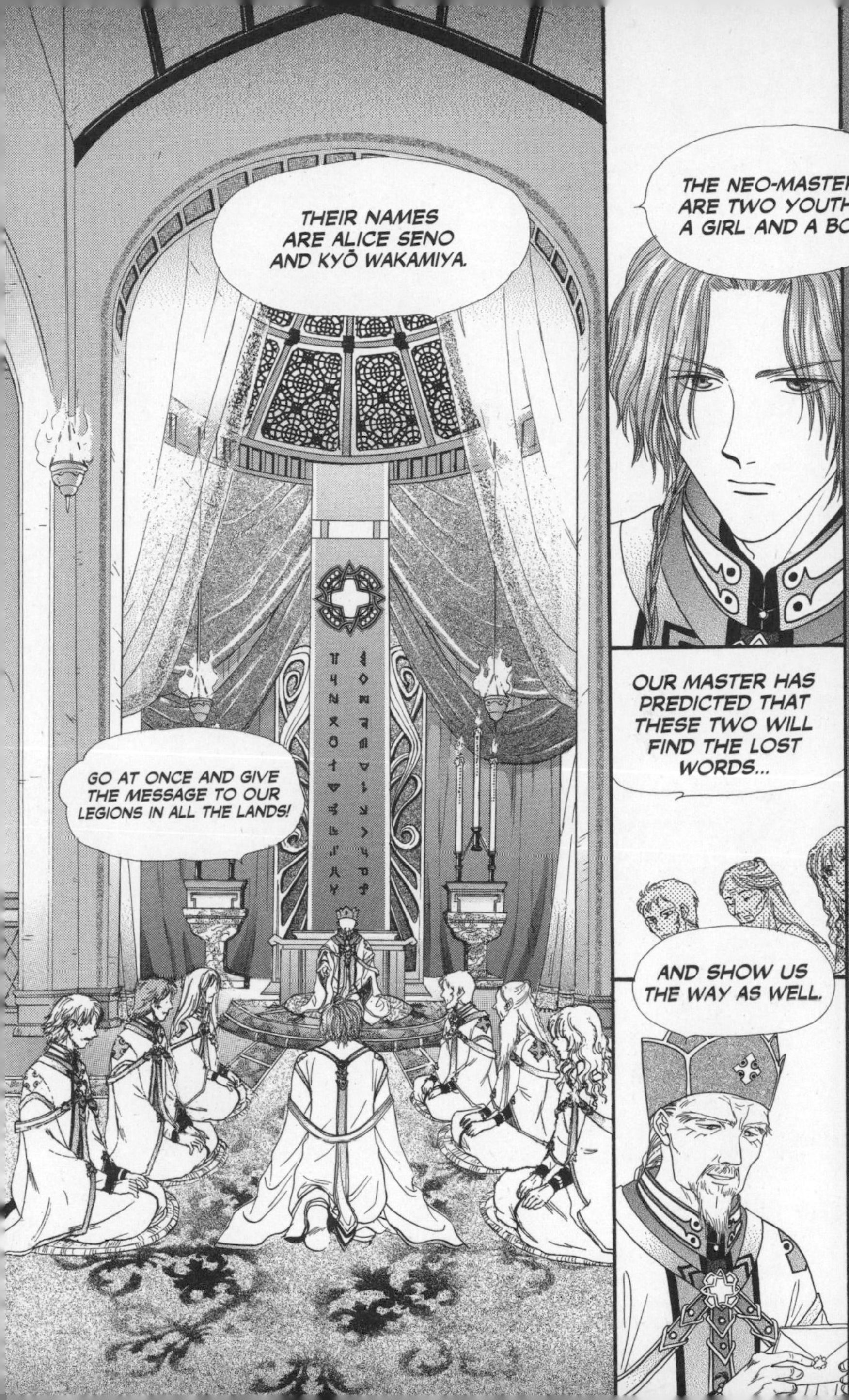
THE NEO-MASTERS ARE TWO YOUTHS, A GIRL AND A BOY.
OUR MASTER HAS PREDICTED THAT THESE TWO WILL FIND THE LOST WORDS...
AND SHOW US THE WAY AS WELL.
THEIR NAMES ARE ALICE SENO AND KYŌ WAKAMIYA.
GO AT ONCE AND GIVE THE MESSAGE TO OUR LEGIONS IN ALL THE LANDS!

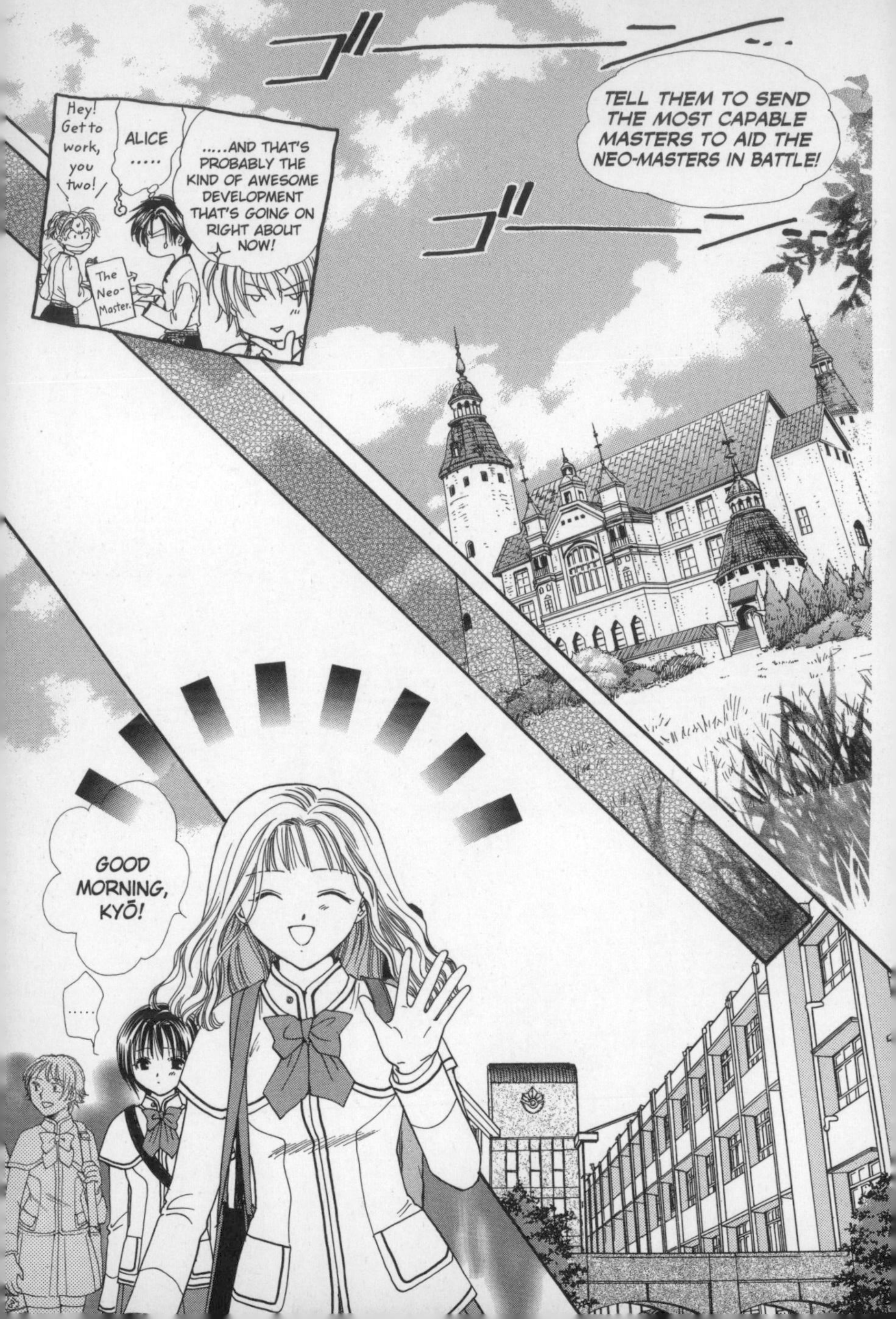

ゴー
TELL THEM TO SEND THE MOST CAPABLE MASTERS TO AID THE NEO-MASTERS IN BATTLE!
ゴー
.....AND THAT'S PROBABLY THE KIND OF AWESOME DEVELOPMENT THAT'S GOING ON RIGHT ABOUT NOW!
ALICE .....
Hey! Get to work, you two!
The Neo-Master.
GOOD MORNING, KYŌ!
......

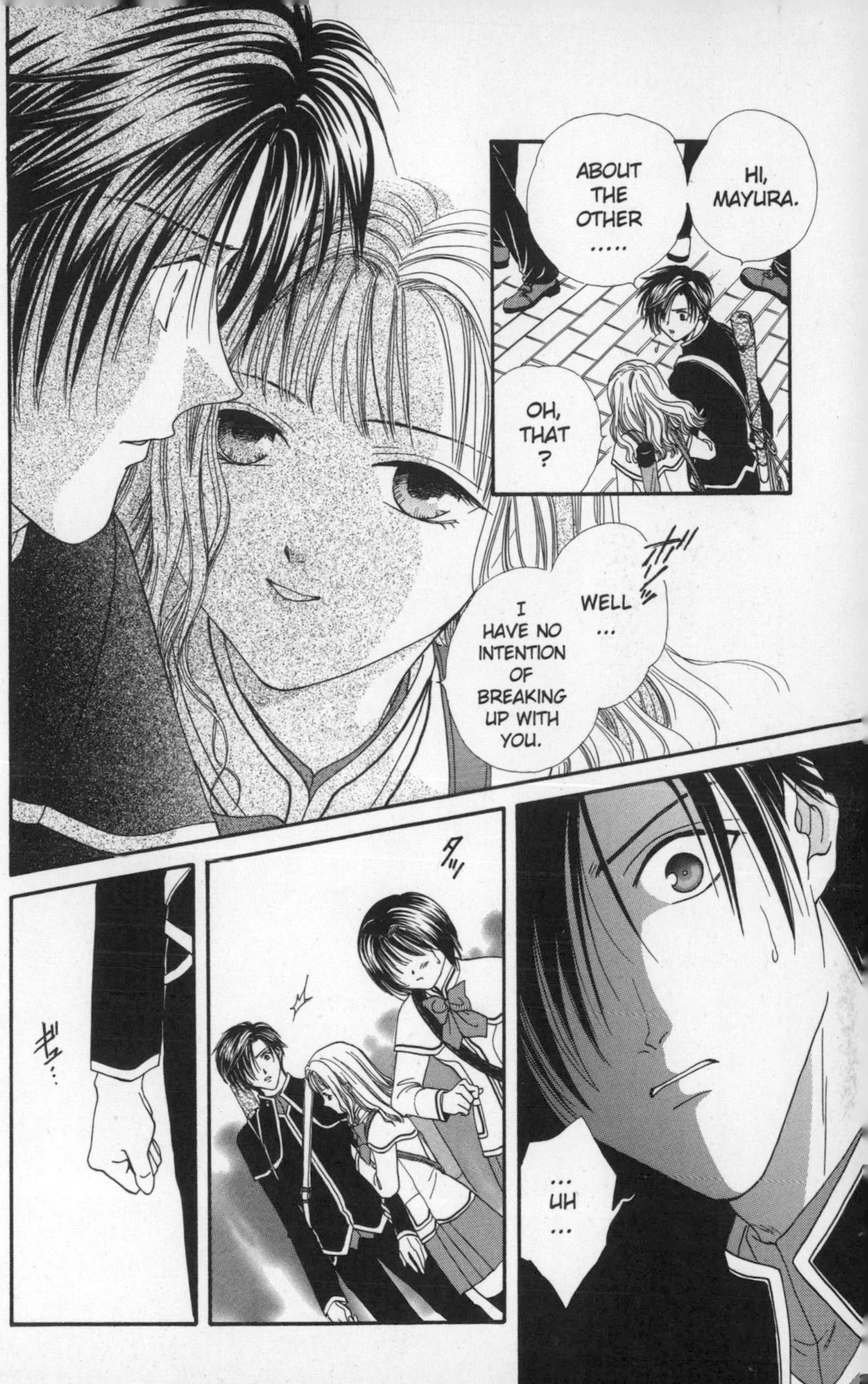
HI, MAYURA.
ABOUT THE OTHER .....
OH, THAT?
WELL ...
I HAVE NO INTENTION OF BREAKING UP WITH YOU.
... UH ...

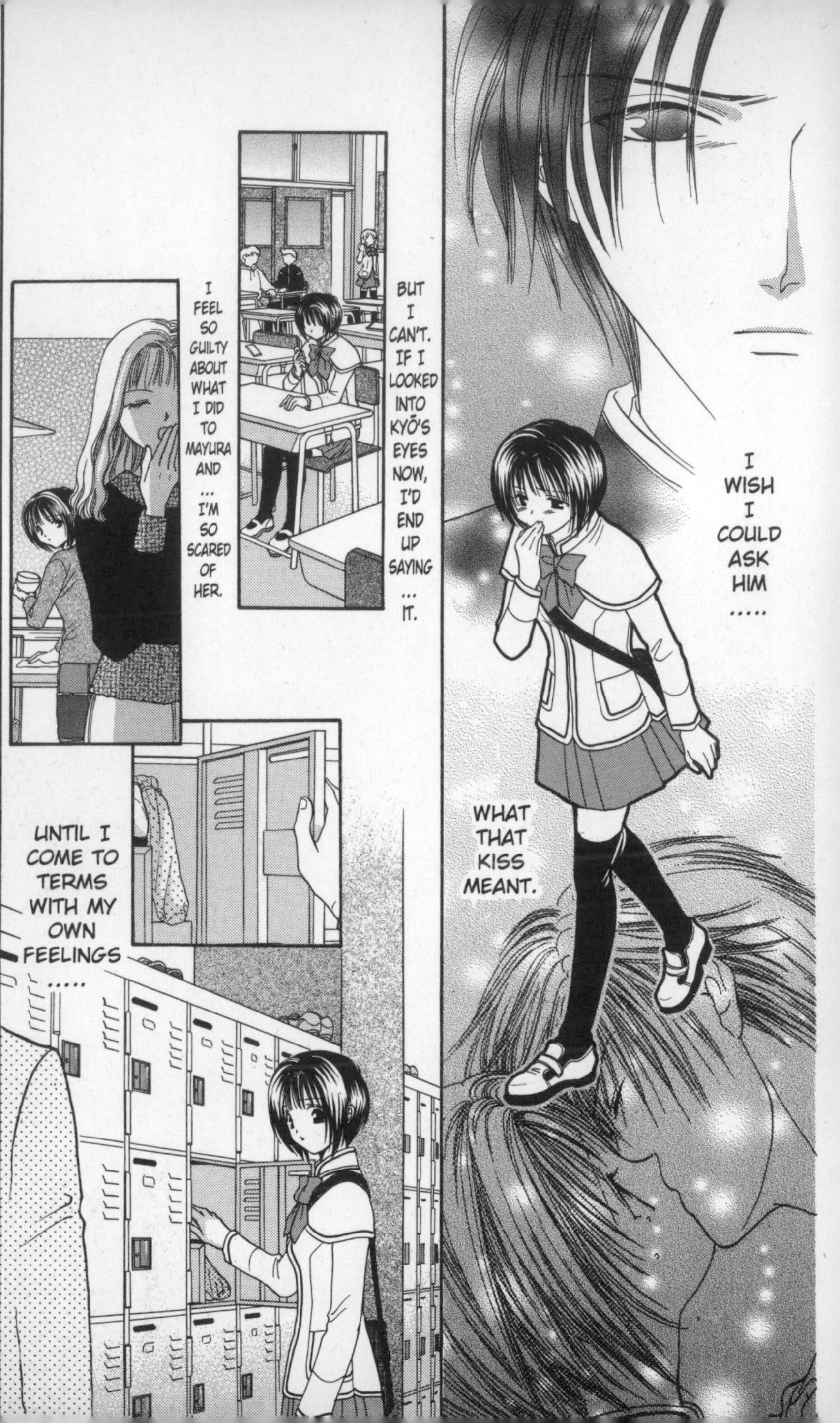

I WISH I COULD ASK HIM .....
WHAT THAT KISS MEANT.
BUT I CAN'T. IF I LOOKED INTO KYŌ'S EYES NOW, I'D END UP SAYING ... IT.
I FEEL SO GUILTY ABOUT WHAT I DID TO MAYURA AND ... I'M SO SCARED OF HER.
UNTIL I COME TO TERMS WITH MY OWN FEELINGS .....

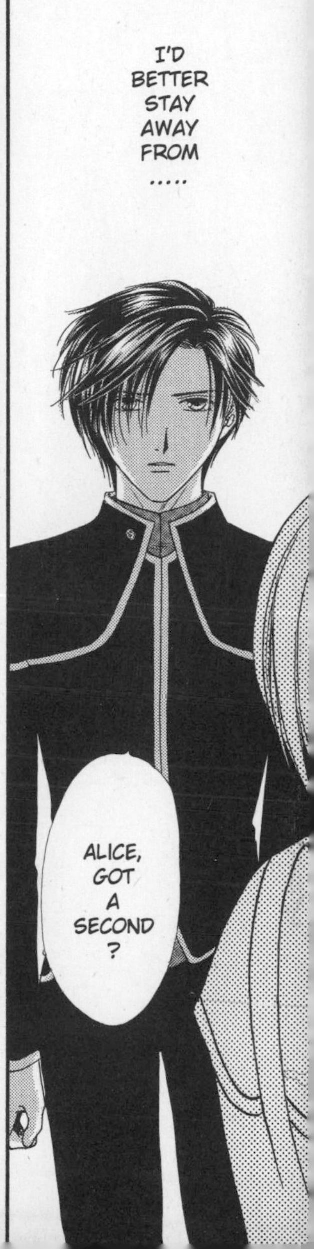
I'D BETTER STAY AWAY FROM .....
ALICE, GOT A SECOND ?

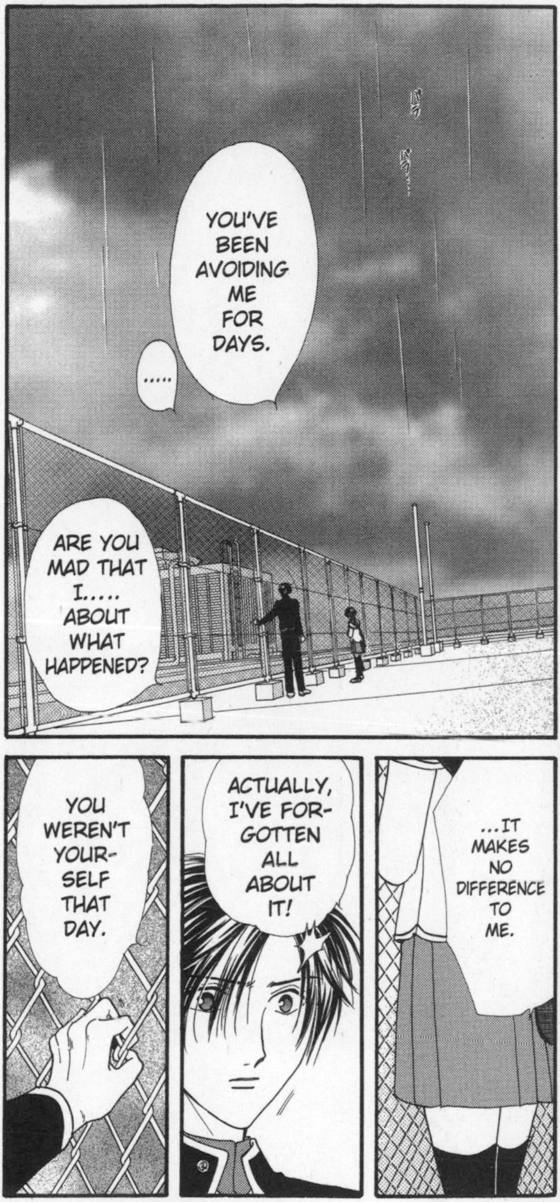
パラ パラ…
YOU'VE BEEN AVOIDING ME FOR DAYS.
.....
ARE YOU MAD THAT I..... ABOUT WHAT HAPPENED?
...IT MAKES NO DIFFERENCE TO ME.
ACTUALLY, I'VE FOR-GOTTEN ALL ABOUT IT!
YOU WEREN'T YOUR-SELF THAT DAY.

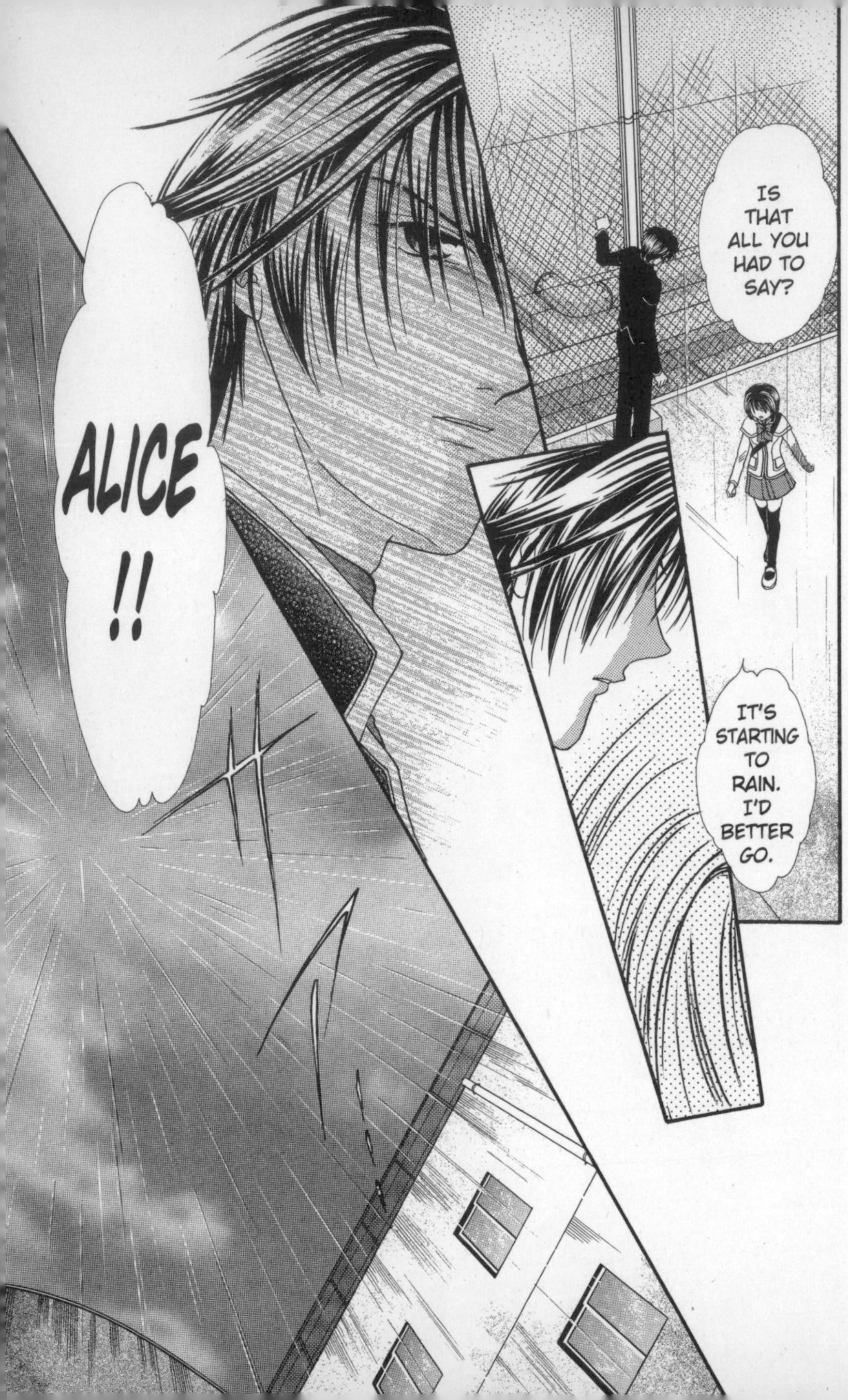
IS THAT ALL YOU HAD TO SAY?
IT'S STARTING TO RAIN. I'D BETTER GO.
ALICE!!

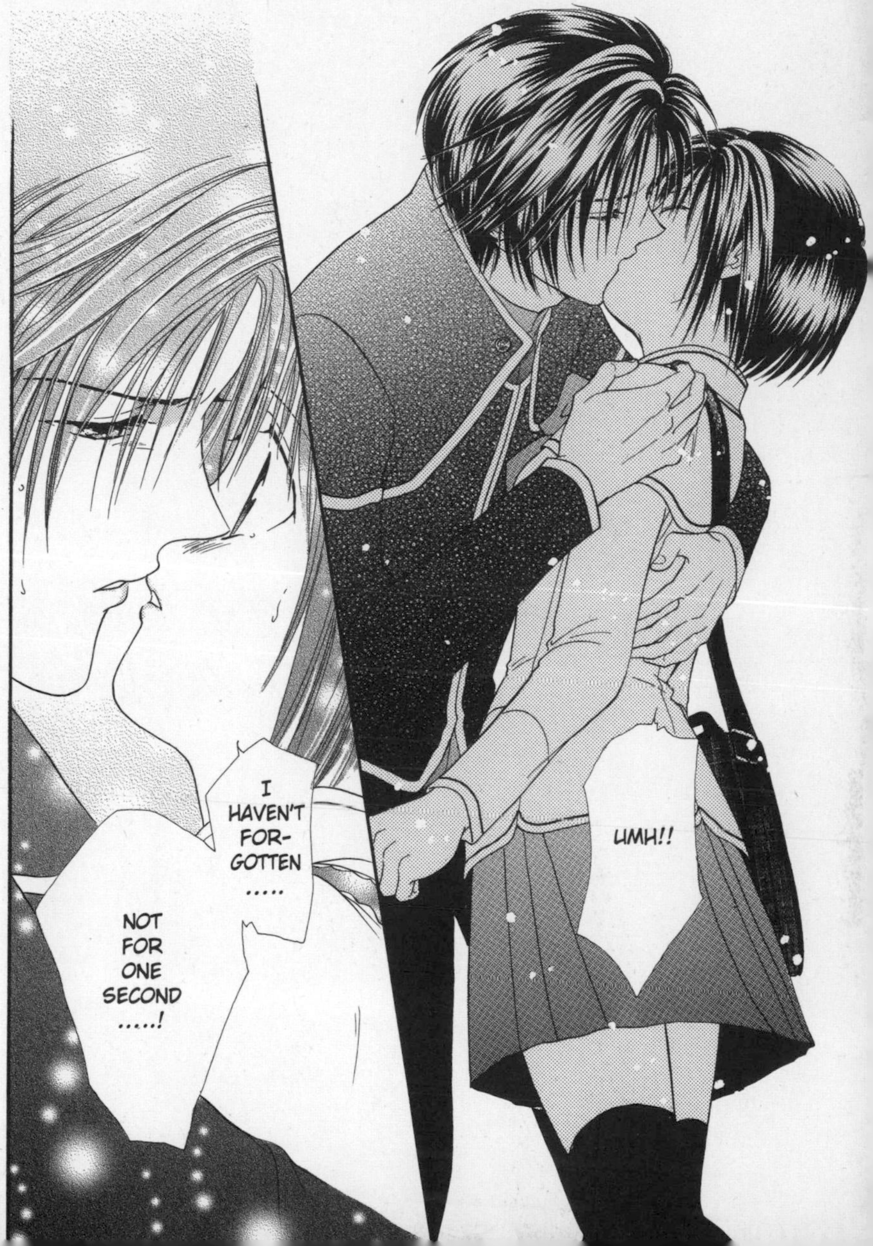
UMH!!
I HAVEN'T FORGOTTEN .....
NOT FOR ONE SECOND .....!

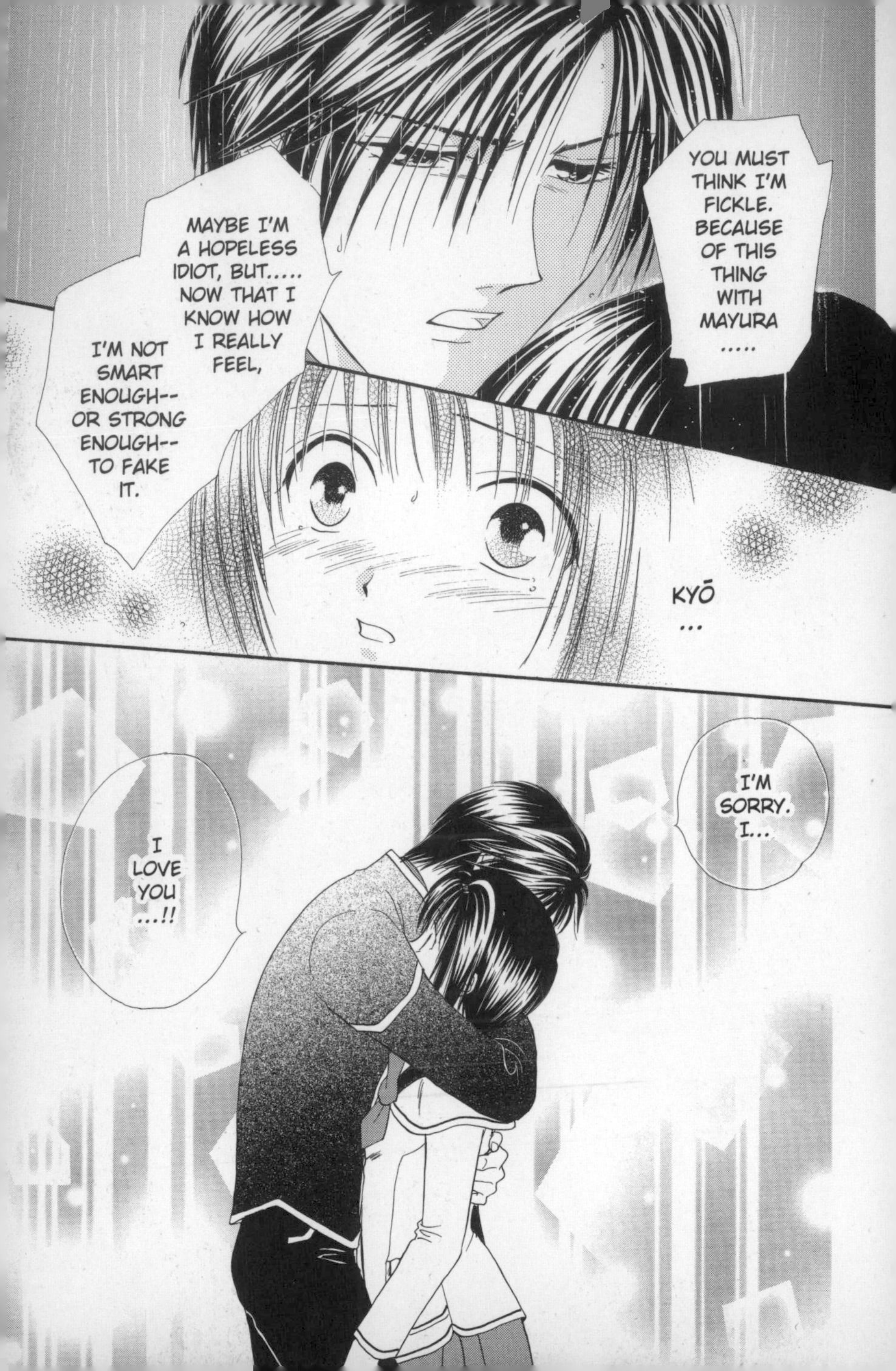
YOU MUST THINK I'M FICKLE. BECAUSE OF THIS THING WITH MAYURA .....
MAYBE I'M A HOPELESS IDIOT, BUT..... NOW THAT I KNOW HOW I REALLY FEEL,
I'M NOT SMART ENOUGH-- OR STRONG ENOUGH-- TO FAKE IT.
KYŌ ...
I'M SORRY. I...
I LOVE YOU ...!!

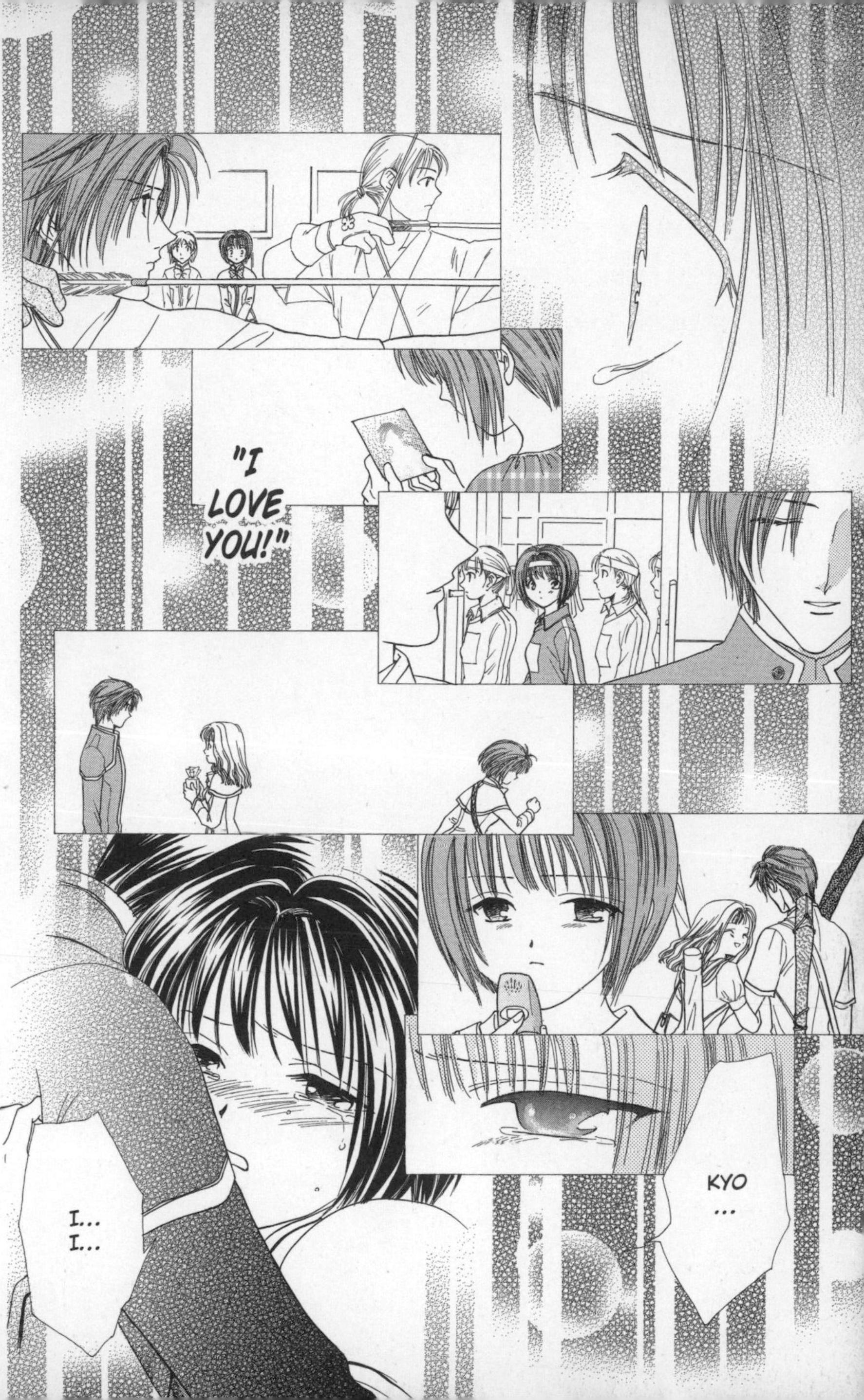
"I LOVE YOU!"
KYO ...
I... I...

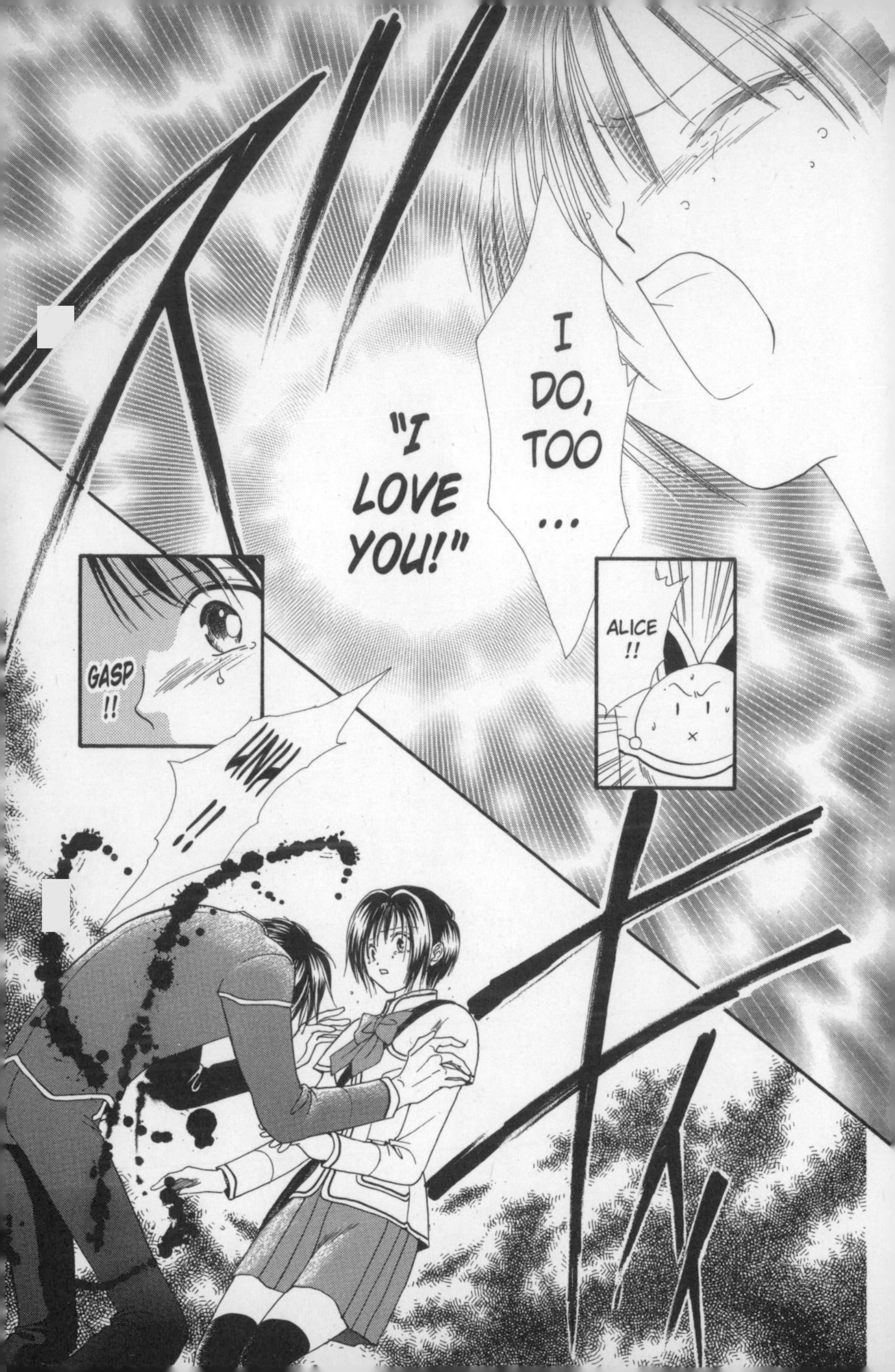
I DO, TOO ...
"I LOVE YOU!"
ALICE !!
GASP !!
UNH !!

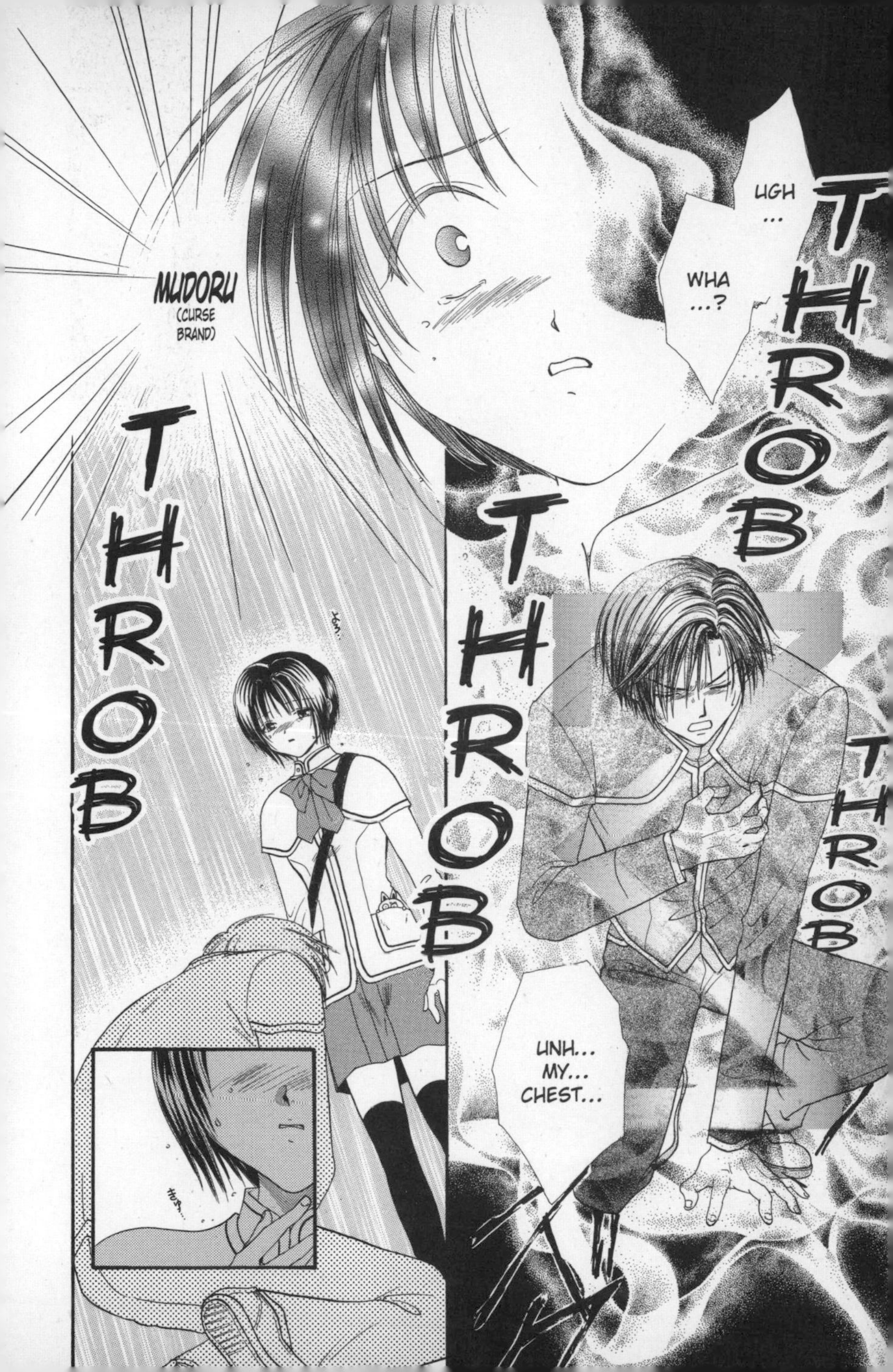
UGH...
WHA...?
THROB
THROB
THROB
UNH... MY... CHEST...
MUDORU
(CURSE BRAND)
THROB

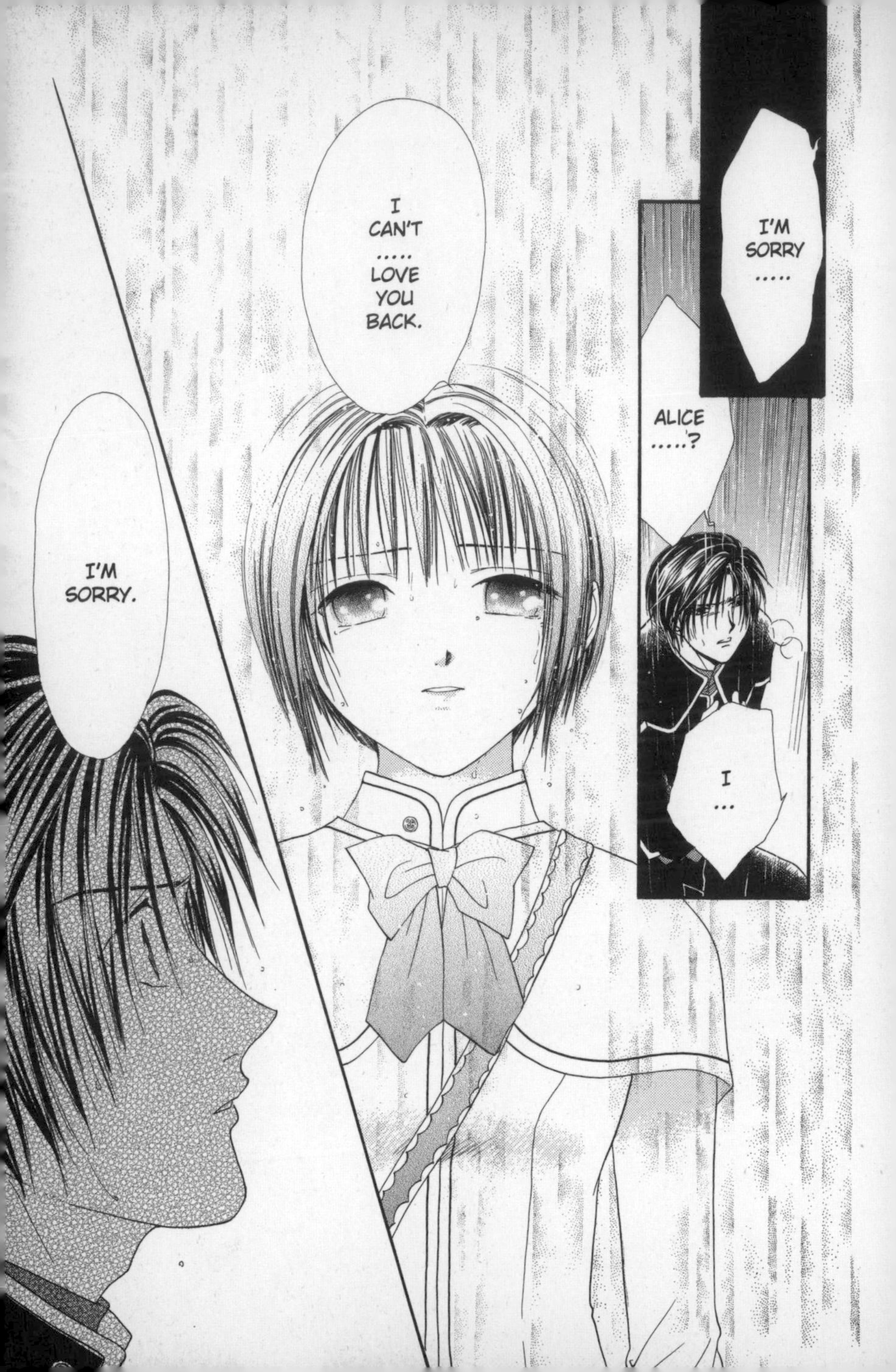
I'M SORRY .....
ALICE .....?
I ...
I CAN'T ..... LOVE YOU BACK.
I'M SORRY.

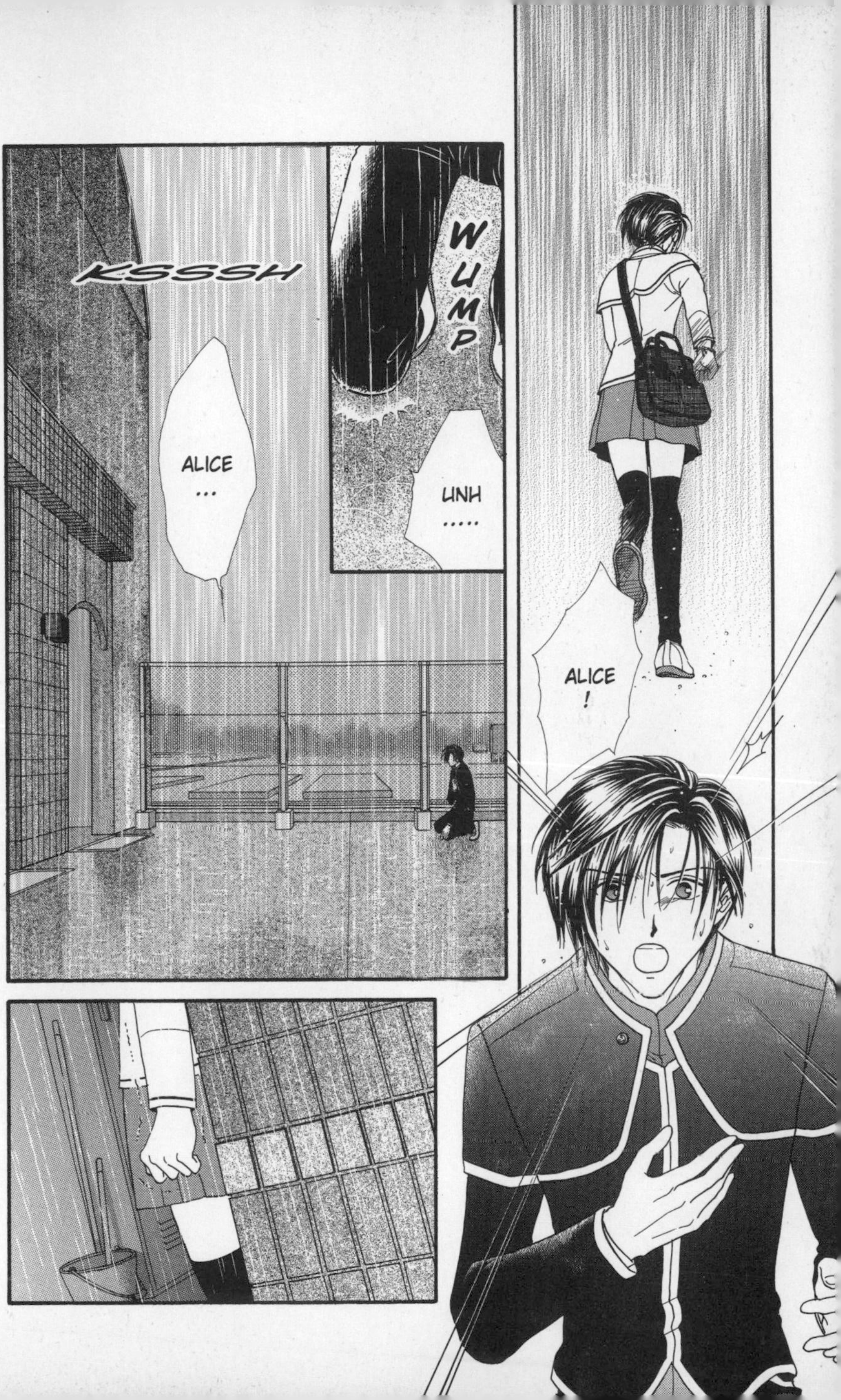
ALICE !
WUMP
UNH .....
KSSSH
ALICE ...

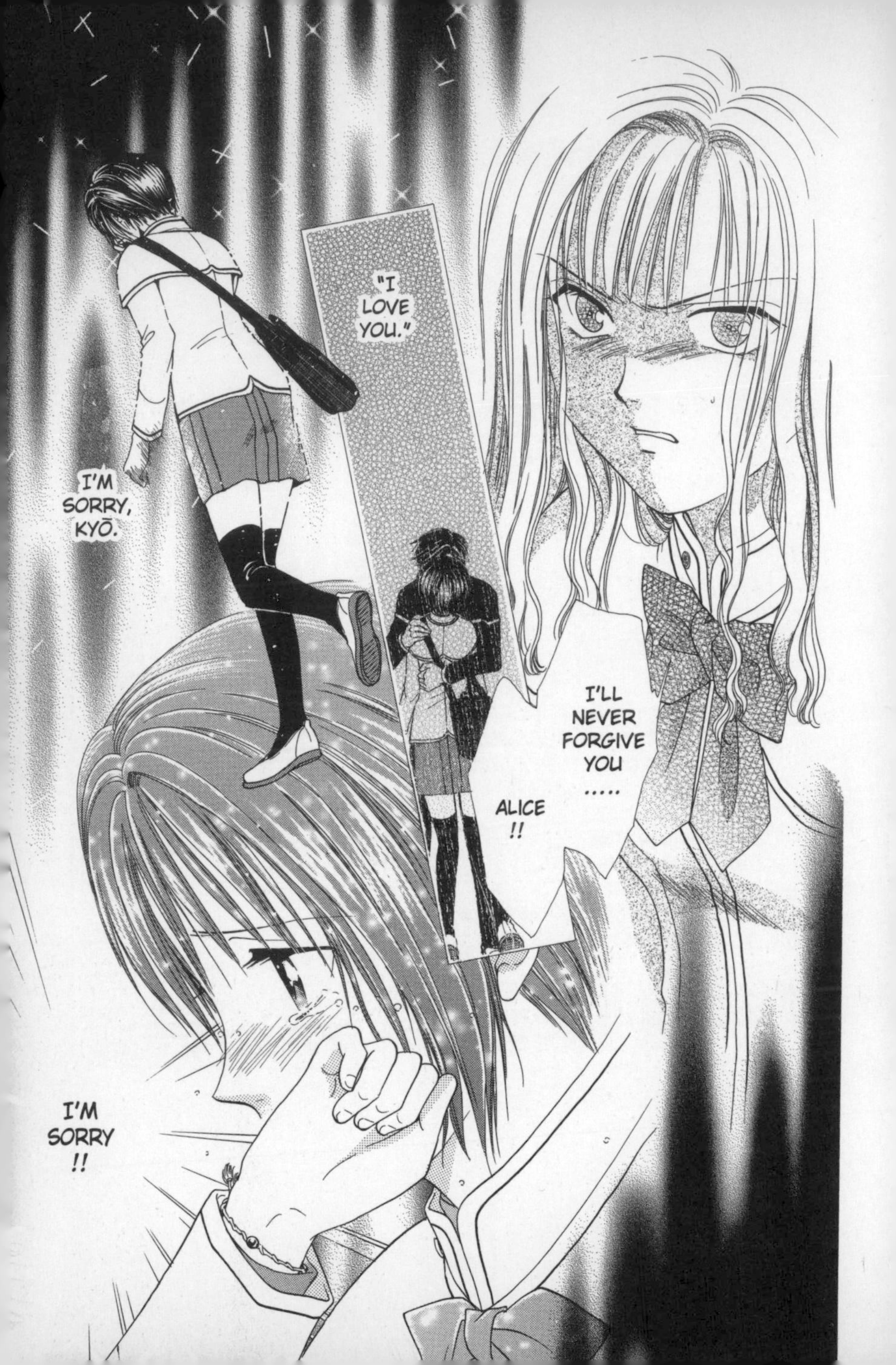
"I LOVE YOU."
I'LL NEVER FORGIVE YOU .....
ALICE !!
I'M SORRY, KYŌ.
I'M SORRY !!

MAYURA SENO

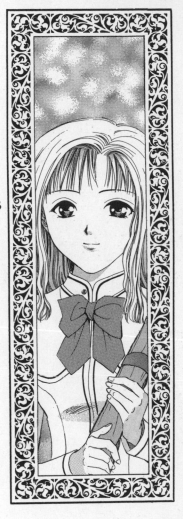

- HEIGHT: 163 CM

- BUST: 83 WAIST: 59 HIPS: 87

- SIGN: ARIES (4/7)

- BLOOD TYPE: O

- HOBBIES: SPORTS, SHOPPING

- ACCOMPLISHES EVERYTHING SHE UNDERTAKES WITH EASE. ALL-AROUND GOOD STUDENT. ALWAYS GETS GOOD GRADES.

- PRETTY, POPULAR WITH BOYS. AGGRESSIVE IN ROMANCE AND IN FRIENDSHIP. DISLIKES BEING ALONE.

- SAYS EXACTLY WHAT SHE THINKS, EVEN WHEN IT MIGHT HURT OTHER PEOPLE. PERHAPS BECAUSE SHE'S RELIABLE AND FRIENDLY, PEOPLE SELDOM HOLD A GRUDGE.

- BECAUSE SHE HATES TO LOSE, AND BECAUSE HER PARENTS DEPEND ON HER SO MUCH, SHE WORKS HARD TO BE DEPENDABLE AND ALWAYS HAS TO MAINTAIN THAT EDGE.

- THOUGH SHE GETS EXASPERATED WITH HER QUIET SISTER AT TIMES, SHE SOMETIMES ENVIES HER.

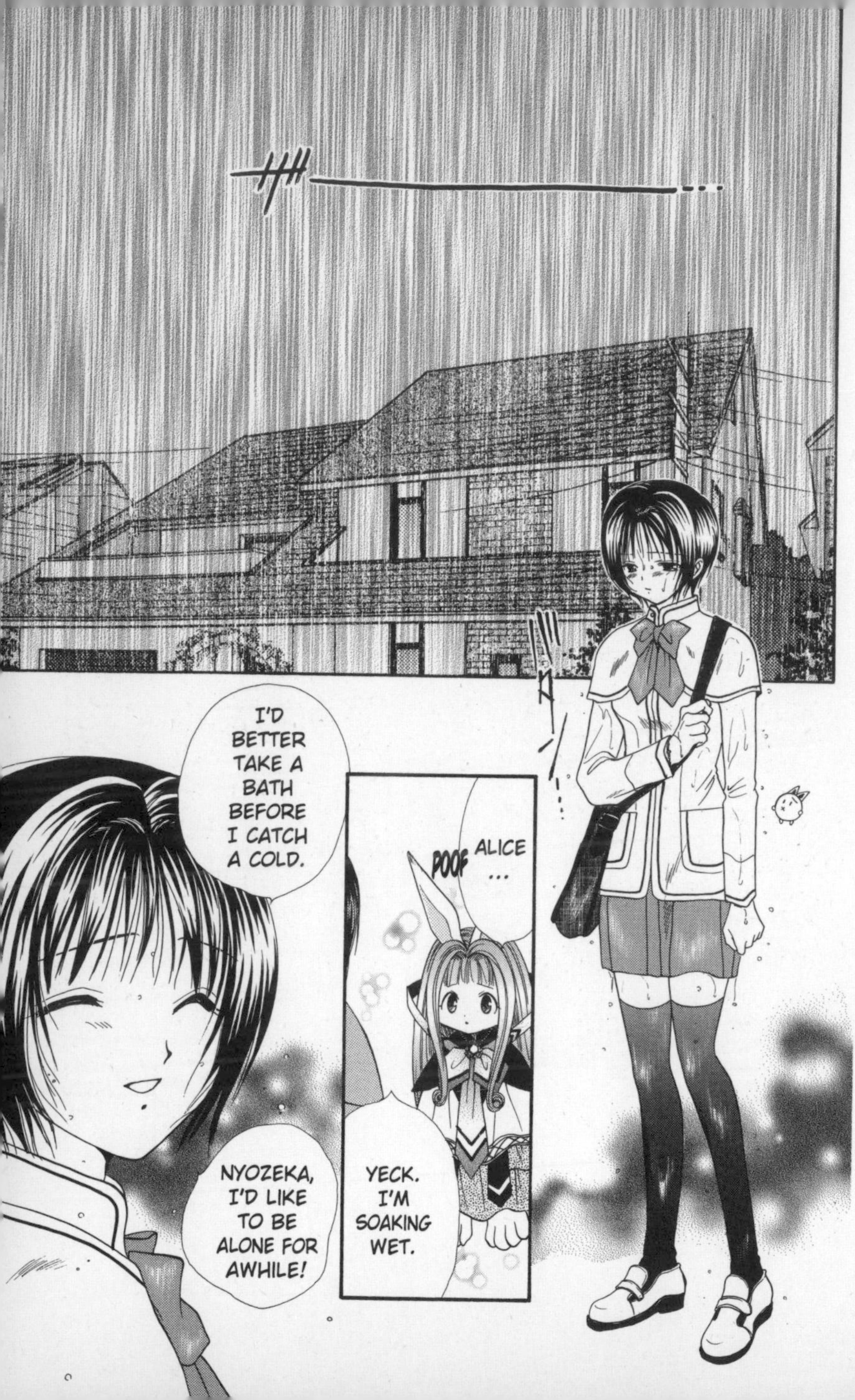
ALICE ...
POOF
YECK. I'M SOAKING WET.
I'D BETTER TAKE A BATH BEFORE I CATCH A COLD.
NYOZEKA, I'D LIKE TO BE ALONE FOR AWHILE!

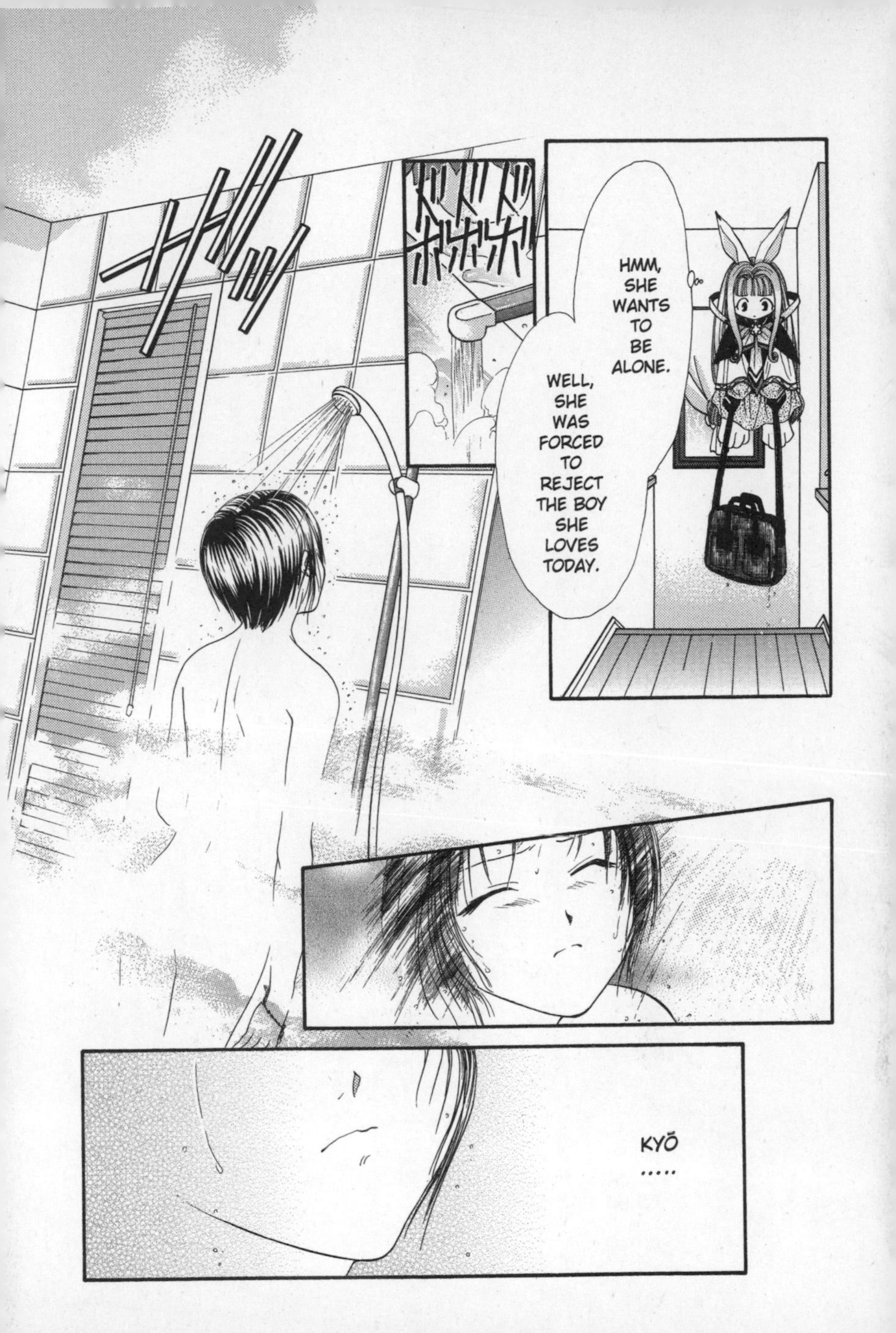
HMM, SHE WANTS TO BE ALONE.
WELL, SHE WAS FORCED TO REJECT THE BOY SHE LOVES TODAY.
KYŌ .....

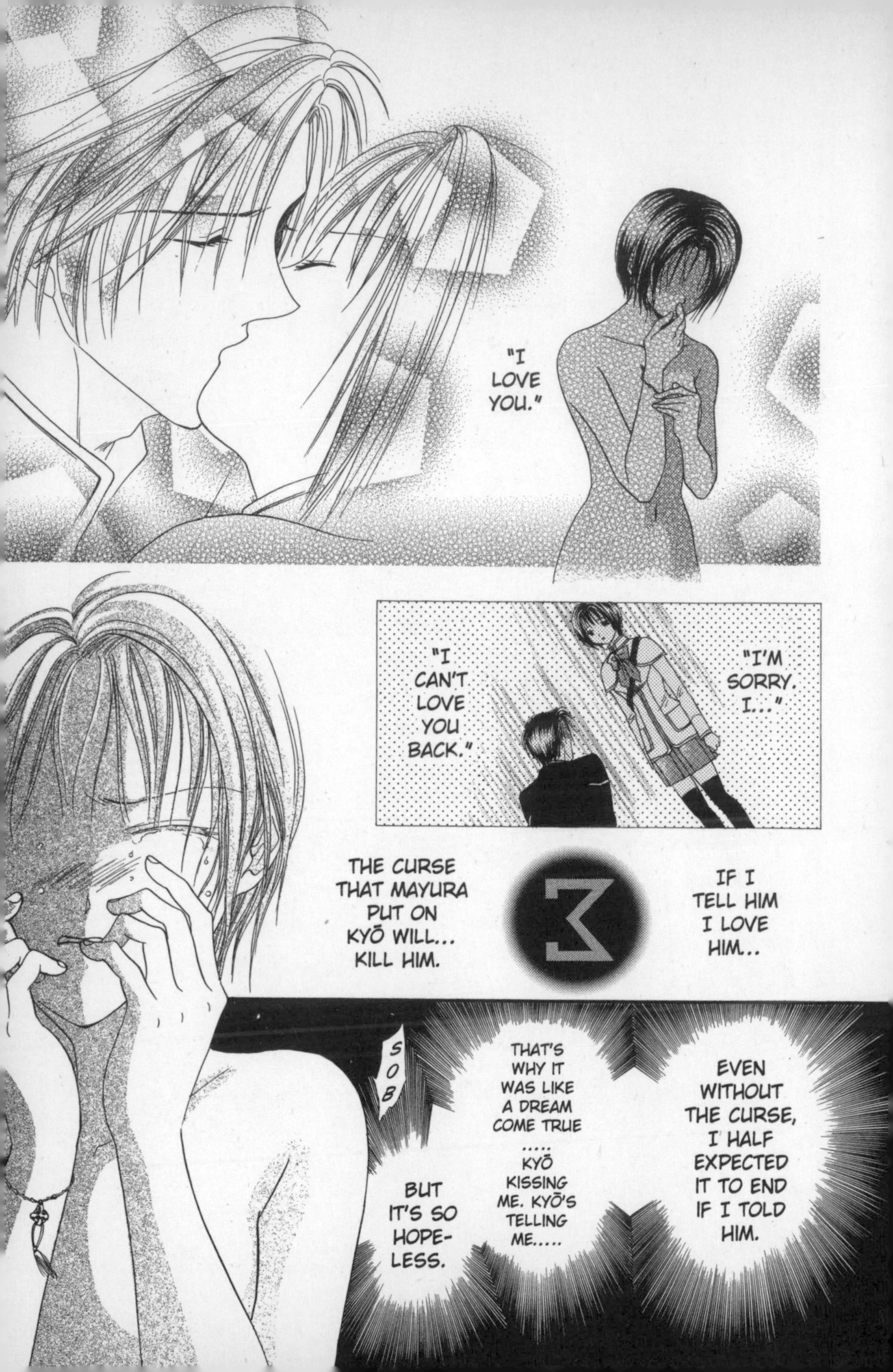
"I LOVE YOU."
"I'M SORRY. I..."
"I CAN'T LOVE YOU BACK."
IF I TELL HIM I LOVE HIM...
3
THE CURSE THAT MAYURA PUT ON KYŌ WILL... KILL HIM.
EVEN WITHOUT THE CURSE, I HALF EXPECTED IT TO END IF I TOLD HIM.
THAT'S WHY IT WAS LIKE A DREAM COME TRUE ..... KYŌ KISSING ME. KYŌ'S TELLING ME.....
SOB
BUT IT'S SO HOPE-LESS.

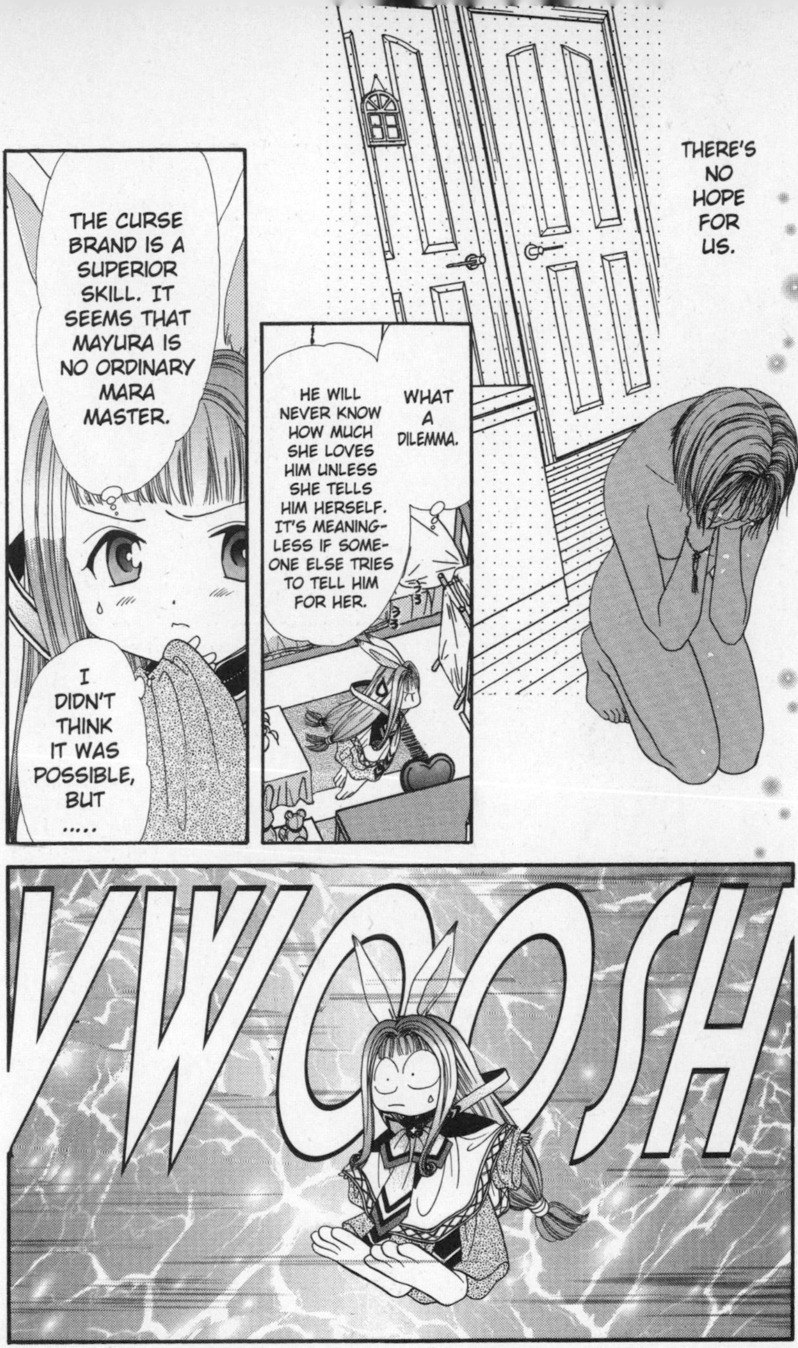
THERE'S NO HOPE FOR US.
WHAT A DILEMMA.
HE WILL NEVER KNOW HOW MUCH SHE LOVES HIM UNLESS SHE TELLS HIM HERSELF. IT'S MEANING-LESS IF SOME-ONE ELSE TRIES TO TELL HIM FOR HER.
THE CURSE BRAND IS A SUPERIOR SKILL. IT SEEMS THAT MAYURA IS NO ORDINARY MARA MASTER.
I DIDN'T THINK IT WAS POSSIBLE, BUT .....
VWOOSH

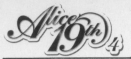

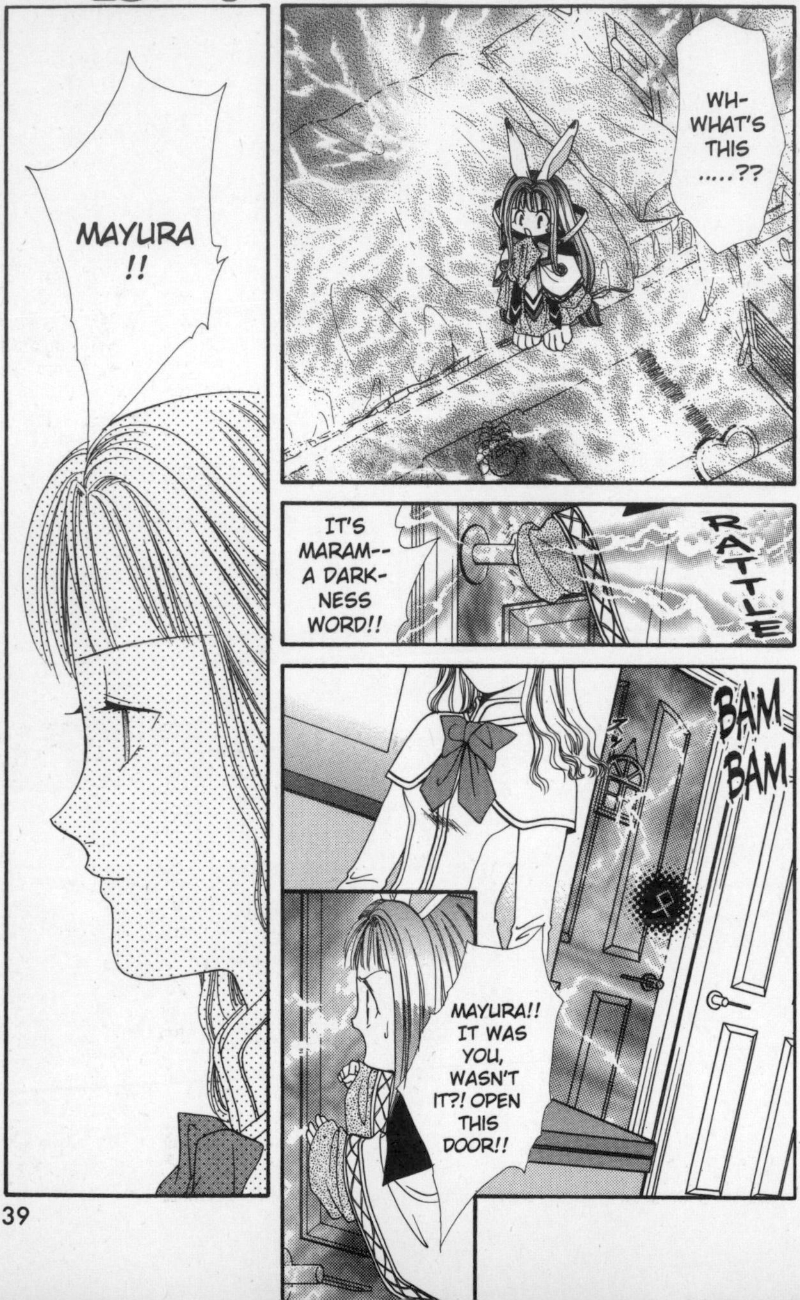
WH-WHAT'S THIS .....??
RATTLE
IT'S MARAM--A DARKNESS WORD!!
BAM BAM
MAYURA!! IT WAS YOU, WASN'T IT?! OPEN THIS DOOR!!
MAYURA !!

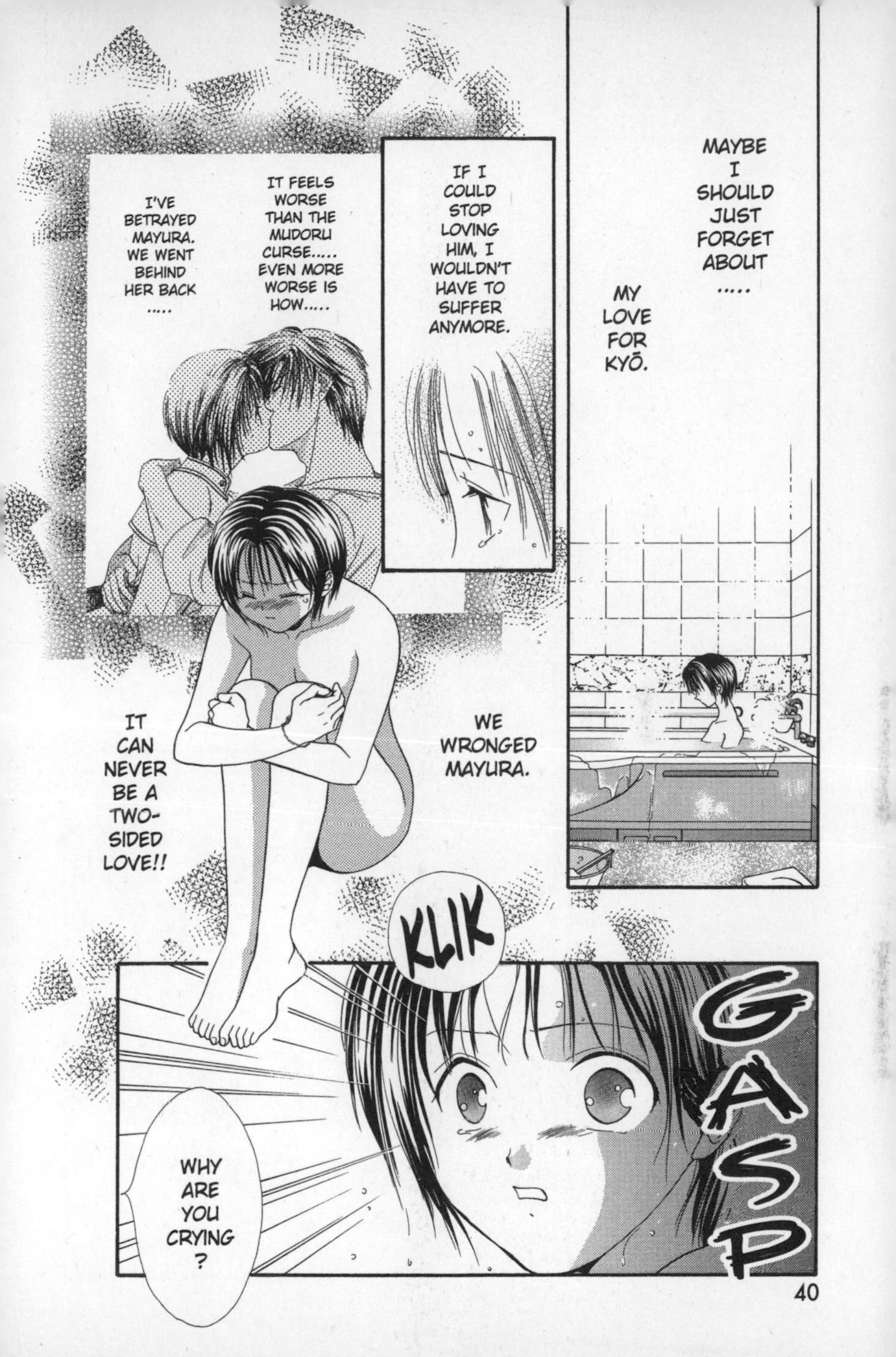
MAYBE I SHOULD JUST FORGET ABOUT .....
MY LOVE FOR KYŌ.
IF I COULD STOP LOVING HIM, I WOULDN'T HAVE TO SUFFER ANYMORE.
IT FEELS WORSE THAN THE MUDORU CURSE..... EVEN MORE WORSE IS HOW.....
I'VE BETRAYED MAYURA. WE WENT BEHIND HER BACK .....
WE WRONGED MAYURA.
IT CAN NEVER BE A TWO-SIDED LOVE!!
KLIK
GASP
WHY ARE YOU CRYING ?

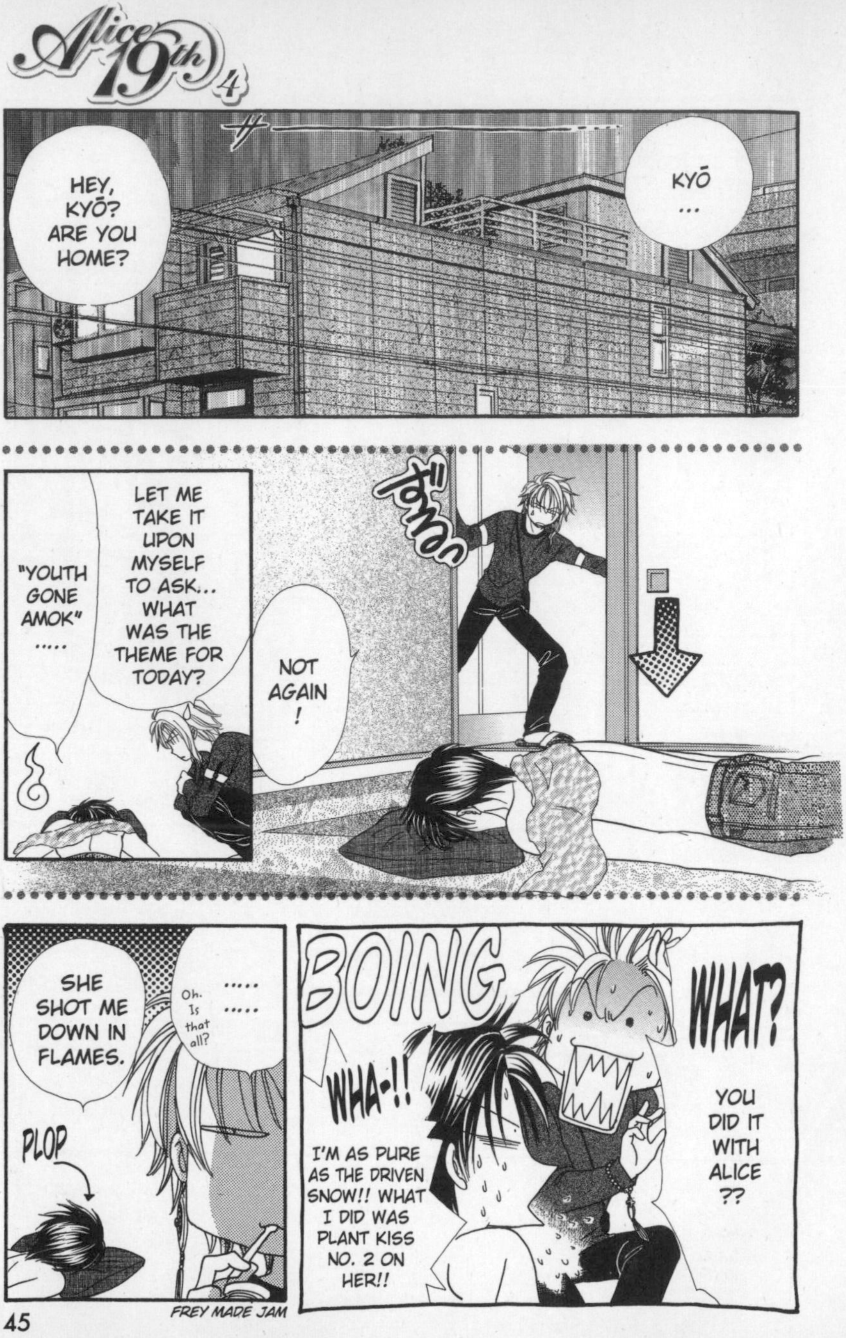
KYŌ
...
HEY, KYŌ? ARE YOU HOME?
ずるっ
NOT AGAIN
!
LET ME TAKE IT UPON MYSELF TO ASK... WHAT WAS THE THEME FOR TODAY?
"YOUTH GONE AMOK"
.....
WHAT?
BOING
YOU DID IT WITH ALICE
??
WHA-!!
I'M AS PURE AS THE DRIVEN SNOW!! WHAT I DID WAS PLANT KISS NO. 2 ON HER!!
.....
.....
Oh. Is that all?
SHE SHOT ME DOWN IN FLAMES.
PLOP

FREY MADE JAM

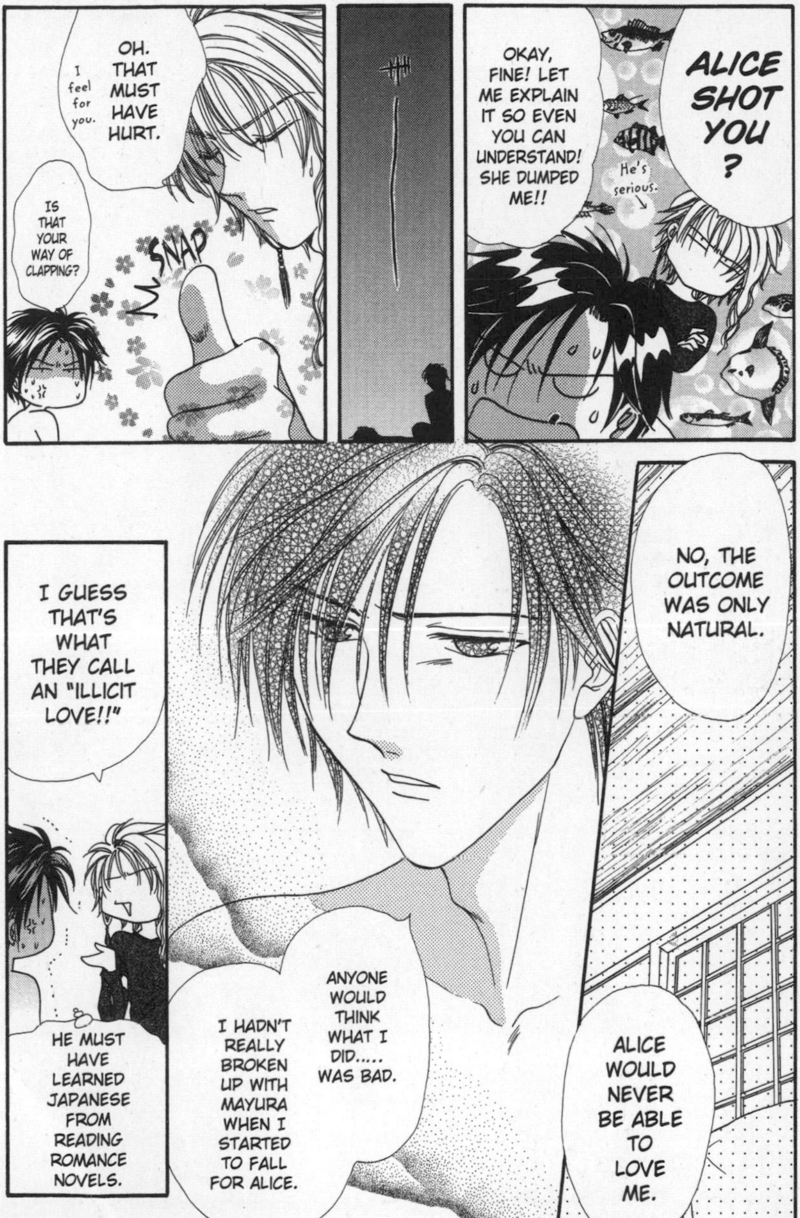
ALICE SHOT YOU ?
OKAY, FINE! LET ME EXPLAIN IT SO EVEN YOU CAN UNDERSTAND! SHE DUMPED ME!!
He's serious.
OH. THAT MUST HAVE HURT.
I feel for you.
SNAP
IS THAT YOUR WAY OF CLAPPING?
NO, THE OUTCOME WAS ONLY NATURAL.
ALICE WOULD NEVER BE ABLE TO LOVE ME.
ANYONE WOULD THINK WHAT I DID..... WAS BAD.
I HADN'T REALLY BROKEN UP WITH MAYURA WHEN I STARTED TO FALL FOR ALICE.
I GUESS THAT'S WHAT THEY CALL AN "ILLICIT LOVE!!"
HE MUST HAVE LEARNED JAPANESE FROM READING ROMANCE NOVELS.

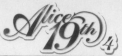

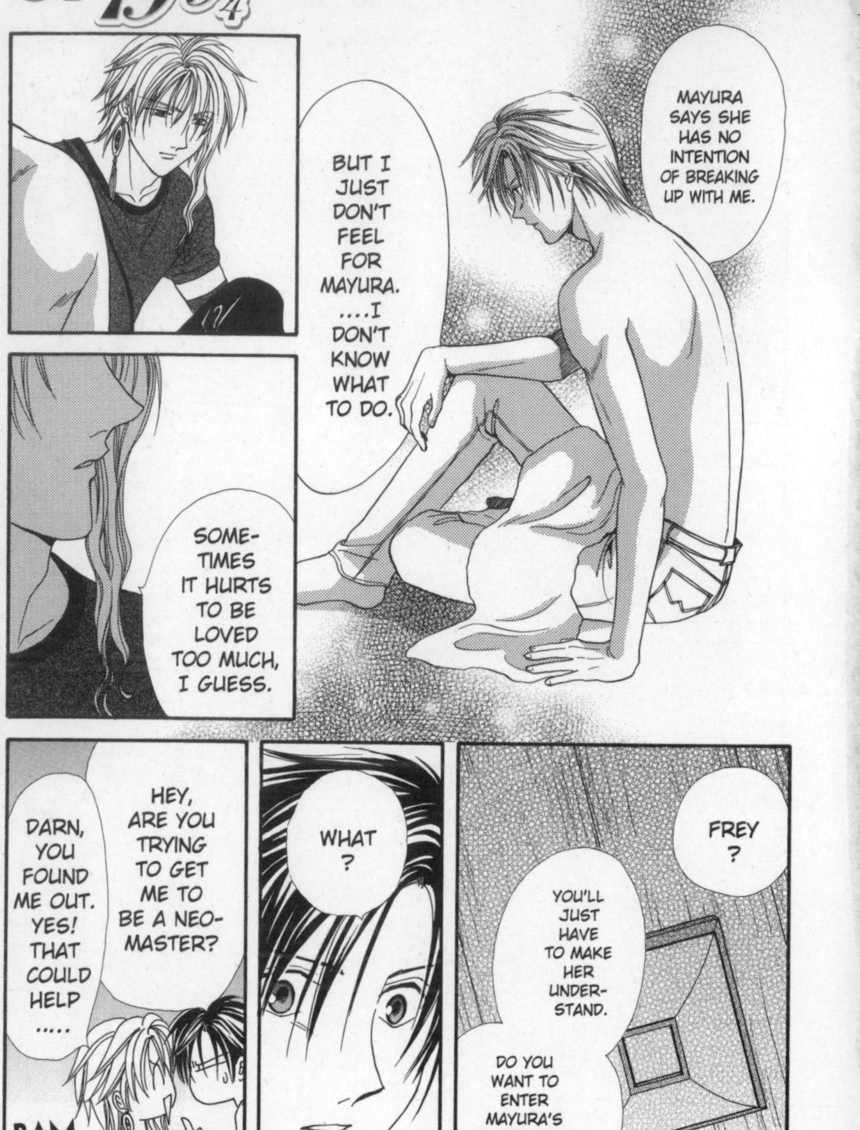
MAYURA SAYS SHE HAS NO INTENTION OF BREAKING UP WITH ME.
BUT I JUST DON'T FEEL FOR MAYURA. ....I DON'T KNOW WHAT TO DO.
SOME-TIMES IT HURTS TO BE LOVED TOO MUCH, I GUESS.
FREY ?
YOU'LL JUST HAVE TO MAKE HER UNDER-STAND.
DO YOU WANT TO ENTER MAYURA'S INNER HEART AND CONVINCE HER DIRECTLY?
WHAT ?
HEY, ARE YOU TRYING TO GET ME TO BE A NEO-MASTER?
DARN, YOU FOUND ME OUT. YES! THAT COULD HELP .....
BAM BAM BAM

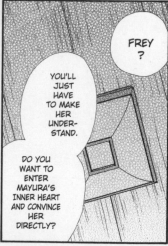

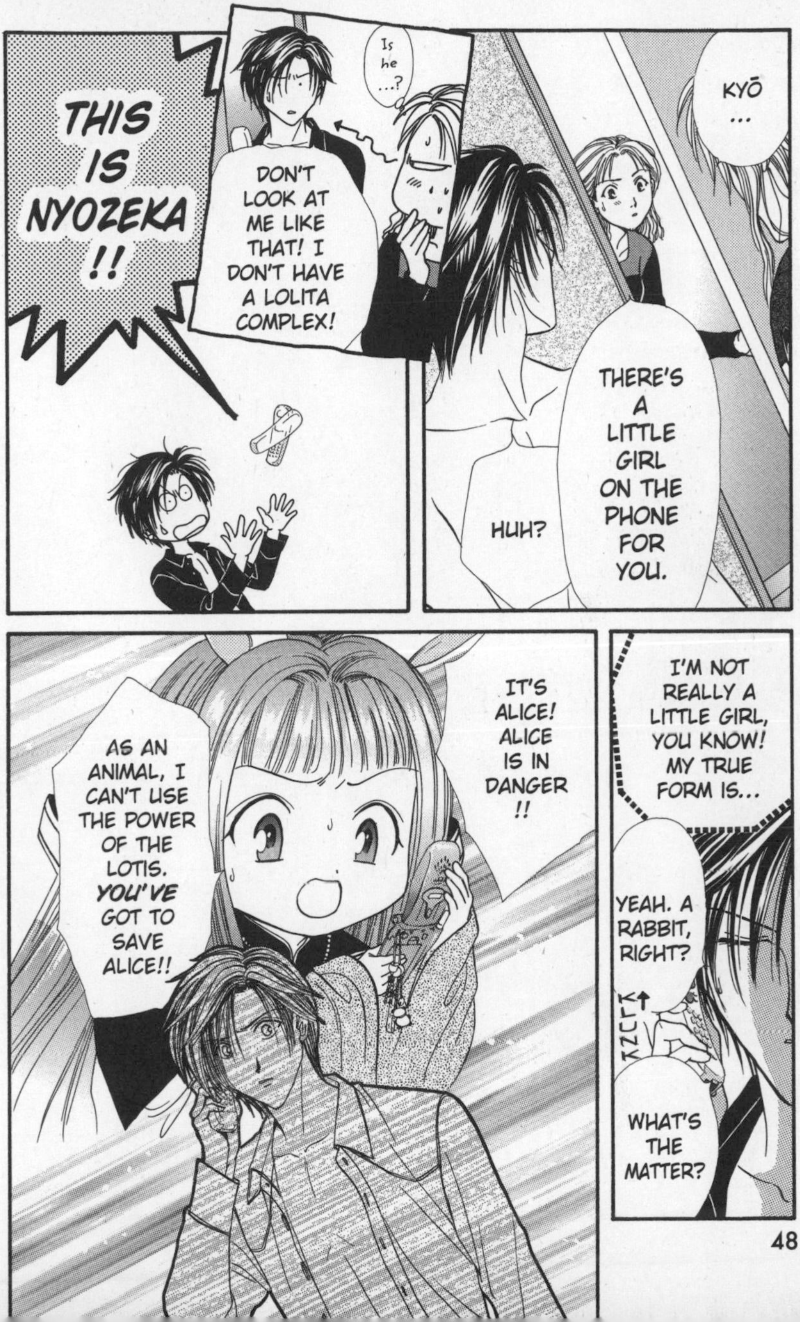
KYŌ...
THERE'S A LITTLE GIRL ON THE PHONE FOR YOU.
HUH?
Is he ...?
DON'T LOOK AT ME LIKE THAT! I DON'T HAVE A LOLITA COMPLEX!
THIS IS NYOZEKA!!
I'M NOT REALLY A LITTLE GIRL, YOU KNOW! MY TRUE FORM IS...
YEAH. A RABBIT, RIGHT?
KRUNK
WHAT'S THE MATTER?
IT'S ALICE! ALICE IS IN DANGER!!
AS AN ANIMAL, I CAN'T USE THE POWER OF THE LOTIS. *YOU'VE* GOT TO SAVE ALICE!!

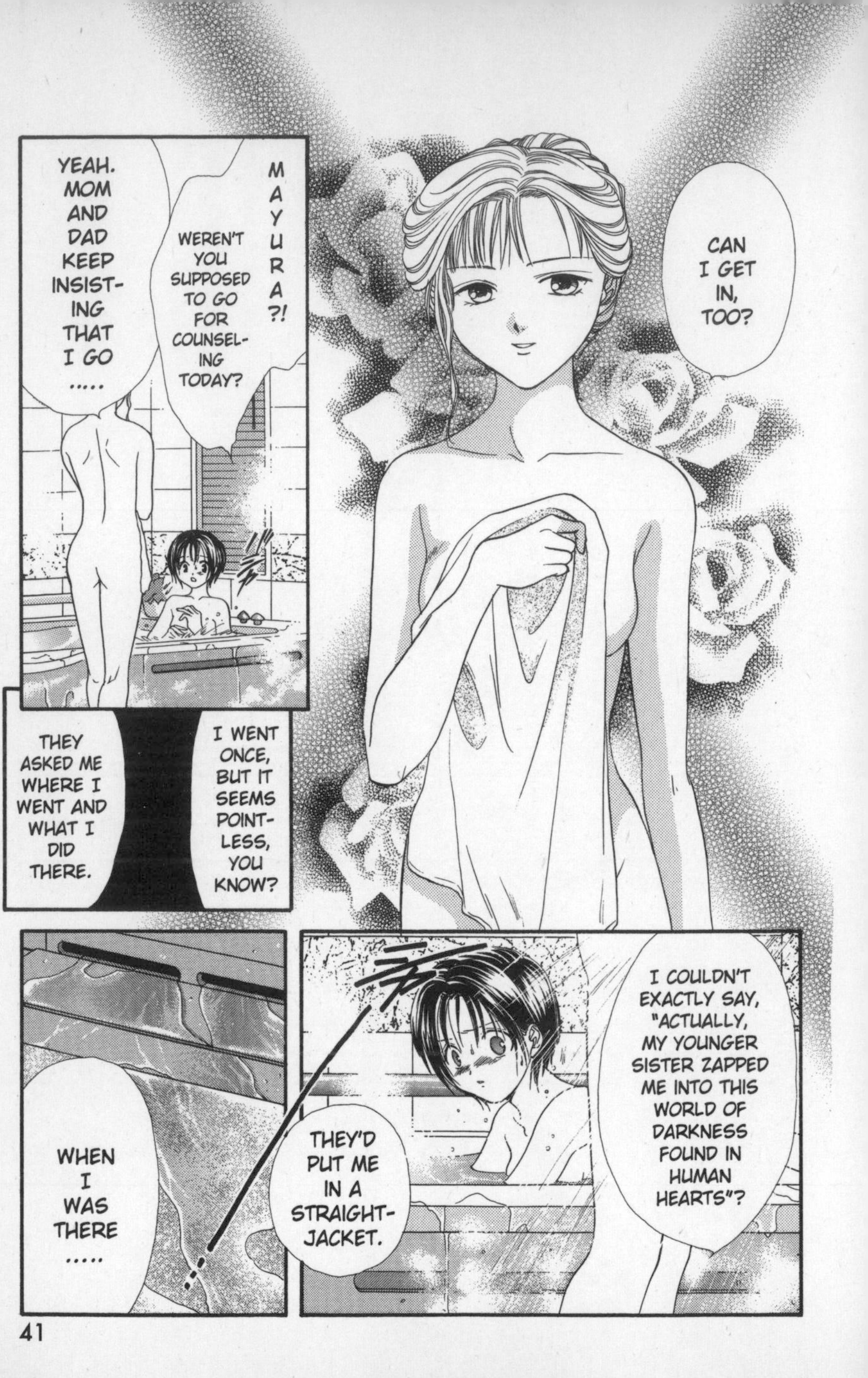
CAN I GET IN, TOO?
MAYURA?!
WEREN'T YOU SUPPOSED TO GO FOR COUNSELING TODAY?
YEAH. MOM AND DAD KEEP INSISTING THAT I GO .....
I WENT ONCE, BUT IT SEEMS POINTLESS, YOU KNOW?
THEY ASKED ME WHERE I WENT AND WHAT I DID THERE.
I COULDN'T EXACTLY SAY, "ACTUALLY, MY YOUNGER SISTER ZAPPED ME INTO THIS WORLD OF DARKNESS FOUND IN HUMAN HEARTS"?
THEY'D PUT ME IN A STRAIGHT-JACKET.
WHEN I WAS THERE .....

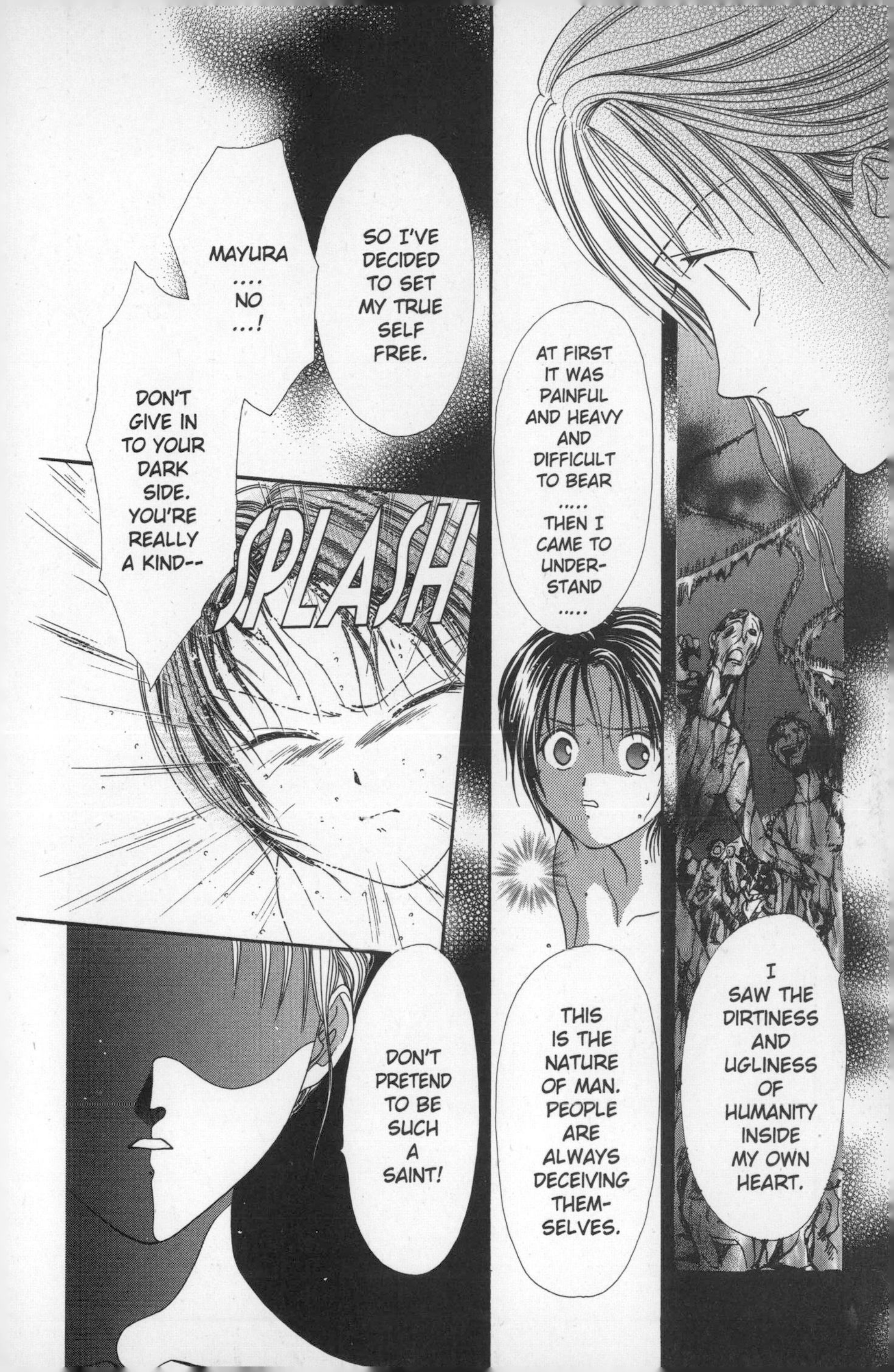
AT FIRST IT WAS PAINFUL AND HEAVY AND DIFFICULT TO BEAR ..... THEN I CAME TO UNDER-STAND .....
I SAW THE DIRTINESS AND UGLINESS OF HUMANITY INSIDE MY OWN HEART.
THIS IS THE NATURE OF MAN. PEOPLE ARE ALWAYS DECEIVING THEM-SELVES.
SO I'VE DECIDED TO SET MY TRUE SELF FREE.
MAYURA .... NO ...!
DON'T GIVE IN TO YOUR DARK SIDE. YOU'RE REALLY A KIND--
SPLASH
DON'T PRETEND TO BE SUCH A SAINT!

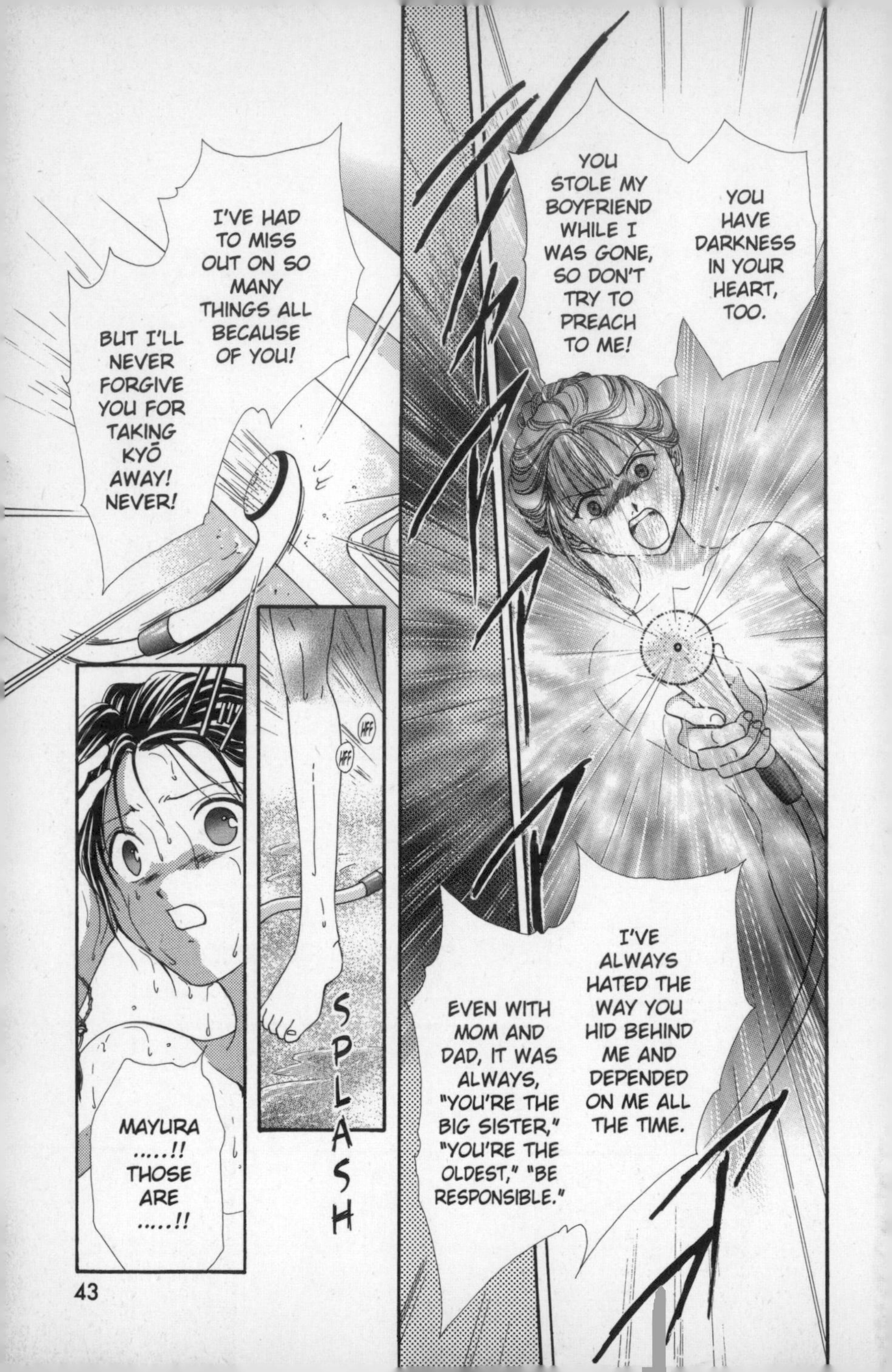
YOU HAVE DARKNESS IN YOUR HEART, TOO.
YOU STOLE MY BOYFRIEND WHILE I WAS GONE, SO DON'T TRY TO PREACH TO ME!
I'VE ALWAYS HATED THE WAY YOU HID BEHIND ME AND DEPENDED ON ME ALL THE TIME.
EVEN WITH MOM AND DAD, IT WAS ALWAYS, "YOU'RE THE BIG SISTER," "YOU'RE THE OLDEST," "BE RESPONSIBLE."
I'VE HAD TO MISS OUT ON SO MANY THINGS ALL BECAUSE OF YOU!
BUT I'LL NEVER FORGIVE YOU FOR TAKING KYŌ AWAY! NEVER!
HFF
HFF
SPLASH
MAYURA .....!! THOSE ARE .....!!

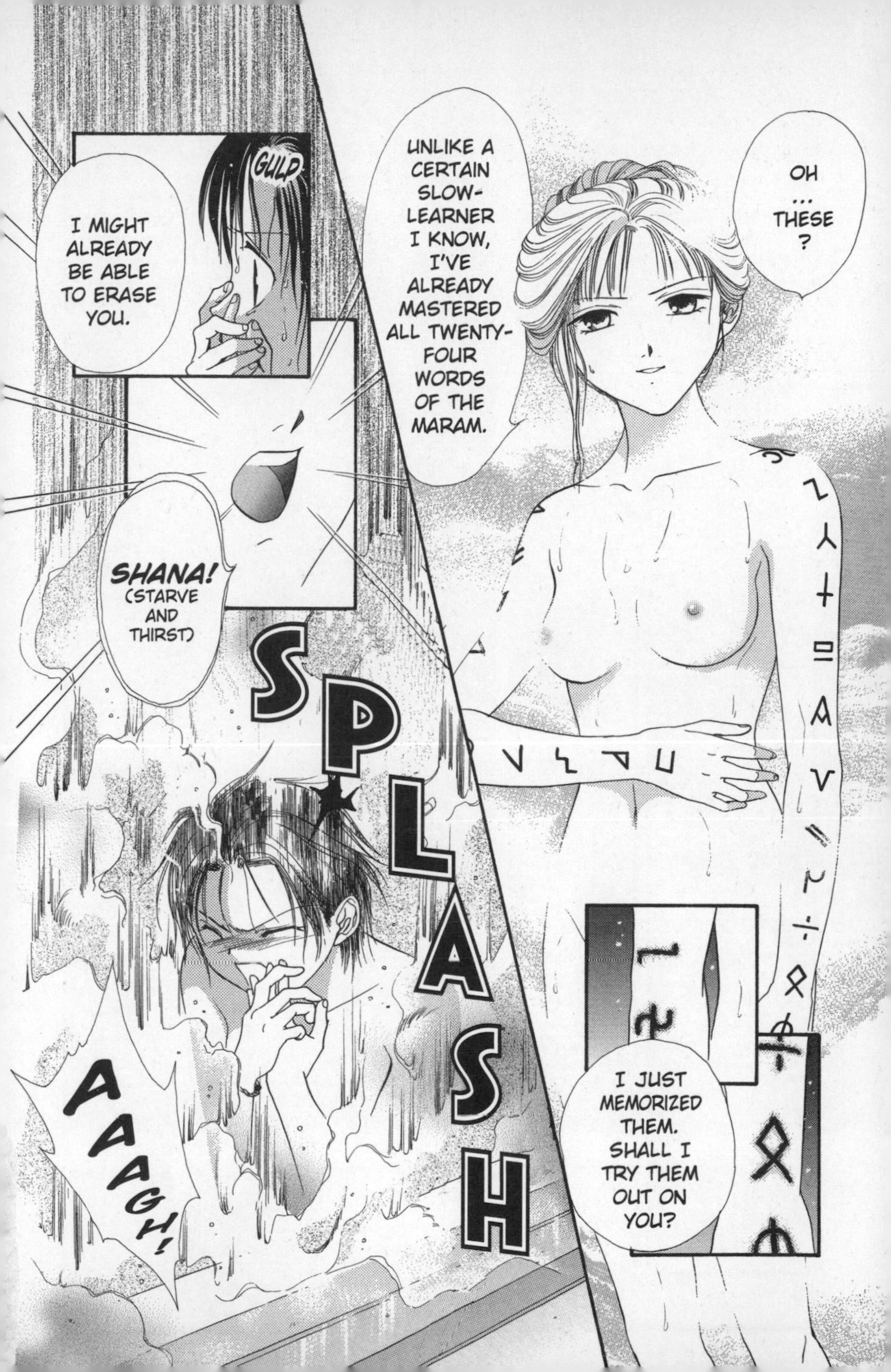

OH ... THESE ?
UNLIKE A CERTAIN SLOW-LEARNER I KNOW, I'VE ALREADY MASTERED ALL TWENTY-FOUR WORDS OF THE MARAM.
I JUST MEMORIZED THEM. SHALL I TRY THEM OUT ON YOU?
I MIGHT ALREADY BE ABLE TO ERASE YOU.
GULP
SHANA! (STARVE AND THIRST)
SPLASH
AAAGH!

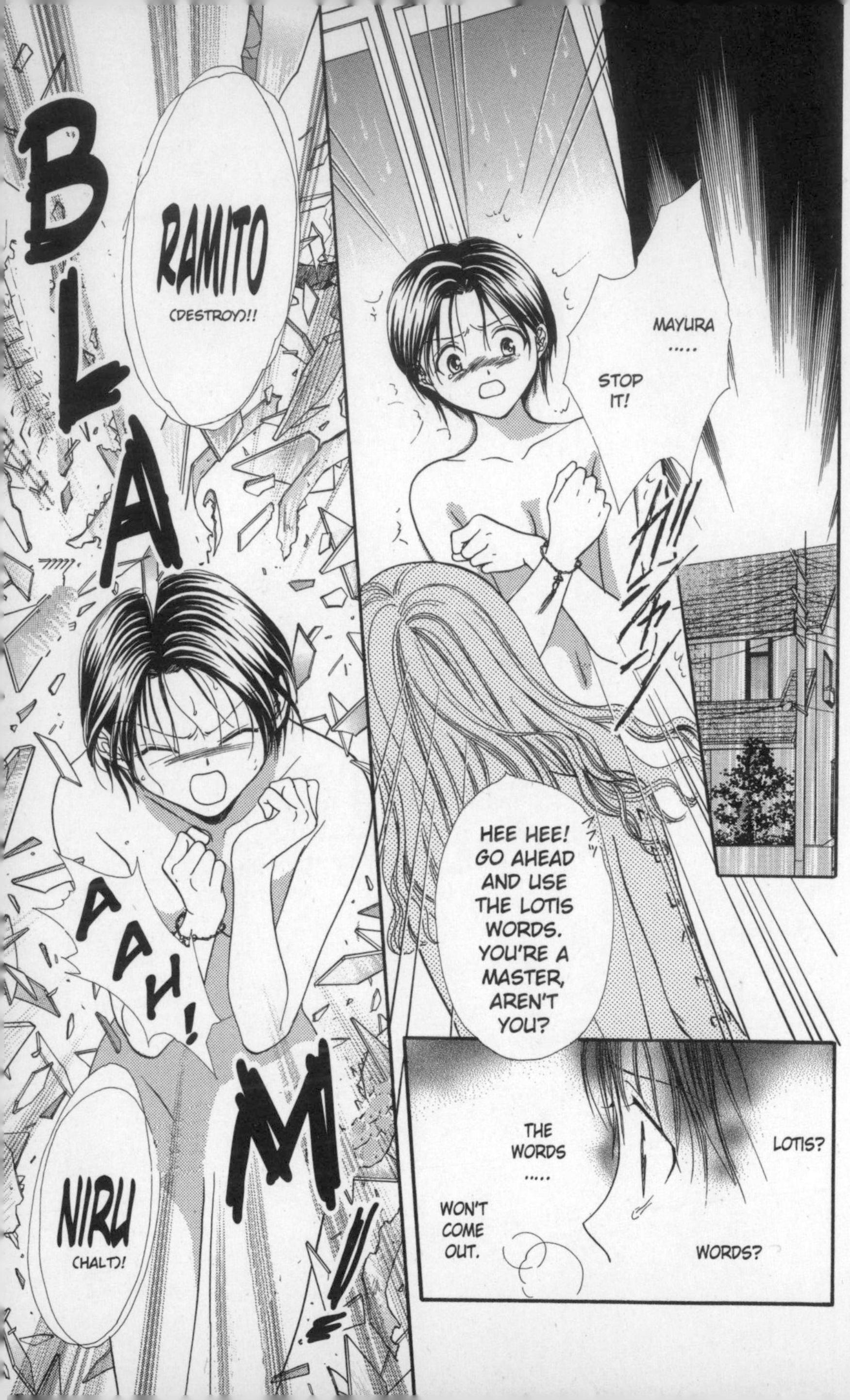
MAYURA .....
STOP IT!
HEE HEE! GO AHEAD AND USE THE LOTIS WORDS. YOU'RE A MASTER, AREN'T YOU?
LOTIS?
WORDS?
THE WORDS .....
WON'T COME OUT.
RAMITO (DESTROY)!!
BLAM!!
AAH!
NIRU (HALT)!

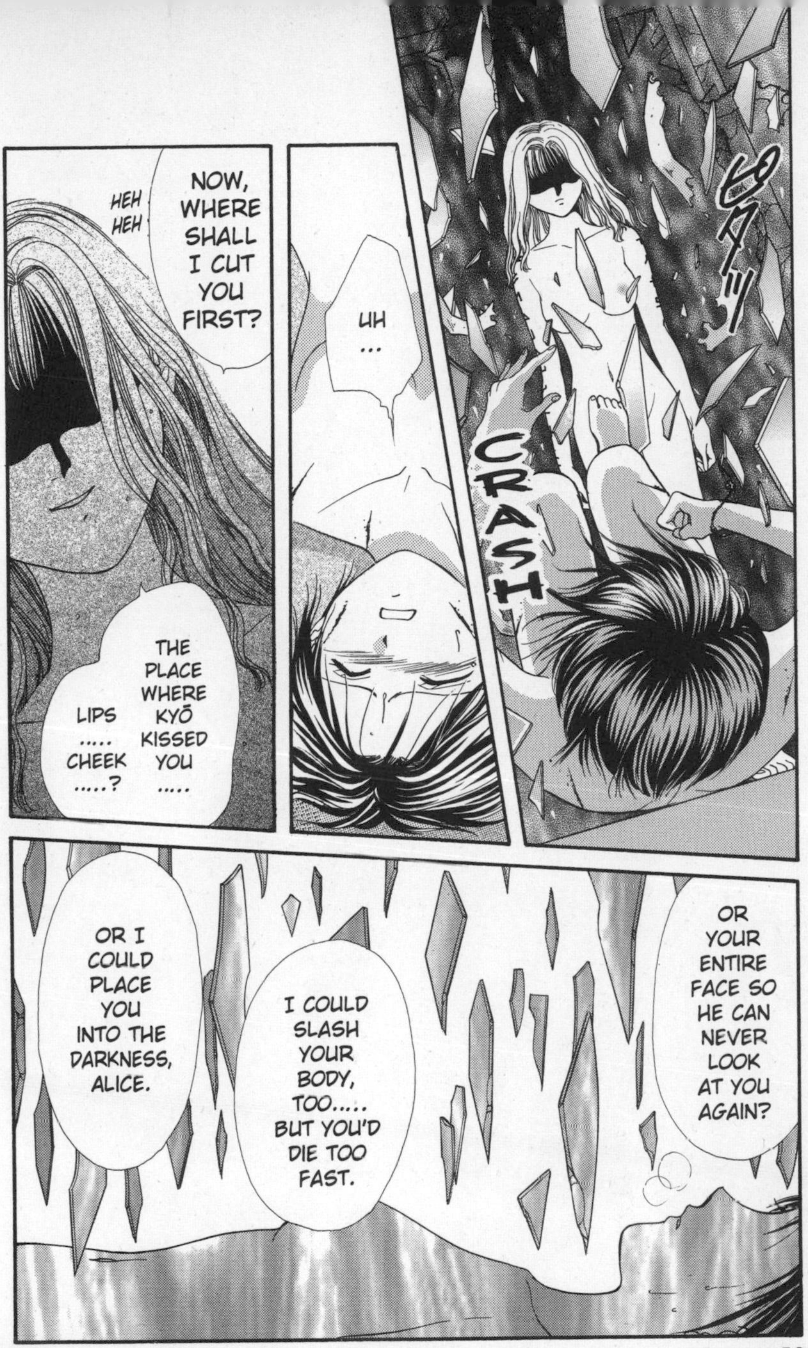
CRASH
UH ...
NOW, WHERE SHALL I CUT YOU FIRST?
HEH HEH
THE PLACE WHERE KYŌ KISSED YOU .....
LIPS ..... CHEEK .....?
OR YOUR ENTIRE FACE SO HE CAN NEVER LOOK AT YOU AGAIN?
I COULD SLASH YOUR BODY, TOO..... BUT YOU'D DIE TOO FAST.
OR I COULD PLACE YOU INTO THE DARKNESS, ALICE.

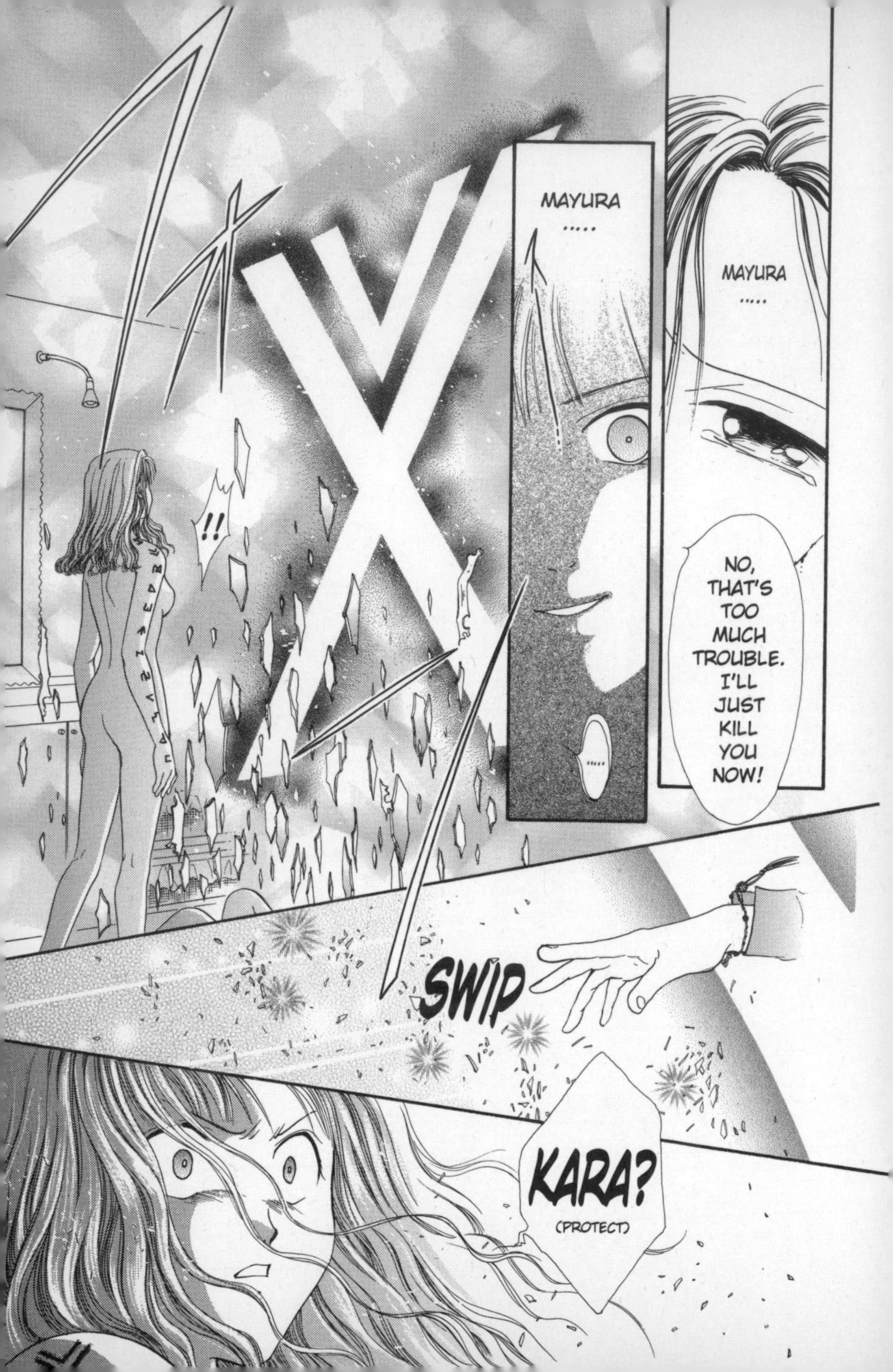
MAYURA .....
NO, THAT'S TOO MUCH TROUBLE. I'LL JUST KILL YOU NOW!
MAYURA .....
.....
!!
SWIP
KARA?
(PROTECT)

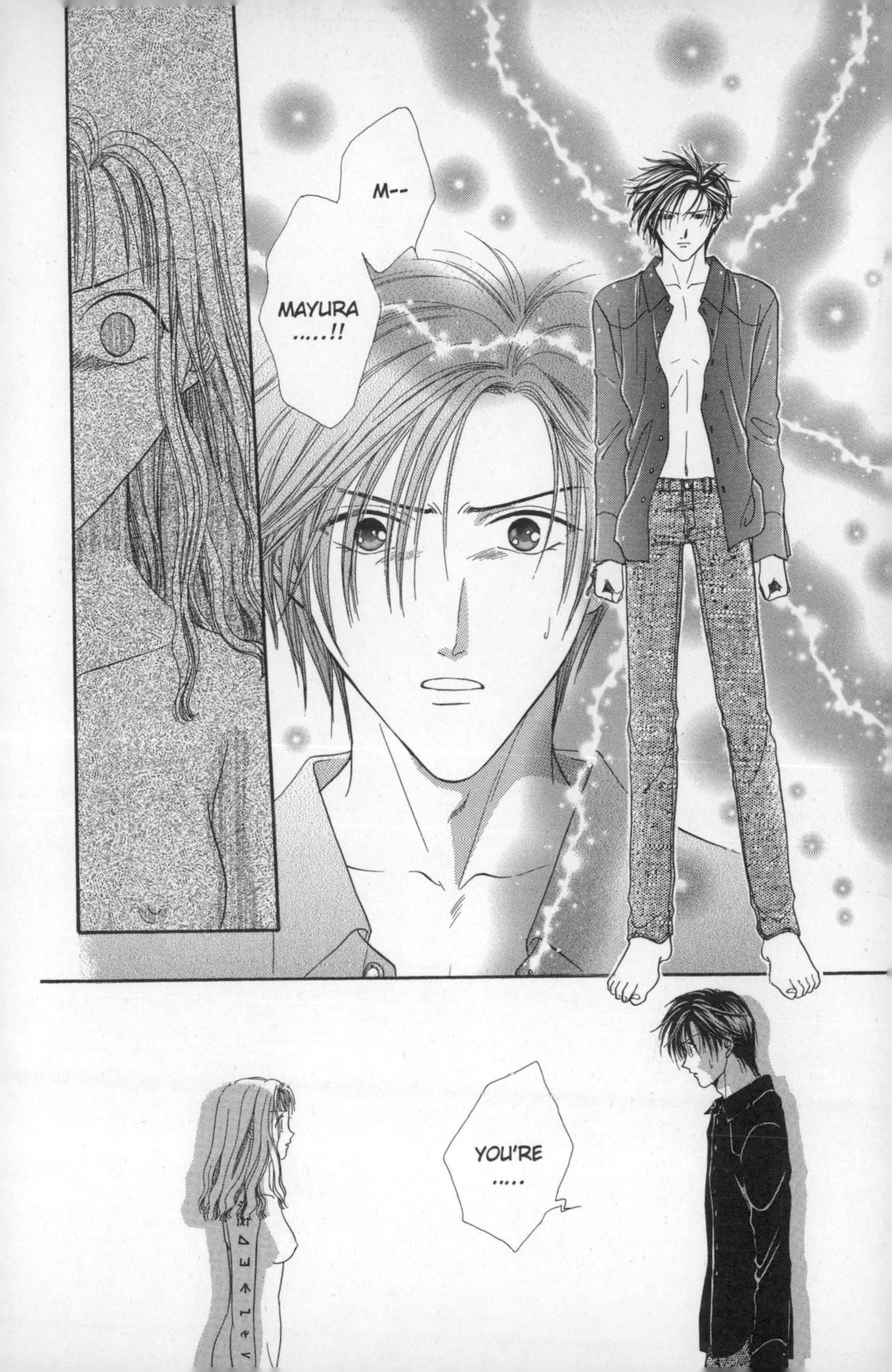
M--
MAYURA .....!!
YOU'RE .....

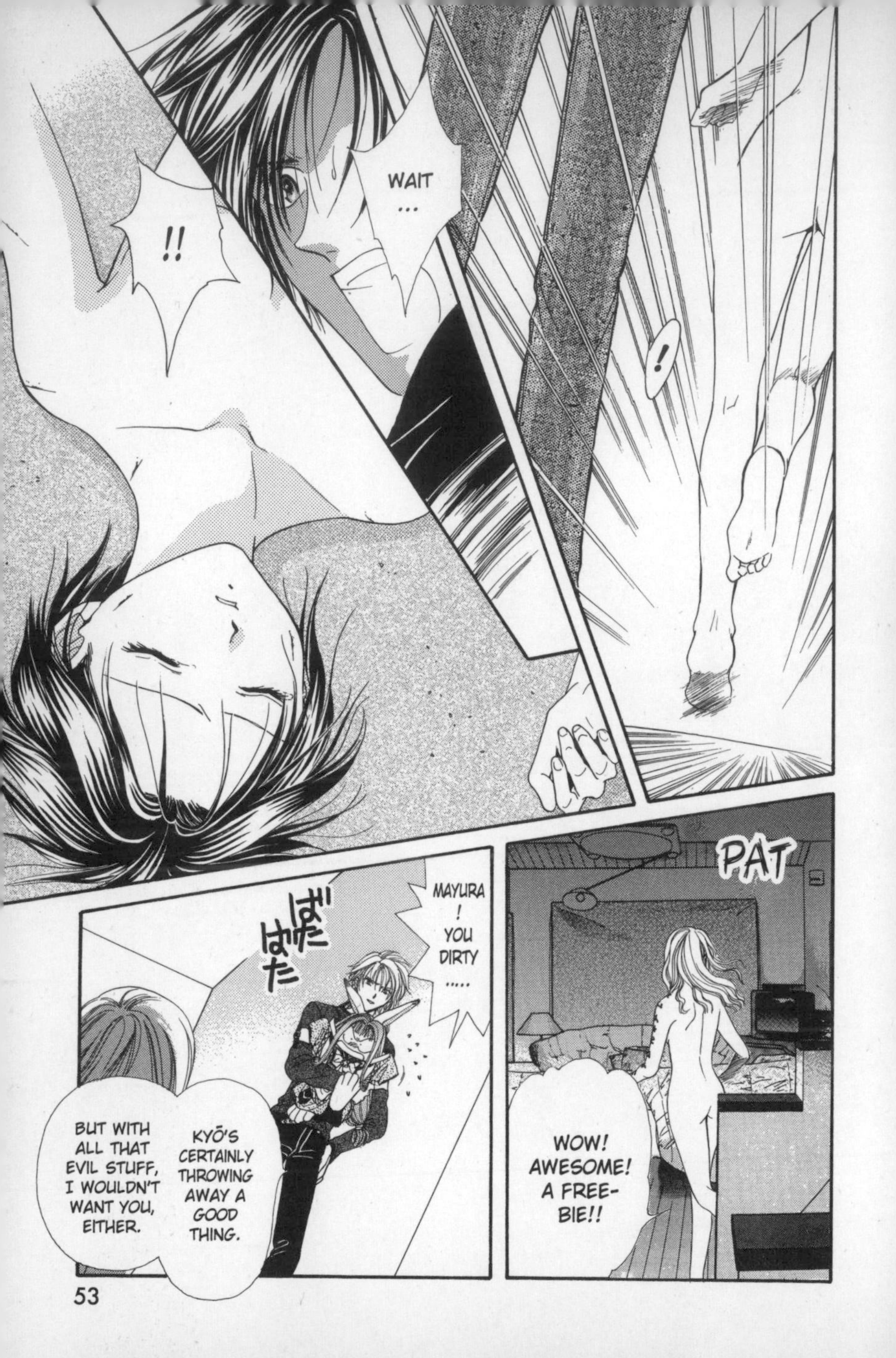

!
WAIT ...
!!
PAT
WOW! AWESOME! A FREE-BIE!!
MAYURA ! YOU DIRTY .....
ばた はた
KYŌ'S CERTAINLY THROWING AWAY A GOOD THING.
BUT WITH ALL THAT EVIL STUFF, I WOULDN'T WANT YOU, EITHER.

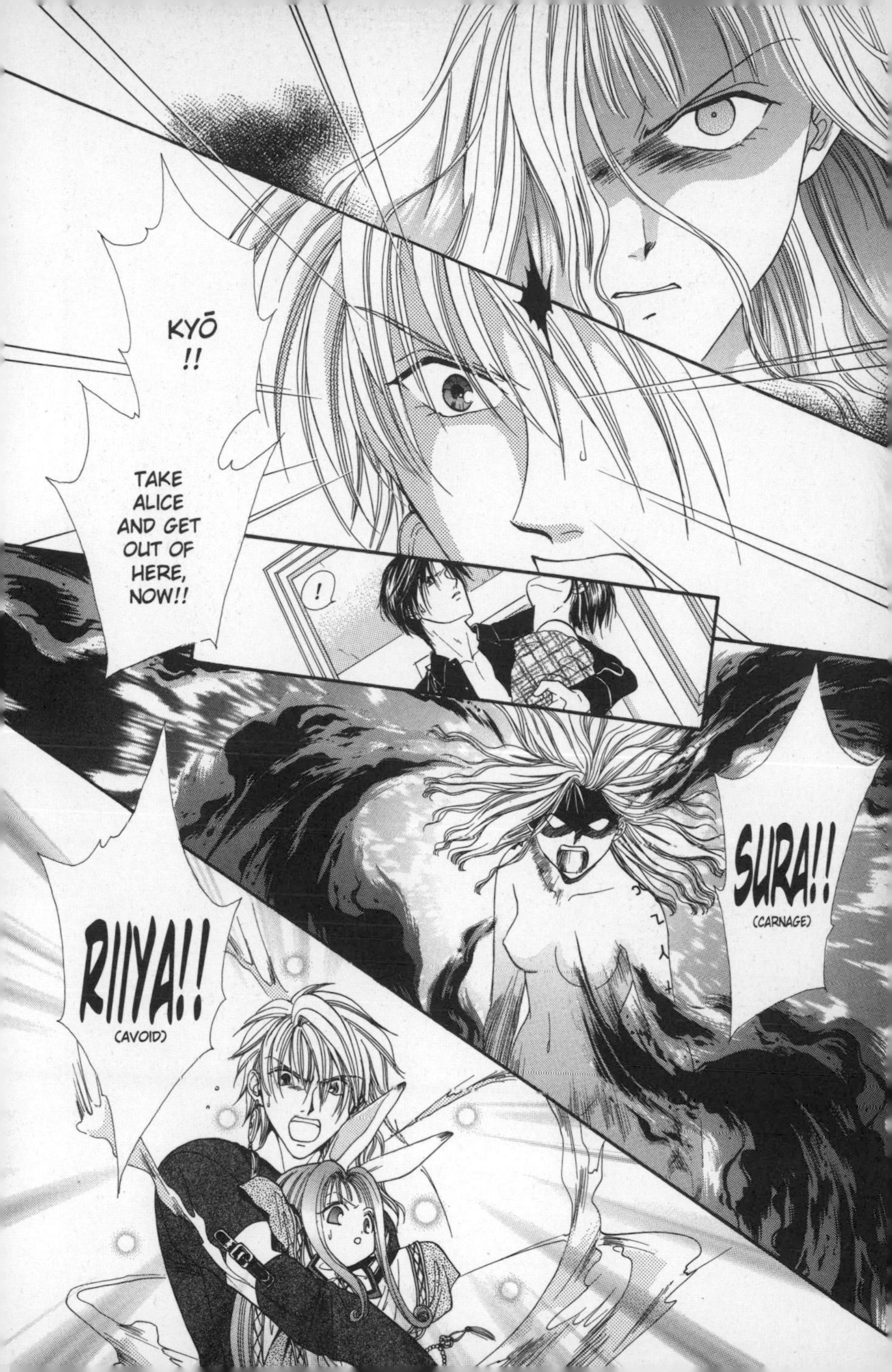
KYŌ !!
TAKE ALICE AND GET OUT OF HERE, NOW!!
!
SURA!!
(CARNAGE)
RIIYA!!
(AVOID)

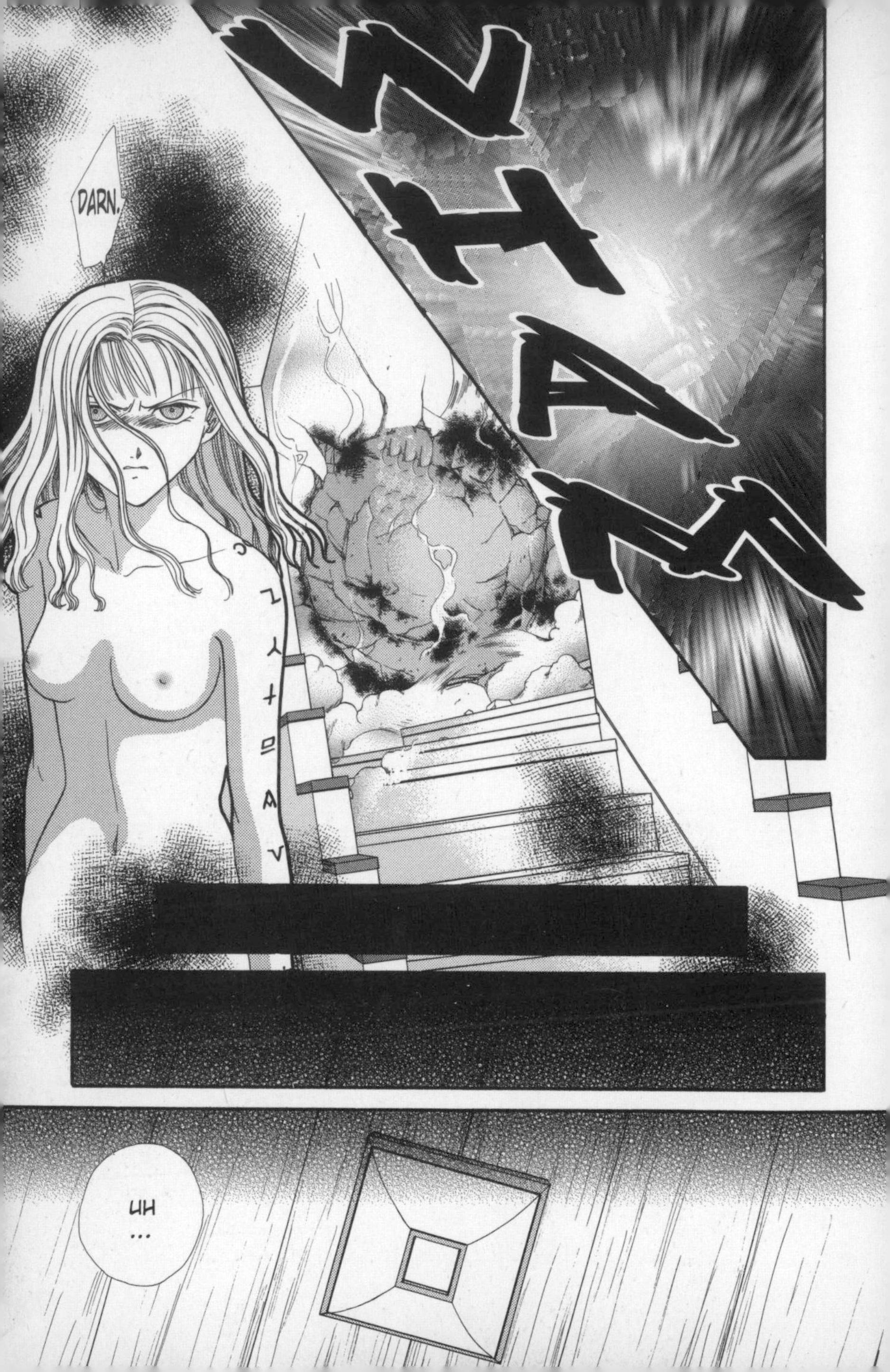
WHAM
DARN.
UH ...

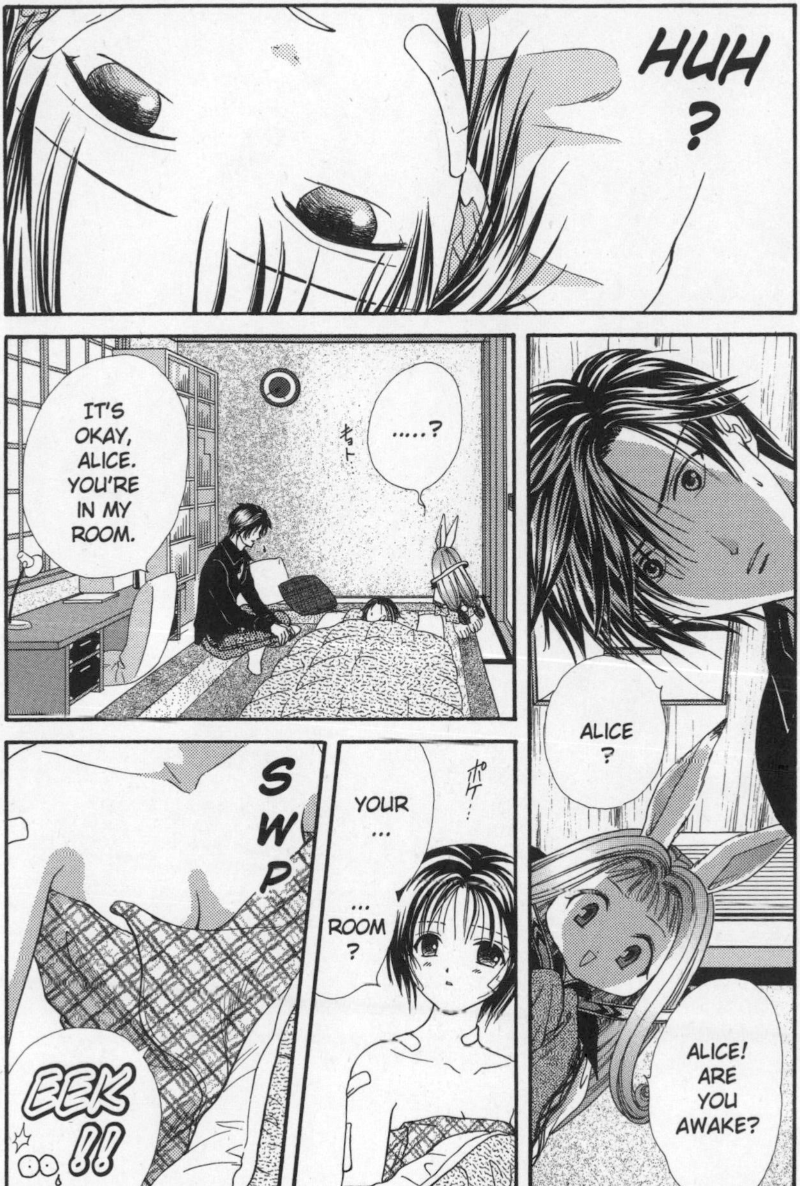
HUH ?
ALICE ?
ALICE! ARE YOU AWAKE?
.....?
IT'S OKAY, ALICE. YOU'RE IN MY ROOM.
YOUR ... ... ROOM ?
SWP
EEK !!

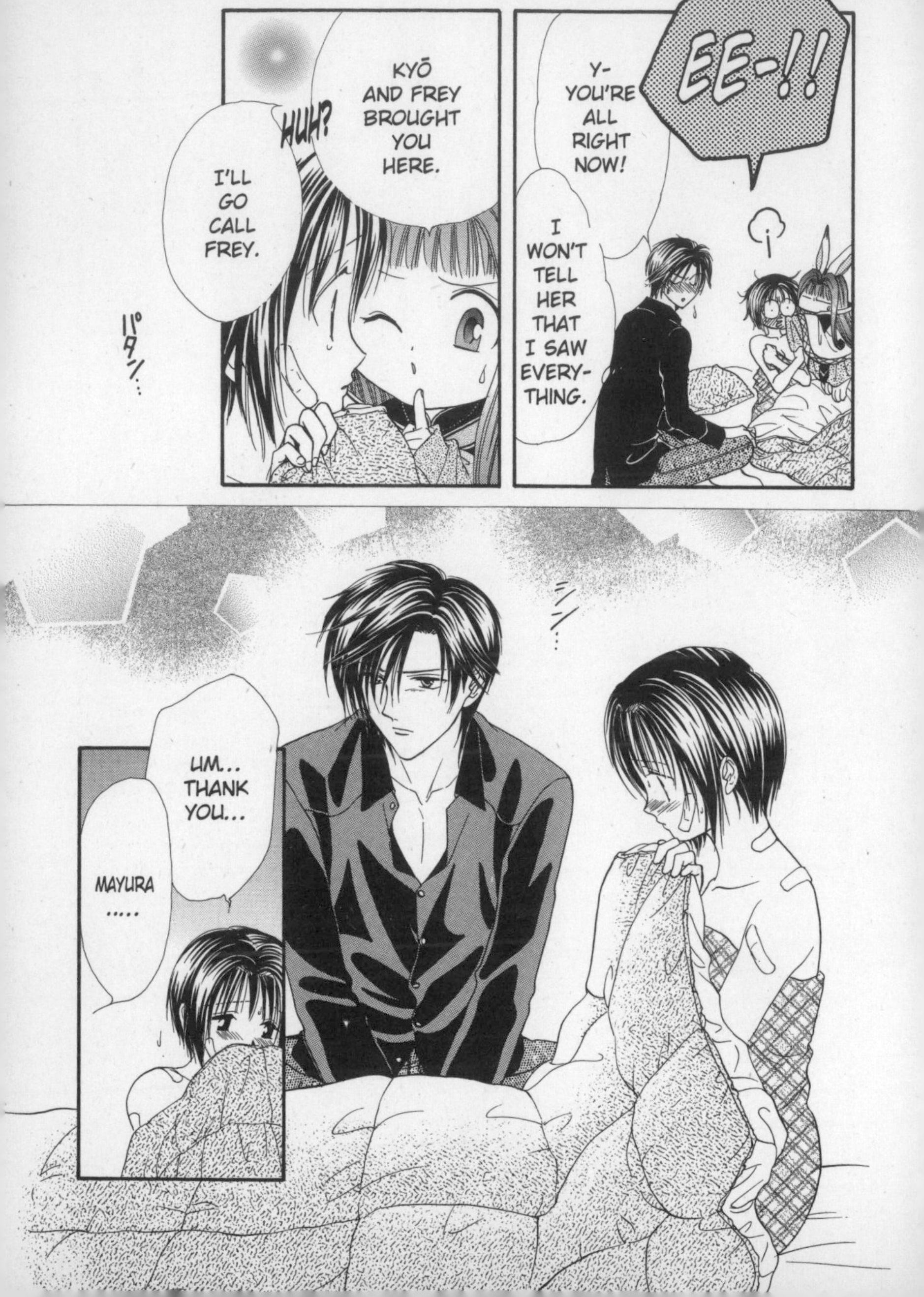
EE-!!
Y- YOU'RE ALL RIGHT NOW!
I WON'T TELL HER THAT I SAW EVERYTHING.
KYŌ AND FREY BROUGHT YOU HERE.
HUH?
I'LL GO CALL FREY.
UM... THANK YOU...
MAYURA .....

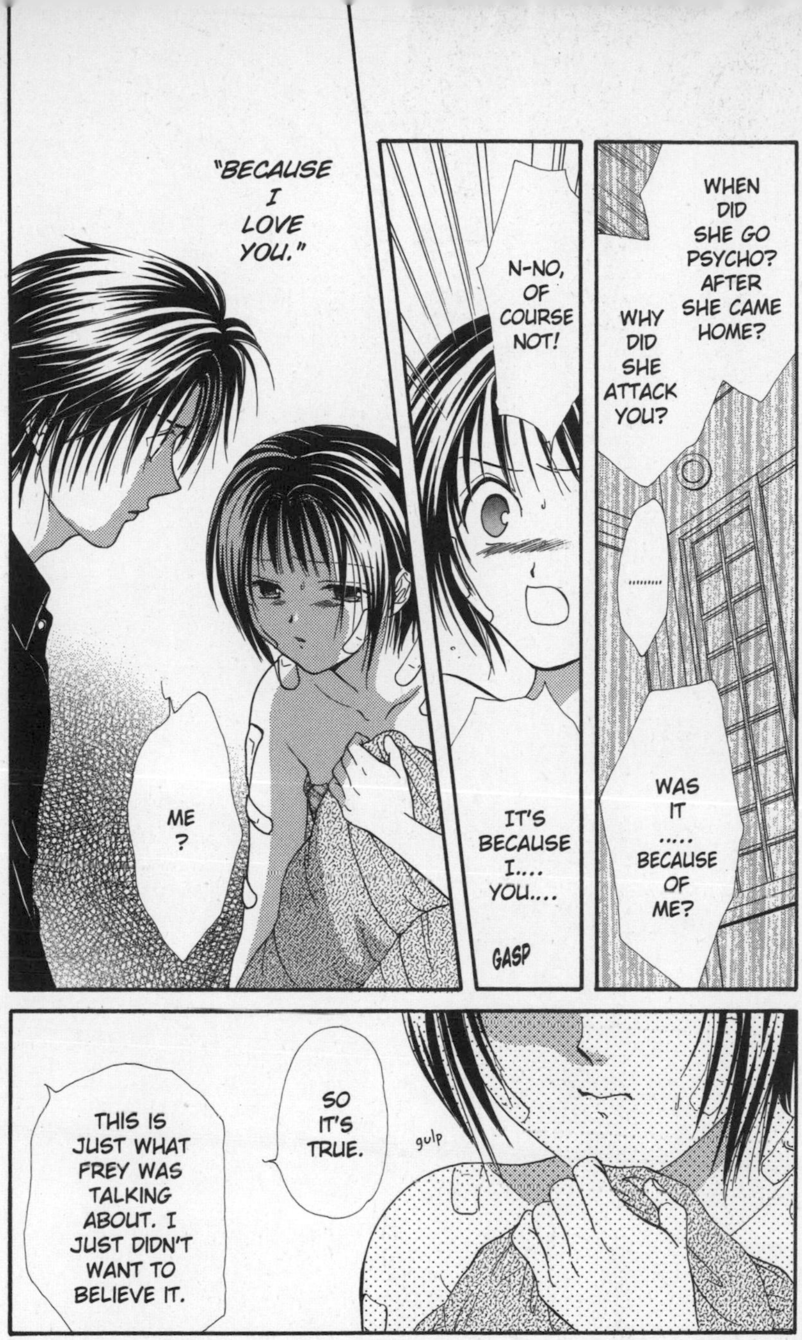
WHEN DID SHE GO PSYCHO? AFTER SHE CAME HOME?
WHY DID SHE ATTACK YOU?
....
WAS IT ..... BECAUSE OF ME?
N-NO, OF COURSE NOT!
IT'S BECAUSE I.... YOU....
GASP
"BECAUSE I LOVE YOU."
ME ?
gulp
SO IT'S TRUE.
THIS IS JUST WHAT FREY WAS TALKING ABOUT. I JUST DIDN'T WANT TO BELIEVE IT.

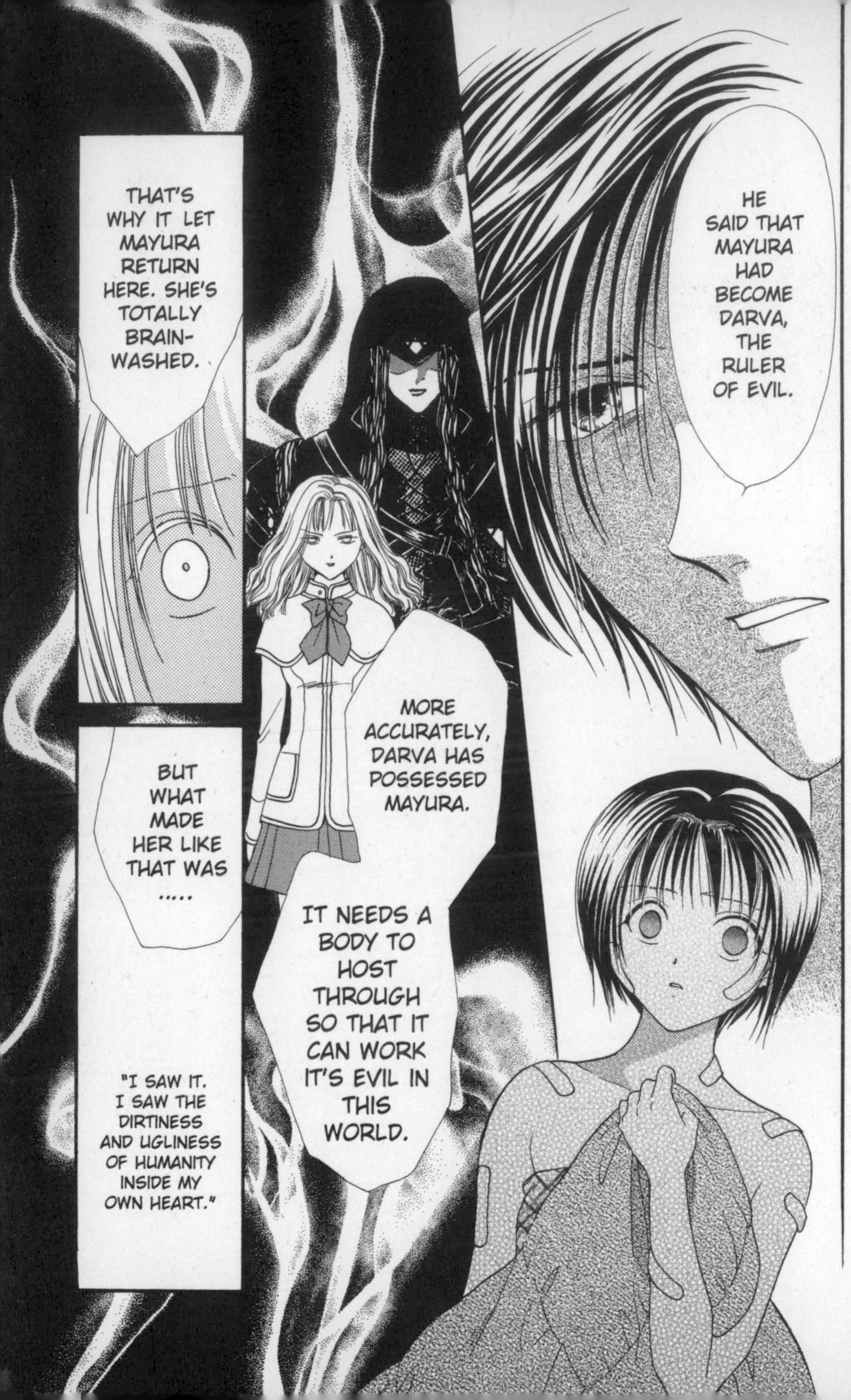
HE SAID THAT MAYURA HAD BECOME DARVA, THE RULER OF EVIL.
MORE ACCURATELY, DARVA HAS POSSESSED MAYURA.
IT NEEDS A BODY TO HOST THROUGH SO THAT IT CAN WORK IT'S EVIL IN THIS WORLD.
THAT'S WHY IT LET MAYURA RETURN HERE. SHE'S TOTALLY BRAIN-WASHED.
BUT WHAT MADE HER LIKE THAT WAS .....
"I SAW IT. I SAW THE DIRTINESS AND UGLINESS OF HUMANITY INSIDE MY OWN HEART."

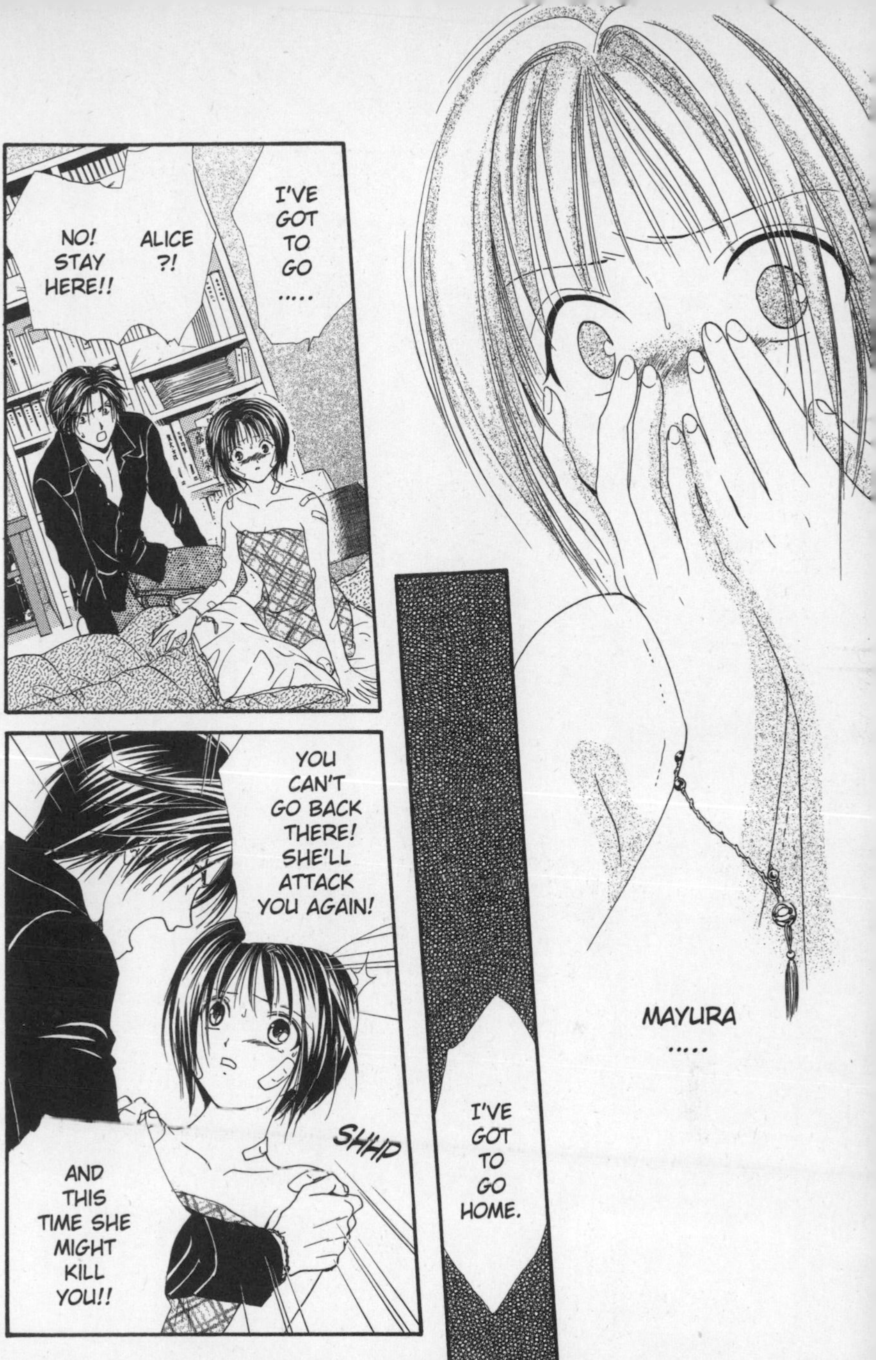
MAYURA .....
I'VE GOT TO GO HOME.
I'VE GOT TO GO .....
ALICE ?!
NO! STAY HERE!!
YOU CAN'T GO BACK THERE! SHE'LL ATTACK YOU AGAIN!
SHHP
AND THIS TIME SHE MIGHT KILL YOU!!

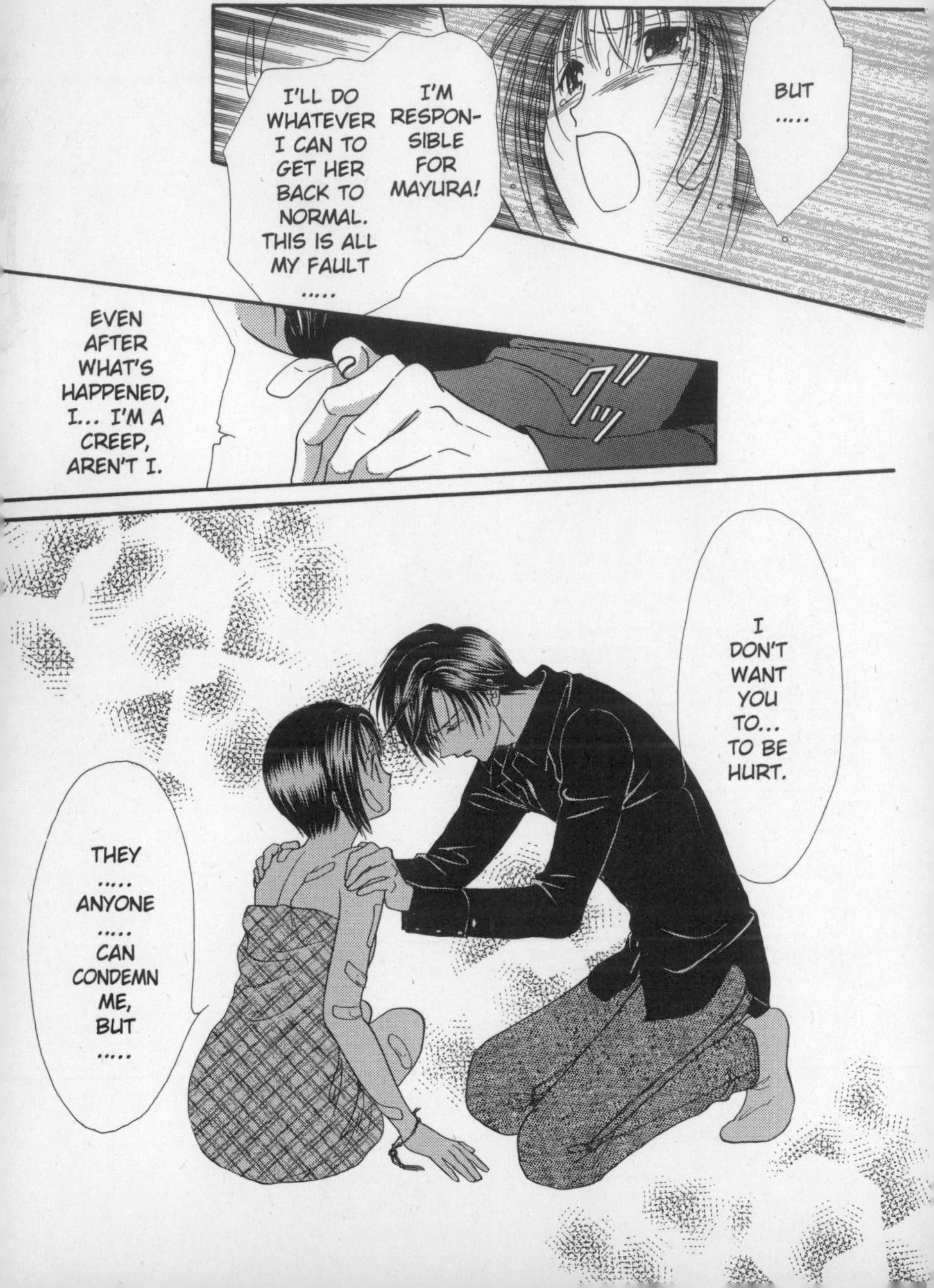
BUT .....
I'M RESPONSIBLE FOR MAYURA!
I'LL DO WHATEVER I CAN TO GET HER BACK TO NORMAL. THIS IS ALL MY FAULT .....
EVEN AFTER WHAT'S HAPPENED, I... I'M A CREEP, AREN'T I.
I DON'T WANT YOU TO... TO BE HURT.
THEY ..... ANYONE ..... CAN CONDEMN ME, BUT .....

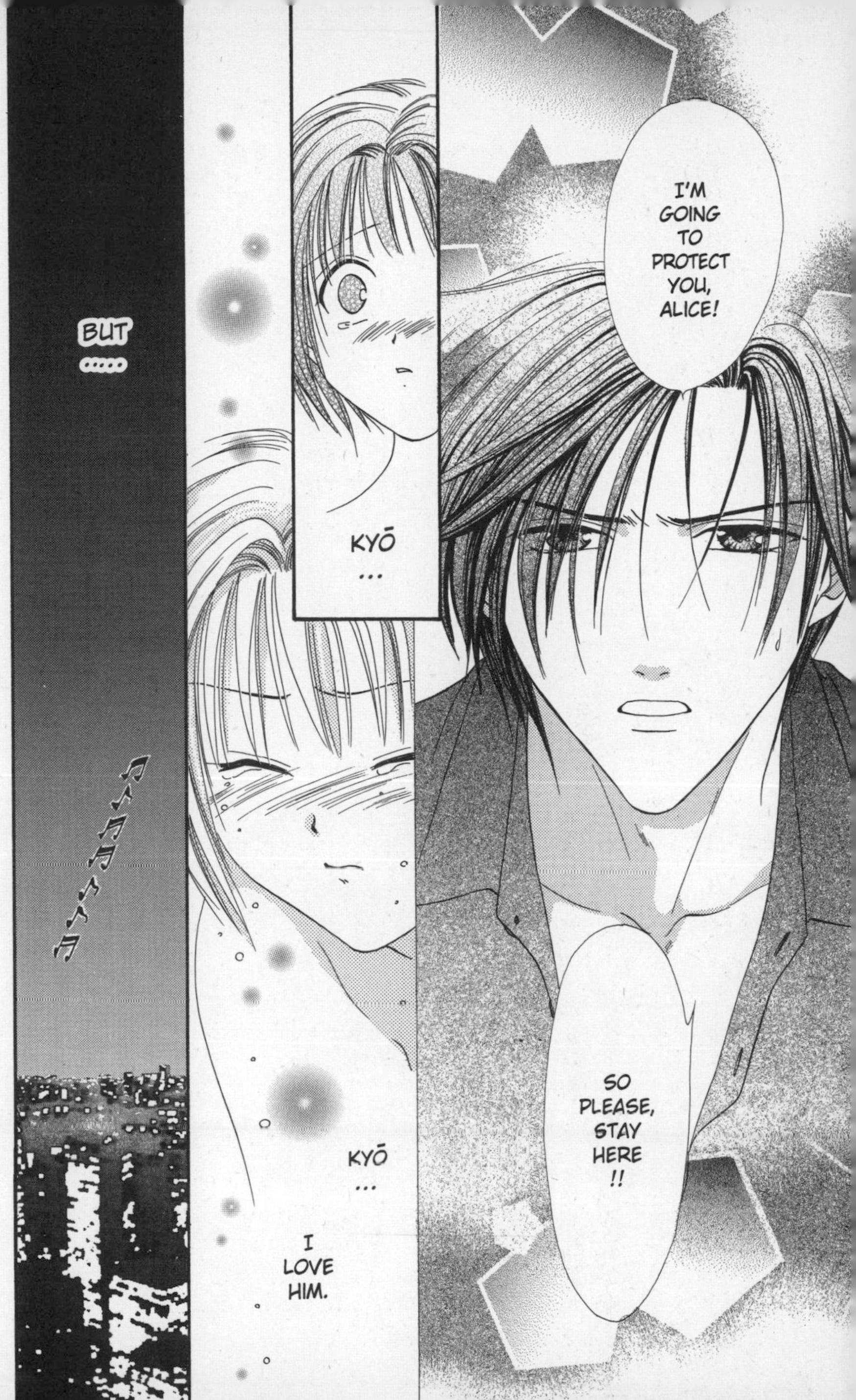
I'M GOING TO PROTECT YOU, ALICE!
SO PLEASE, STAY HERE !!
KYŌ ...
KYŌ ...
I LOVE HIM.
BUT ......

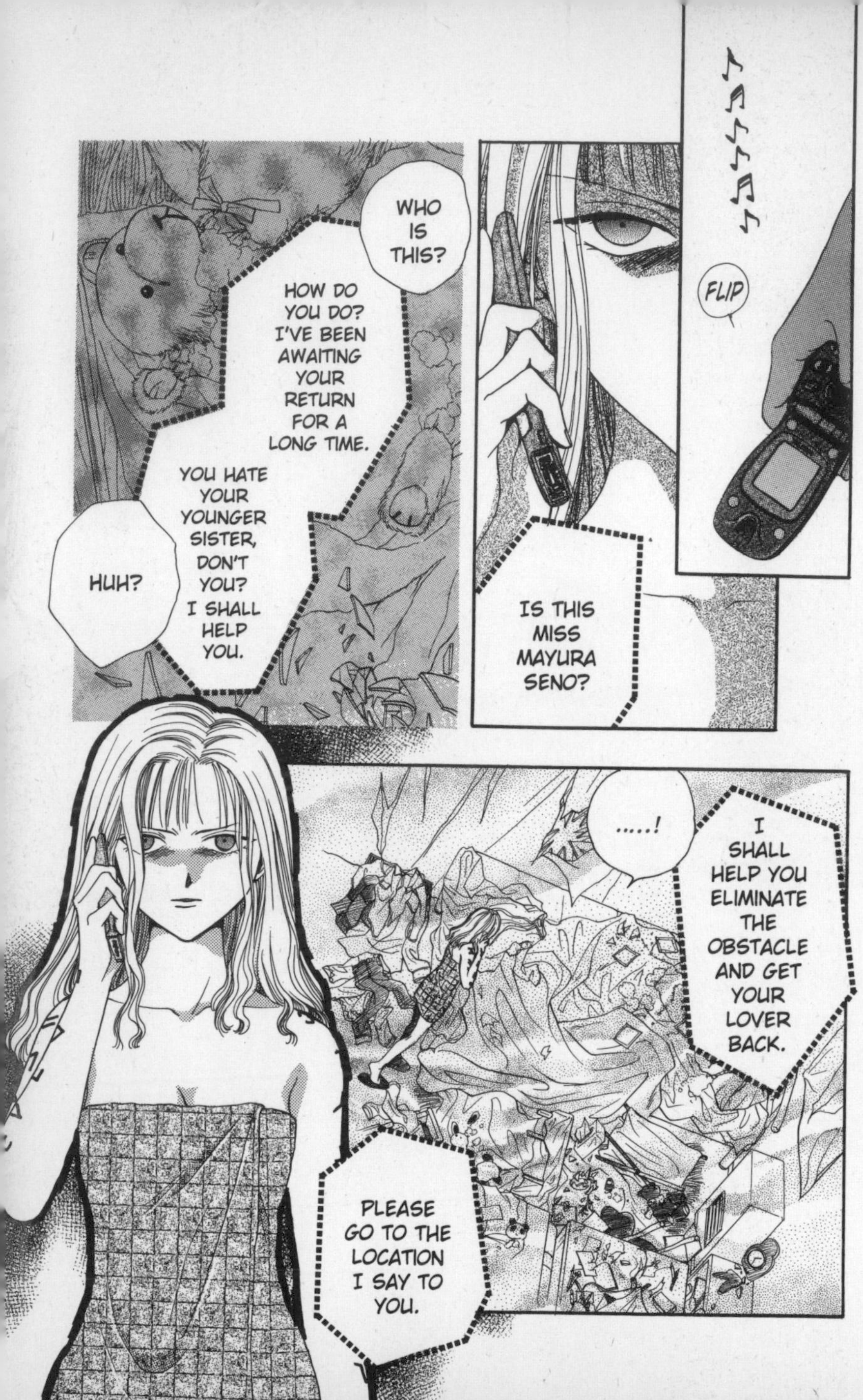
FLIP
IS THIS MISS MAYURA SENO?
WHO IS THIS?
HOW DO YOU DO? I'VE BEEN AWAITING YOUR RETURN FOR A LONG TIME.
YOU HATE YOUR YOUNGER SISTER, DON'T YOU? I SHALL HELP YOU.
HUH?
I SHALL HELP YOU ELIMINATE THE OBSTACLE AND GET YOUR LOVER BACK.
.....!
PLEASE GO TO THE LOCATION I SAY TO YOU.

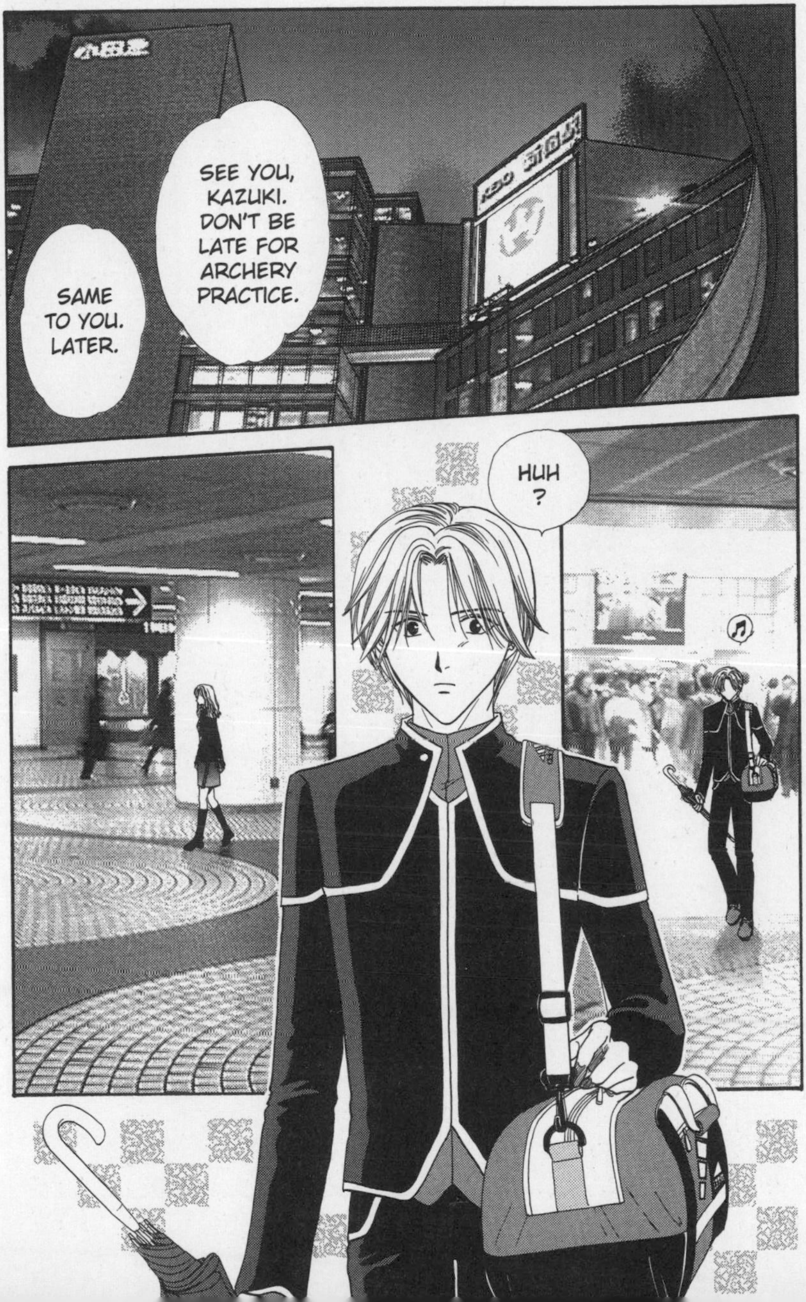
SEE YOU, KAZUKI. DON'T BE LATE FOR ARCHERY PRACTICE.
SAME TO YOU. LATER.
HUH?

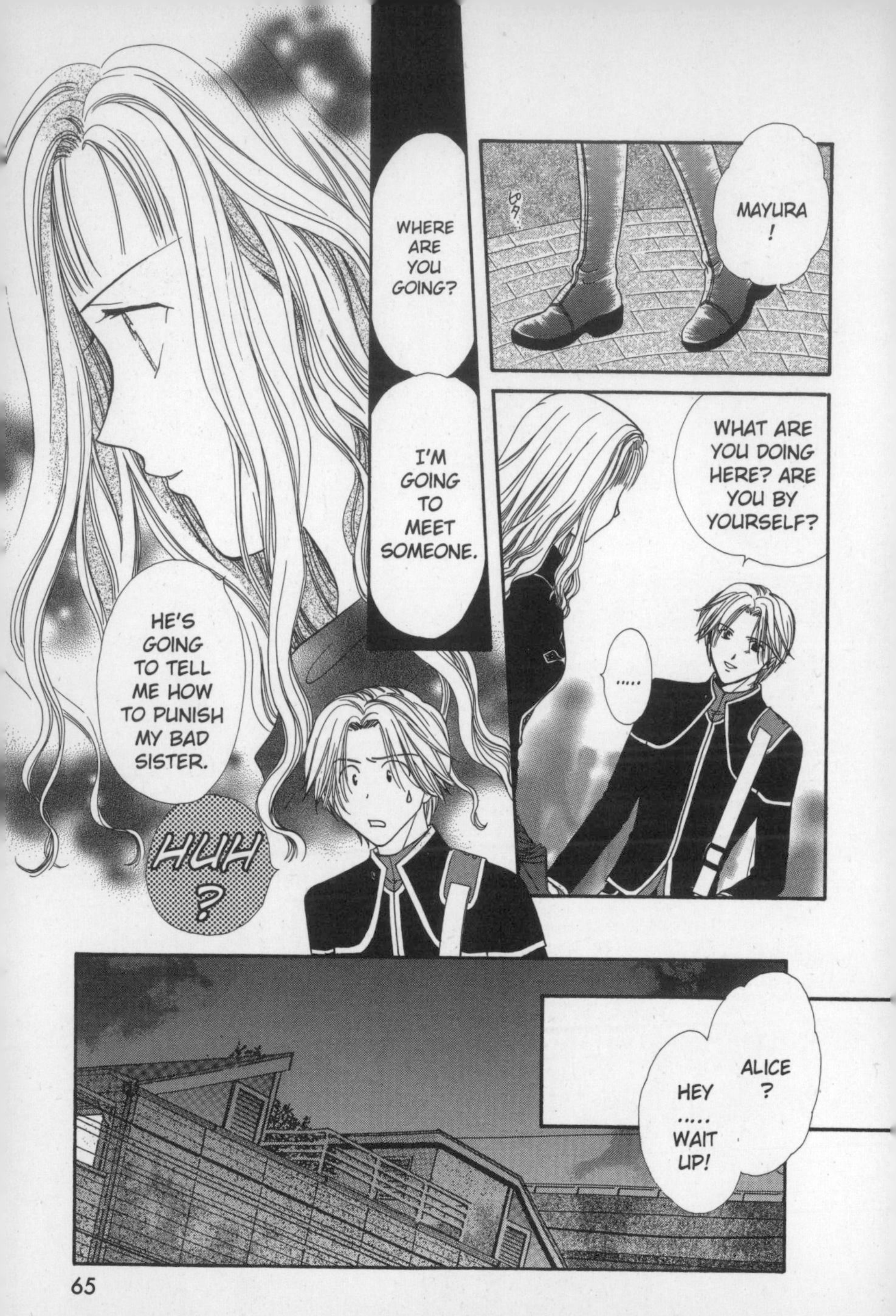
MAYURA!
WHAT ARE YOU DOING HERE? ARE YOU BY YOURSELF?
.....
WHERE ARE YOU GOING?
I'M GOING TO MEET SOMEONE.
HE'S GOING TO TELL ME HOW TO PUNISH MY BAD SISTER.
HUH?
ALICE?
HEY..... WAIT UP!

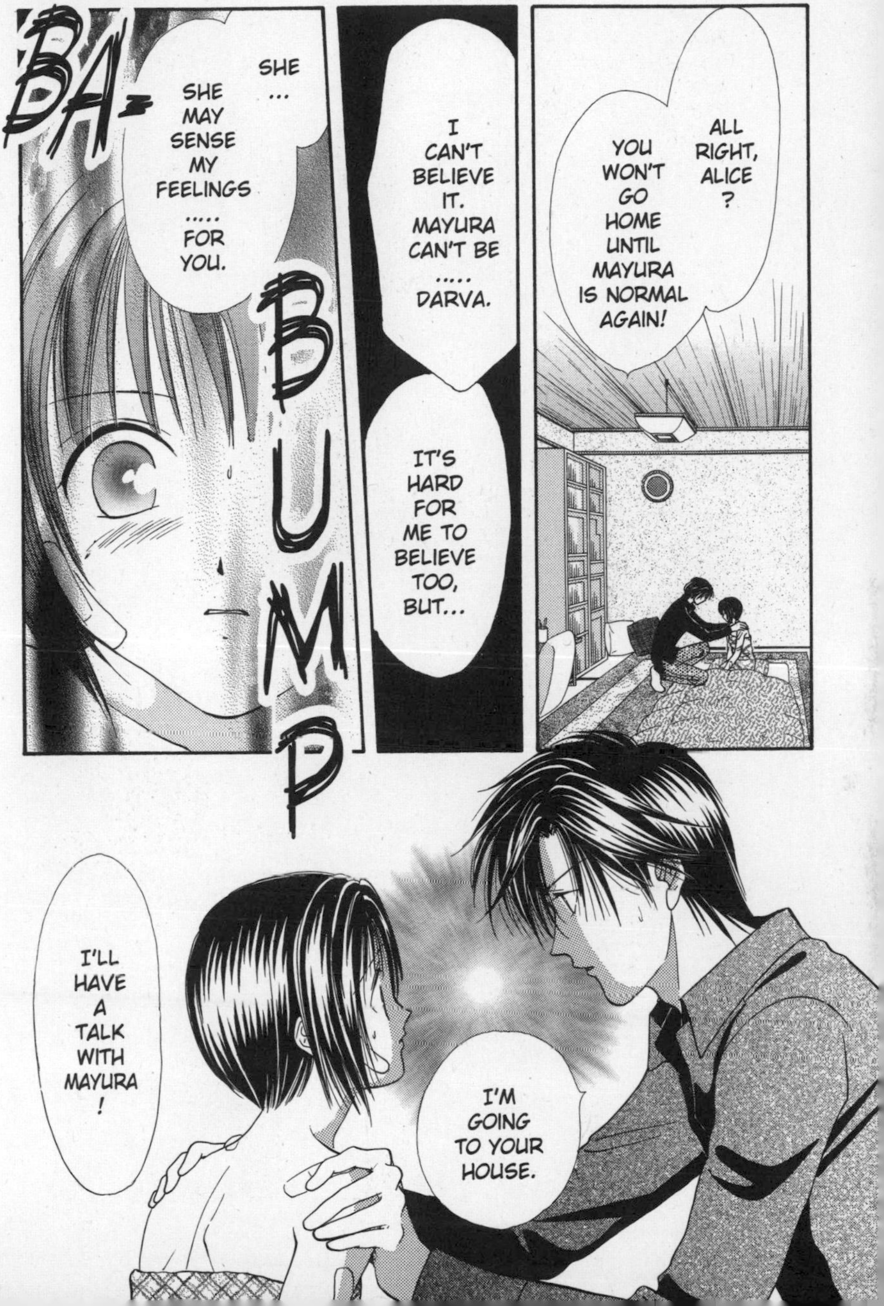
ALL RIGHT, ALICE?
YOU WON'T GO HOME UNTIL MAYURA IS NORMAL AGAIN!
I CAN'T BELIEVE IT. MAYURA CAN'T BE ..... DARVA.
IT'S HARD FOR ME TO BELIEVE TOO, BUT...
SHE ...
SHE MAY SENSE MY FEELINGS ..... FOR YOU.
BA-BUMP
I'M GOING TO YOUR HOUSE.
I'LL HAVE A TALK WITH MAYURA!

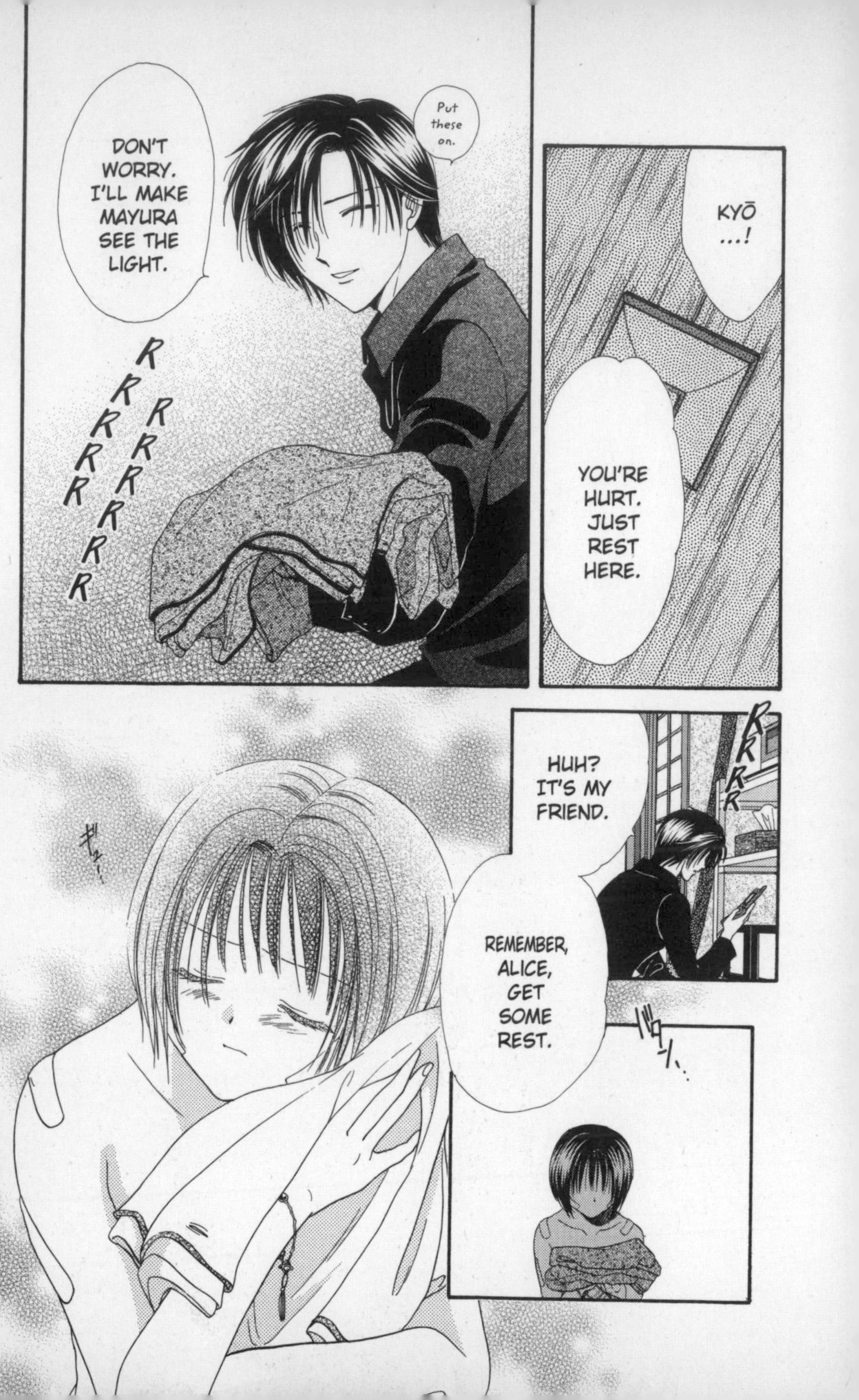
KYŌ ...!
YOU'RE HURT. JUST REST HERE.
Put these on.
DON'T WORRY. I'LL MAKE MAYURA SEE THE LIGHT.
RRRRRRRR
RRRRRR
RRRR
HUH? IT'S MY FRIEND.
REMEMBER, ALICE, GET SOME REST.

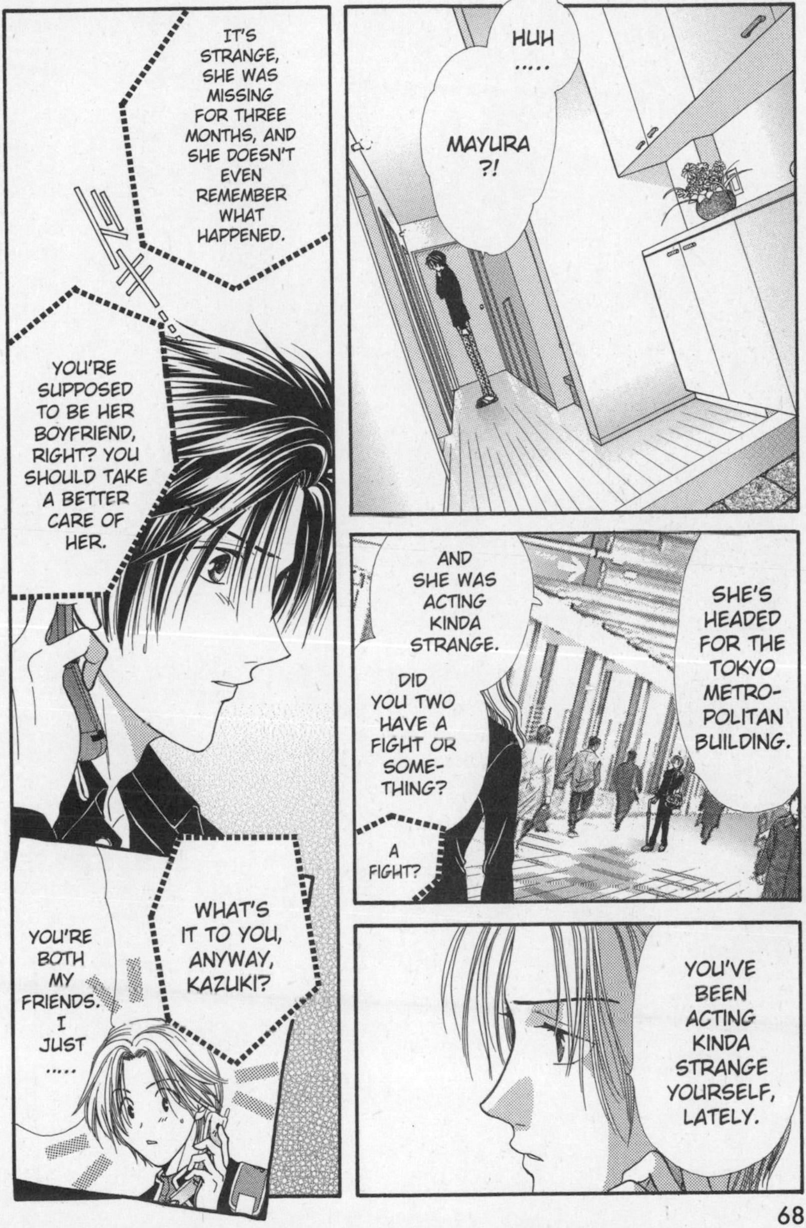
HUH .....
MAYURA ?!
SHE'S HEADED FOR THE TOKYO METRO-POLITAN BUILDING.
AND SHE WAS ACTING KINDA STRANGE.
DID YOU TWO HAVE A FIGHT OR SOME-THING?
A FIGHT?
YOU'VE BEEN ACTING KINDA STRANGE YOURSELF, LATELY.
IT'S STRANGE, SHE WAS MISSING FOR THREE MONTHS, AND SHE DOESN'T EVEN REMEMBER WHAT HAPPENED.
YOU'RE SUPPOSED TO BE HER BOYFRIEND, RIGHT? YOU SHOULD TAKE A BETTER CARE OF HER.
WHAT'S IT TO YOU, ANYWAY, KAZUKI?
YOU'RE BOTH MY FRIENDS. I JUST .....

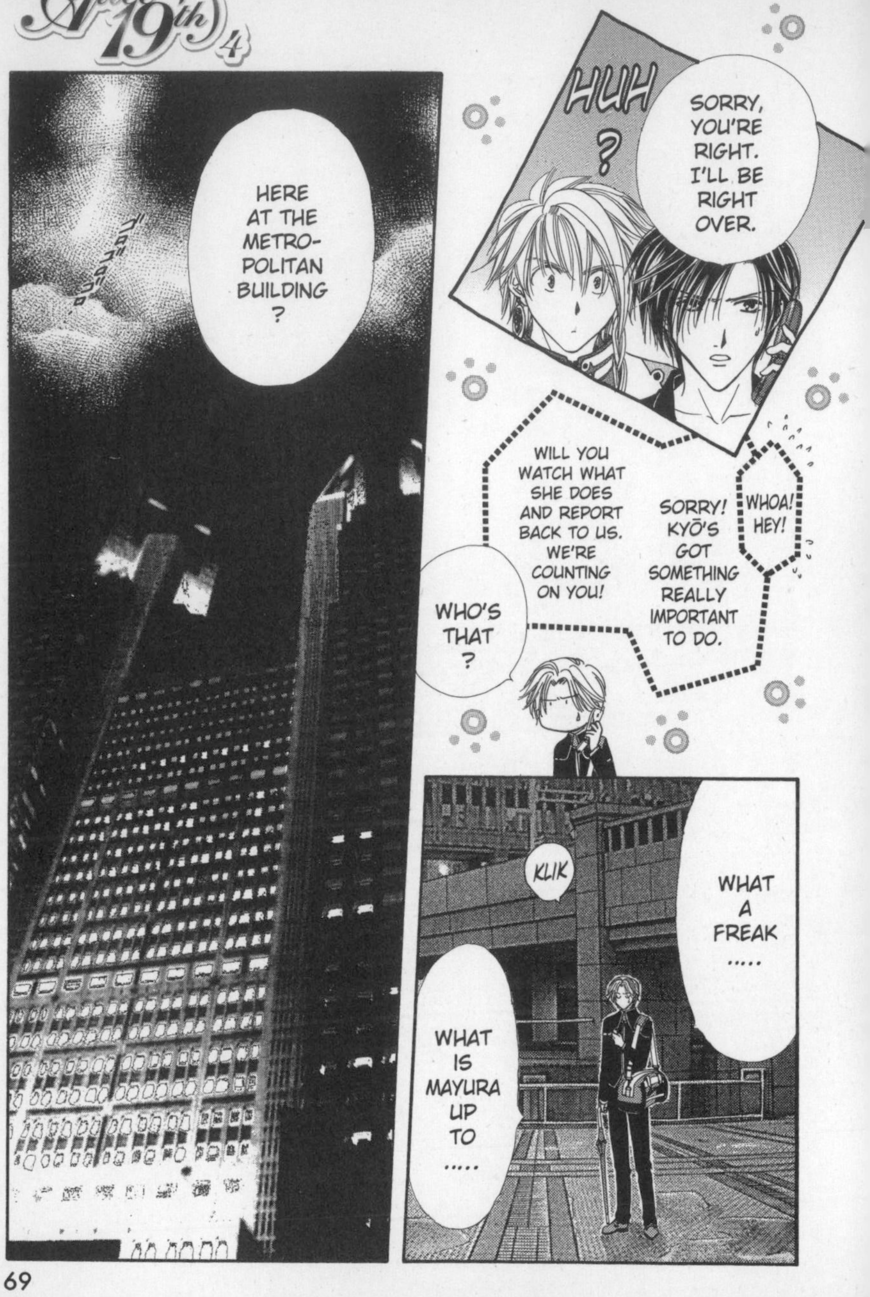
HUH ?
SORRY, YOU'RE RIGHT. I'LL BE RIGHT OVER.
WHOA! HEY!
SORRY! KYŌ'S GOT SOMETHING REALLY IMPORTANT TO DO.
WILL YOU WATCH WHAT SHE DOES AND REPORT BACK TO US. WE'RE COUNTING ON YOU!
WHO'S THAT ?
KLIK
WHAT A FREAK .....
WHAT IS MAYURA UP TO .....
HERE AT THE METRO-POLITAN BUILDING ?

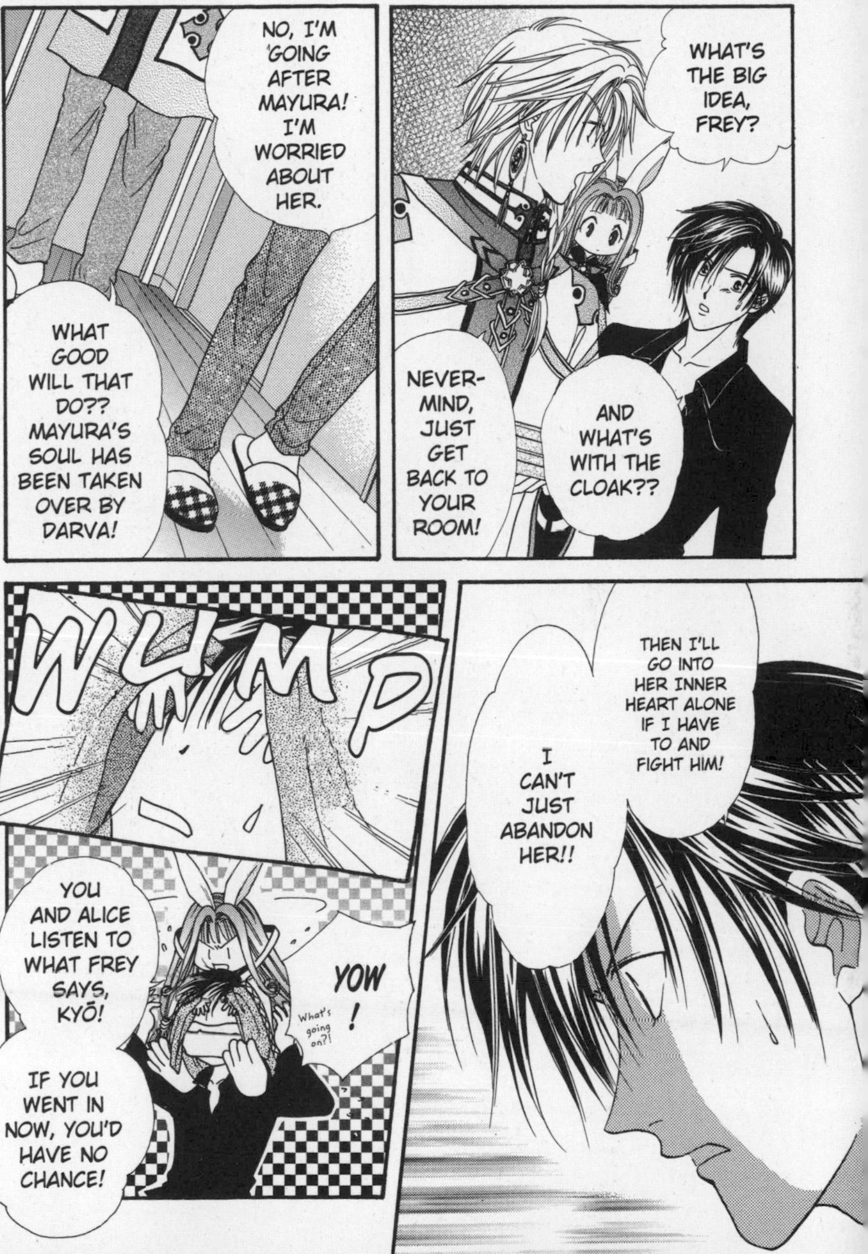
WHAT'S THE BIG IDEA, FREY?
AND WHAT'S WITH THE CLOAK??
NEVER-MIND, JUST GET BACK TO YOUR ROOM!
NO, I'M GOING AFTER MAYURA! I'M WORRIED ABOUT HER.
WHAT GOOD WILL THAT DO?? MAYURA'S SOUL HAS BEEN TAKEN OVER BY DARVA!
THEN I'LL GO INTO HER INNER HEART ALONE IF I HAVE TO AND FIGHT HIM!
I CAN'T JUST ABANDON HER!!
WUMP
YOW!
What's going on?!
YOU AND ALICE LISTEN TO WHAT FREY SAYS, KYŌ!
IF YOU WENT IN NOW, YOU'D HAVE NO CHANCE!

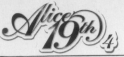

Continuing from the last part--What made me really laugh was the story about a former inmate from Alcatraz who visits the prison every once in a while to do autograph sessions for a book that he wrote.
He didn't come when we were there, but it would have been nice if you could see him when you're on Alcatraz. Although, I'm not sure what would be so nice about it.
Also, while on my trip, I saw some movies. I saw Star Wars: Episode II and Spiderman, which just opened in Japan. (This was the end of May 2002.)
I won't go into the plots, but American theaters are great! First of all, you can see over the heads of people in front of you! And the seats recline! But the movies were only in English! I couldn't understa-a-a-nd!
Best of all, it was only 700 yen for a movie ticket. It's soo expensive in Japan!! All the good theaters in Japan are getting expensive, and they're still too small! It's still too hard to see!! If a big guy sits in front of you, it's all over!! The US theaters have great acoustics too, it's awesome. America is great. That's my story.....

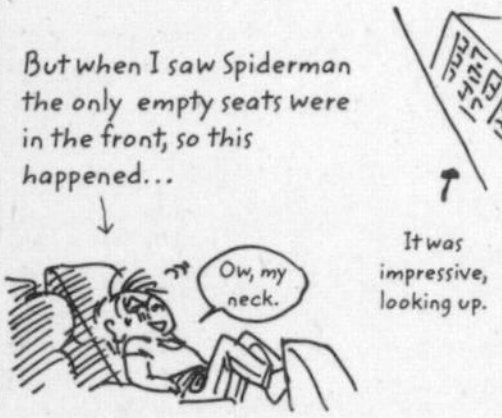
But when I saw Spiderman the only empty seats were in the front, so this happened...
Ow, my neck.
It was impressive, looking up.

Oh, I almost forgot...! They showed the trailer for Matrix Revolutions, my friends and I were thrilled!!
It looked really cool!! I'm looking forward to its opening in 2003. That Keanu is neat!!
Whenever I come to the U.S., I see the American flag waving here and there. And they're big! Patriotism is strong here...
I got the feeling that last year's events of 9/11 had taken firm root in the hearts of Americans. Even fans asked me, "How do you feel about it?"
I wonder if the problem with India and Pakistan will be solved by the time this Volume 4 hits the stands....
There's big excitement over the World Cup right now.
Let's all talk things over peacefully.

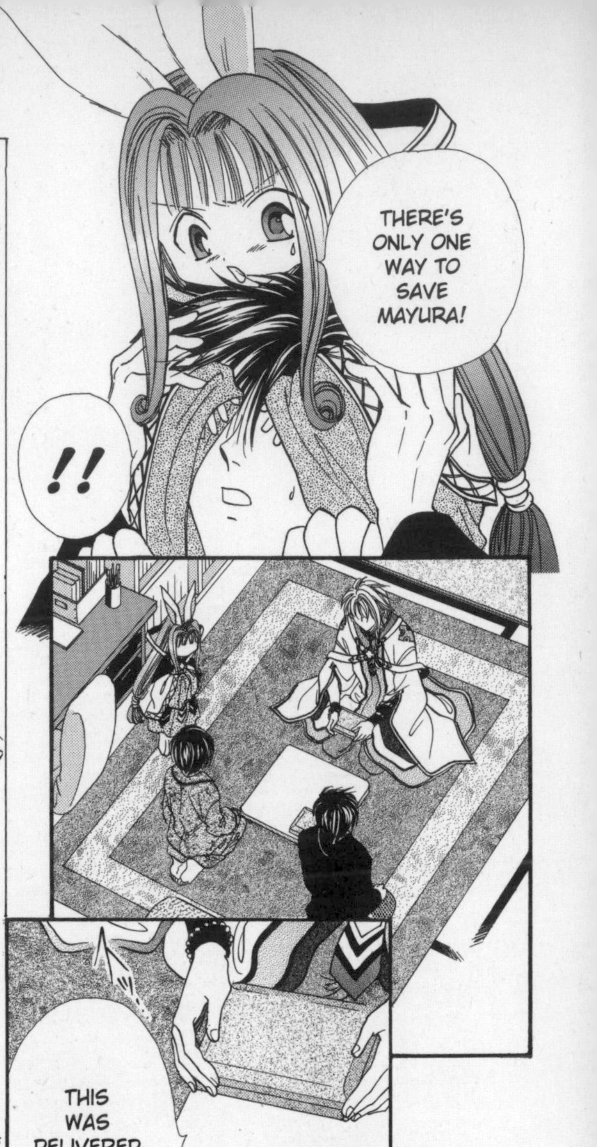
THERE'S ONLY ONE WAY TO SAVE MAYURA!
!!
THIS WAS DELIVERED TODAY BY A MESSENGER FROM OUR SCANDINAVIAN SANCTUARY.

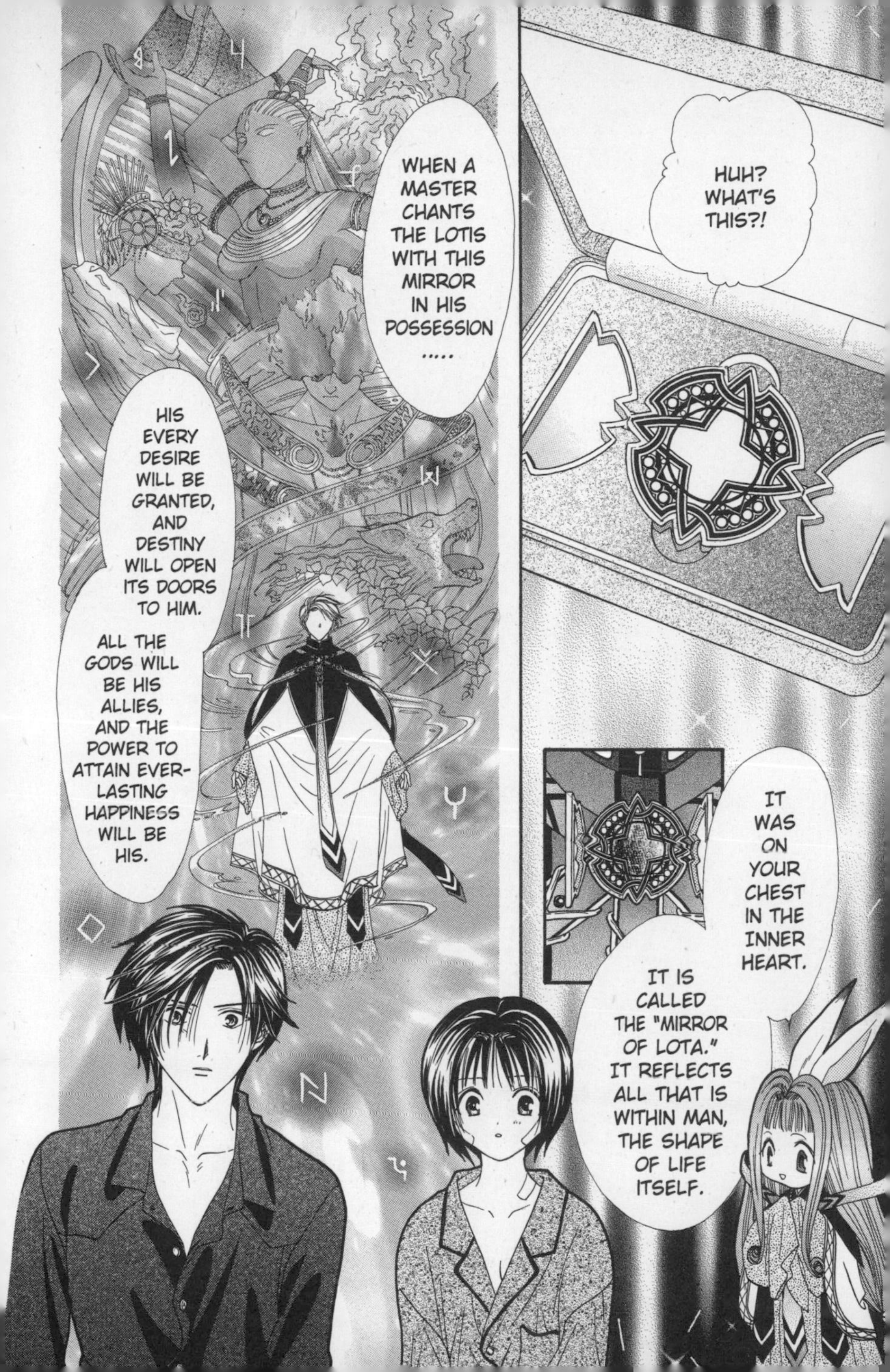

HUH? WHAT'S THIS?!
IT WAS ON YOUR CHEST IN THE INNER HEART.
IT IS CALLED THE "MIRROR OF LOTA." IT REFLECTS ALL THAT IS WITHIN MAN, THE SHAPE OF LIFE ITSELF.
WHEN A MASTER CHANTS THE LOTIS WITH THIS MIRROR IN HIS POSSESSION .....
HIS EVERY DESIRE WILL BE GRANTED, AND DESTINY WILL OPEN ITS DOORS TO HIM.
ALL THE GODS WILL BE HIS ALLIES, AND THE POWER TO ATTAIN EVER-LASTING HAPPINESS WILL BE HIS.

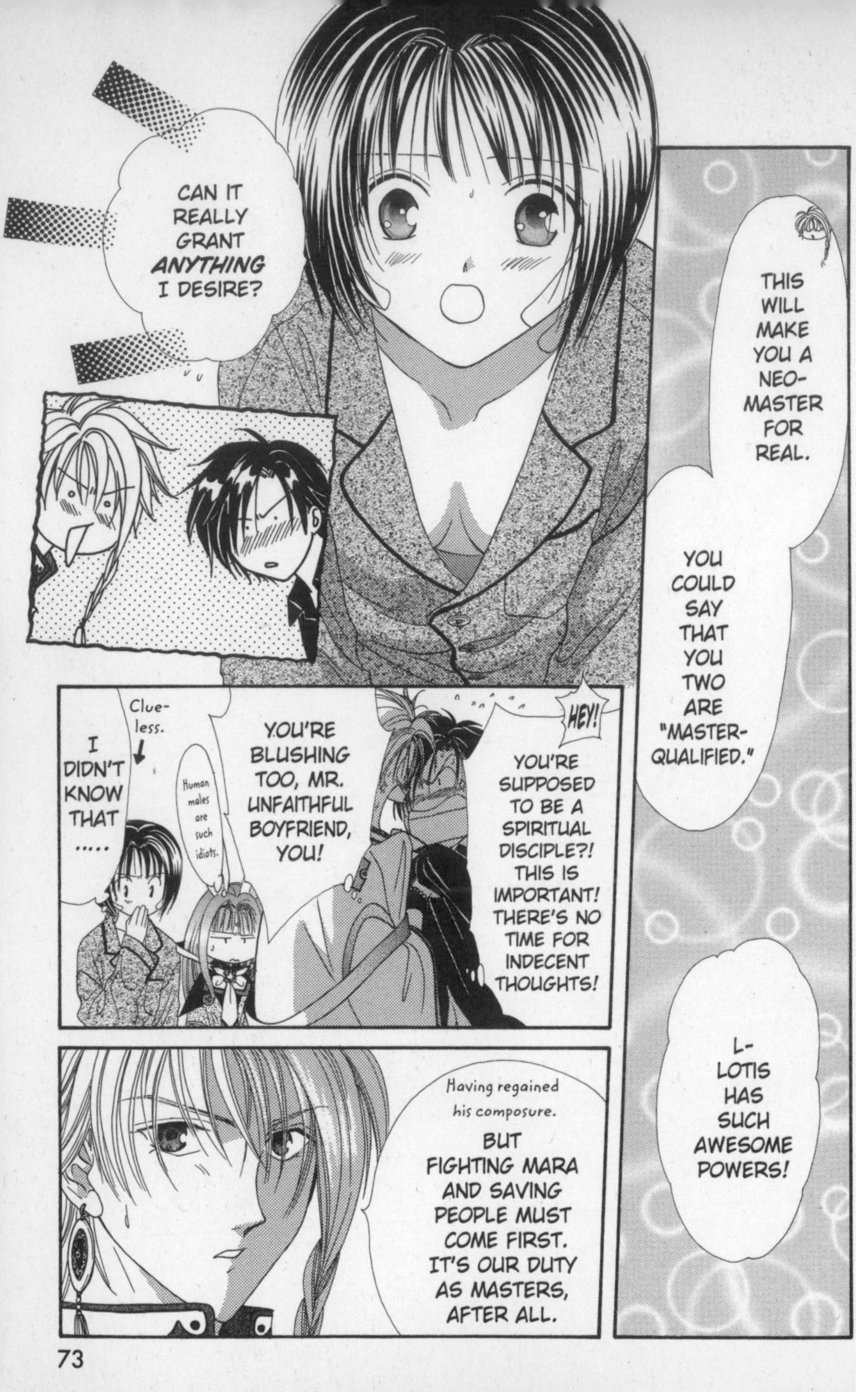
THIS WILL MAKE YOU A NEO-MASTER FOR REAL.
YOU COULD SAY THAT YOU TWO ARE "MASTER-QUALIFIED."
L-LOTIS HAS SUCH AWESOME POWERS!
CAN IT REALLY GRANT ANYTHING I DESIRE?
HEY!
YOU'RE SUPPOSED TO BE A SPIRITUAL DISCIPLE?! THIS IS IMPORTANT! THERE'S NO TIME FOR INDECENT THOUGHTS!
YOU'RE BLUSHING TOO, MR. UNFAITHFUL BOYFRIEND, YOU!
Human males are such idiots.
Clue-less.
I DIDN'T KNOW THAT.....
Having regained his composure.
BUT FIGHTING MARA AND SAVING PEOPLE MUST COME FIRST. IT'S OUR DUTY AS MASTERS, AFTER ALL.

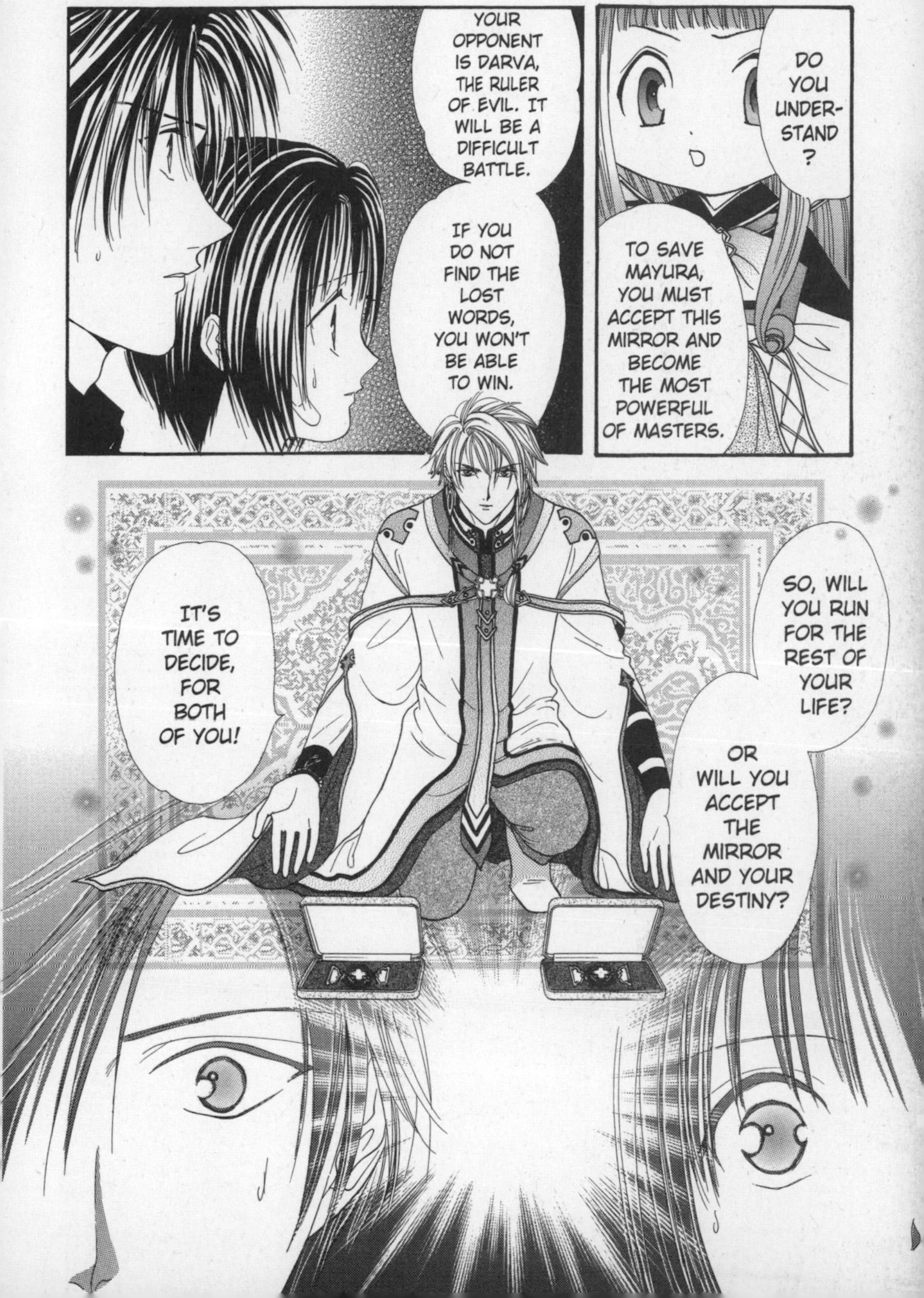
DO YOU UNDER-STAND?
TO SAVE MAYURA, YOU MUST ACCEPT THIS MIRROR AND BECOME THE MOST POWERFUL OF MASTERS.
YOUR OPPONENT IS DARVA, THE RULER OF EVIL. IT WILL BE A DIFFICULT BATTLE.
IF YOU DO NOT FIND THE LOST WORDS, YOU WON'T BE ABLE TO WIN.
SO, WILL YOU RUN FOR THE REST OF YOUR LIFE?
OR WILL YOU ACCEPT THE MIRROR AND YOUR DESTINY?
IT'S TIME TO DECIDE, FOR BOTH OF YOU!

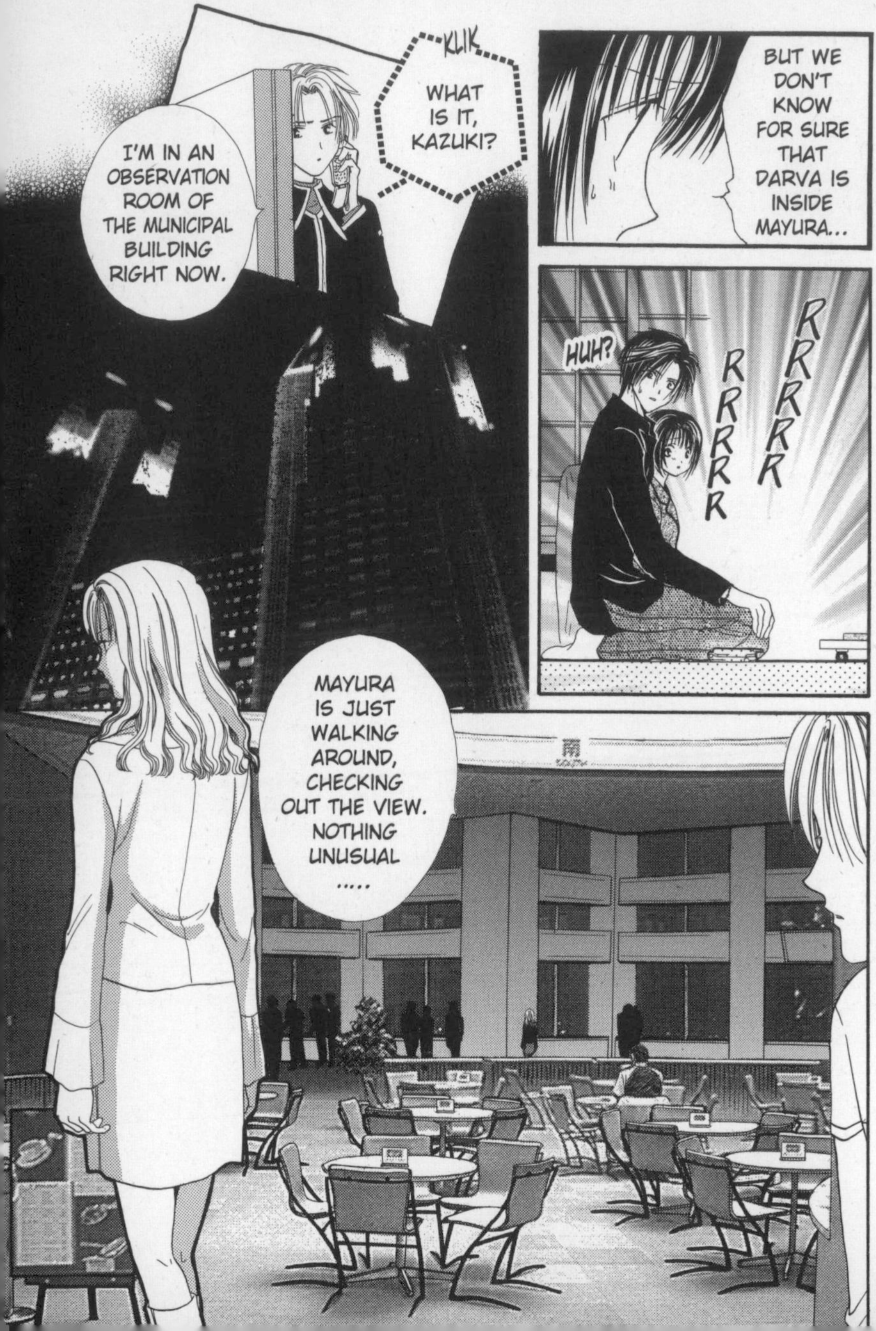
BUT WE DON'T KNOW FOR SURE THAT DARVA IS INSIDE MAYURA...
HUH?
RRRRR
RRRR
KLIK
WHAT IS IT, KAZUKI?
I'M IN AN OBSERVATION ROOM OF THE MUNICIPAL BUILDING RIGHT NOW.
MAYURA IS JUST WALKING AROUND, CHECKING OUT THE VIEW. NOTHING UNUSUAL .....

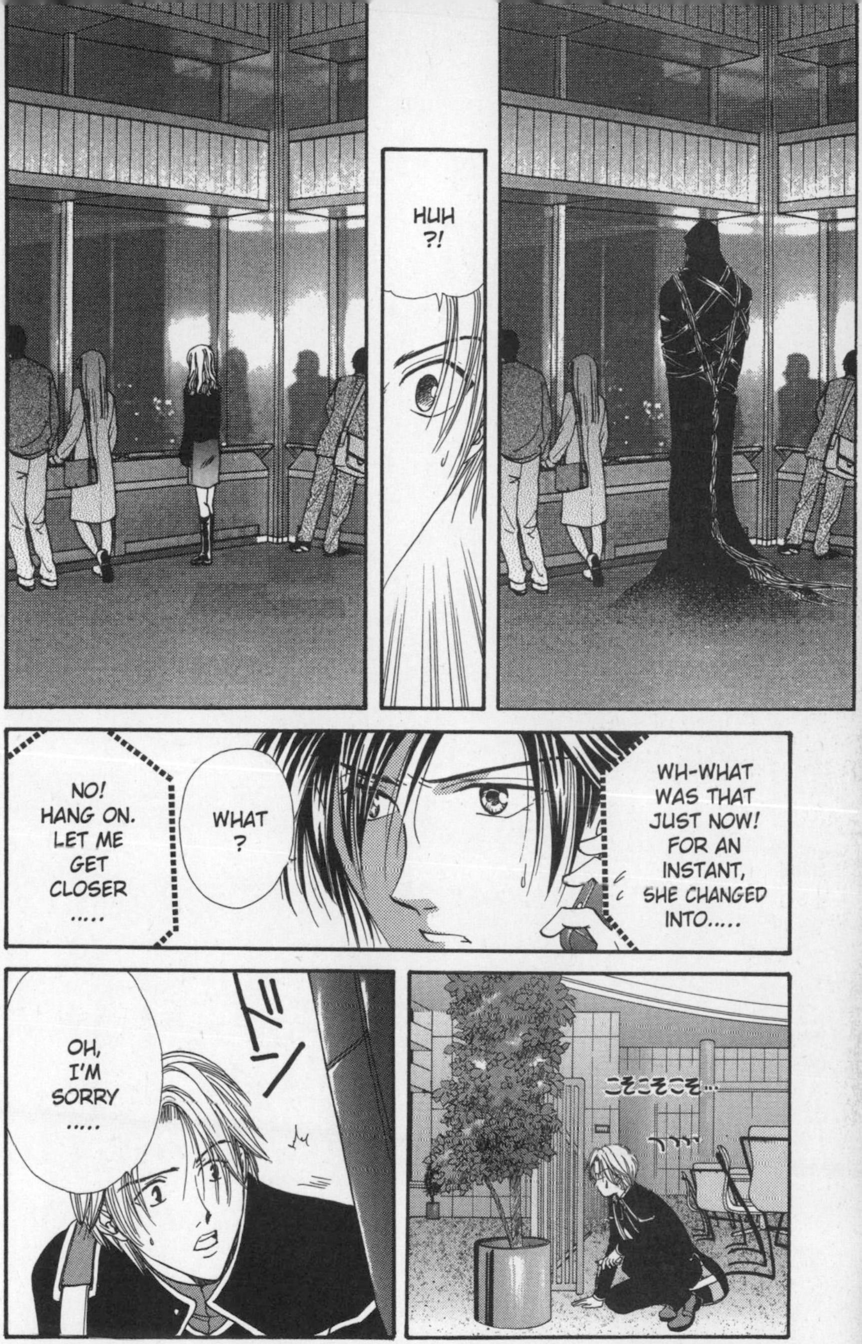
HUH ?!
WH-WHAT WAS THAT JUST NOW! FOR AN INSTANT, SHE CHANGED INTO.....
WHAT ?
NO! HANG ON. LET ME GET CLOSER .....
こそこそこそ…
OH, I'M SORRY .....

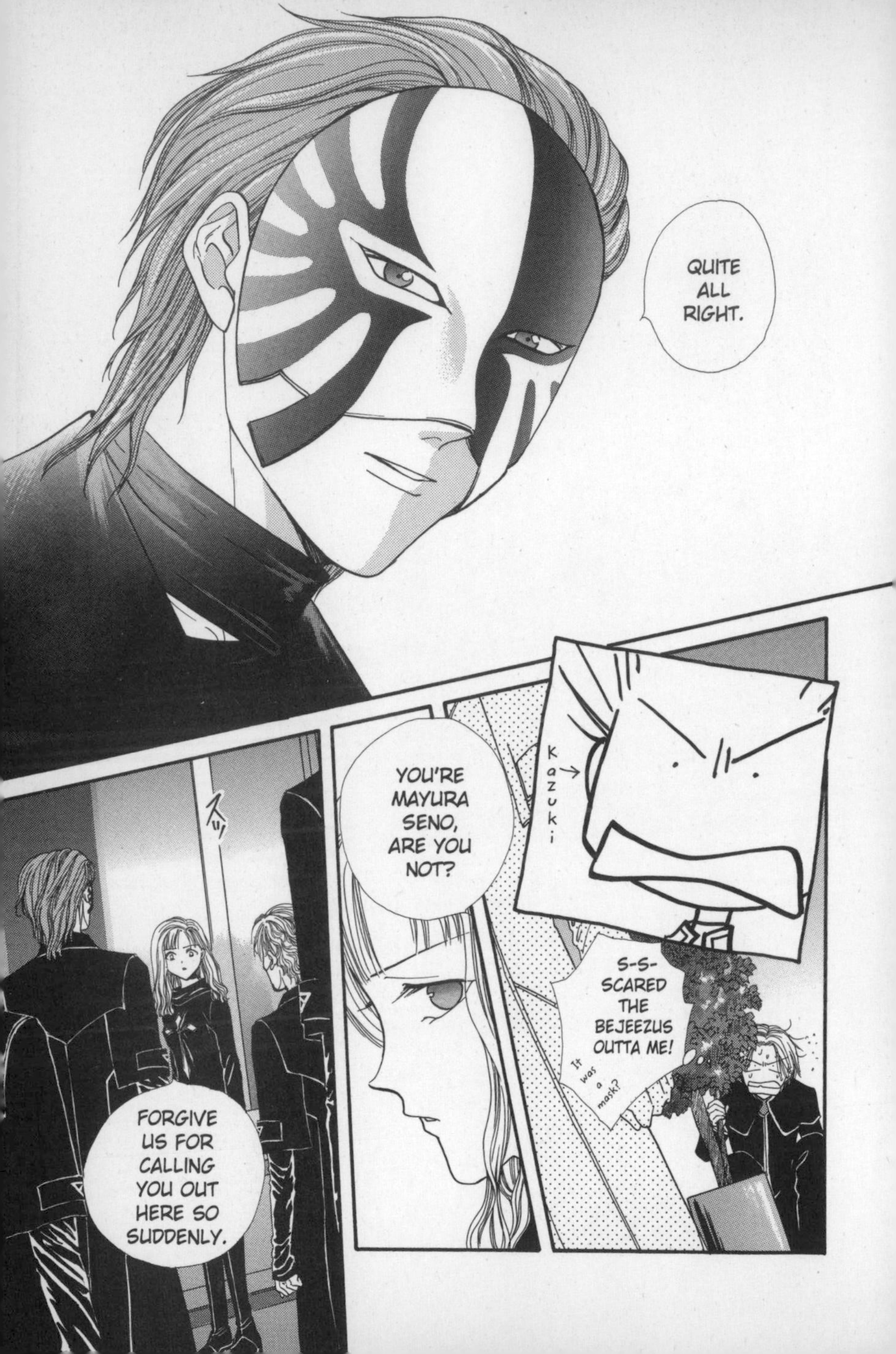
QUITE ALL RIGHT.
Kazuki →
S-S-SCARED THE BEJEEZUS OUTTA ME!
It was a mask?
YOU'RE MAYURA SENO, ARE YOU NOT?
FORGIVE US FOR CALLING YOU OUT HERE SO SUDDENLY.

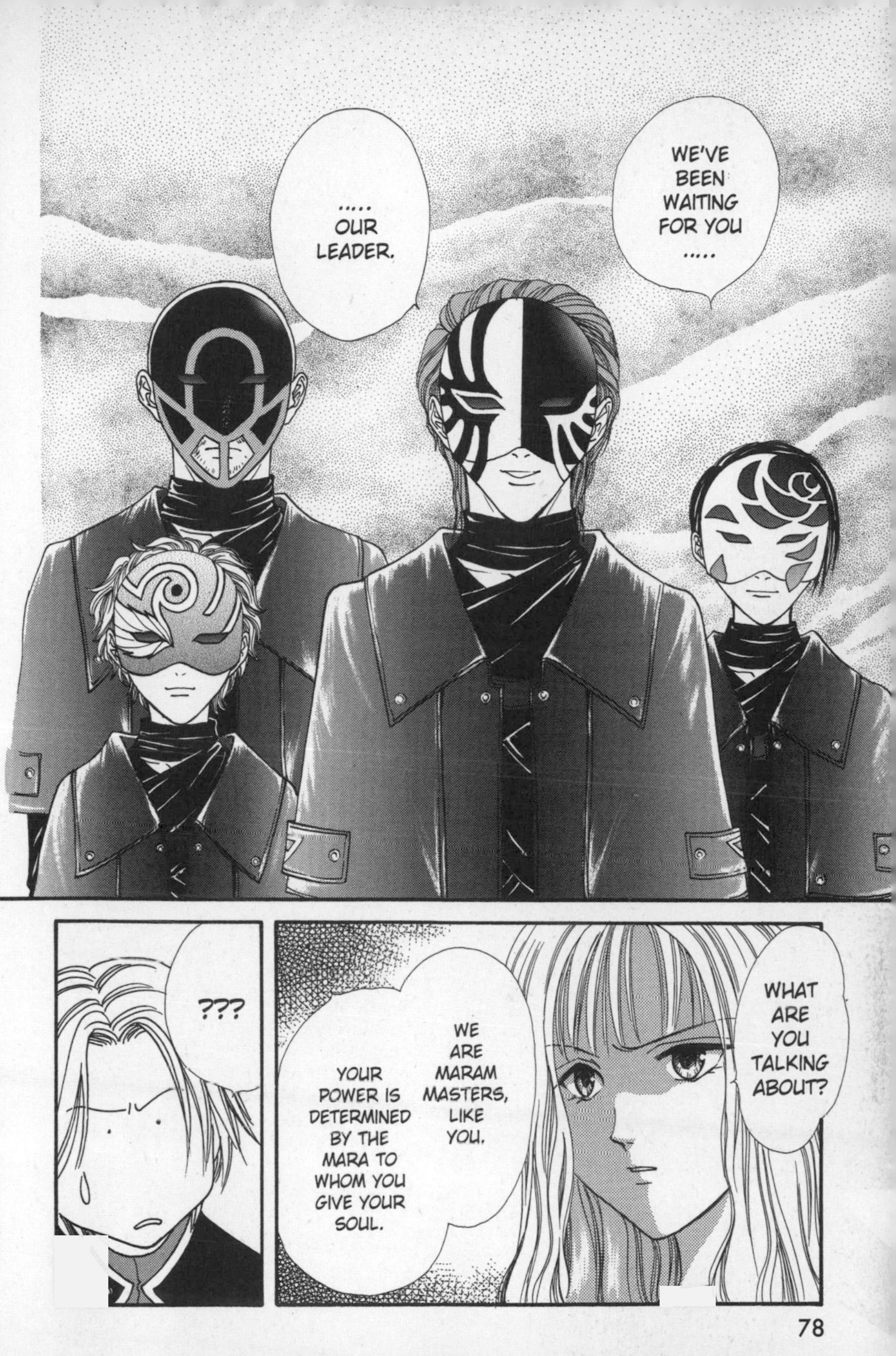
WE'VE BEEN WAITING FOR YOU .....
..... OUR LEADER.
WHAT ARE YOU TALKING ABOUT?
WE ARE MARAM MASTERS, LIKE YOU.
YOUR POWER IS DETERMINED BY THE MARA TO WHOM YOU GIVE YOUR SOUL.
???

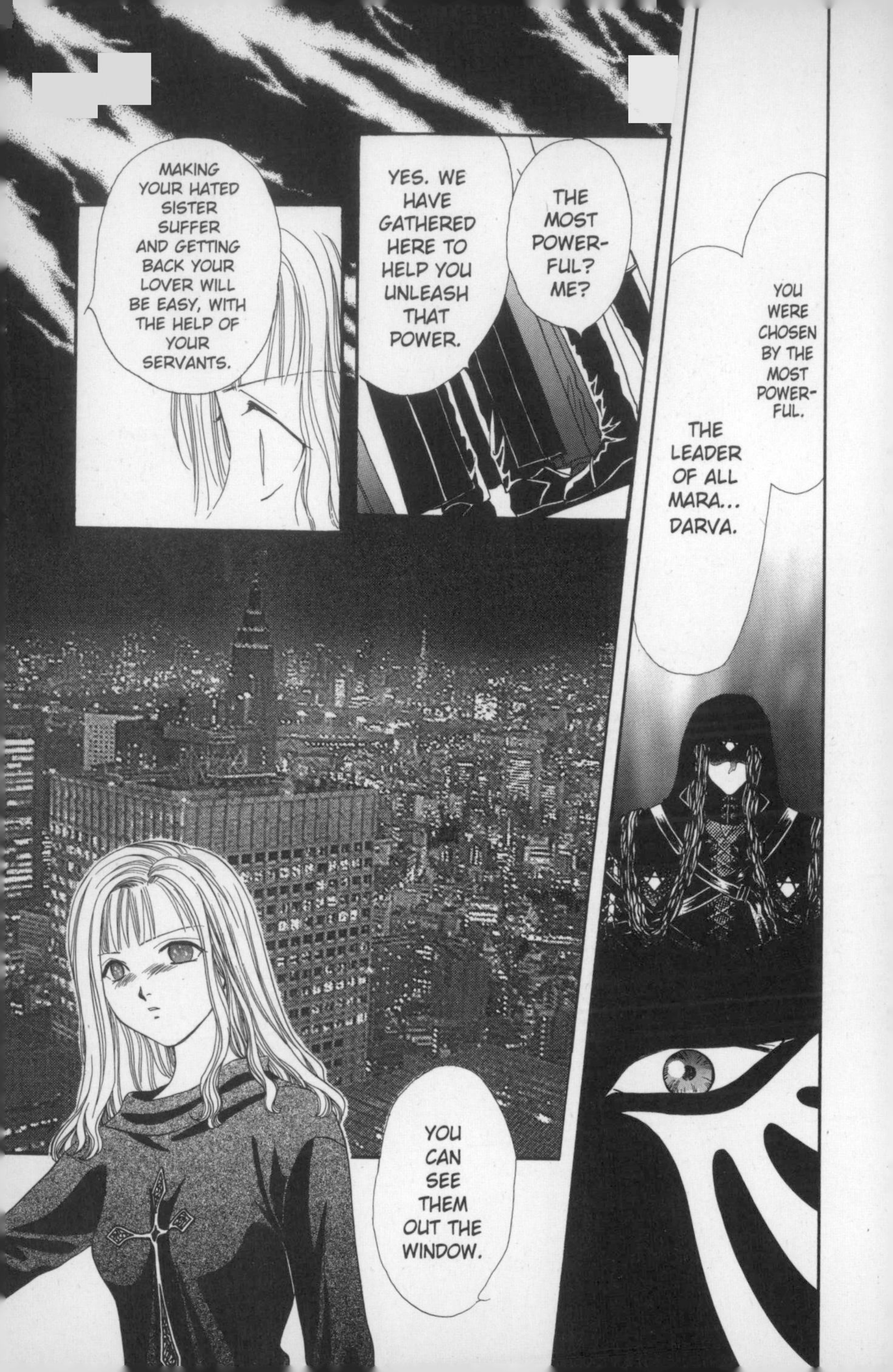
YOU WERE CHOSEN BY THE MOST POWER-FUL.
THE LEADER OF ALL MARA... DARVA.
THE MOST POWER-FUL? ME?
YES. WE HAVE GATHERED HERE TO HELP YOU UNLEASH THAT POWER.
MAKING YOUR HATED SISTER SUFFER AND GETTING BACK YOUR LOVER WILL BE EASY, WITH THE HELP OF YOUR SERVANTS.
YOU CAN SEE THEM OUT THE WINDOW.

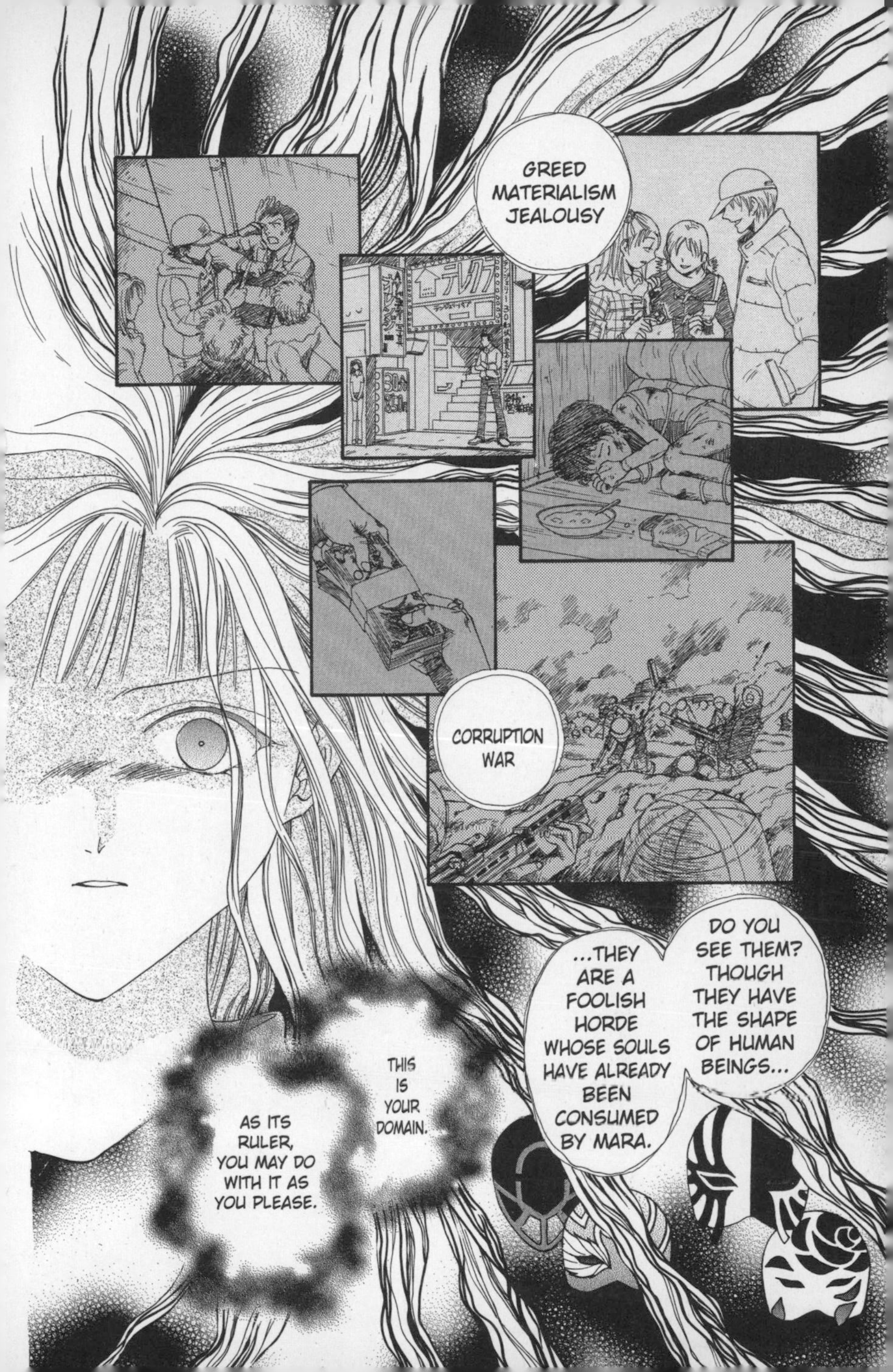
GREED MATERIALISM JEALOUSY
CORRUPTION WAR
DO YOU SEE THEM? THOUGH THEY HAVE THE SHAPE OF HUMAN BEINGS...
...THEY ARE A FOOLISH HORDE WHOSE SOULS HAVE ALREADY BEEN CONSUMED BY MARA.
THIS IS YOUR DOMAIN.
AS ITS RULER, YOU MAY DO WITH IT AS YOU PLEASE.

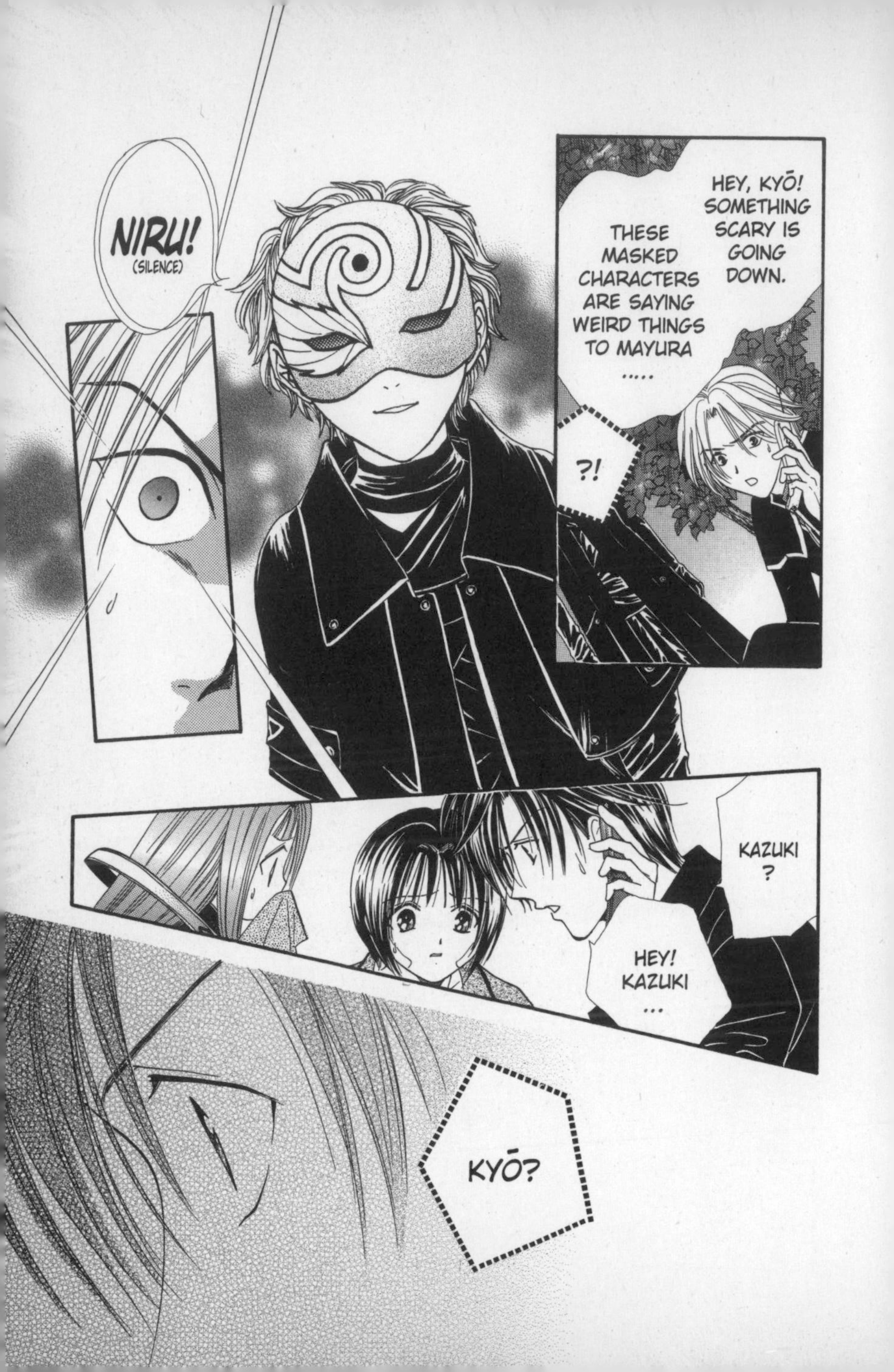
HEY, KYŌ! SOMETHING SCARY IS GOING DOWN.
THESE MASKED CHARACTERS ARE SAYING WEIRD THINGS TO MAYURA .....
?!
NIRU!
(SILENCE)
KAZUKI ?
HEY! KAZUKI ...
KYŌ?

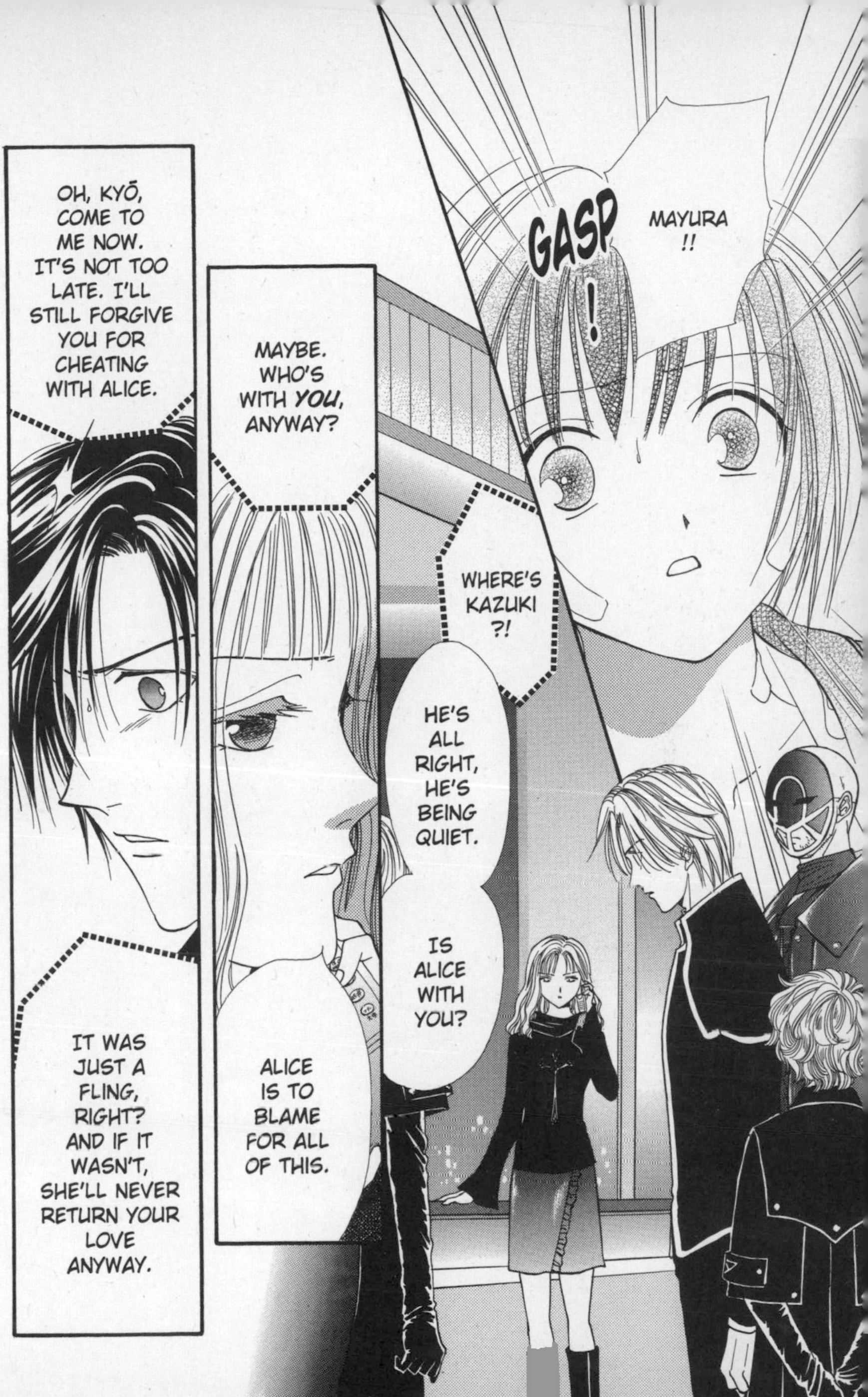
GASP !
MAYURA !!
WHERE'S KAZUKI ?!
HE'S ALL RIGHT, HE'S BEING QUIET.
IS ALICE WITH YOU?
MAYBE. WHO'S WITH *YOU*, ANYWAY?
ALICE IS TO BLAME FOR ALL OF THIS.
OH, KYŌ, COME TO ME NOW. IT'S NOT TOO LATE. I'LL STILL FORGIVE YOU FOR CHEATING WITH ALICE.
IT WAS JUST A FLING, RIGHT? AND IF IT WASN'T, SHE'LL NEVER RETURN YOUR LOVE ANYWAY.

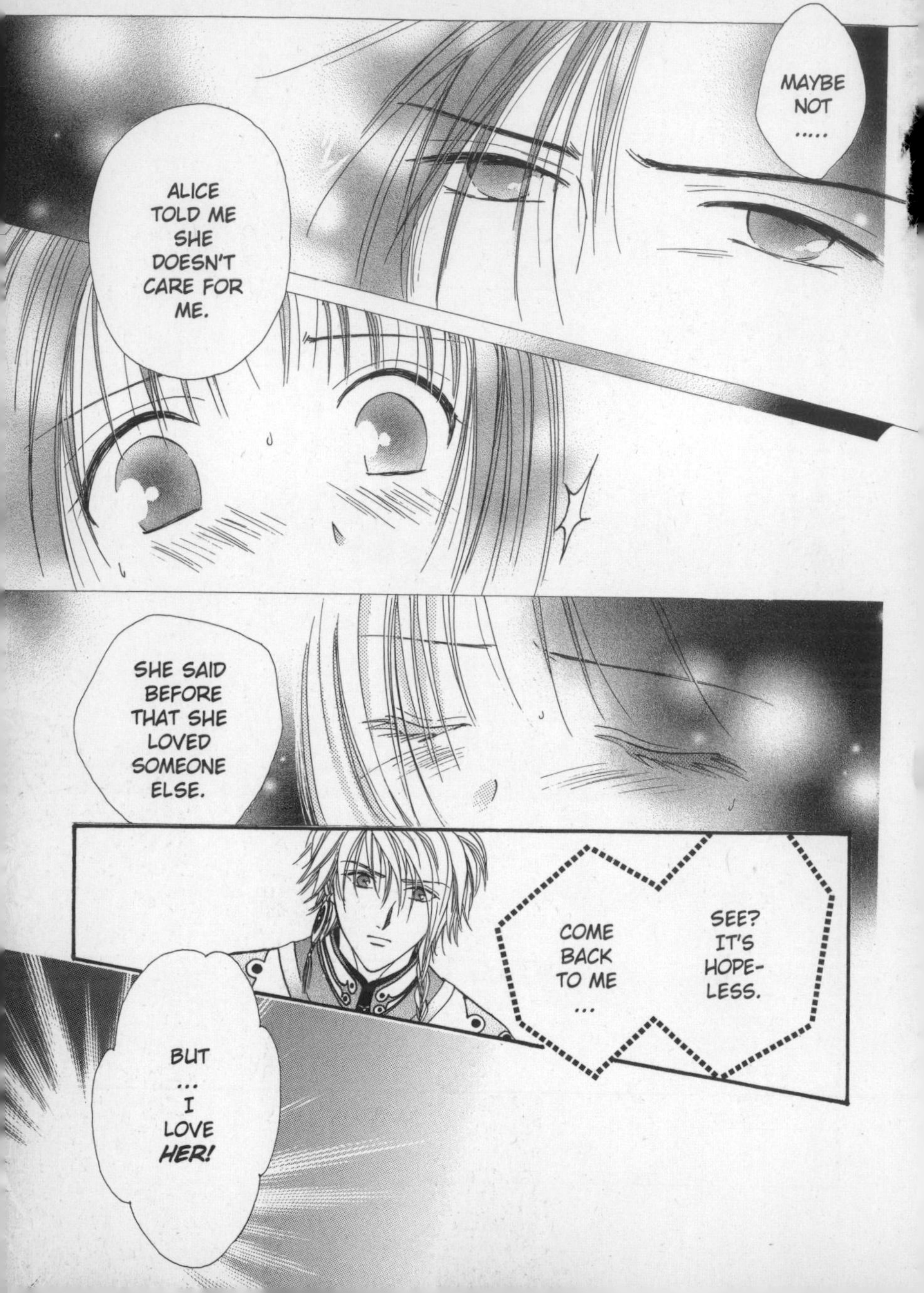

MAYBE NOT .....
ALICE TOLD ME SHE DOESN'T CARE FOR ME.
SHE SAID BEFORE THAT SHE LOVED SOMEONE ELSE.
SEE? IT'S HOPE-LESS.
COME BACK TO ME ...
BUT ... I LOVE *HER!*

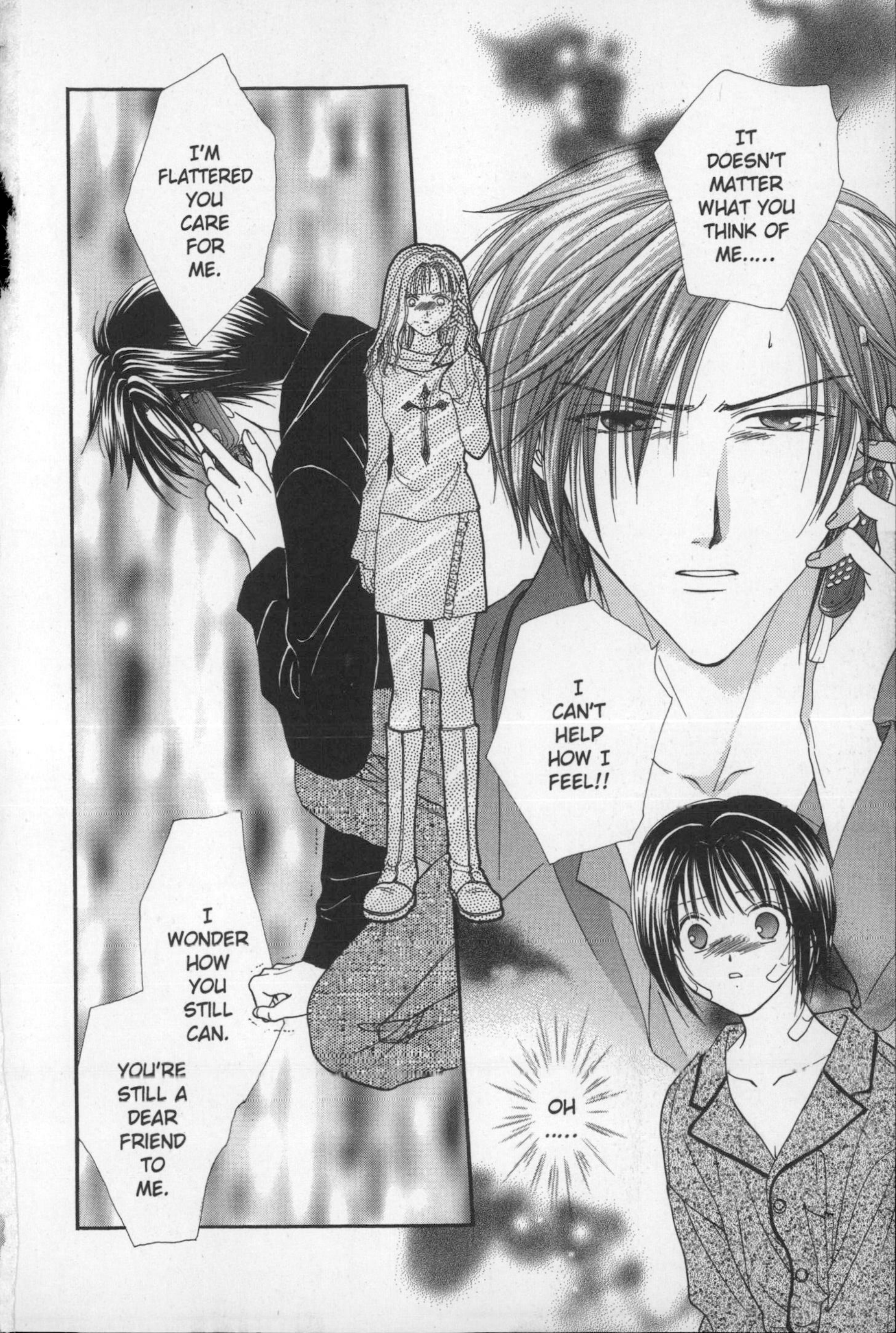
IT DOESN'T MATTER WHAT YOU THINK OF ME.....
I CAN'T HELP HOW I FEEL!!
OH .....
I'M FLATTERED YOU CARE FOR ME.
I WONDER HOW YOU STILL CAN.
YOU'RE STILL A DEAR FRIEND TO ME.

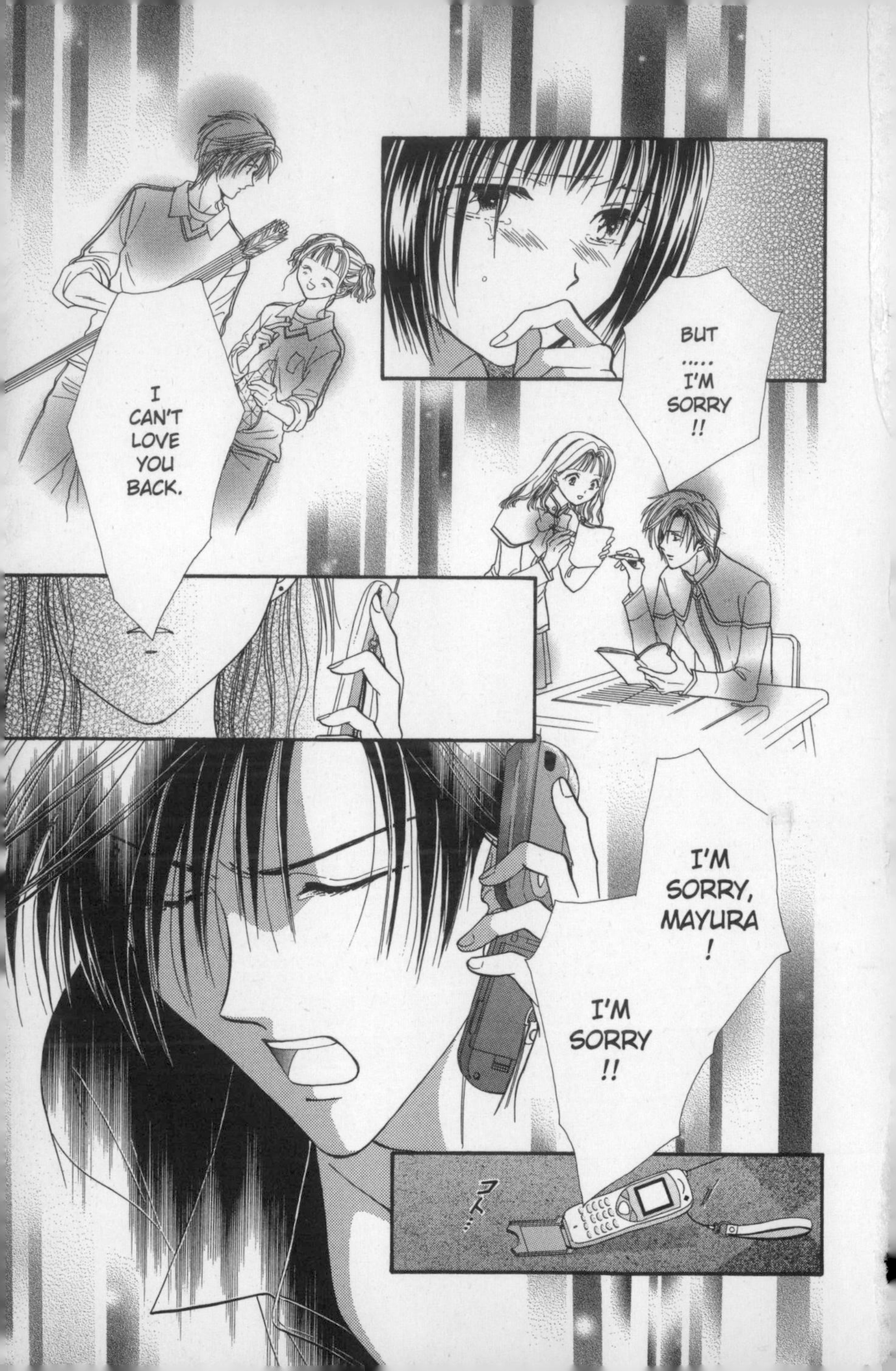
BUT ..... I'M SORRY !!
I CAN'T LOVE YOU BACK.
I'M SORRY, MAYURA !
I'M SORRY !!
コト…

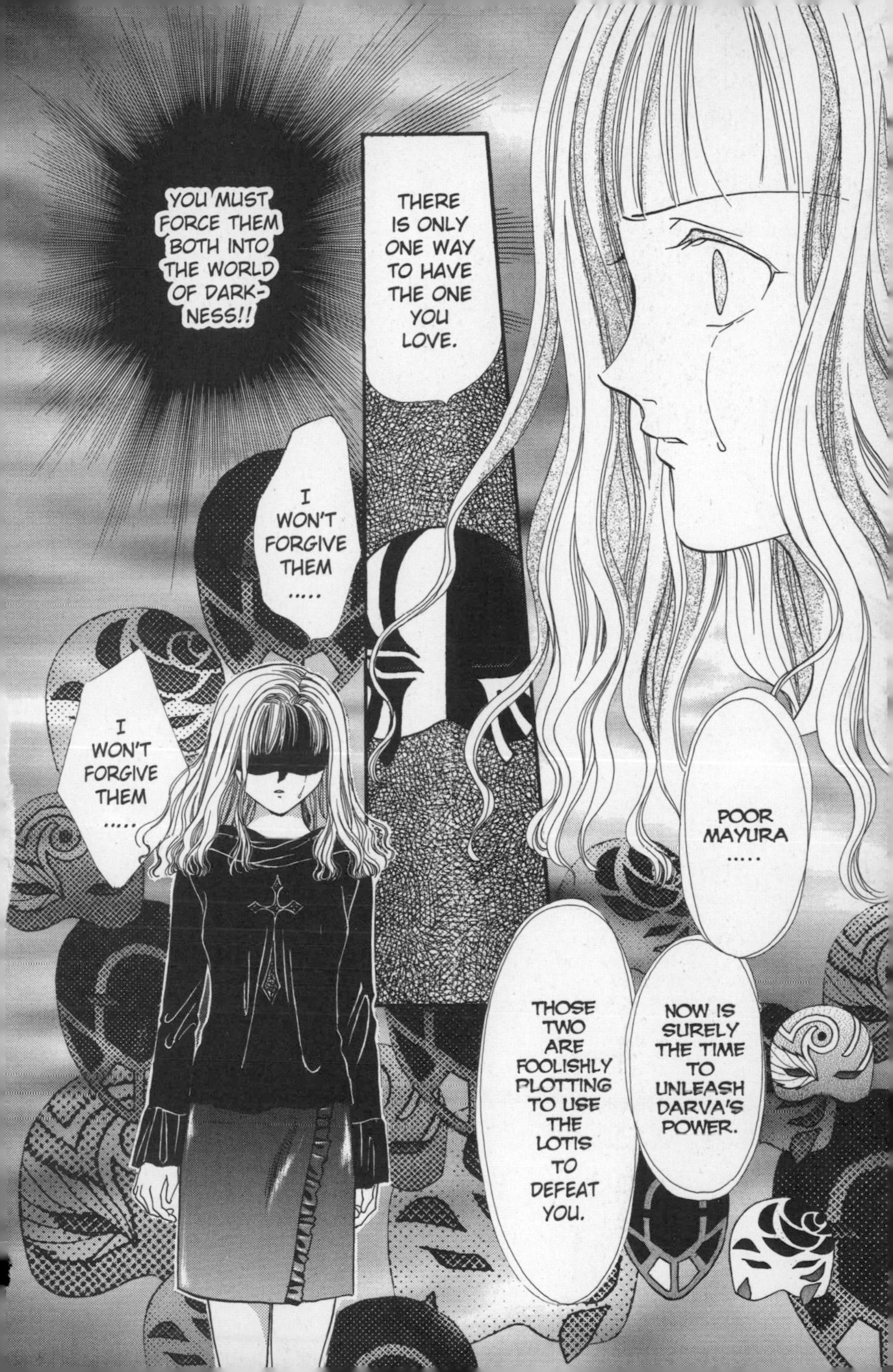
POOR MAYURA .....
NOW IS SURELY THE TIME TO UNLEASH DARVA'S POWER.
THOSE TWO ARE FOOLISHLY PLOTTING TO USE THE LOTIS TO DEFEAT YOU.
THERE IS ONLY ONE WAY TO HAVE THE ONE YOU LOVE.
YOU MUST FORCE THEM BOTH INTO THE WORLD OF DARK-NESS!!
I WON'T FORGIVE THEM .....
I WON'T FORGIVE THEM .....

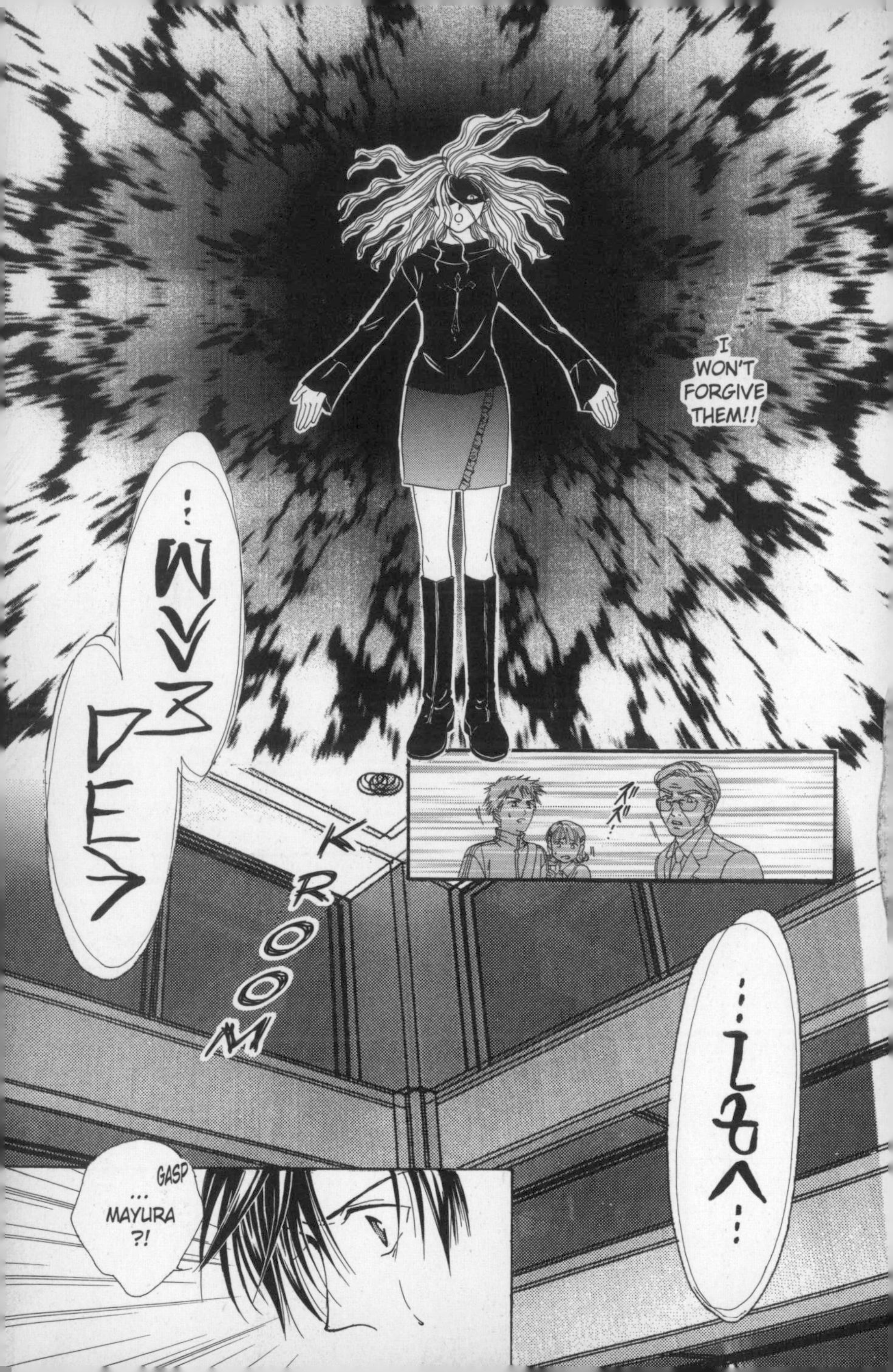
I WON'T FORGIVE THEM!!
KROOM
GASP
... MAYURA ?!

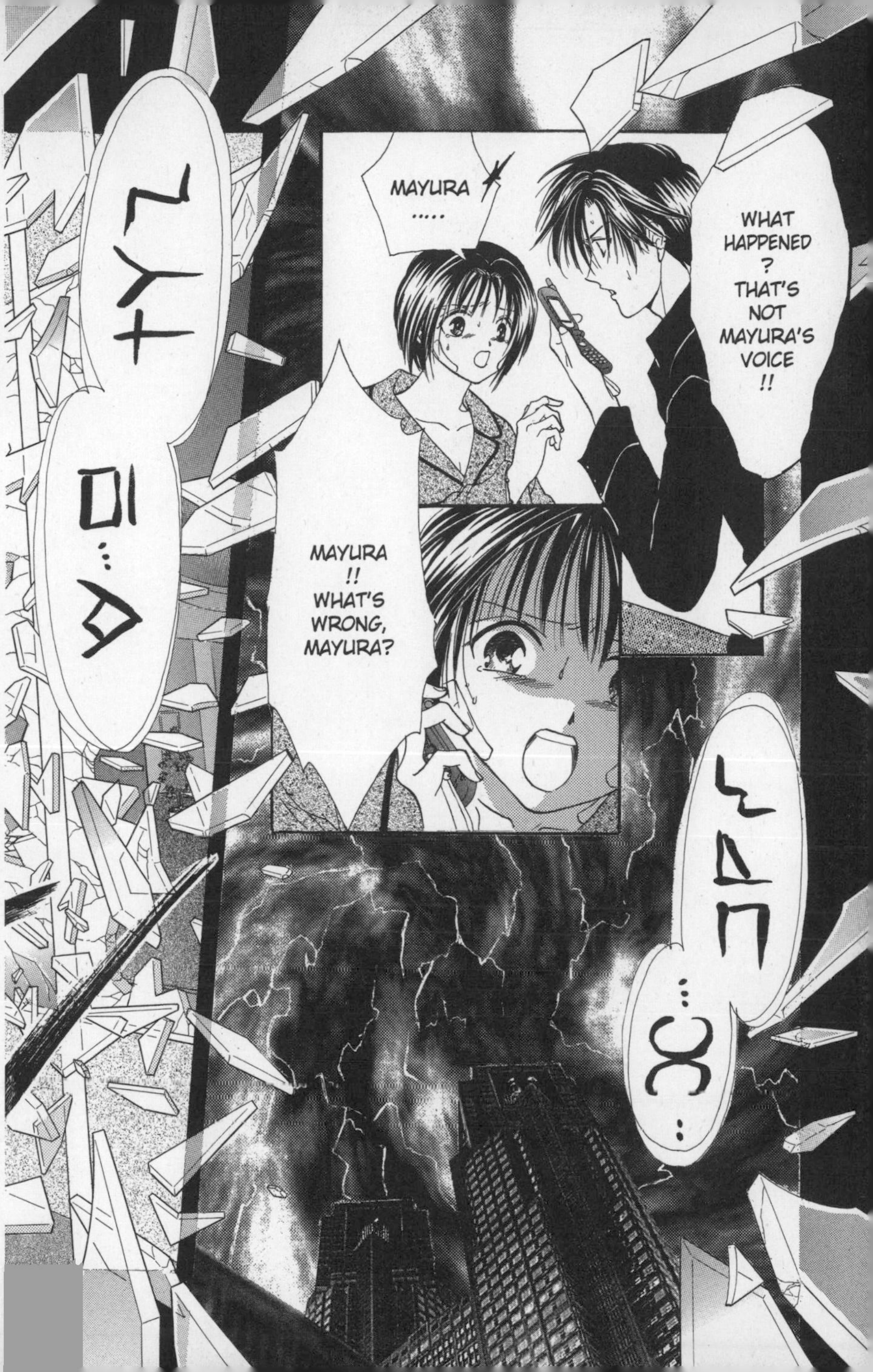
WHAT HAPPENED ? THAT'S NOT MAYURA'S VOICE !!
MAYURA .....
MAYURA !! WHAT'S WRONG, MAYURA?

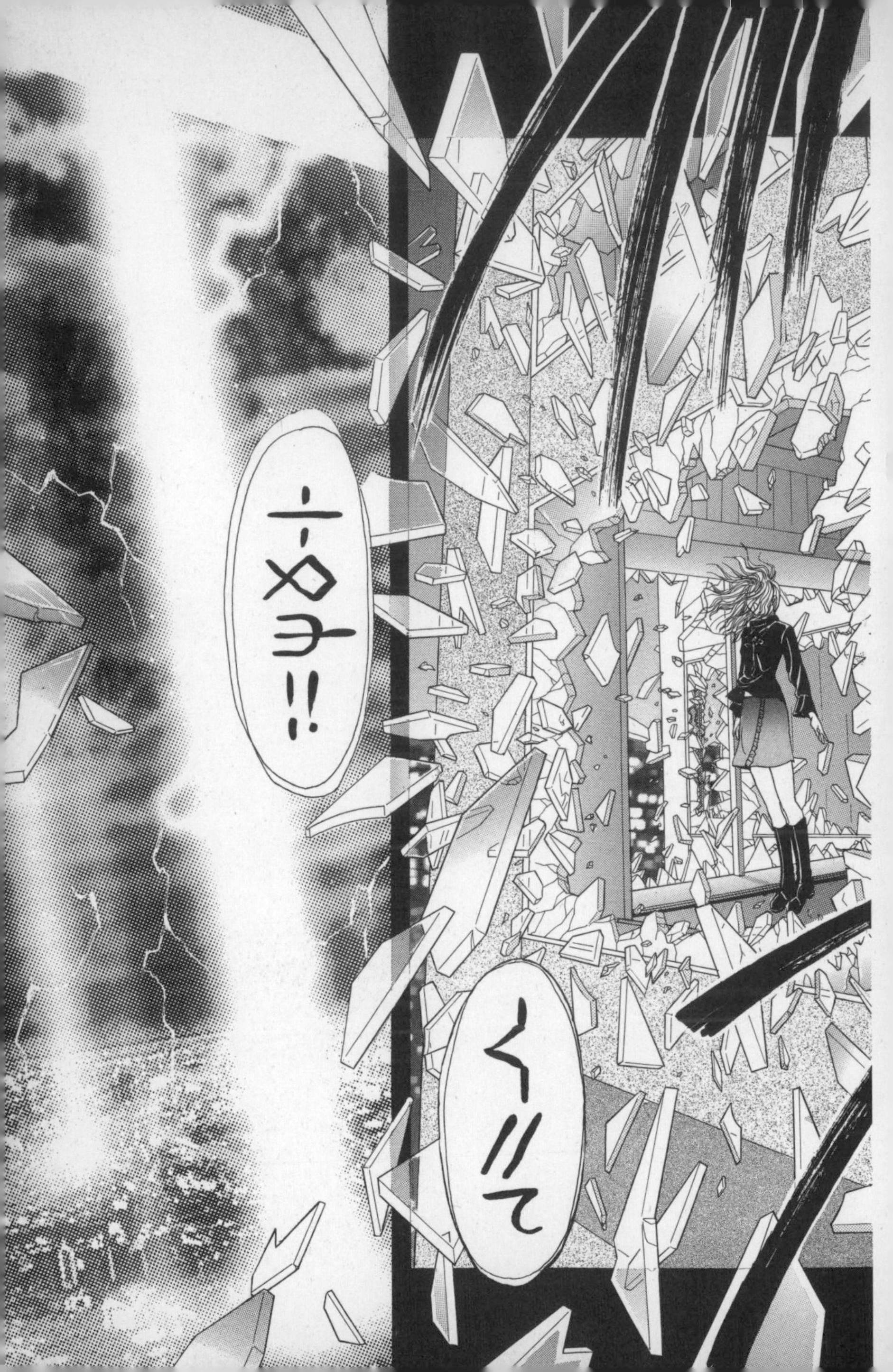

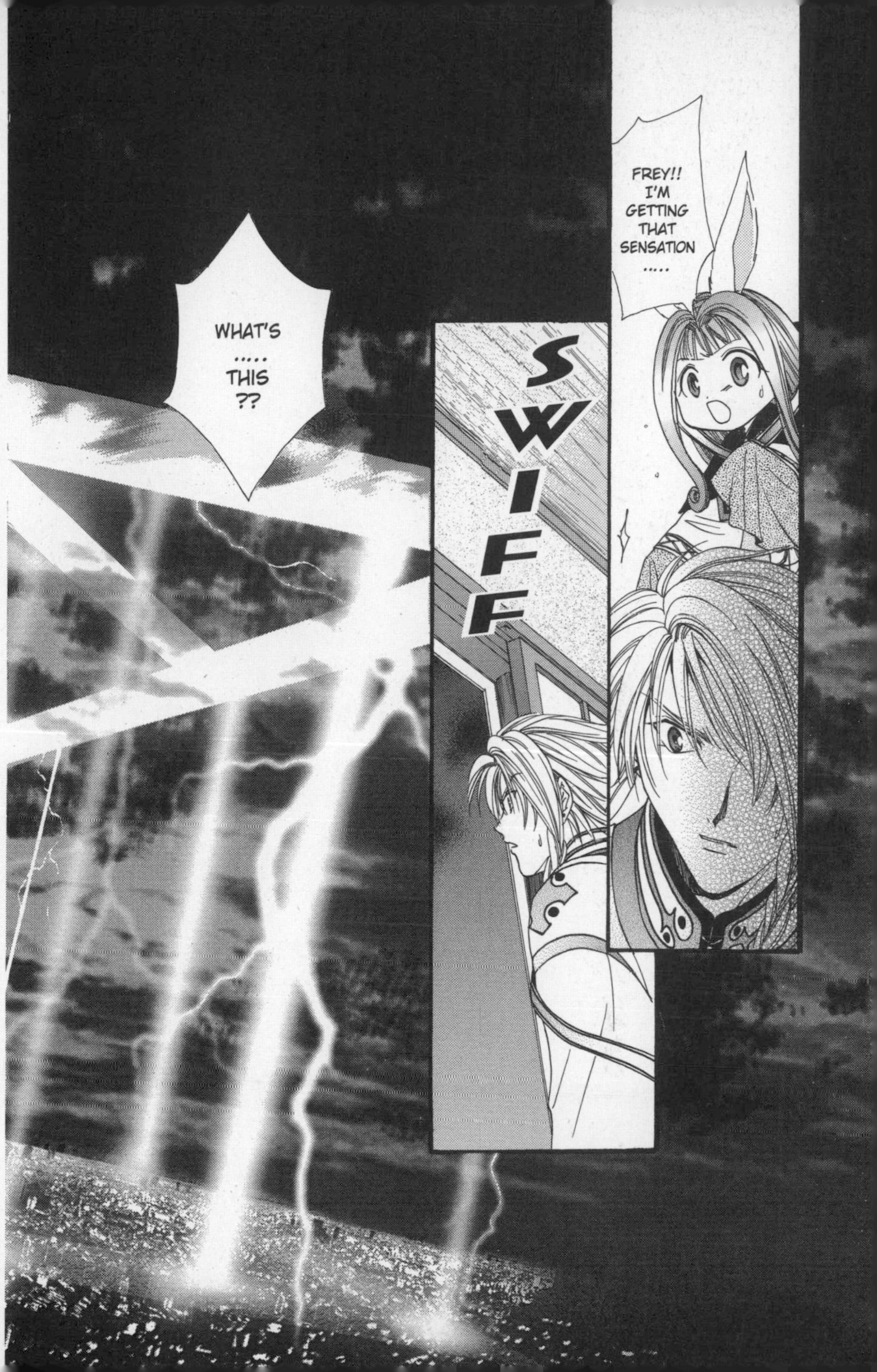
FREY!! I'M GETTING THAT SENSATION .....
SWIFF
WHAT'S ..... THIS ??

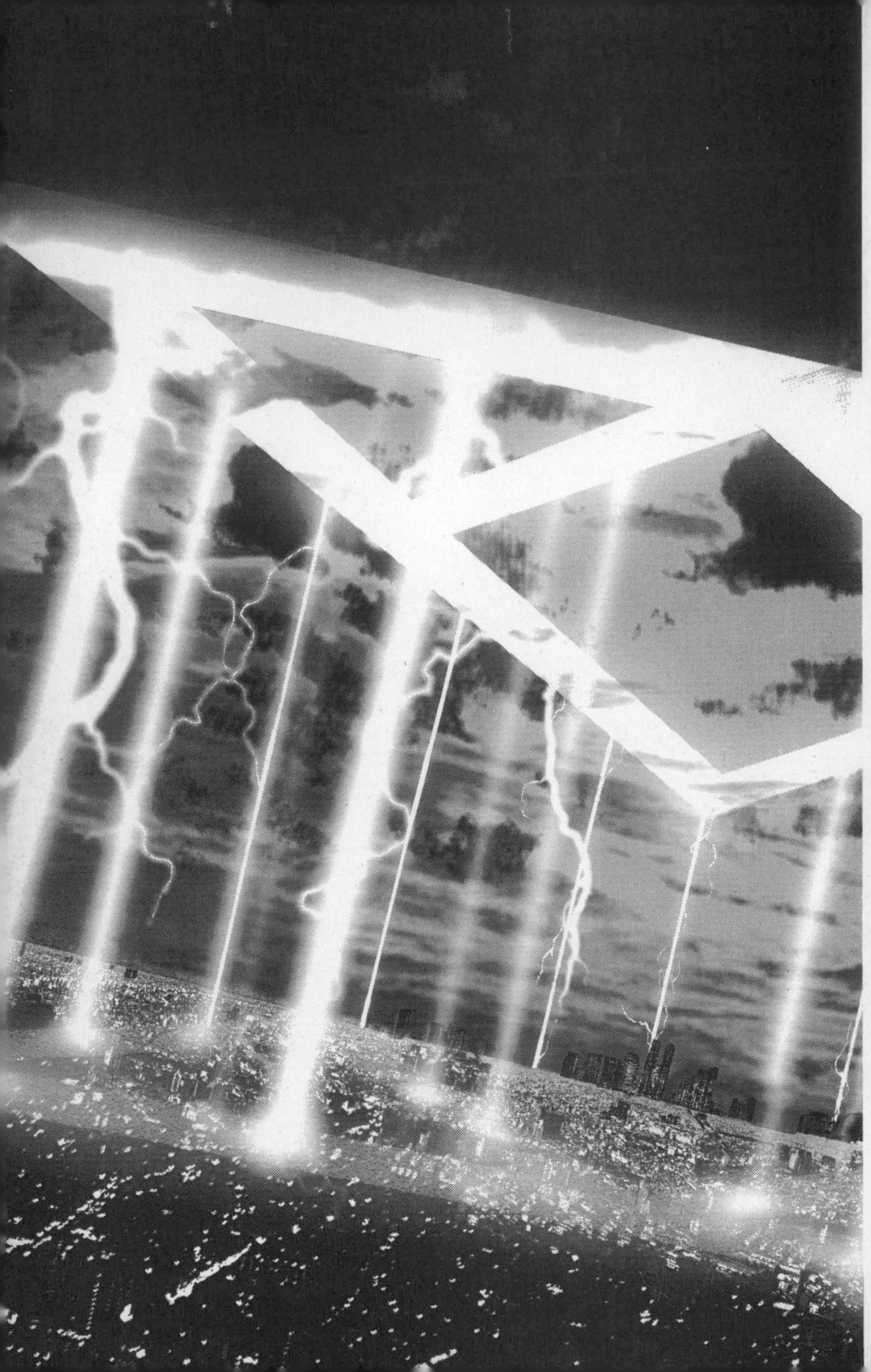

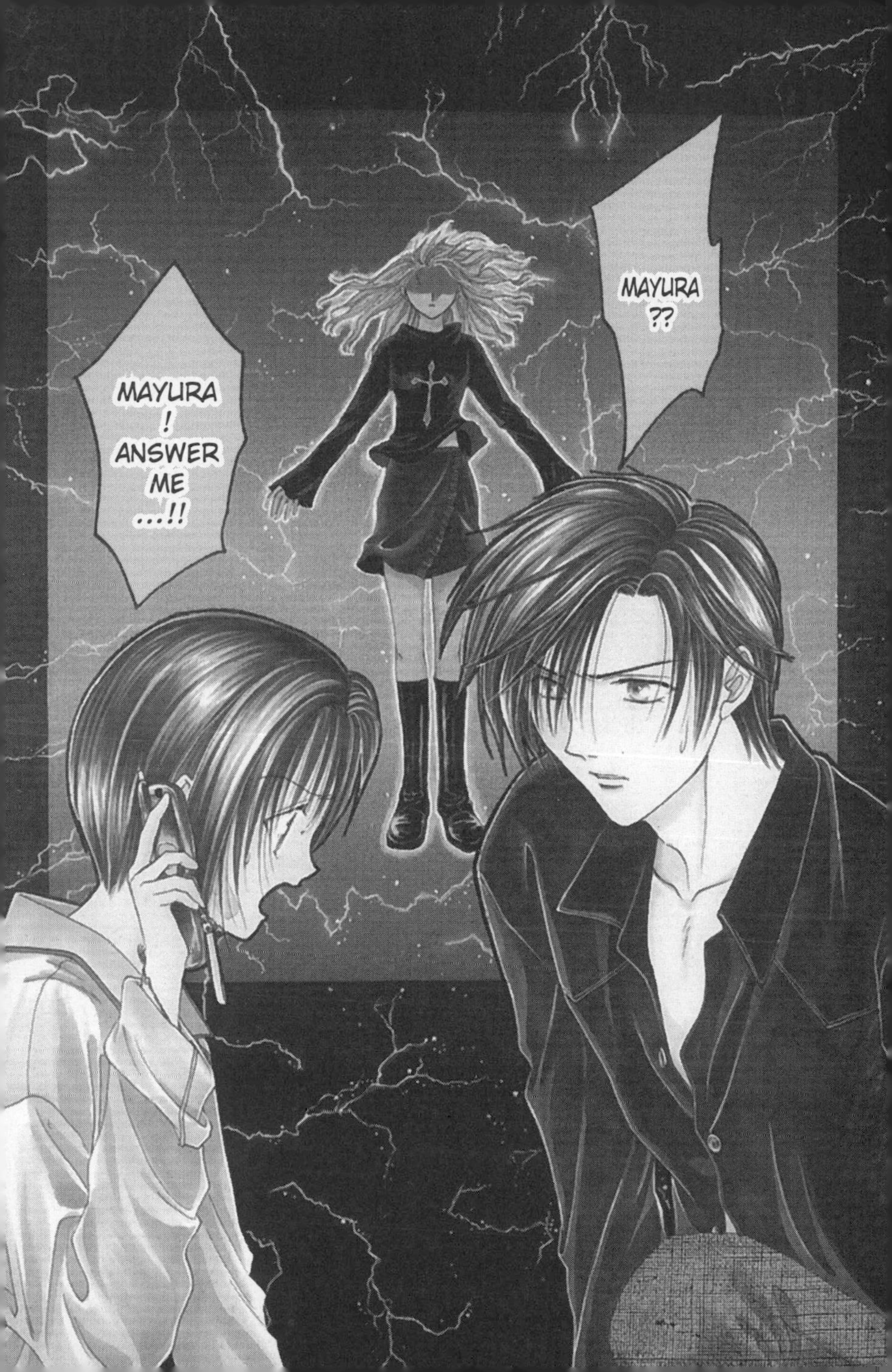
MAYURA ??
MAYURA ! ANSWER ME ...!!

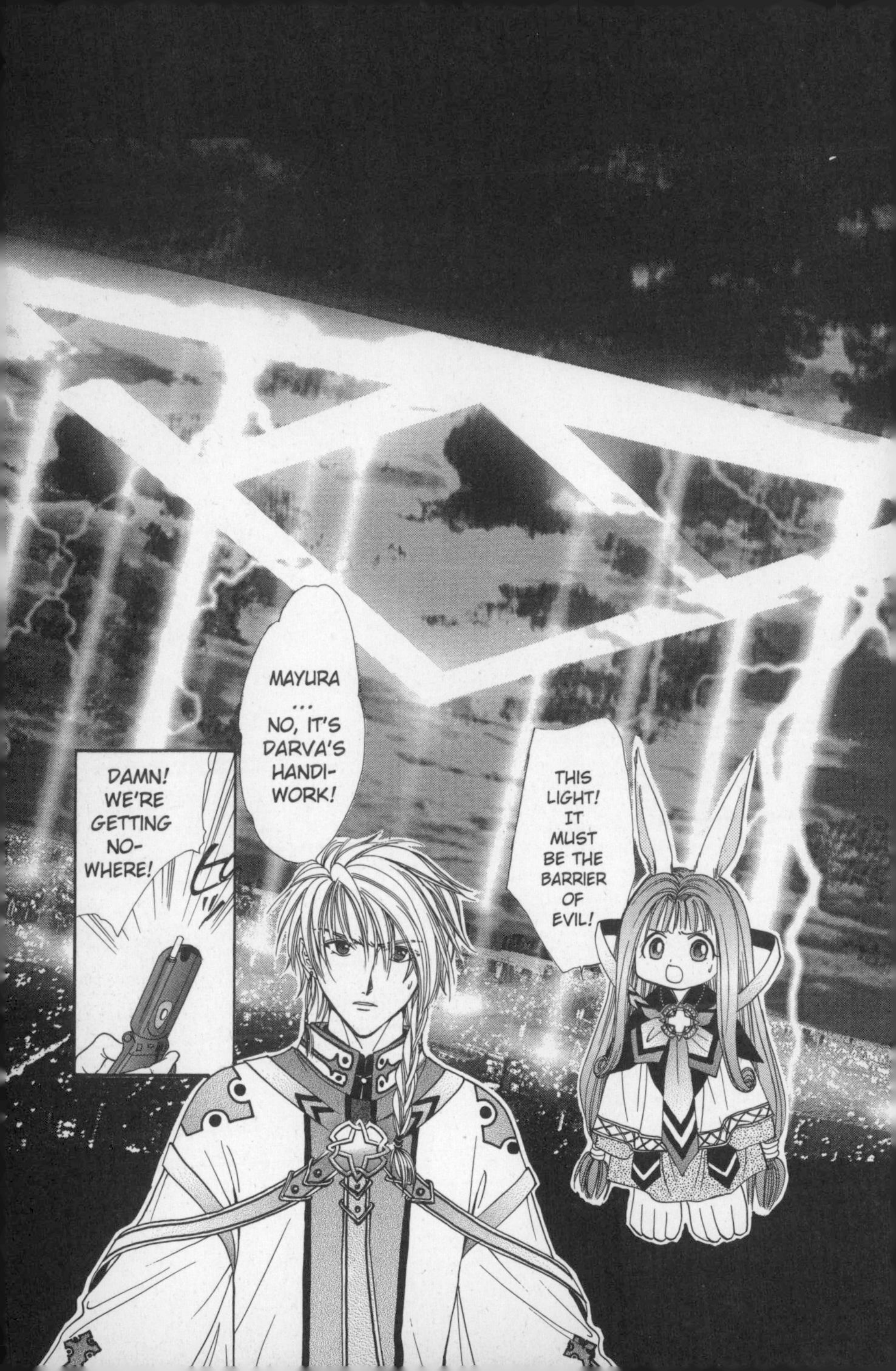
THIS LIGHT! IT MUST BE THE BARRIER OF EVIL!
MAYURA ... NO, IT'S DARVA'S HANDI-WORK!
DAMN! WE'RE GETTING NO-WHERE!

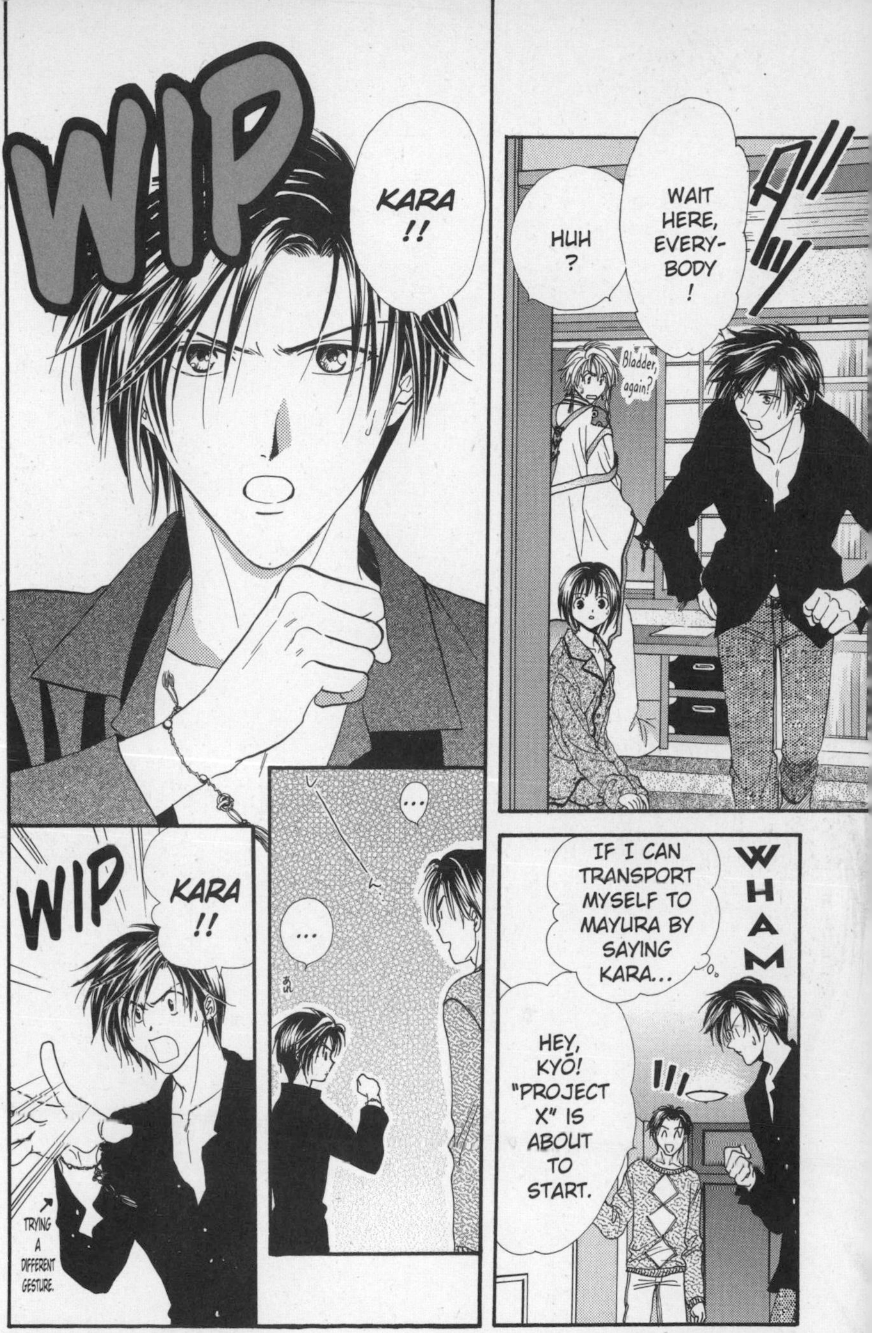
WAIT HERE, EVERY-BODY!
HUH?
Bladder, again?
WIP
KARA!!
WHAM
IF I CAN TRANSPORT MYSELF TO MAYURA BY SAYING KARA...
HEY, KYŌ! "PROJECT X" IS ABOUT TO START.
...
...
WIP
KARA!!
TRYING A DIFFERENT GESTURE.

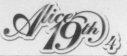

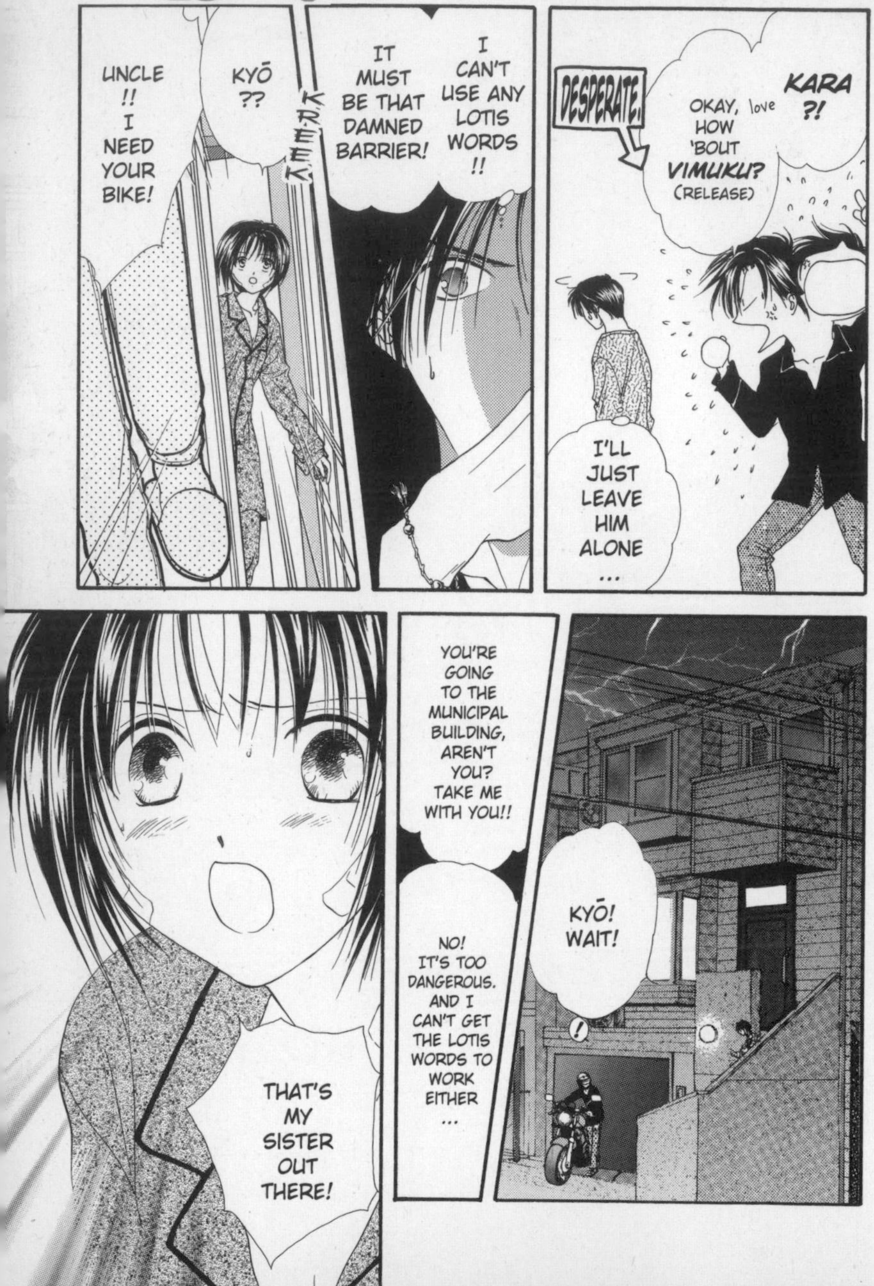
KARA ?!
OKAY, love HOW 'BOUT VIMUKU? (RELEASE)
DESPERATE.
I'LL JUST LEAVE HIM ALONE ...
I CAN'T USE ANY LOTIS WORDS !!
IT MUST BE THAT DAMNED BARRIER!
KREEK
KYŌ ??
UNCLE !! I NEED YOUR BIKE!
KYŌ! WAIT!
!
YOU'RE GOING TO THE MUNICIPAL BUILDING, AREN'T YOU? TAKE ME WITH YOU!!
NO! IT'S TOO DANGEROUS. AND I CAN'T GET THE LOTIS WORDS TO WORK EITHER ...
THAT'S MY SISTER OUT THERE!

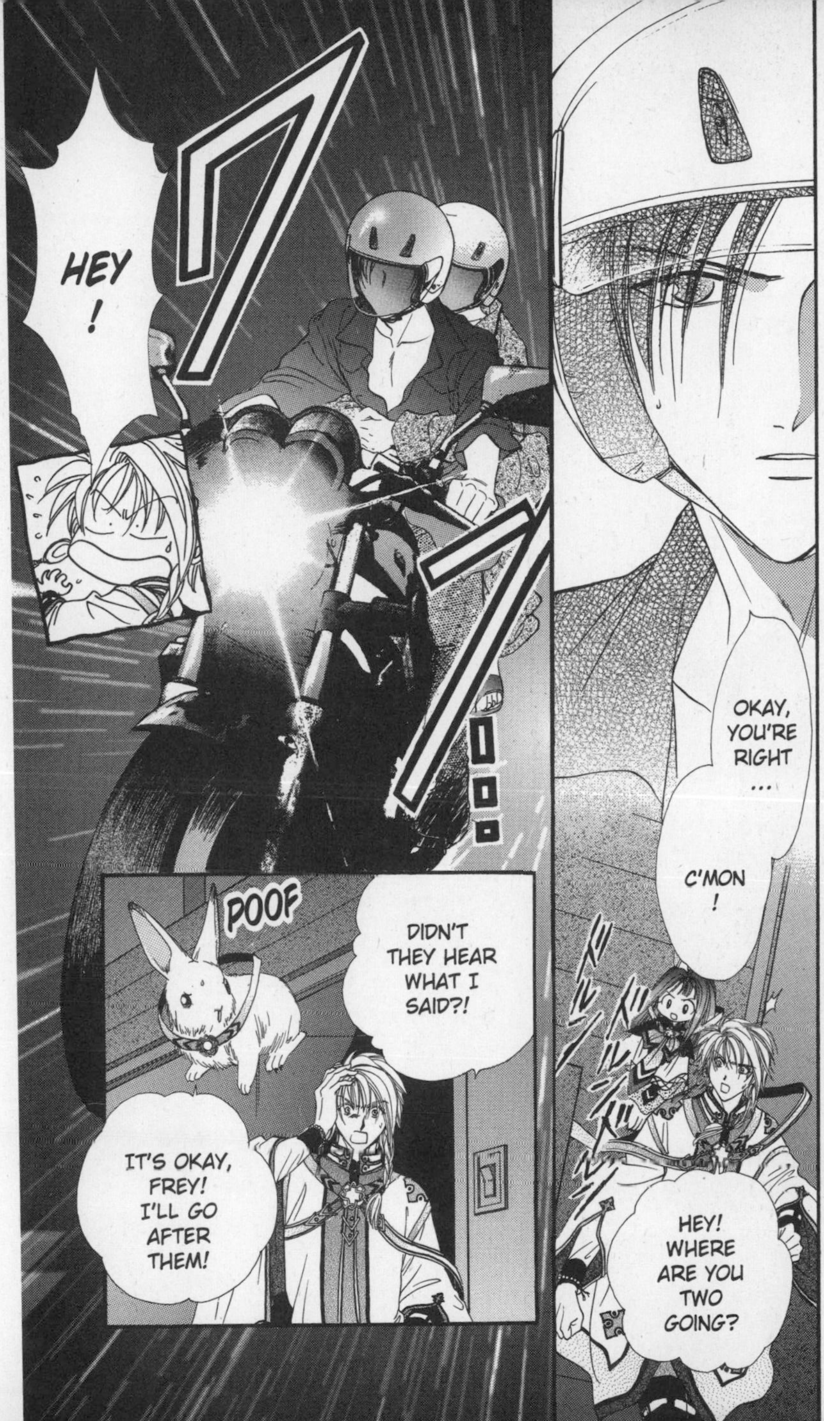
OKAY, YOU'RE RIGHT ...
C'MON !
HEY! WHERE ARE YOU TWO GOING?
HEY !
POOF
DIDN'T THEY HEAR WHAT I SAID?!
IT'S OKAY, FREY! I'LL GO AFTER THEM!

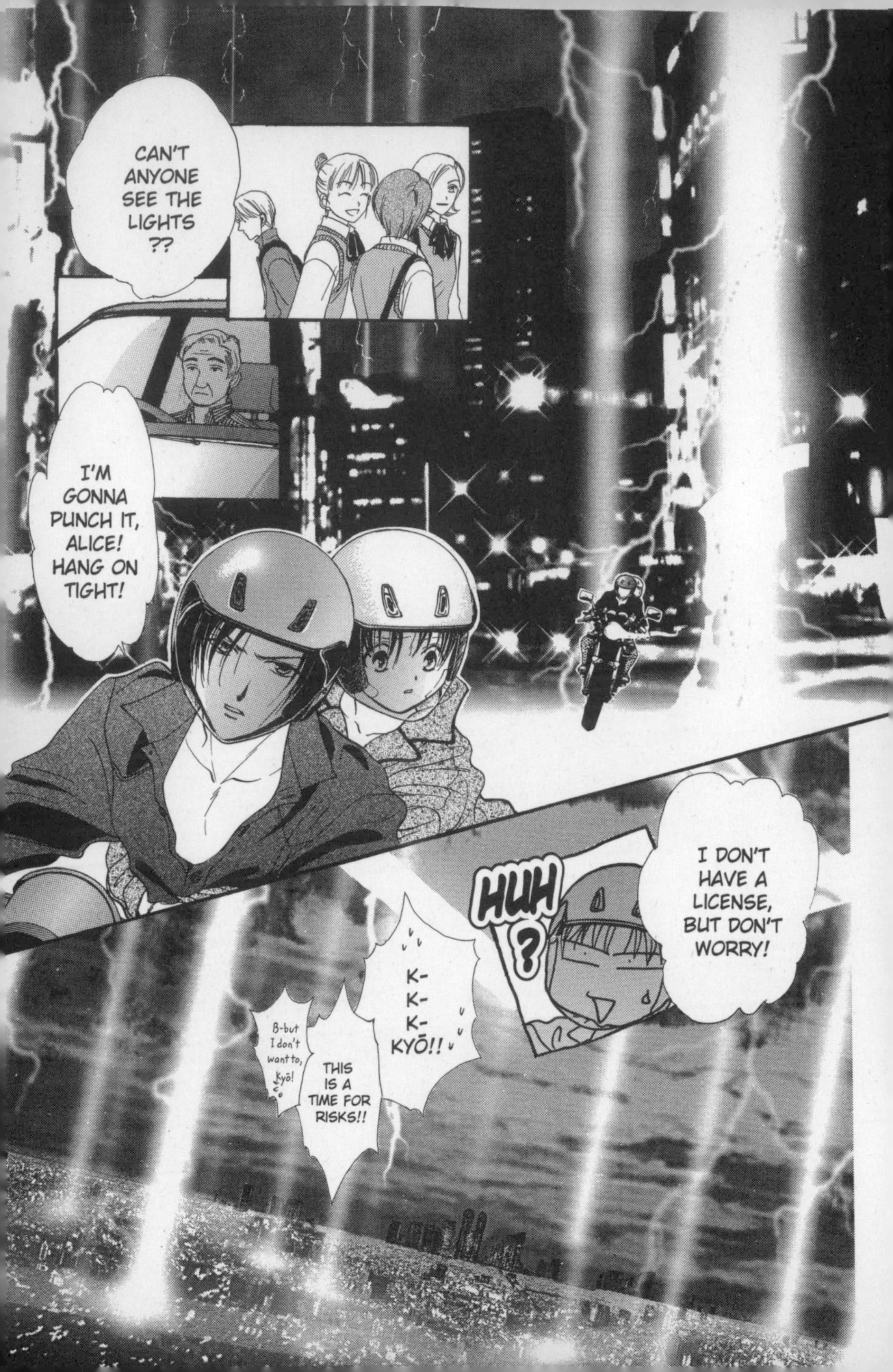
CAN'T ANYONE SEE THE LIGHTS ??
I'M GONNA PUNCH IT, ALICE! HANG ON TIGHT!
I DON'T HAVE A LICENSE, BUT DON'T WORRY!
HUH ?
K-K-K-KYŌ!!
THIS IS A TIME FOR RISKS!!
B-but I don't want to, Kyō!

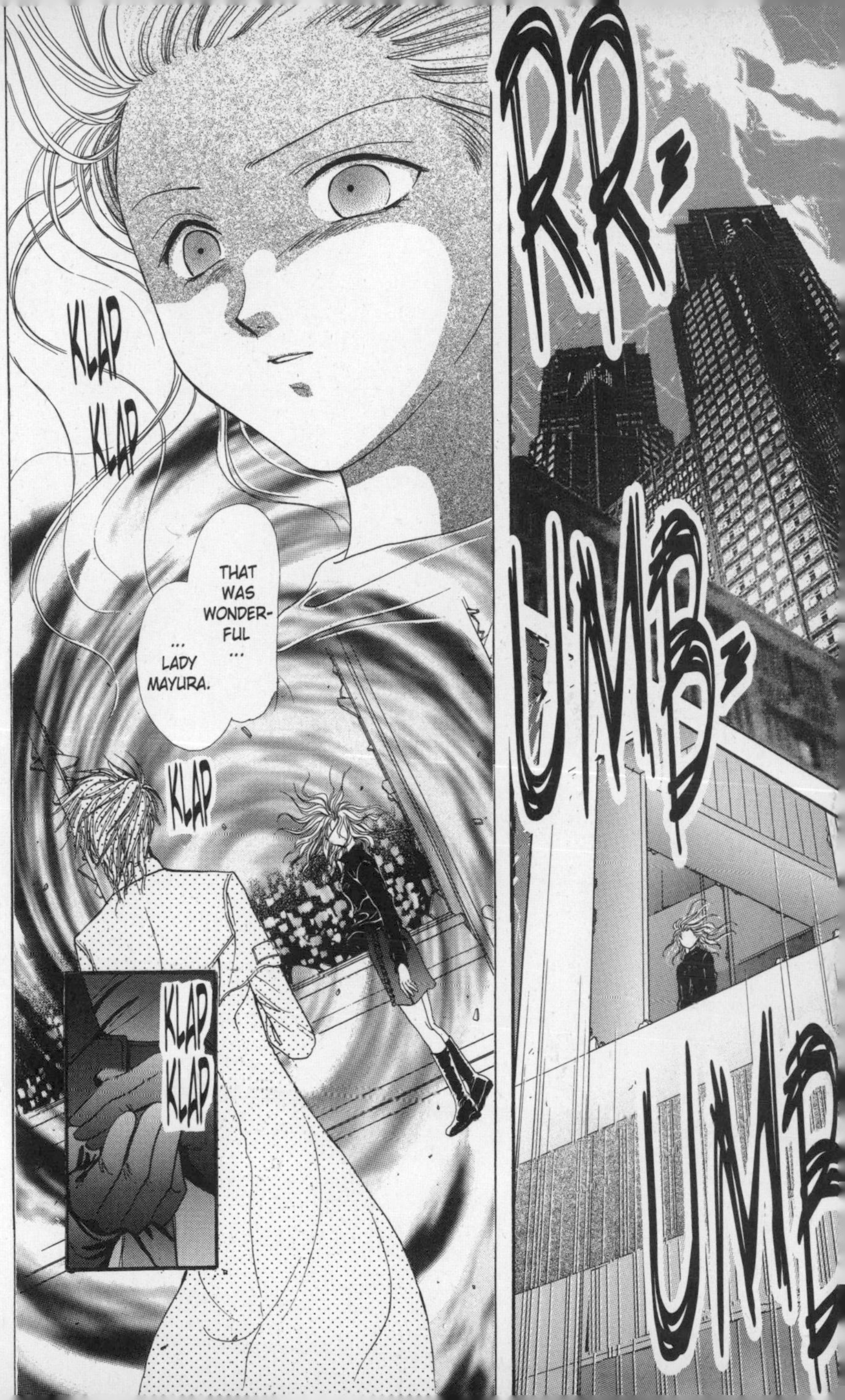
RR
UMB
UMB
KLAP KLAP
THAT WAS WONDERFUL ... ... LADY MAYURA.
KLAP
KLAP KLAP

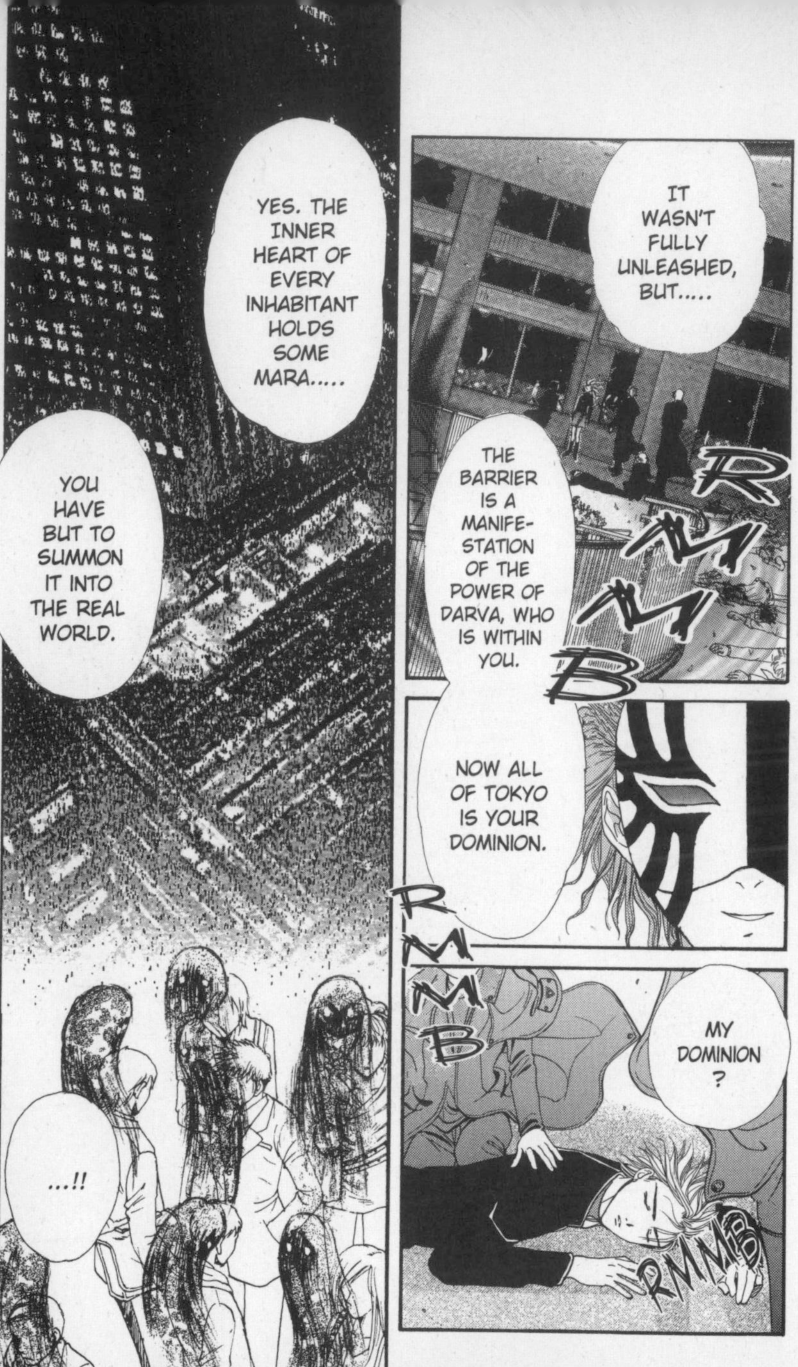
IT WASN'T FULLY UNLEASHED, BUT.....
THE BARRIER IS A MANIFE-STATION OF THE POWER OF DARVA, WHO IS WITHIN YOU.
RMMB
NOW ALL OF TOKYO IS YOUR DOMINION.
RMMB
MY DOMINION ?
RMMB
YES. THE INNER HEART OF EVERY INHABITANT HOLDS SOME MARA.....
YOU HAVE BUT TO SUMMON IT INTO THE REAL WORLD.
...!!

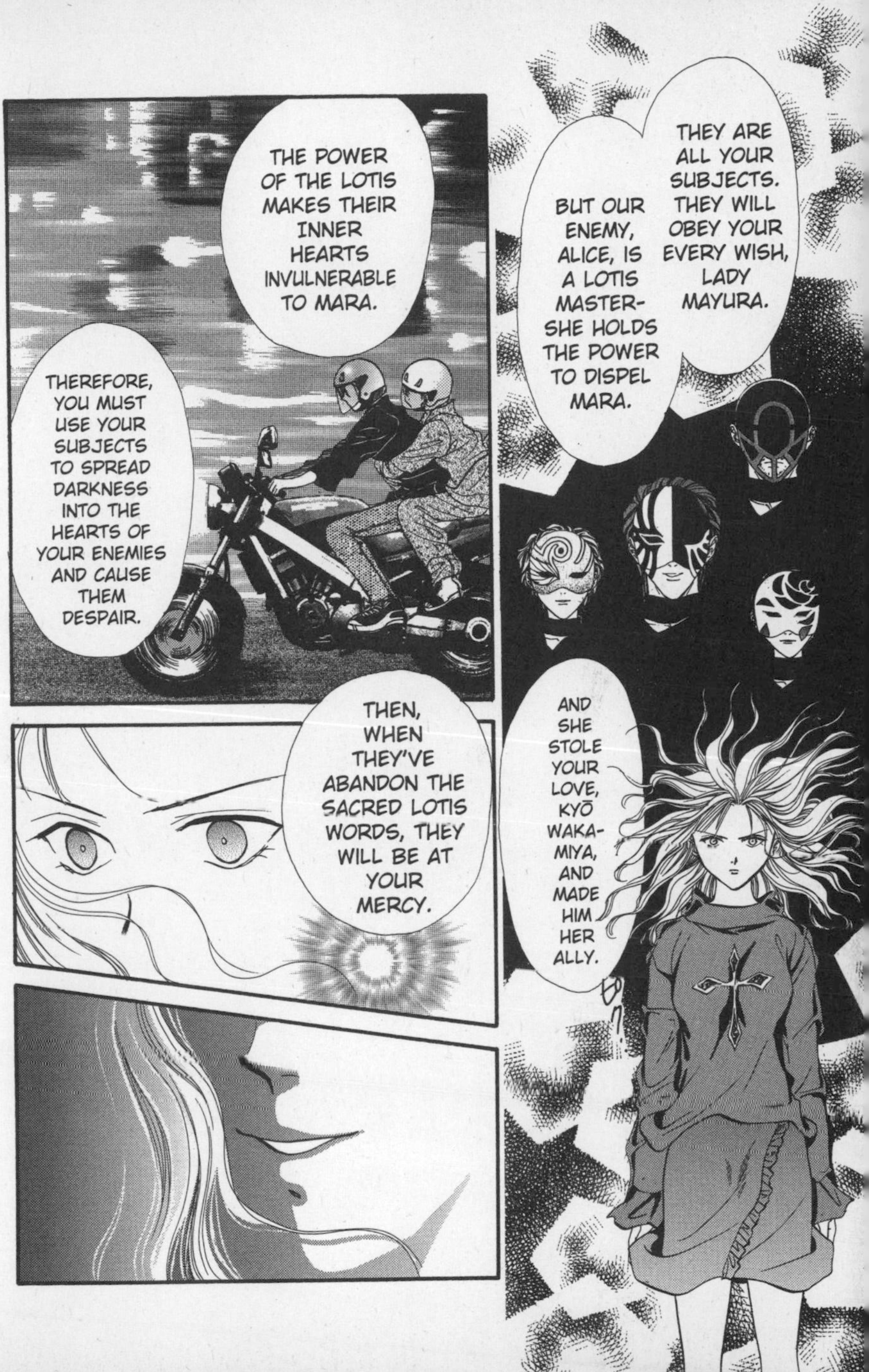
THEY ARE ALL YOUR SUBJECTS. THEY WILL OBEY YOUR EVERY WISH, LADY MAYURA.
BUT OUR ENEMY, ALICE, IS A LOTIS MASTER- SHE HOLDS THE POWER TO DISPEL MARA.
AND SHE STOLE YOUR LOVE, KYŌ WAKA-MIYA, AND MADE HIM HER ALLY.
THE POWER OF THE LOTIS MAKES THEIR INNER HEARTS INVULNERABLE TO MARA.
THEREFORE, YOU MUST USE YOUR SUBJECTS TO SPREAD DARKNESS INTO THE HEARTS OF YOUR ENEMIES AND CAUSE THEM DESPAIR.
THEN, WHEN THEY'VE ABANDON THE SACRED LOTIS WORDS, THEY WILL BE AT YOUR MERCY.

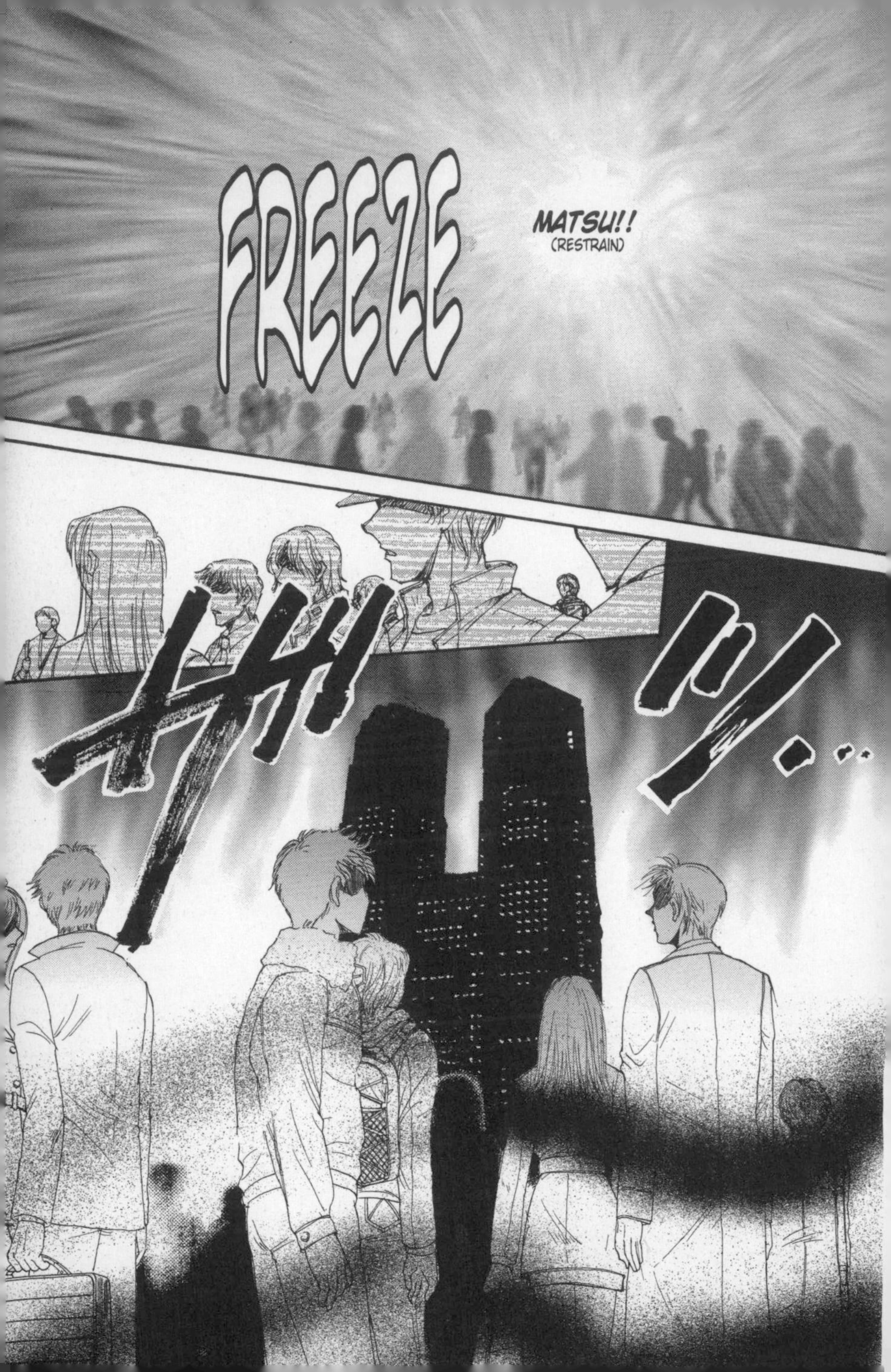
MATSU!!
(RESTRAIN)
FREEZE

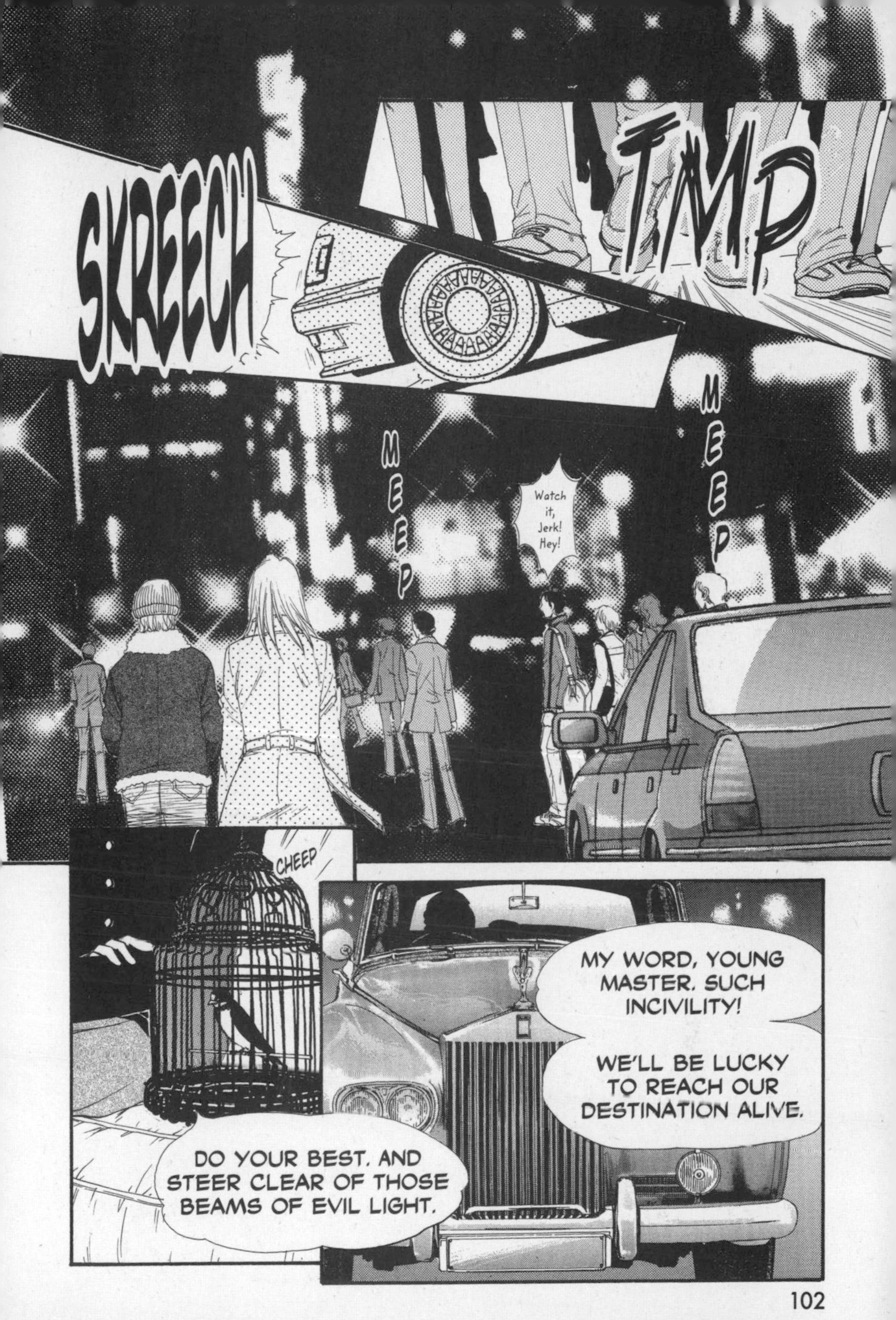
TMP
SKREECH
MEEP
Watch it, Jerk! Hey!
MEEP
MY WORD, YOUNG MASTER. SUCH INCIVILITY!
WE'LL BE LUCKY TO REACH OUR DESTINATION ALIVE.
DO YOUR BEST. AND STEER CLEAR OF THOSE BEAMS OF EVIL LIGHT.
CHEEP

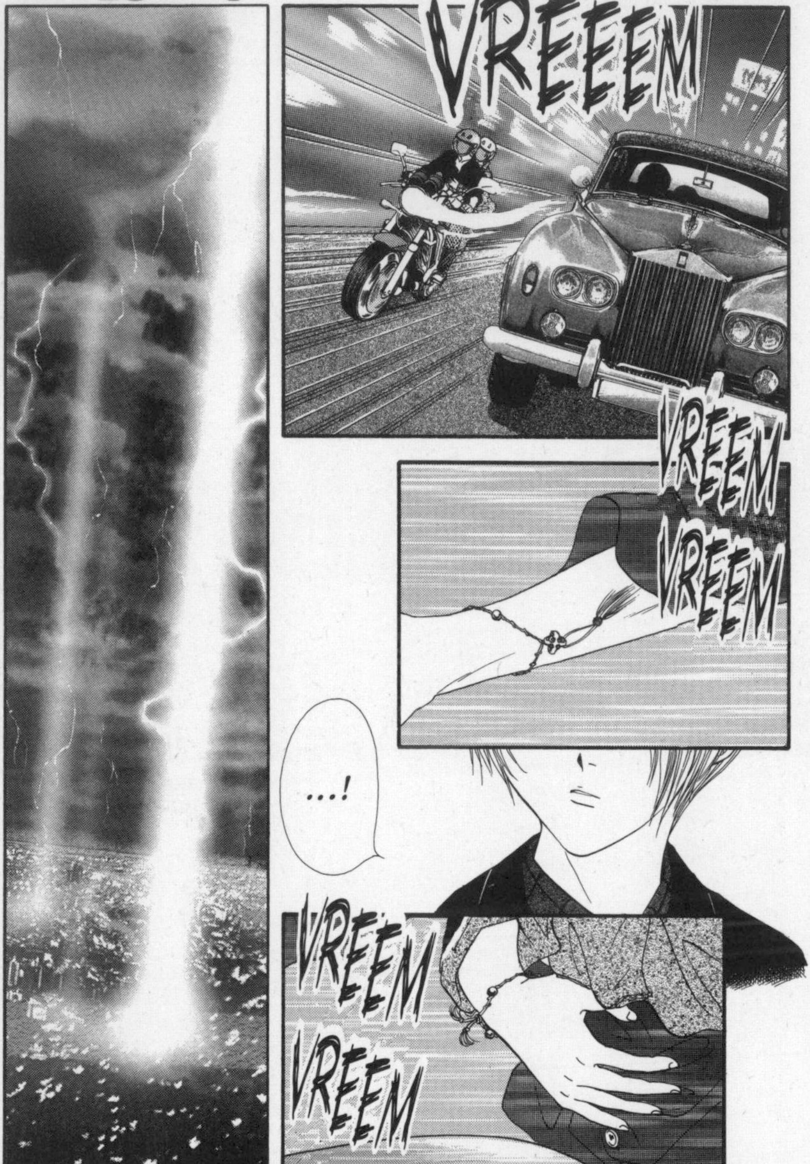
VREEEM
VREEM
VREEM
...!
VREEM
VREEM

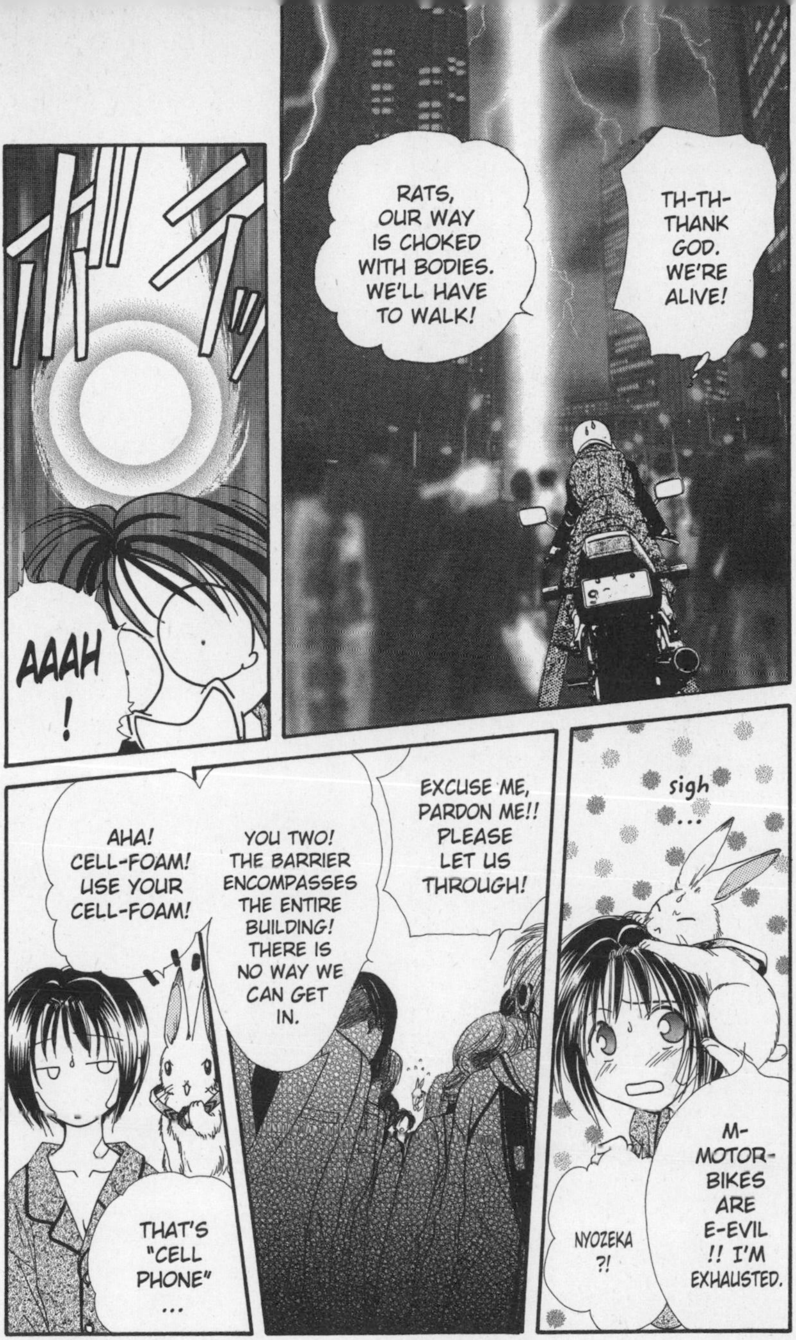
TH-TH-THANK GOD. WE'RE ALIVE!
RATS, OUR WAY IS CHOKED WITH BODIES. WE'LL HAVE TO WALK!
AAAH!
sigh...
M-MOTORBIKES ARE E-EVIL!! I'M EXHAUSTED.
NYOZEKA?!
EXCUSE ME, PARDON ME!! PLEASE LET US THROUGH!
YOU TWO! THE BARRIER ENCOMPASSES THE ENTIRE BUILDING! THERE IS NO WAY WE CAN GET IN.
AHA! CELL-FOAM! USE YOUR CELL-FOAM!
THAT'S "CELL PHONE"...

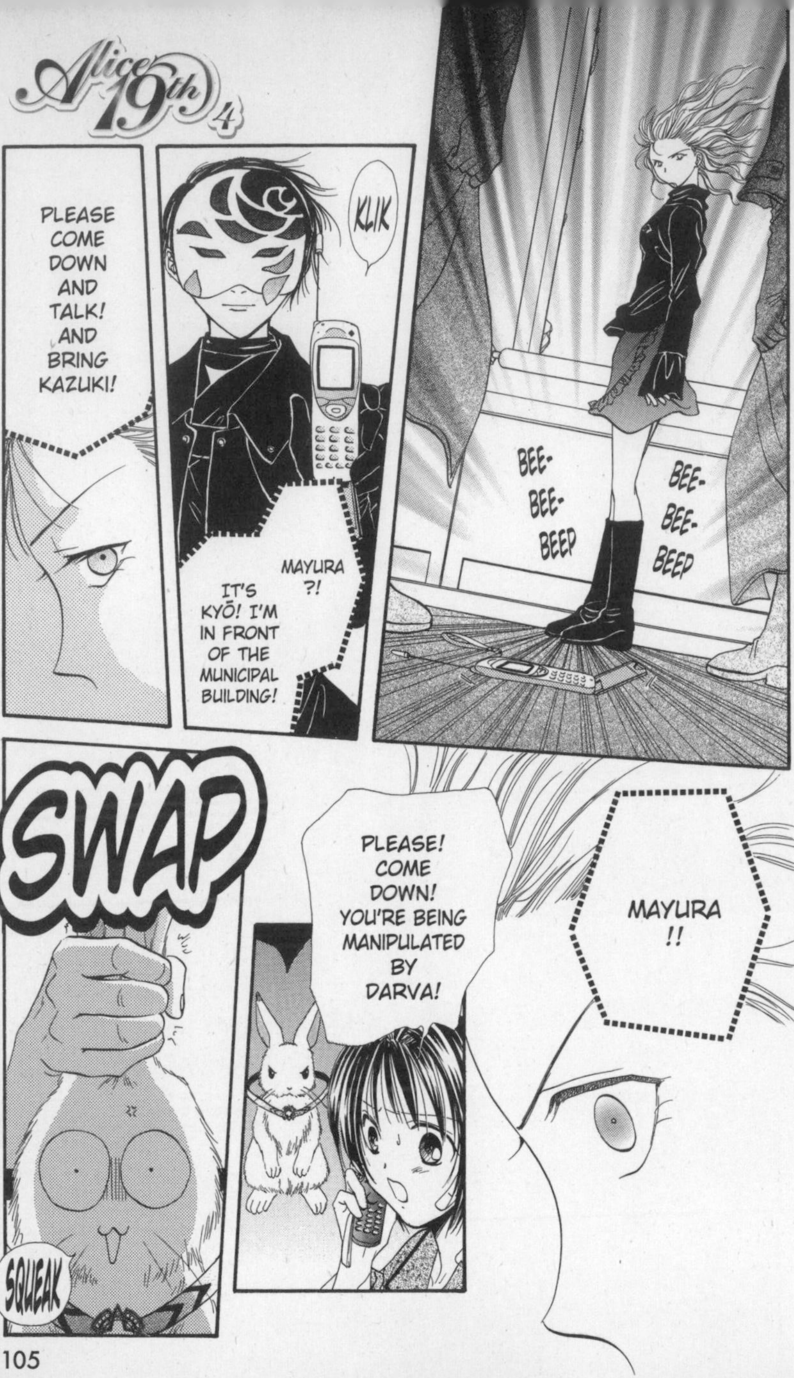
BEE-
BEE-
BEEP
BEE-
BEE-
BEEP
KLIK
MAYURA ?!
IT'S KYŌ! I'M IN FRONT OF THE MUNICIPAL BUILDING!
PLEASE COME DOWN AND TALK! AND BRING KAZUKI!
MAYURA !!
PLEASE! COME DOWN! YOU'RE BEING MANIPULATED BY DARVA!
SWAP
SQUEAK

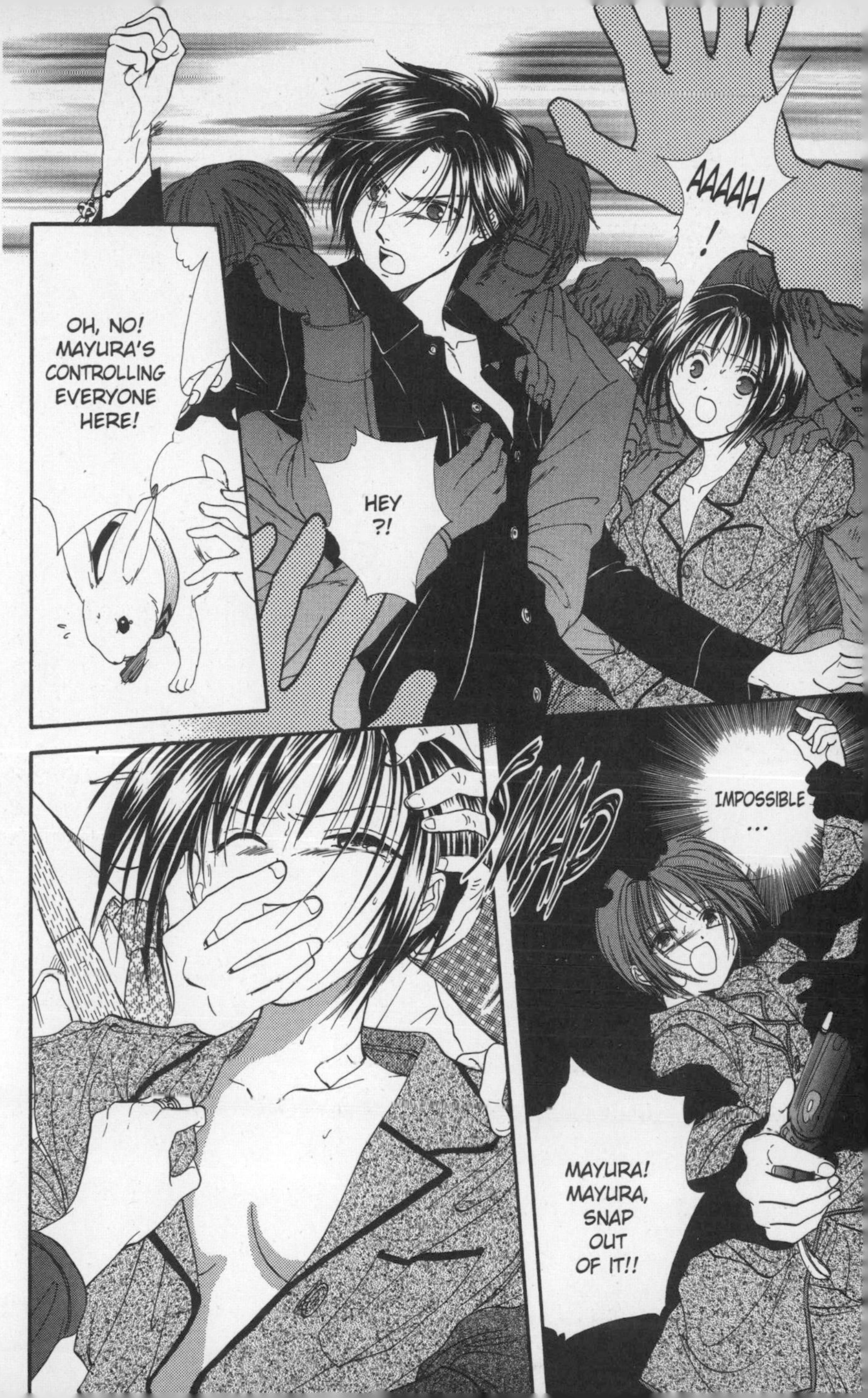
AAAAH!
HEY?!
OH, NO! MAYURA'S CONTROLLING EVERYONE HERE!
IMPOSSIBLE...
MAYURA! MAYURA, SNAP OUT OF IT!!
SNAP

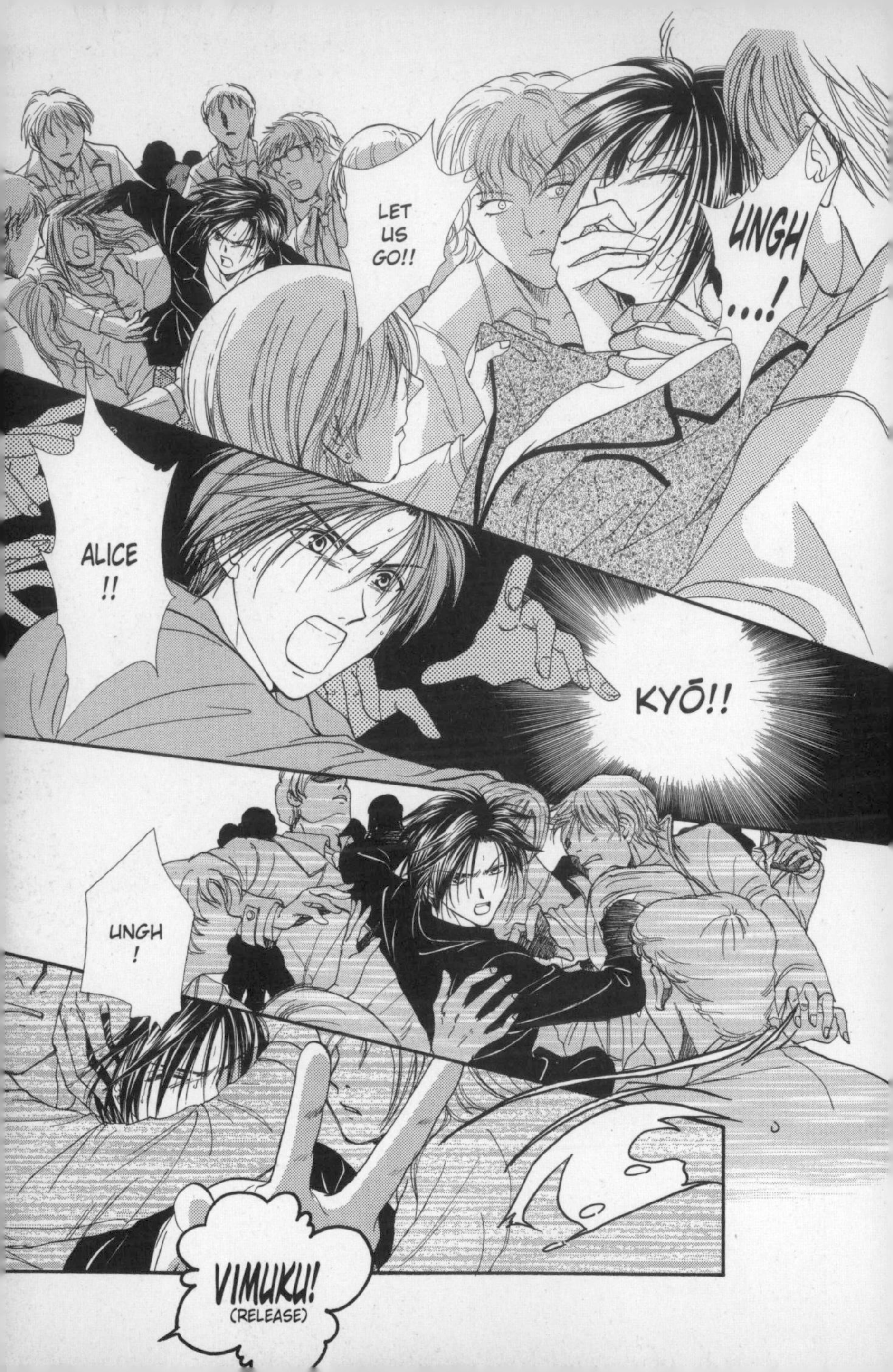
UNGH ...!
LET US GO!!
KYŌ!!
ALICE !!
UNGH !
VIMUKU! (RELEASE)

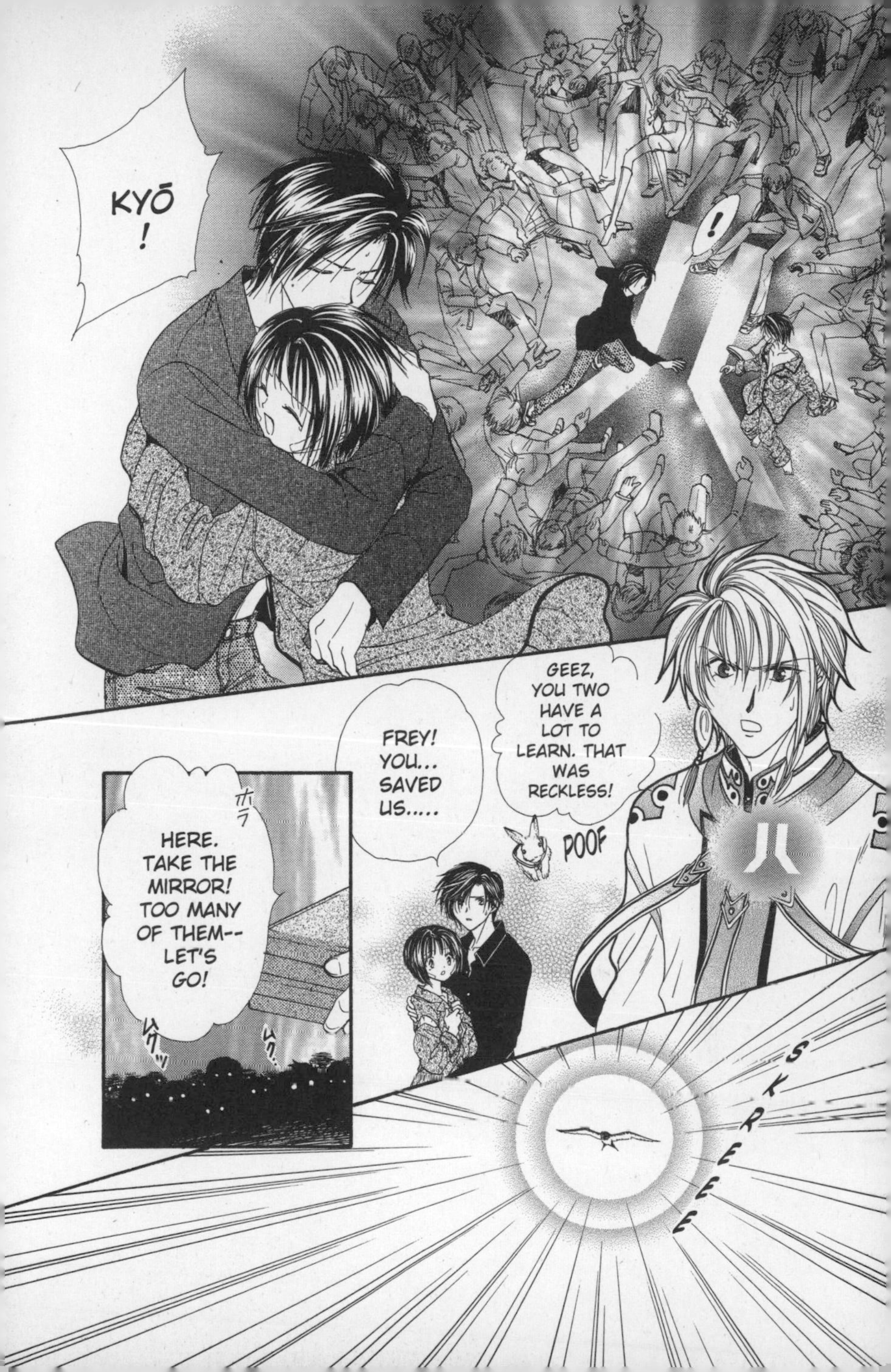
!
KYŌ !
GEEZ, YOU TWO HAVE A LOT TO LEARN. THAT WAS RECKLESS!
POOF
FREY! YOU... SAVED US.....
ホラ
HERE. TAKE THE MIRROR! TOO MANY OF THEM-- LET'S GO!
SKREEEE

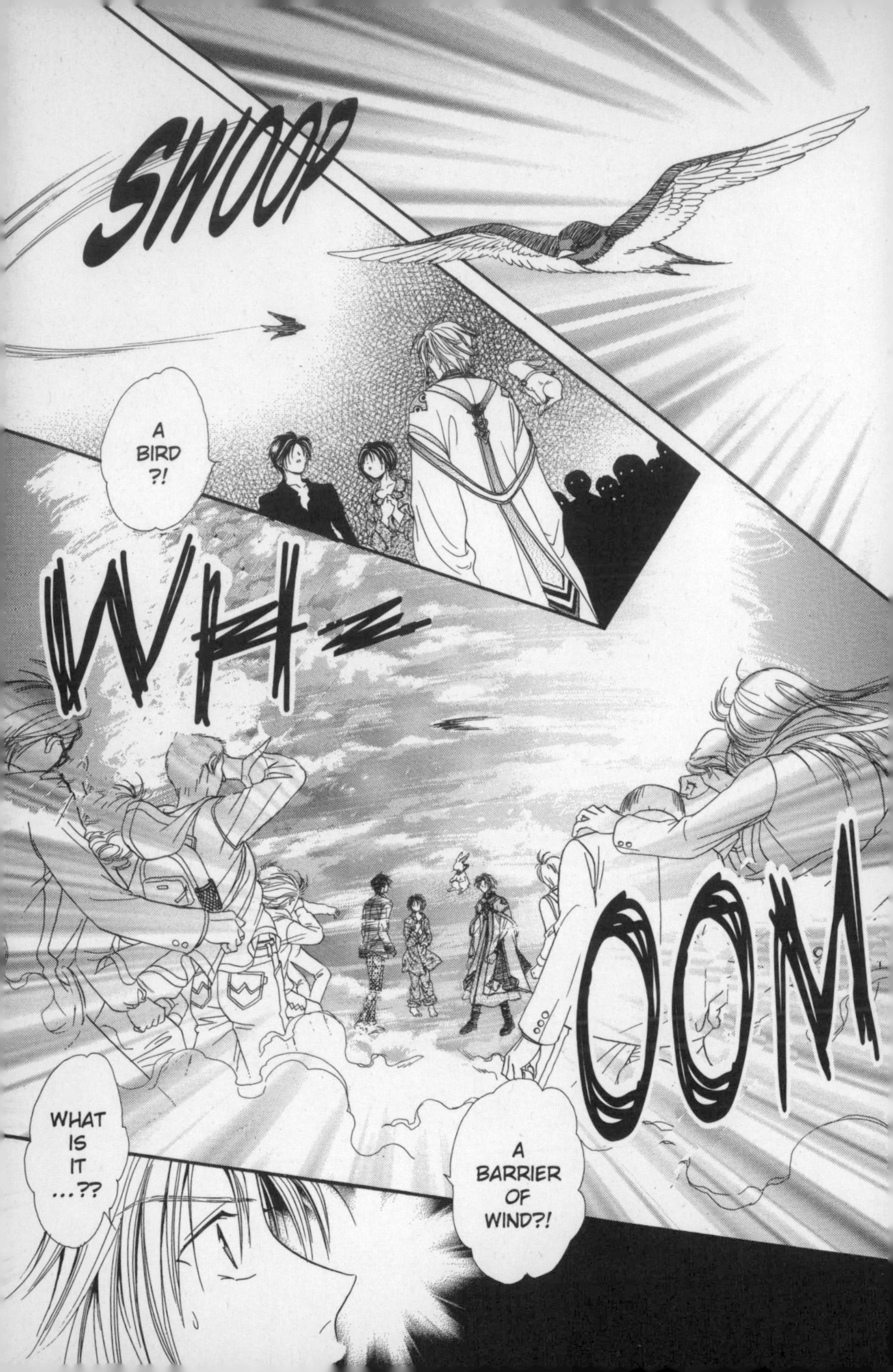
SWOOP
A BIRD ?!
WH-
OOM
A BARRIER OF WIND?!
WHAT IS IT ...??

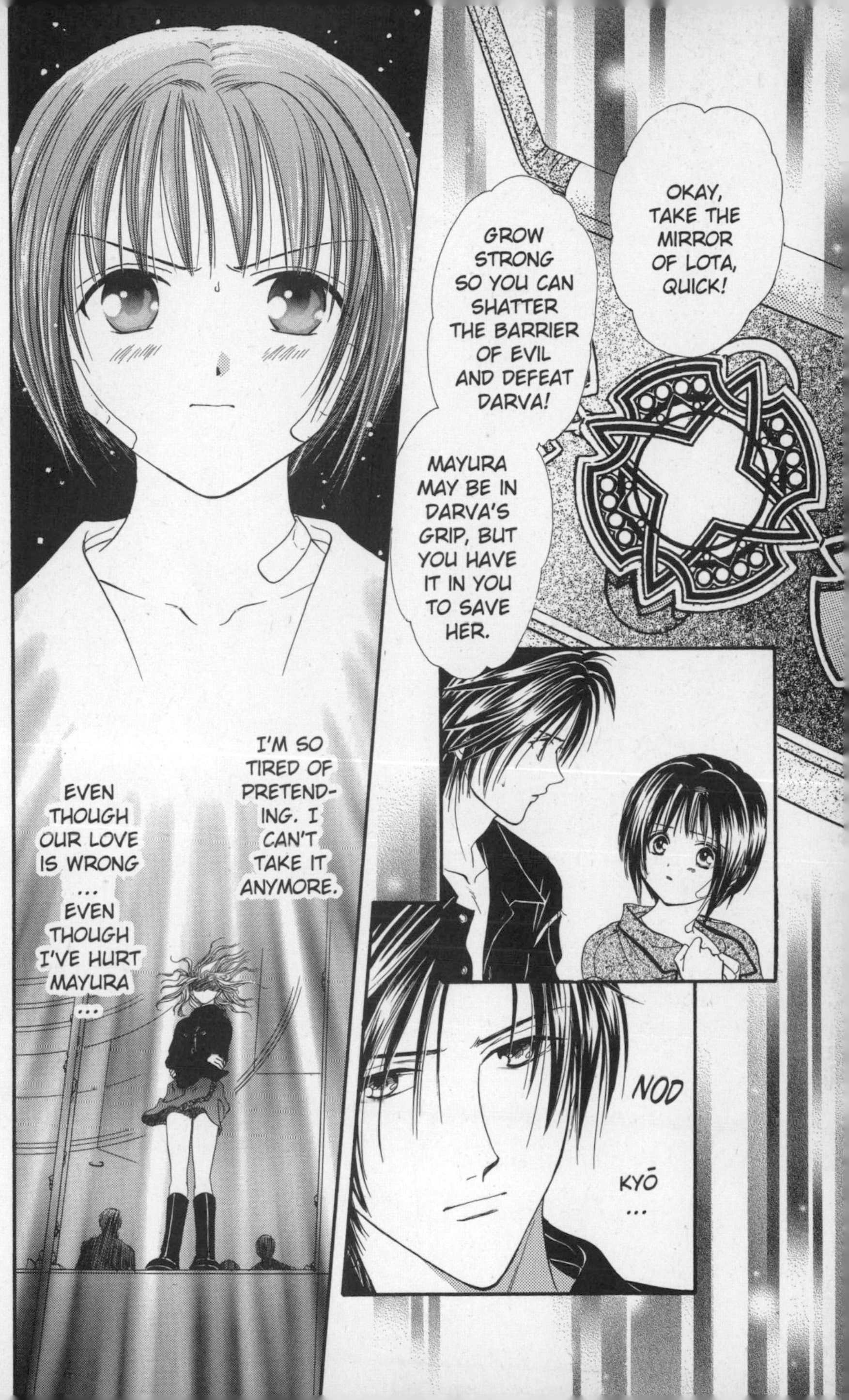

OKAY, TAKE THE MIRROR OF LOTA, QUICK!
GROW STRONG SO YOU CAN SHATTER THE BARRIER OF EVIL AND DEFEAT DARVA!
MAYURA MAY BE IN DARVA'S GRIP, BUT YOU HAVE IT IN YOU TO SAVE HER.
NOD
KYŌ ...
I'M SO TIRED OF PRETEND-ING. I CAN'T TAKE IT ANYMORE.
EVEN THOUGH OUR LOVE IS WRONG ...
EVEN THOUGH I'VE HURT MAYURA ...

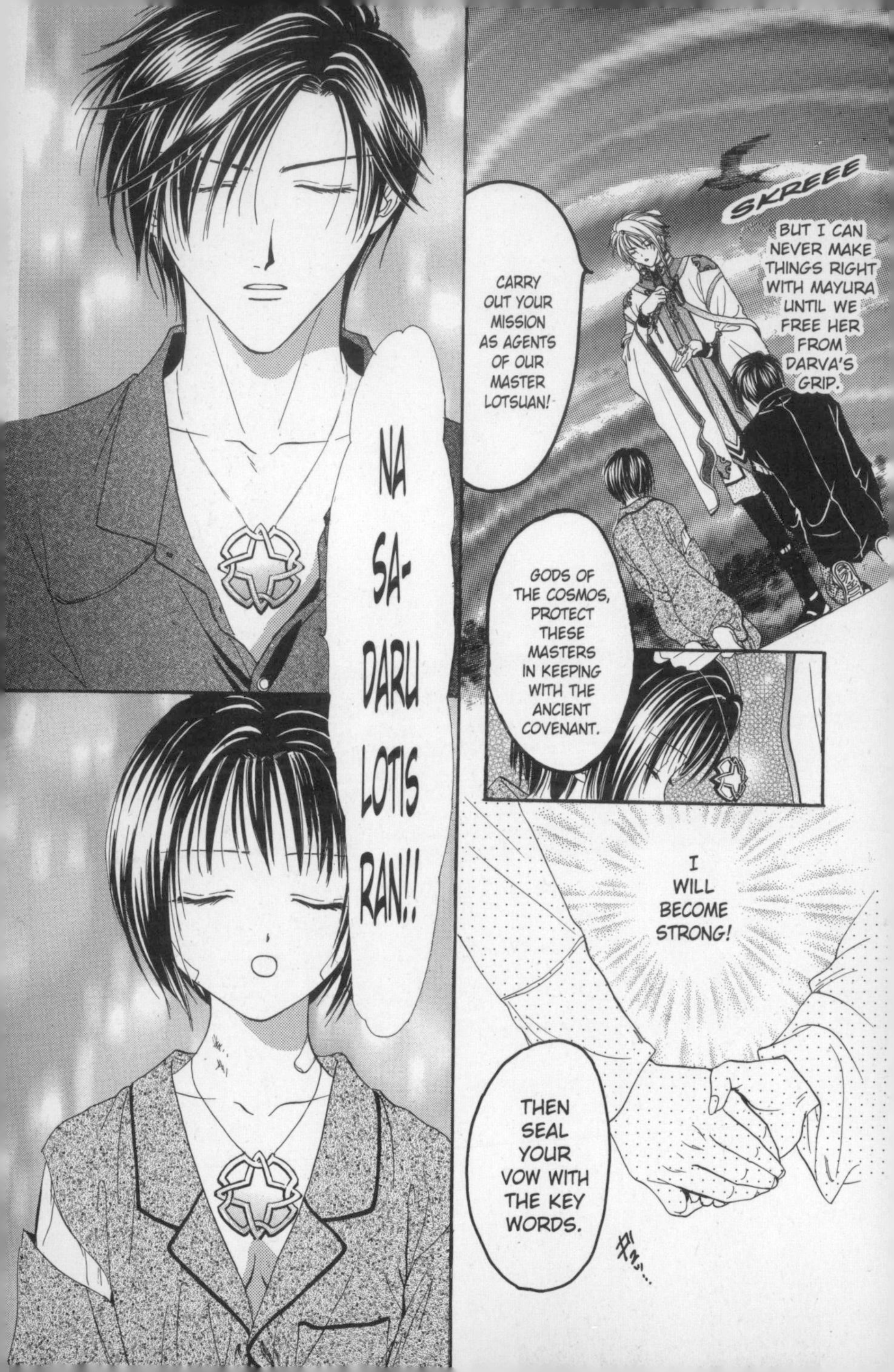
SKREEE
BUT I CAN NEVER MAKE THINGS RIGHT WITH MAYURA UNTIL WE FREE HER FROM DARVA'S GRIP.
CARRY OUT YOUR MISSION AS AGENTS OF OUR MASTER LOTSUAN!
GODS OF THE COSMOS, PROTECT THESE MASTERS IN KEEPING WITH THE ANCIENT COVENANT.
I WILL BECOME STRONG!
THEN SEAL YOUR VOW WITH THE KEY WORDS.
NA SA-DARU LOTIS RAN!!

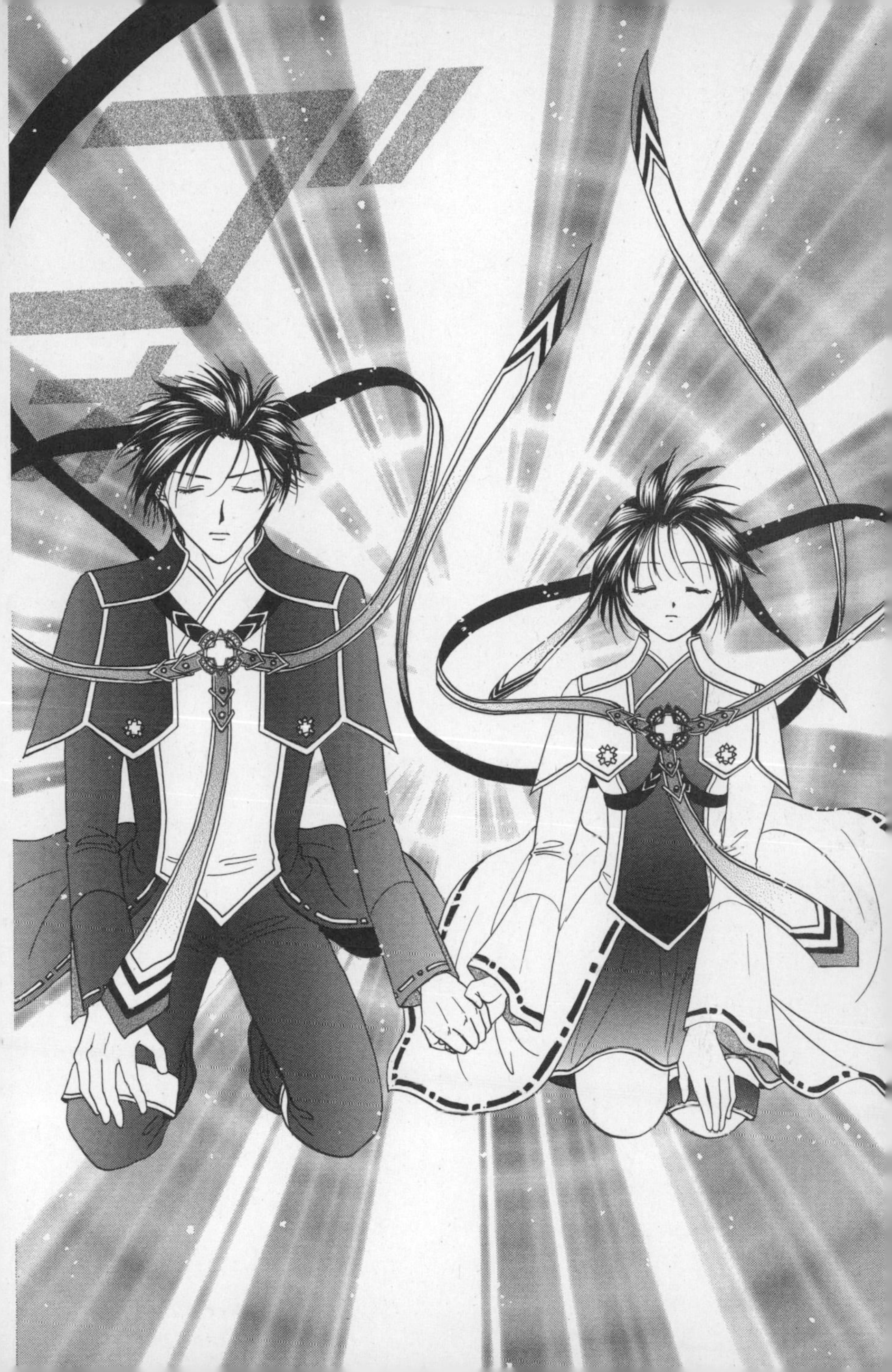

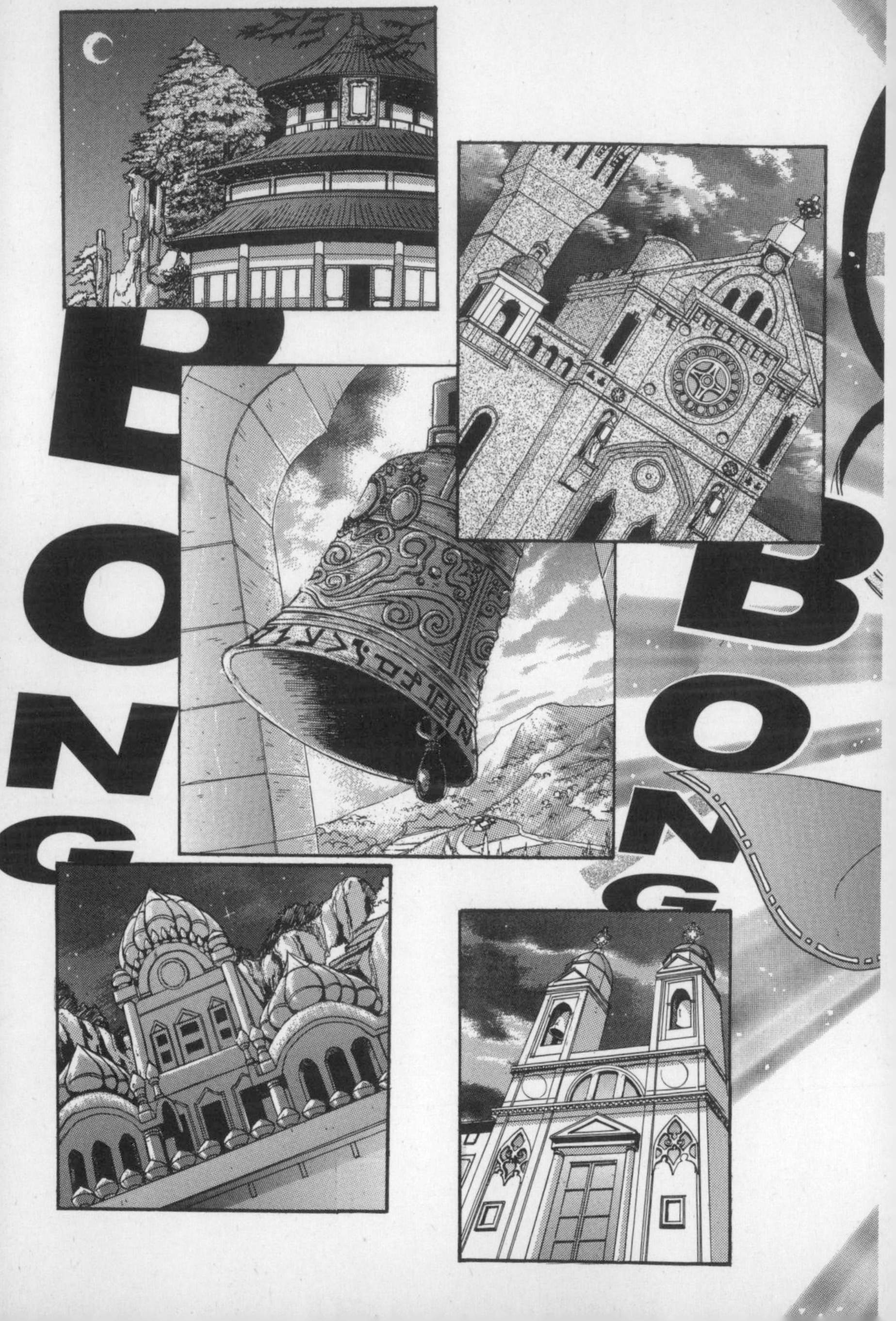
BONG
DONG

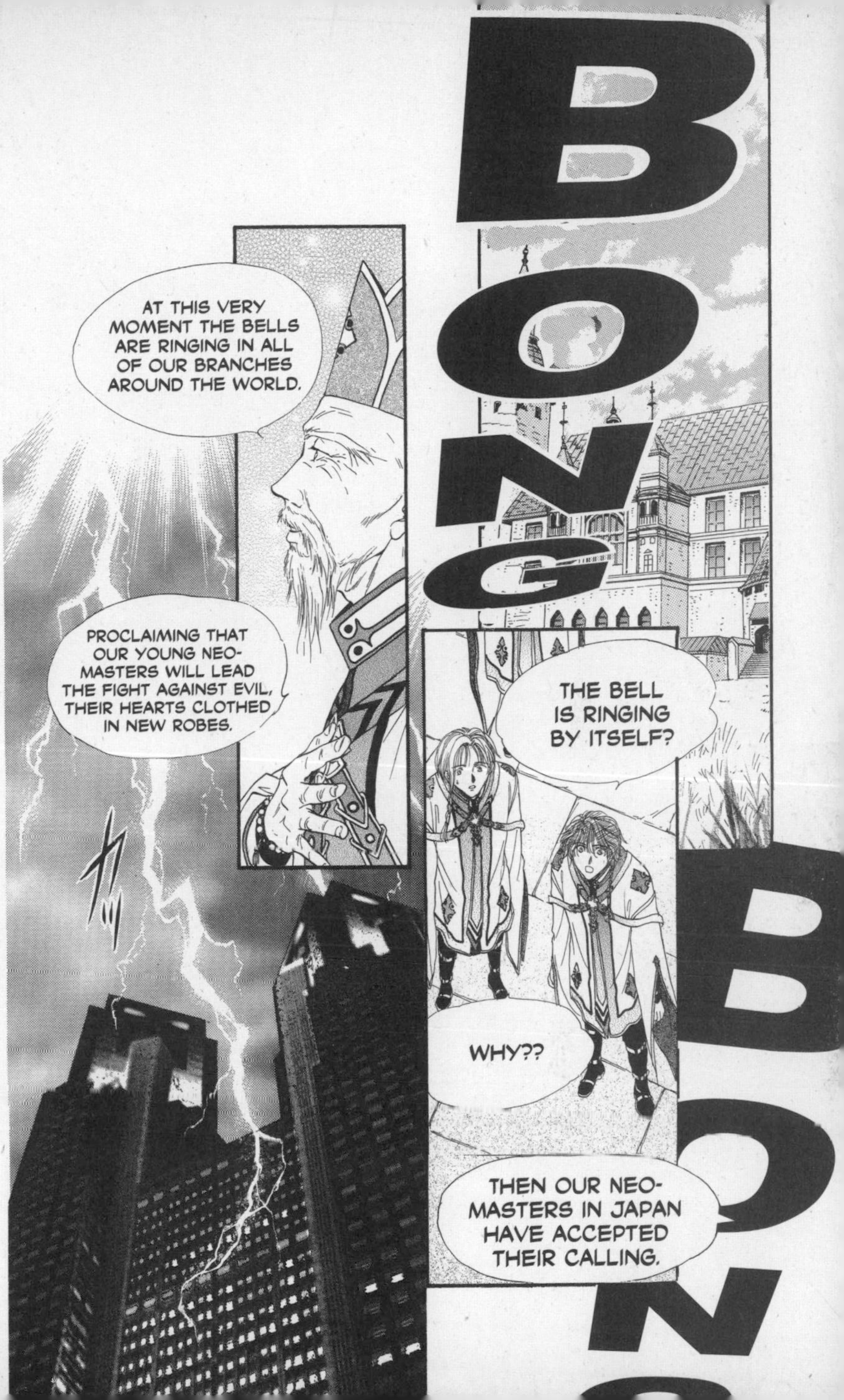

BONG
AT THIS VERY MOMENT THE BELLS ARE RINGING IN ALL OF OUR BRANCHES AROUND THE WORLD.
PROCLAIMING THAT OUR YOUNG NEO-MASTERS WILL LEAD THE FIGHT AGAINST EVIL, THEIR HEARTS CLOTHED IN NEW ROBES.
THE BELL IS RINGING BY ITSELF?
WHY??
THEN OUR NEO-MASTERS IN JAPAN HAVE ACCEPTED THEIR CALLING.
BON

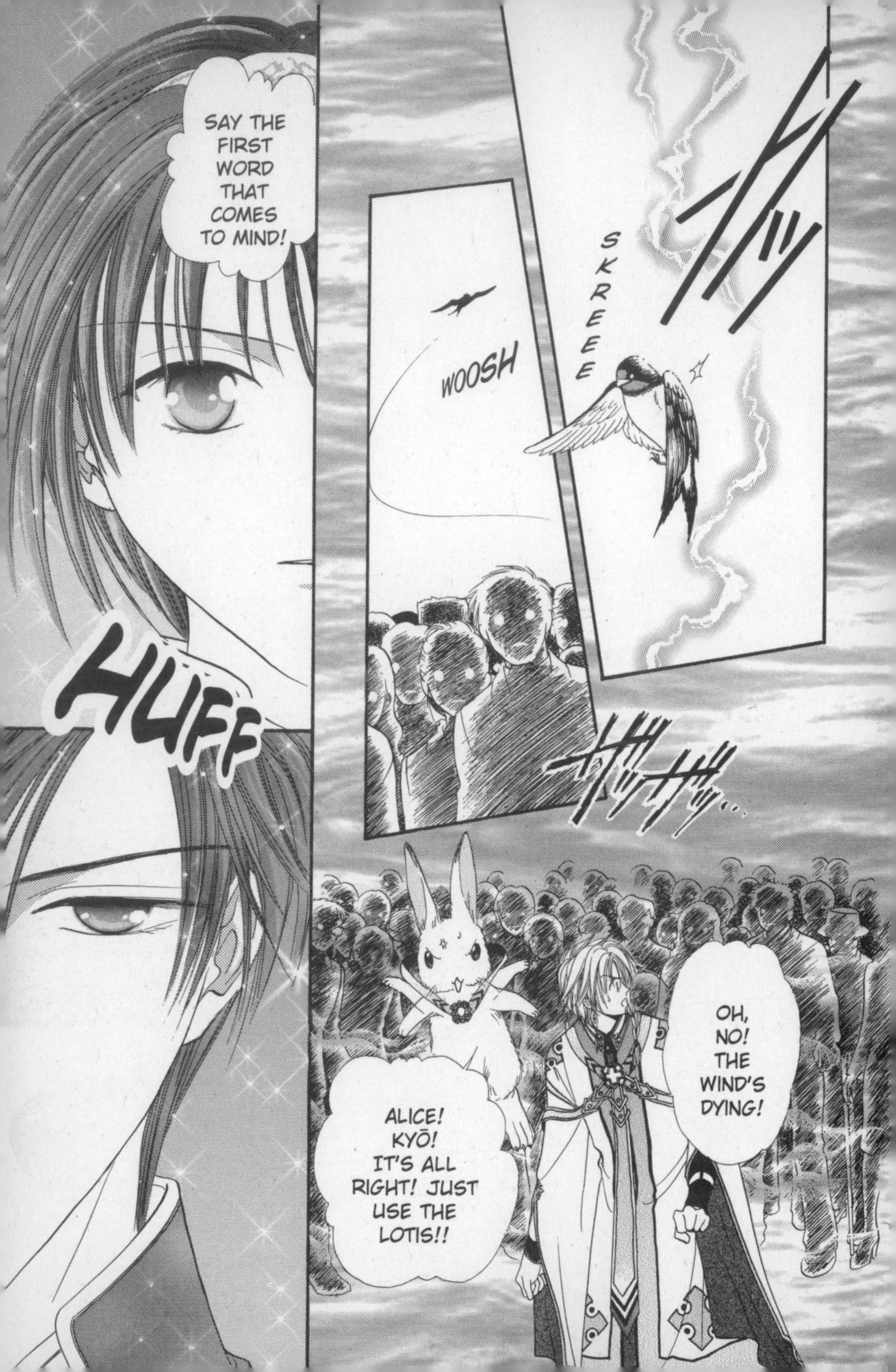
SKREEE
WOOSH
OH, NO! THE WIND'S DYING!
ALICE! KYŌ! IT'S ALL RIGHT! JUST USE THE LOTIS!!
SAY THE FIRST WORD THAT COMES TO MIND!
HUFF

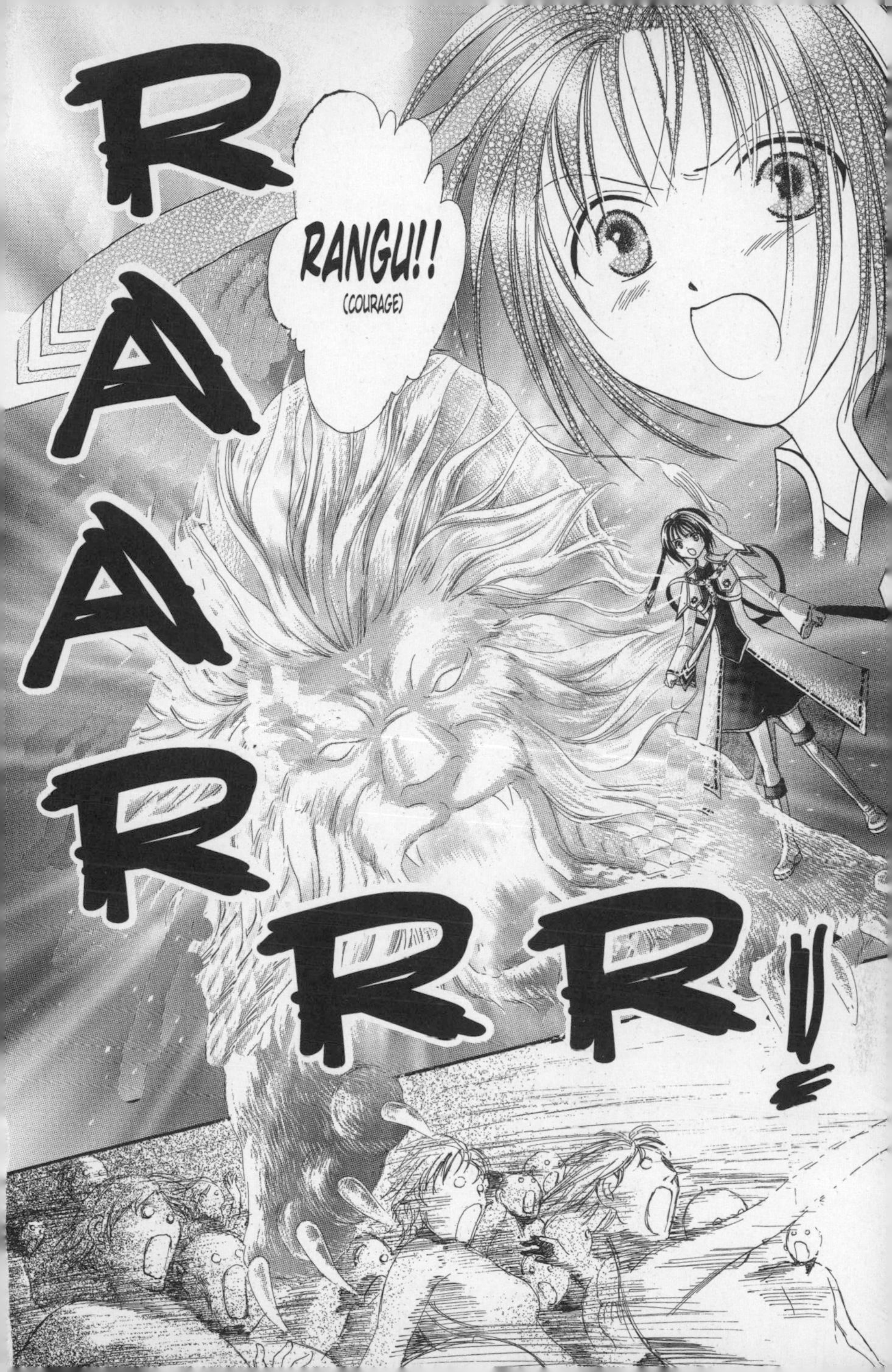
RANGU!!
(COURAGE)
RAARRR!

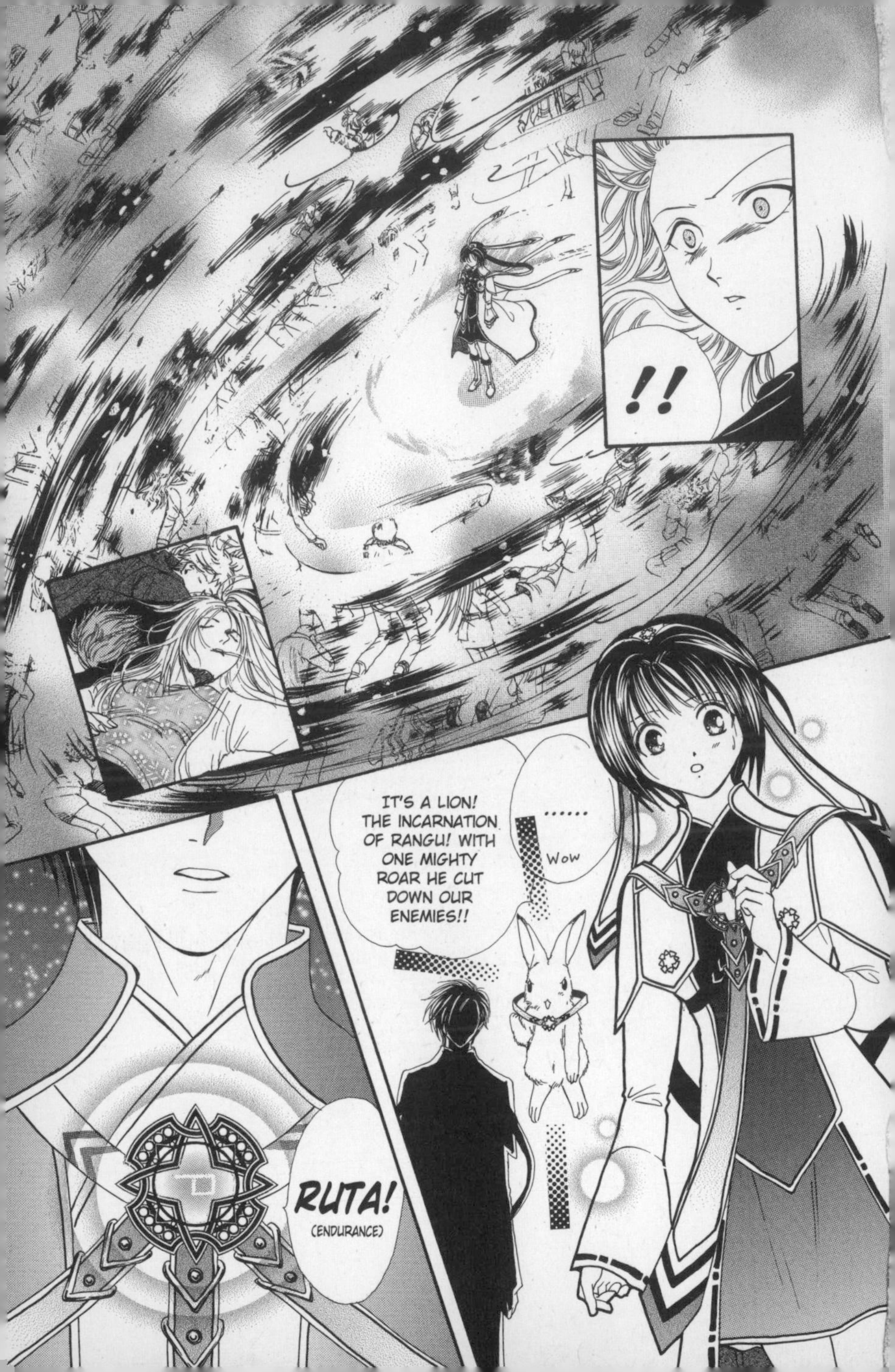
!!
......
Wow
IT'S A LION! THE INCARNATION OF RANGU! WITH ONE MIGHTY ROAR HE CUT DOWN OUR ENEMIES!!
RUTA!
(ENDURANCE)

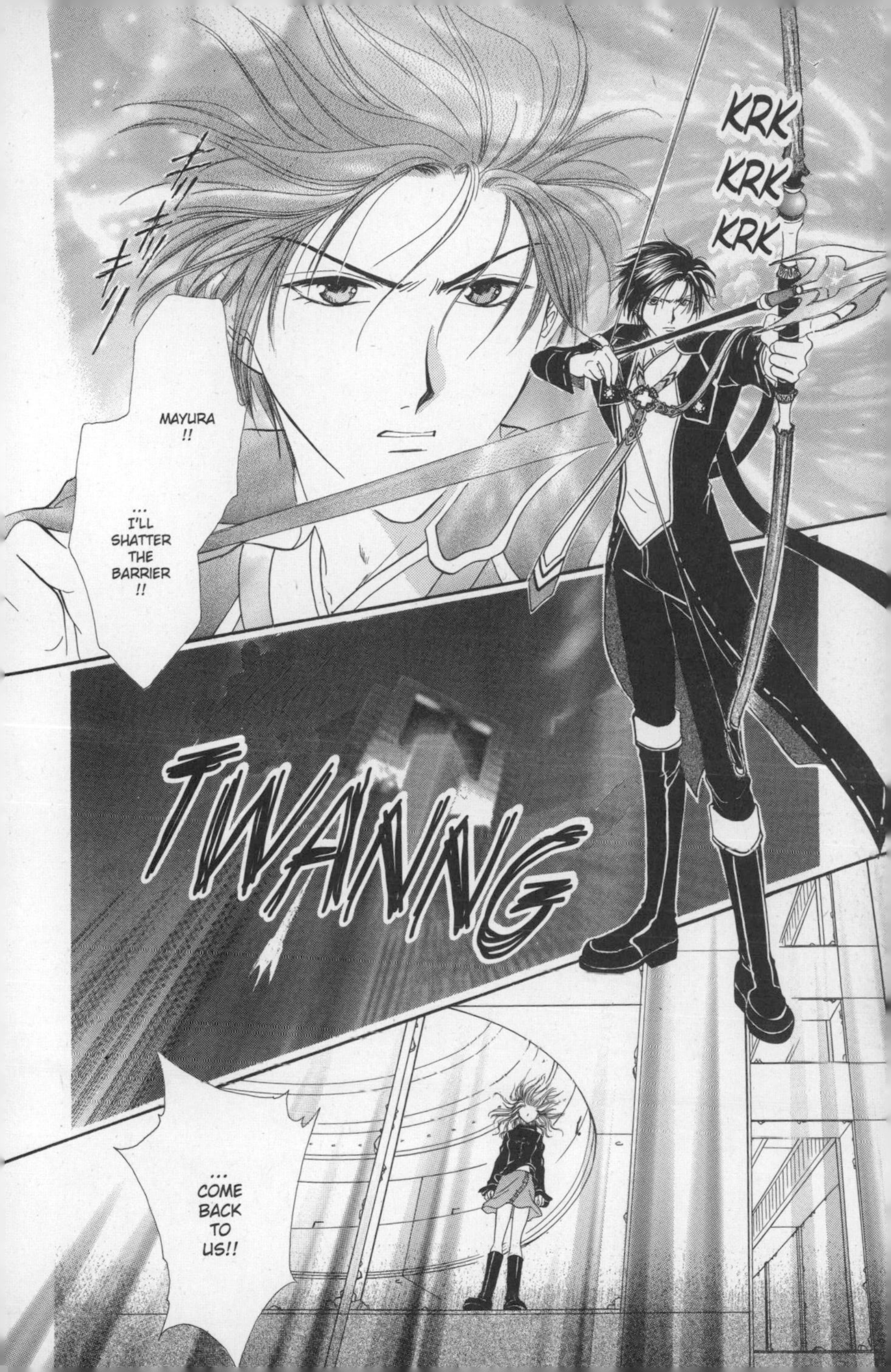
KRK KRK KRK
MAYURA !!
... I'LL SHATTER THE BARRIER !!
TWANNG
... COME BACK TO US!!

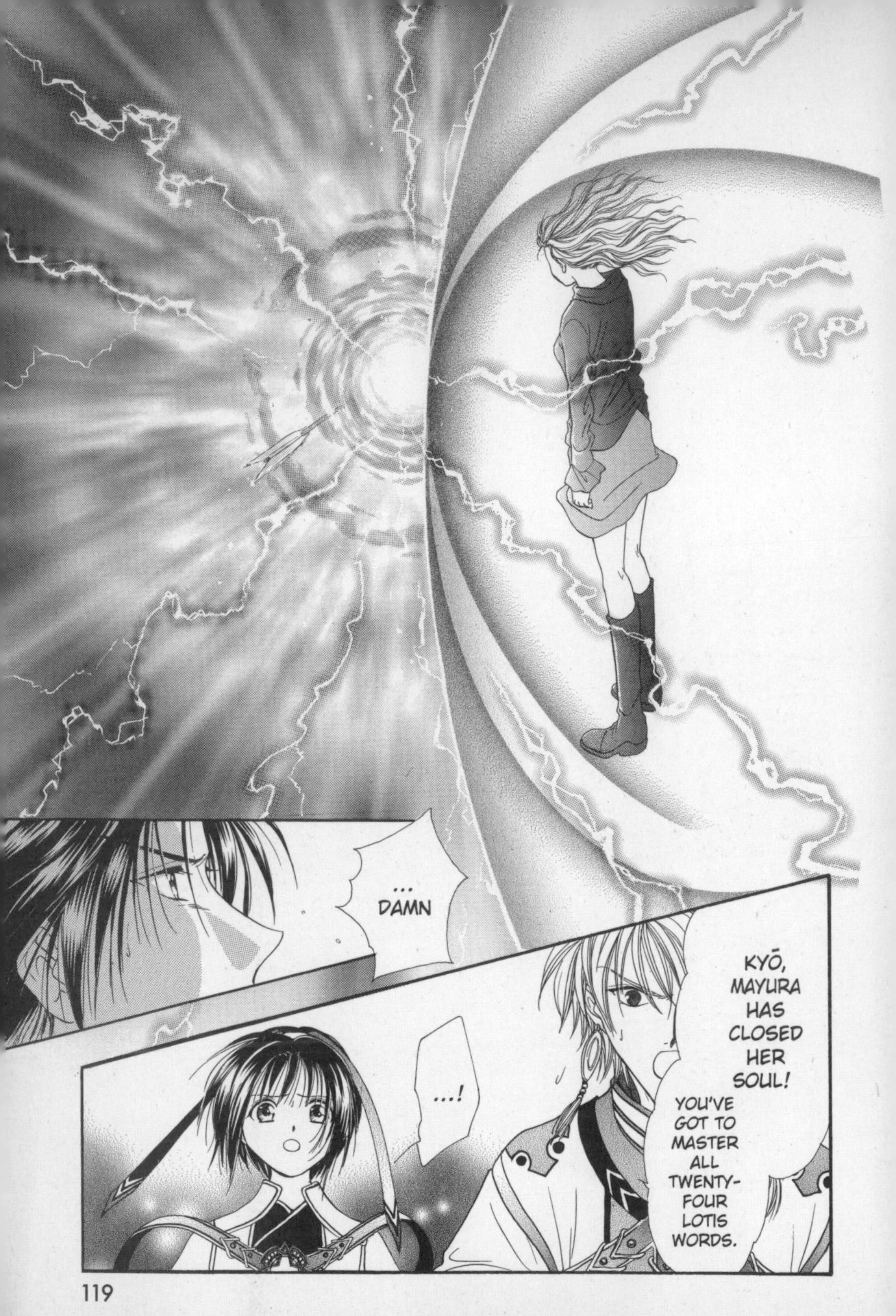
...
DAMN
KYŌ, MAYURA HAS CLOSED HER SOUL!
YOU'VE GOT TO MASTER ALL TWENTY-FOUR LOTIS WORDS.
...!

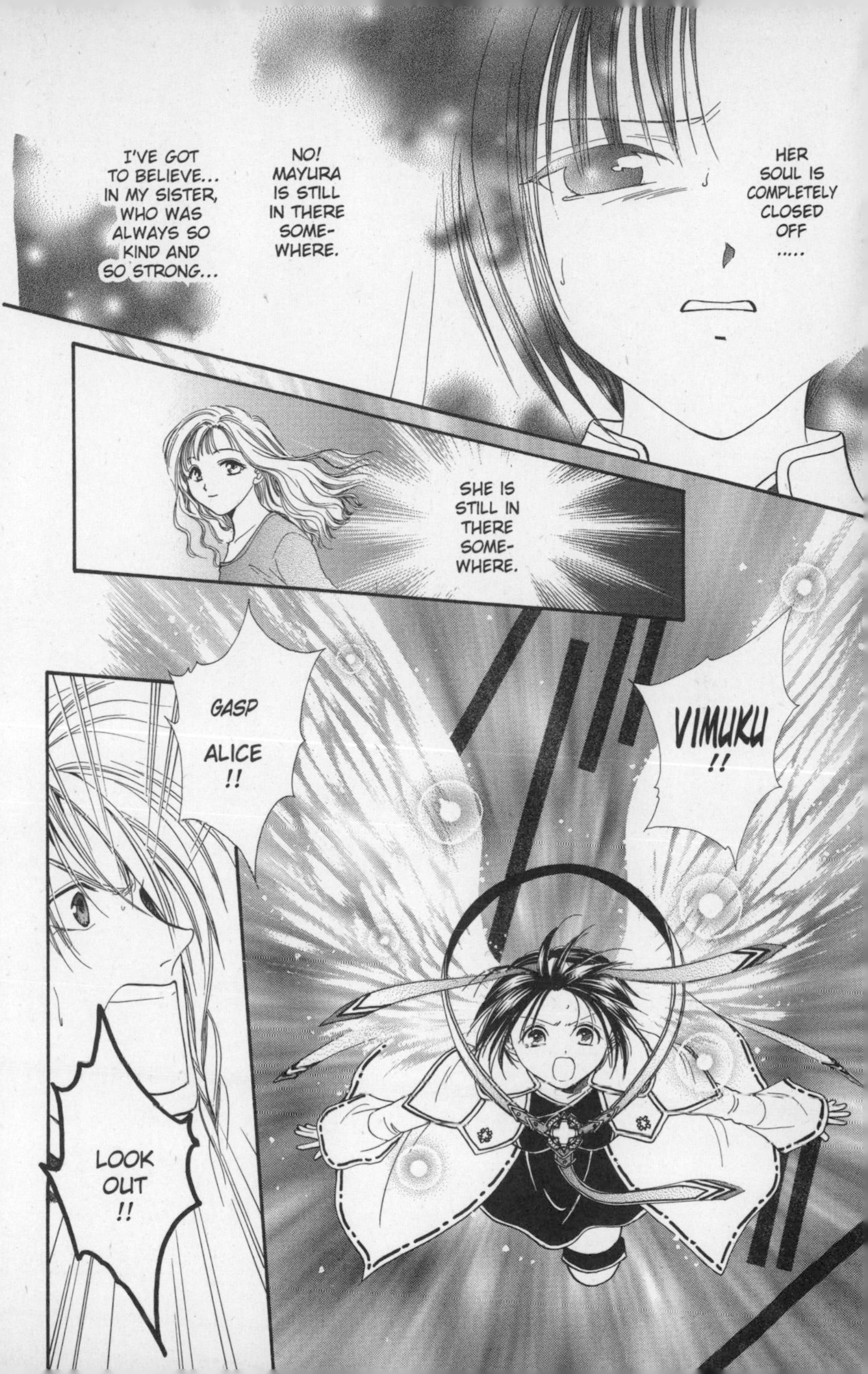
HER SOUL IS COMPLETELY CLOSED OFF .....
NO! MAYURA IS STILL IN THERE SOME-WHERE.
I'VE GOT TO BELIEVE... IN MY SISTER, WHO WAS ALWAYS SO KIND AND SO STRONG...
SHE IS STILL IN THERE SOME-WHERE.
VIMUKU !!
GASP
ALICE !!
LOOK OUT !!

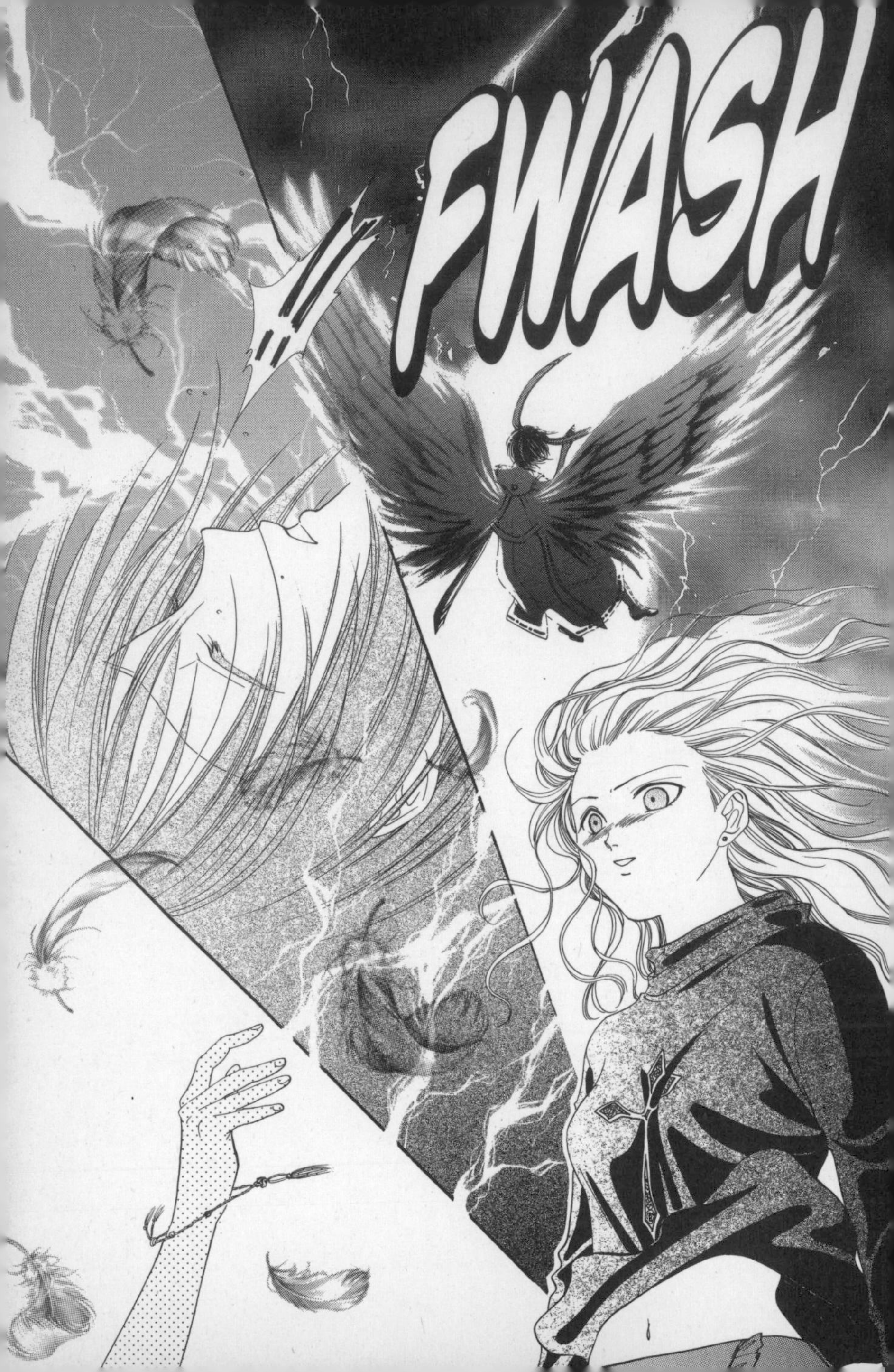
FWASH

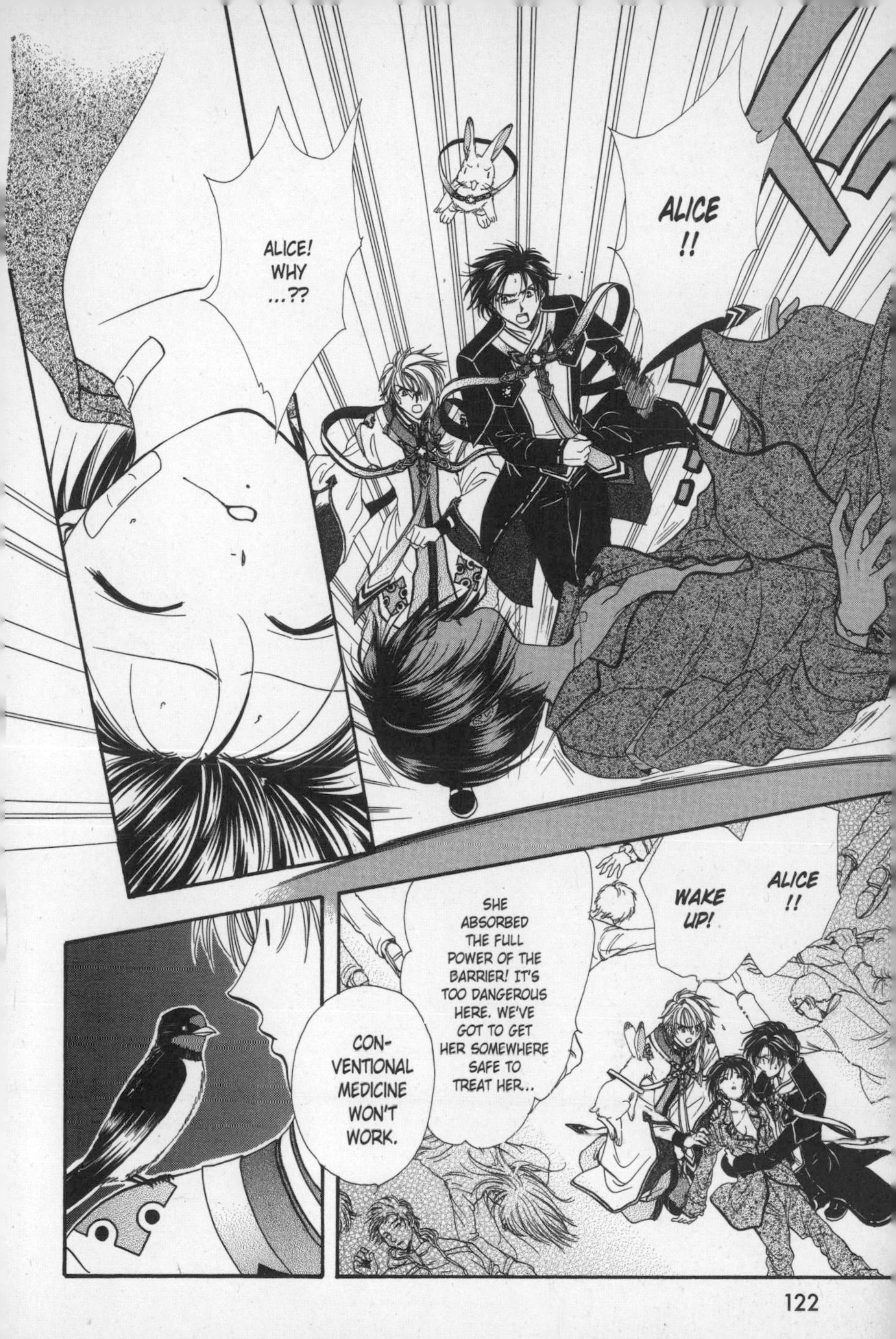
ALICE !!
ALICE! WHY ...??
ALICE !!
WAKE UP!
SHE ABSORBED THE FULL POWER OF THE BARRIER! IT'S TOO DANGEROUS HERE. WE'VE GOT TO GET HER SOMEWHERE SAFE TO TREAT HER...
CON-VENTIONAL MEDICINE WON'T WORK.

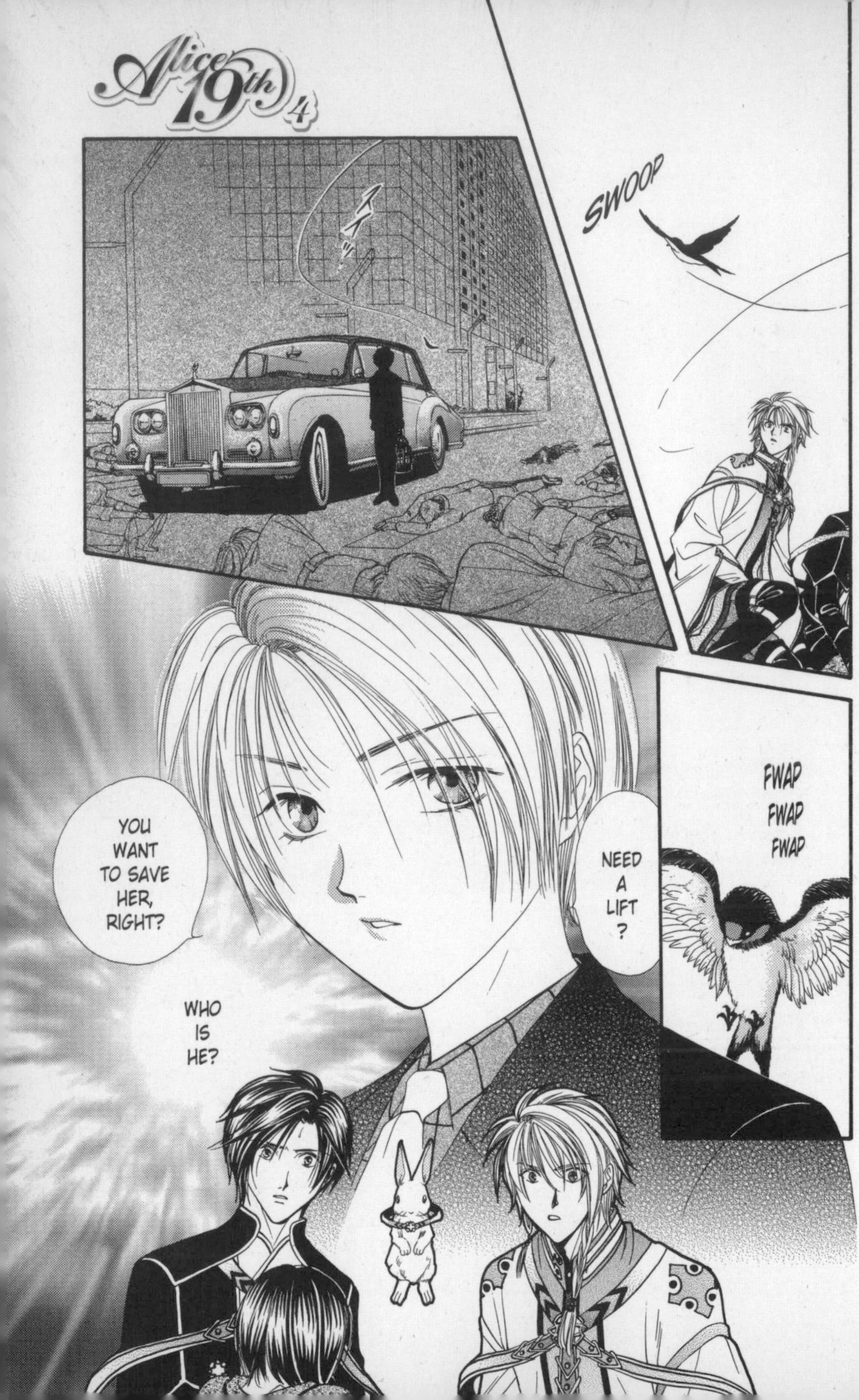
SWOOP
FWAP FWAP FWAP
NEED A LIFT?
YOU WANT TO SAVE HER, RIGHT?
WHO IS HE?

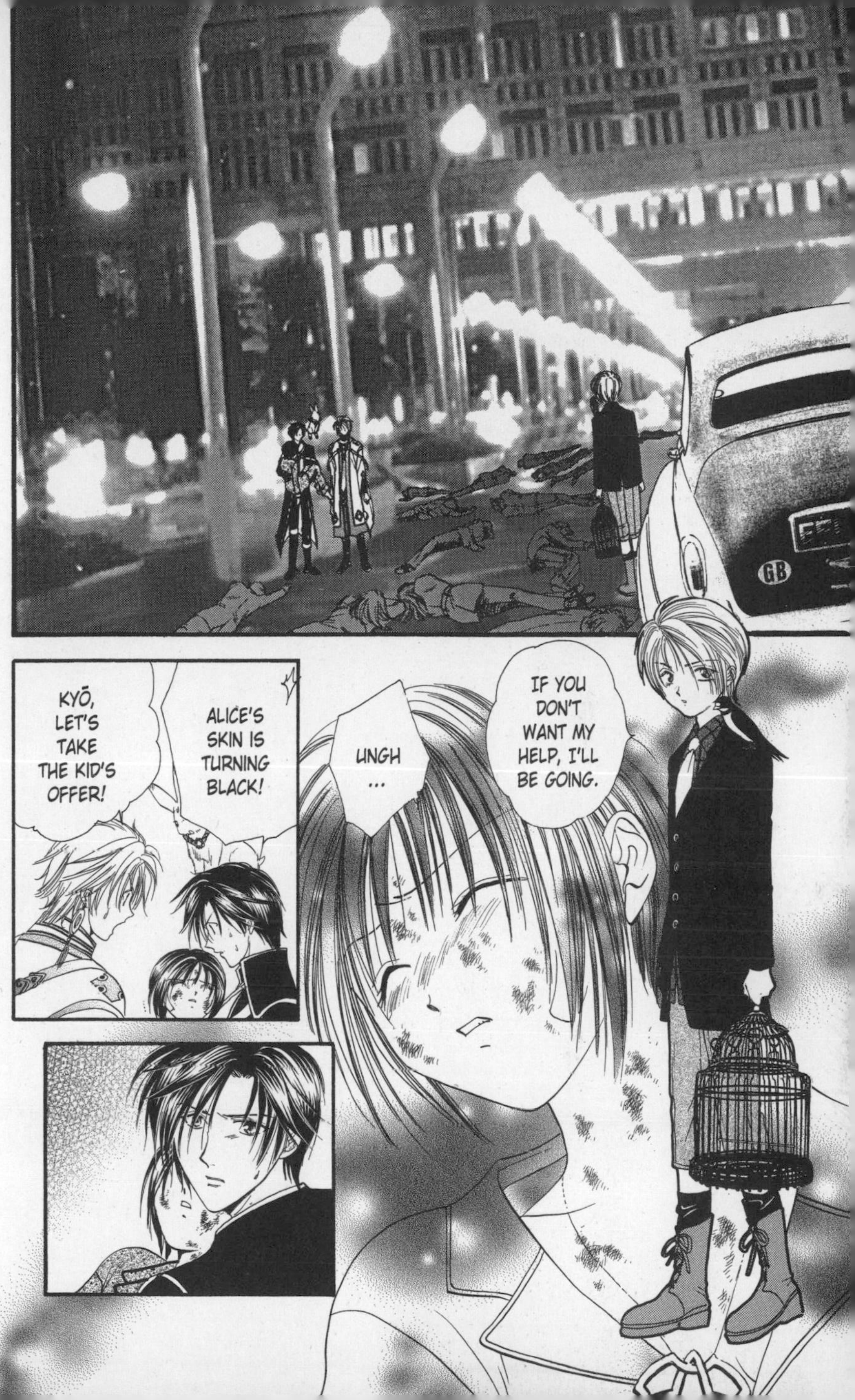
GB
IF YOU DON'T WANT MY HELP, I'LL BE GOING.
UNGH ...
ALICE'S SKIN IS TURNING BLACK!
KYŌ, LET'S TAKE THE KID'S OFFER!

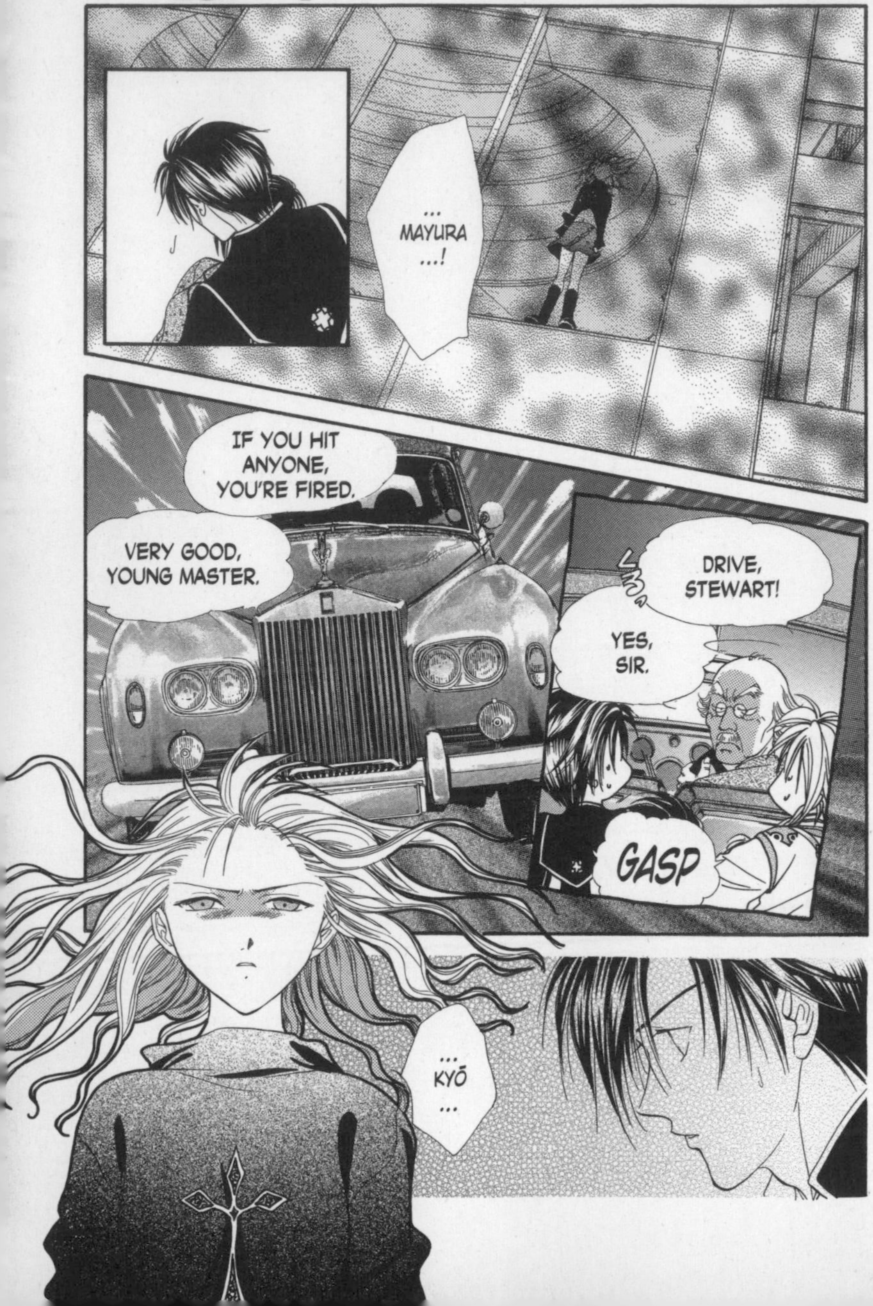
... MAYURA ...!
DRIVE, STEWART!
YES, SIR.
GASP
IF YOU HIT ANYONE, YOU'RE FIRED.
VERY GOOD, YOUNG MASTER.
... KYŌ ...

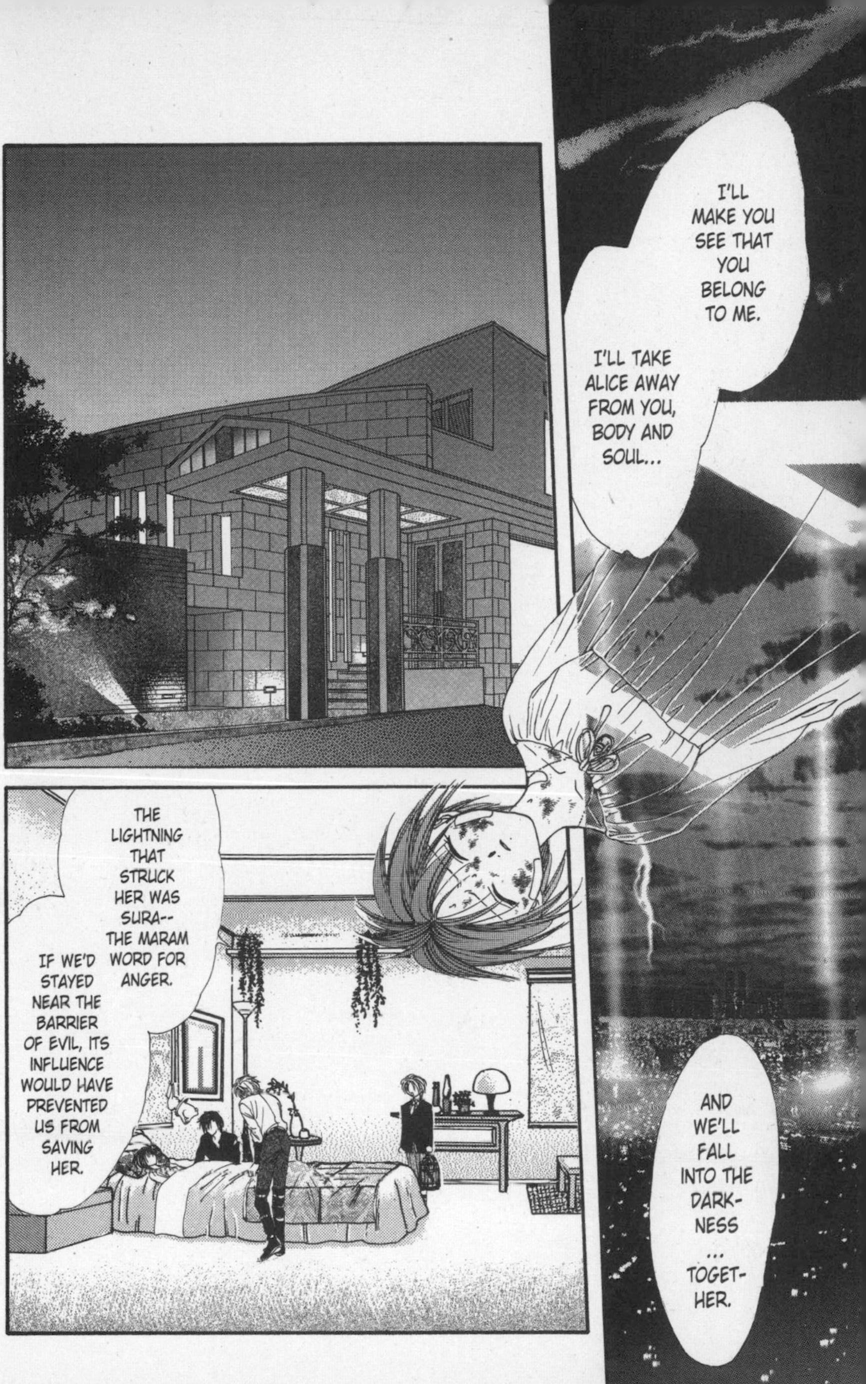
I'LL MAKE YOU SEE THAT YOU BELONG TO ME.
I'LL TAKE ALICE AWAY FROM YOU, BODY AND SOUL...
AND WE'LL FALL INTO THE DARK-NESS ... TOGET-HER.
THE LIGHTNING THAT STRUCK HER WAS SURA-- THE MARAM WORD FOR ANGER.
IF WE'D STAYED NEAR THE BARRIER OF EVIL, ITS INFLUENCE WOULD HAVE PREVENTED US FROM SAVING HER.

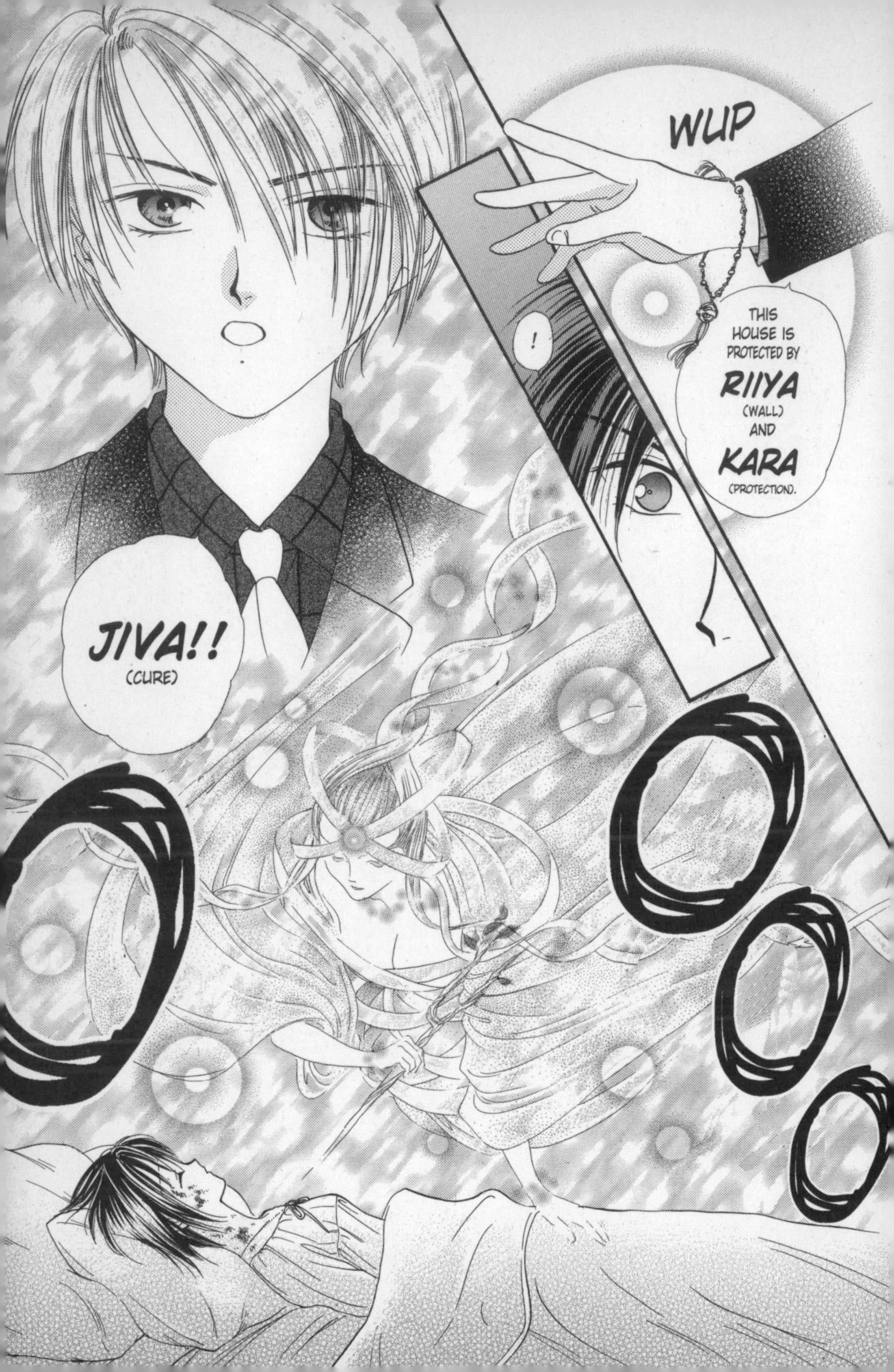
WUP
THIS HOUSE IS PROTECTED BY RIIYA (WALL) AND KARA (PROTECTION).
!
JIVA!! (CURE)

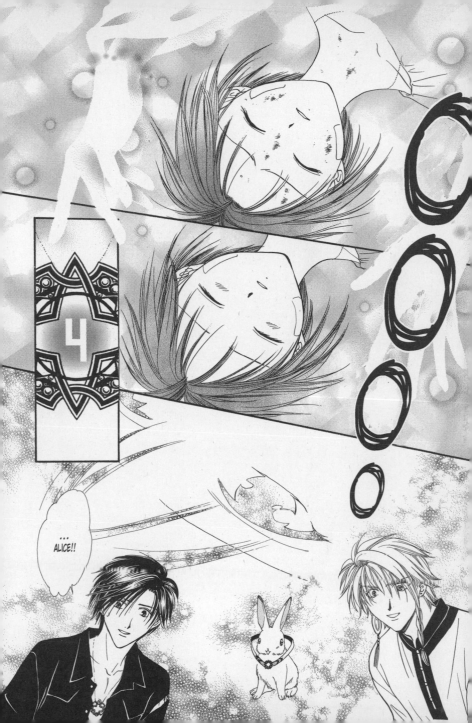

... ALICE!!

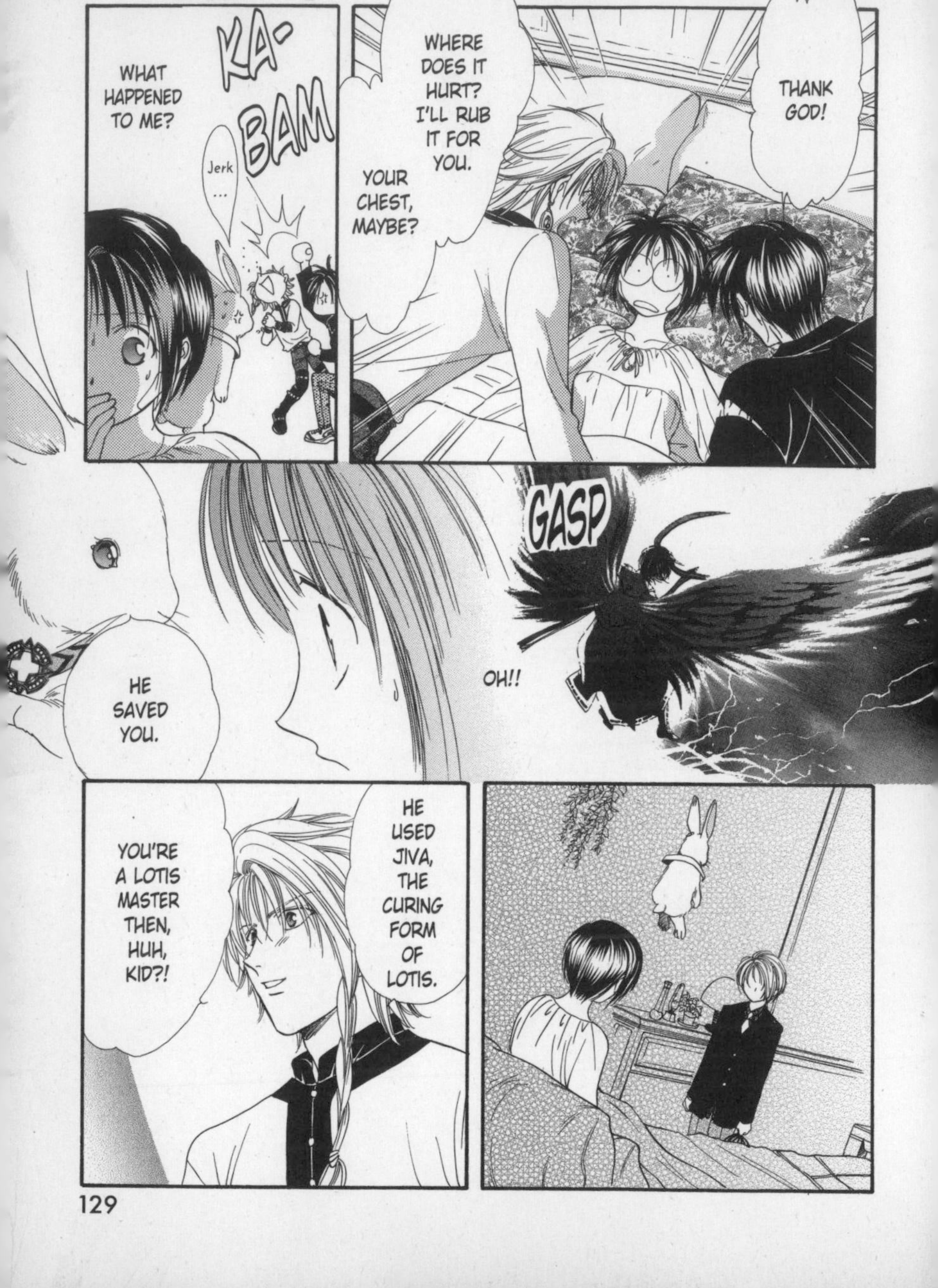
THANK GOD!
WHERE DOES IT HURT? I'LL RUB IT FOR YOU.
YOUR CHEST, MAYBE?
KA-BAM
WHAT HAPPENED TO ME?
Jerk...
GASP
OH!!
HE SAVED YOU.
HE USED JIVA, THE CURING FORM OF LOTIS.
YOU'RE A LOTIS MASTER THEN, HUH, KID?!

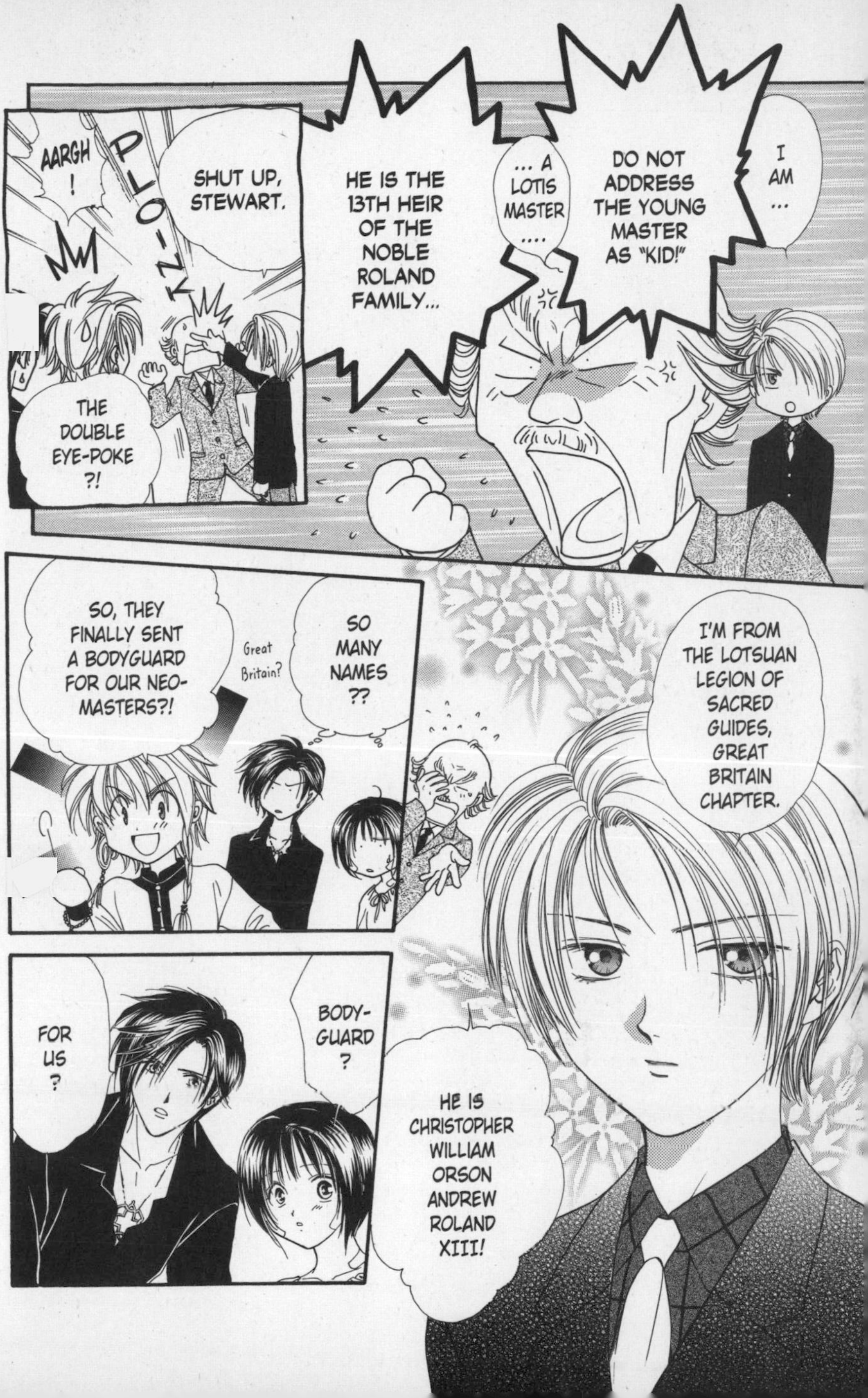
I AM ...
DO NOT ADDRESS THE YOUNG MASTER AS "KID!"
... A LOTIS MASTER ....
HE IS THE 13TH HEIR OF THE NOBLE ROLAND FAMILY...
SHUT UP, STEWART.
PLO-INK
AARGH !
THE DOUBLE EYE-POKE ?!
I'M FROM THE LOTSUAN LEGION OF SACRED GUIDES, GREAT BRITAIN CHAPTER.
HE IS CHRISTOPHER WILLIAM ORSON ANDREW ROLAND XIII!
SO MANY NAMES ??
Great Britain?
SO, THEY FINALLY SENT A BODYGUARD FOR OUR NEO-MASTERS?!
BODY-GUARD ?
FOR US ?

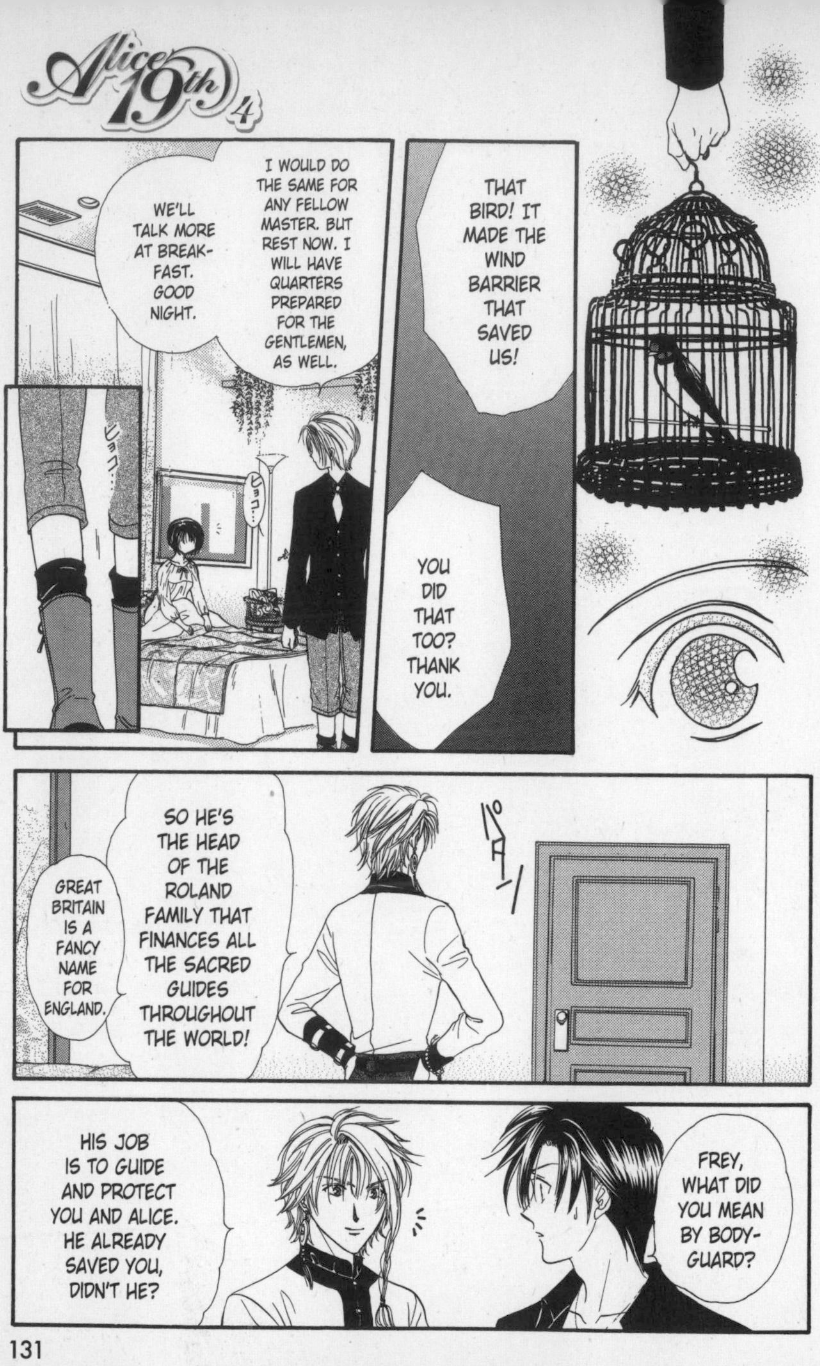
THAT BIRD! IT MADE THE WIND BARRIER THAT SAVED US!
YOU DID THAT TOO? THANK YOU.
I WOULD DO THE SAME FOR ANY FELLOW MASTER. BUT REST NOW. I WILL HAVE QUARTERS PREPARED FOR THE GENTLEMEN, AS WELL.
WE'LL TALK MORE AT BREAK-FAST. GOOD NIGHT.
SO HE'S THE HEAD OF THE ROLAND FAMILY THAT FINANCES ALL THE SACRED GUIDES THROUGHOUT THE WORLD!
GREAT BRITAIN IS A FANCY NAME FOR ENGLAND.
FREY, WHAT DID YOU MEAN BY BODY-GUARD?
HIS JOB IS TO GUIDE AND PROTECT YOU AND ALICE. HE ALREADY SAVED YOU, DIDN'T HE?

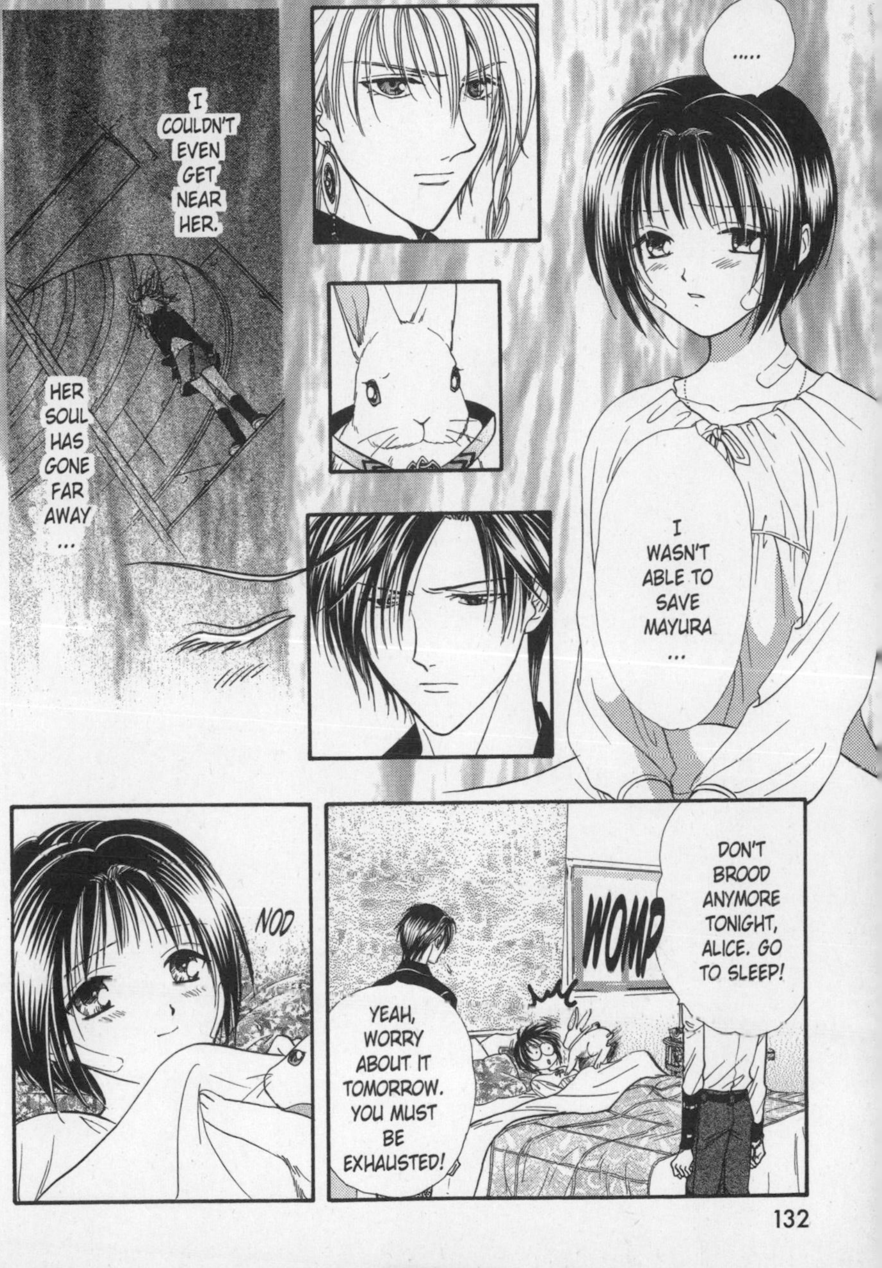
.....
I WASN'T ABLE TO SAVE MAYURA ...
I COULDN'T EVEN GET NEAR HER.
HER SOUL HAS GONE FAR AWAY ...
DON'T BROOD ANYMORE TONIGHT, ALICE. GO TO SLEEP!
WOMP
YEAH, WORRY ABOUT IT TOMORROW. YOU MUST BE EXHAUSTED!
NOD

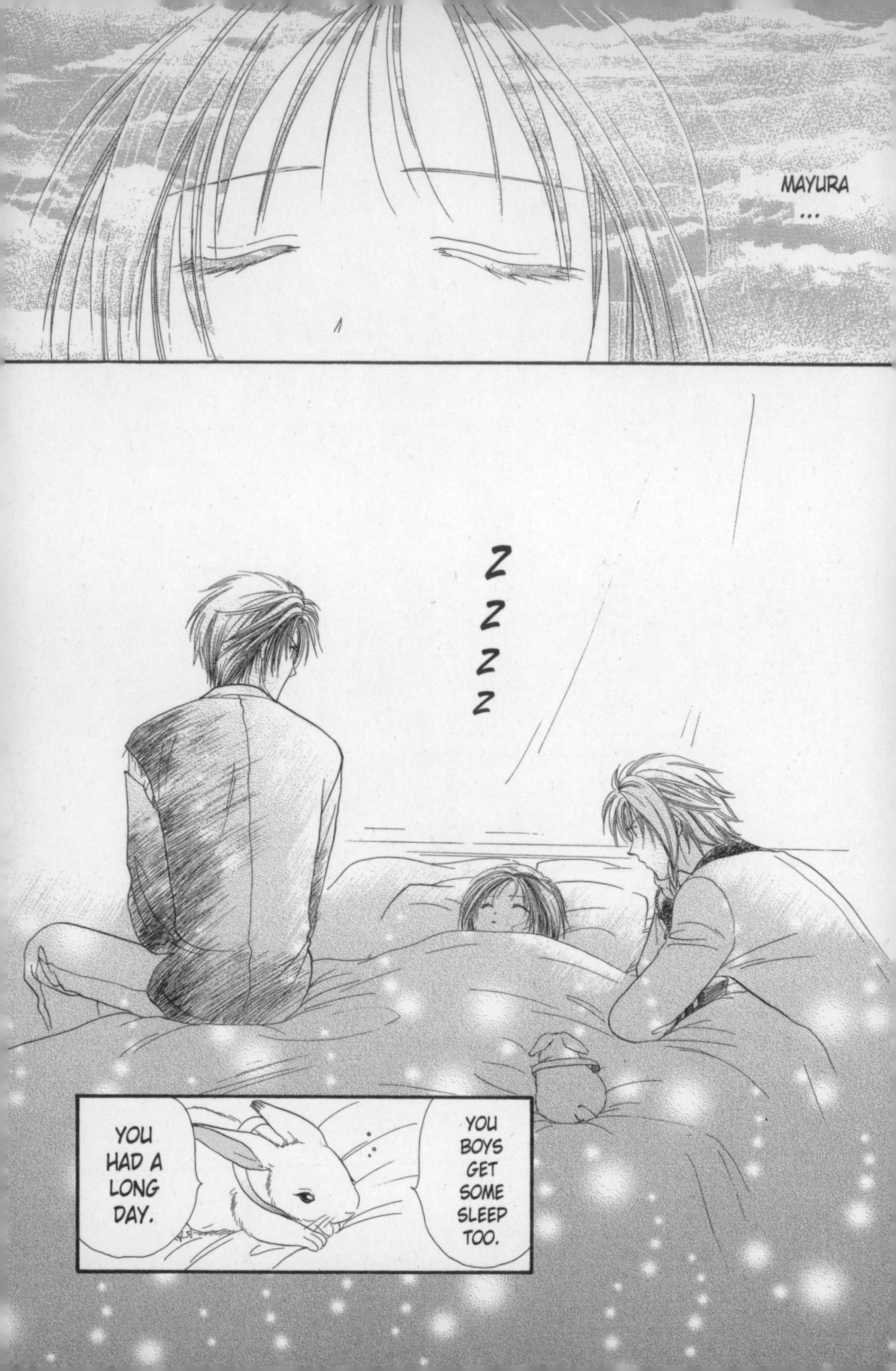
MAYURA ...
ZZZZ
YOU BOYS GET SOME SLEEP TOO.
YOU HAD A LONG DAY.

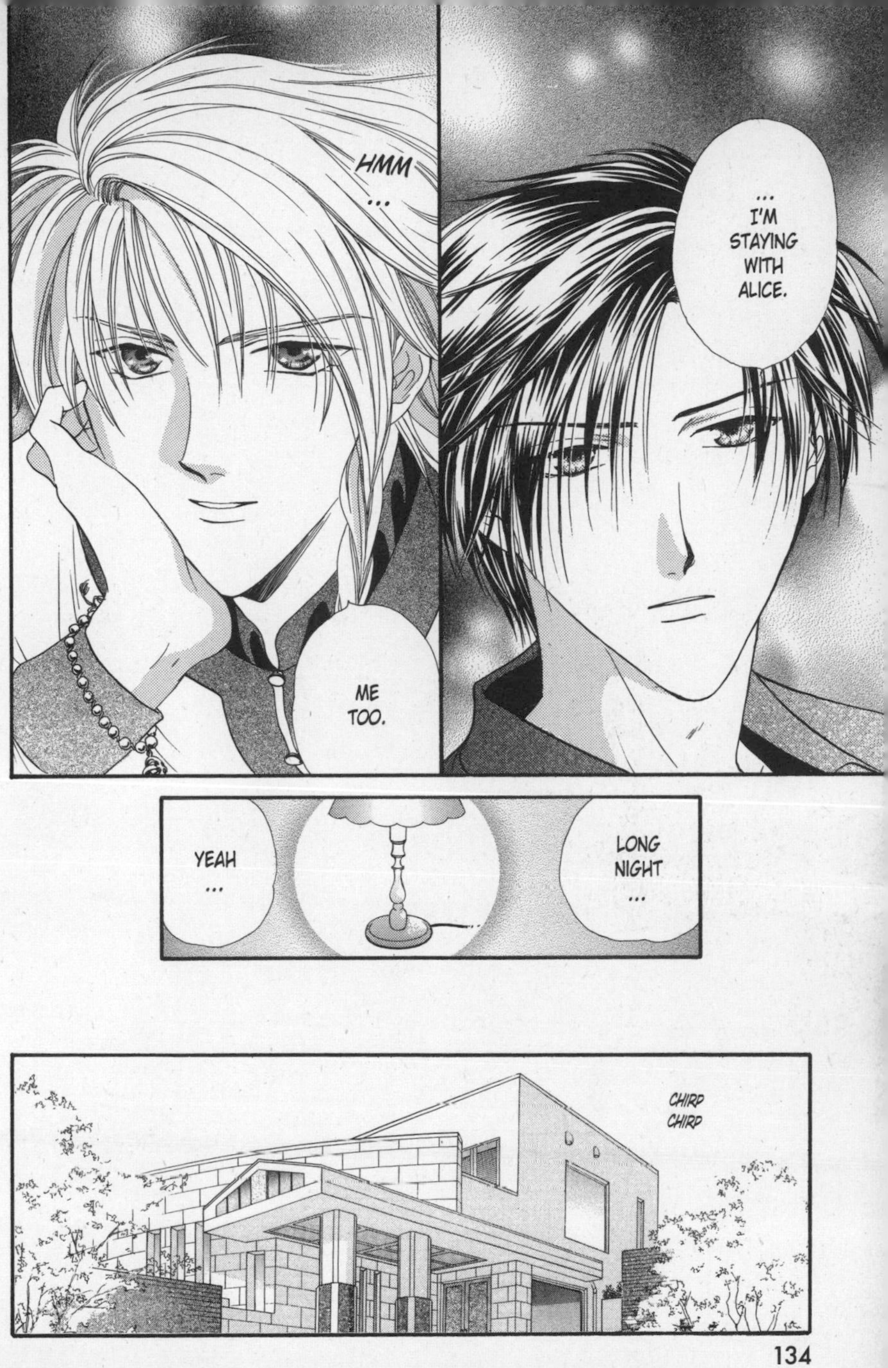
... I'M STAYING WITH ALICE.
HMM ...
ME TOO.
LONG NIGHT ...
YEAH ...
CHIRP CHIRP

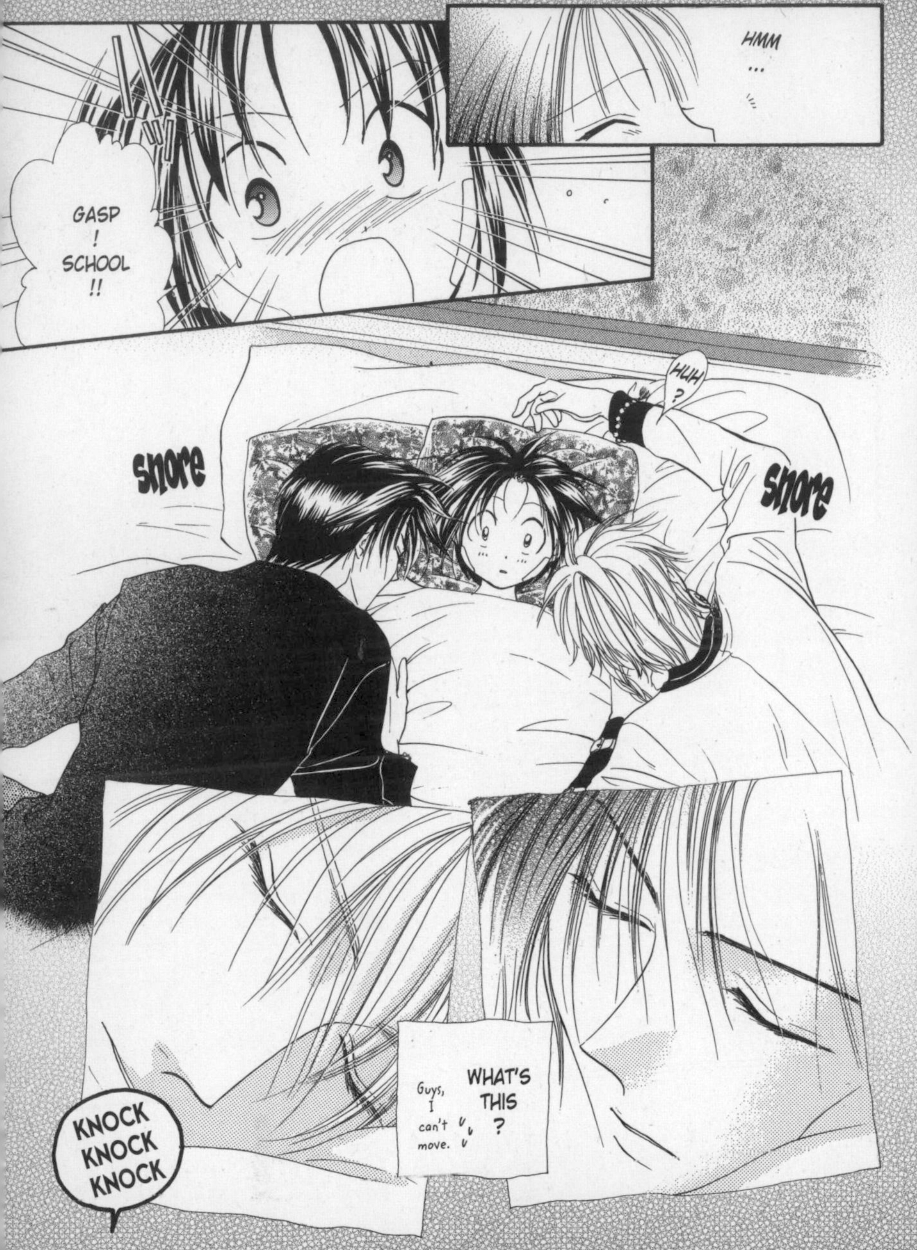
HMM ...
GASP ! SCHOOL !!
HUH ?
snore
snore
WHAT'S THIS ?
Guys, I can't move.
KNOCK KNOCK KNOCK

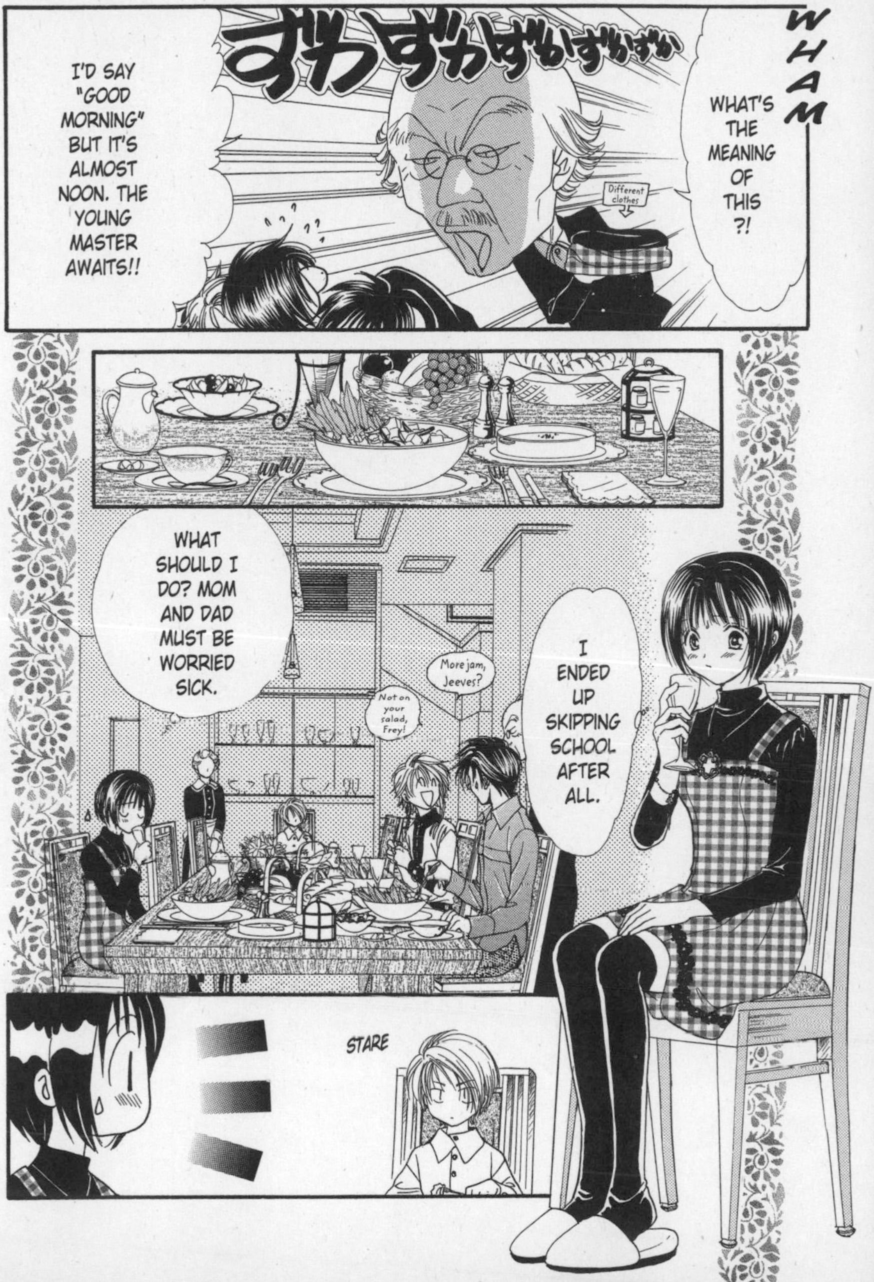
WHAM
WHAT'S THE MEANING OF THIS ?!
Different clothes
I'D SAY "GOOD MORNING" BUT IT'S ALMOST NOON. THE YOUNG MASTER AWAITS!!
I ENDED UP SKIPPING SCHOOL AFTER ALL.
More jam, Jeeves?
Not on your salad, Frey!
WHAT SHOULD I DO? MOM AND DAD MUST BE WORRIED SICK.
STARE

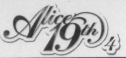

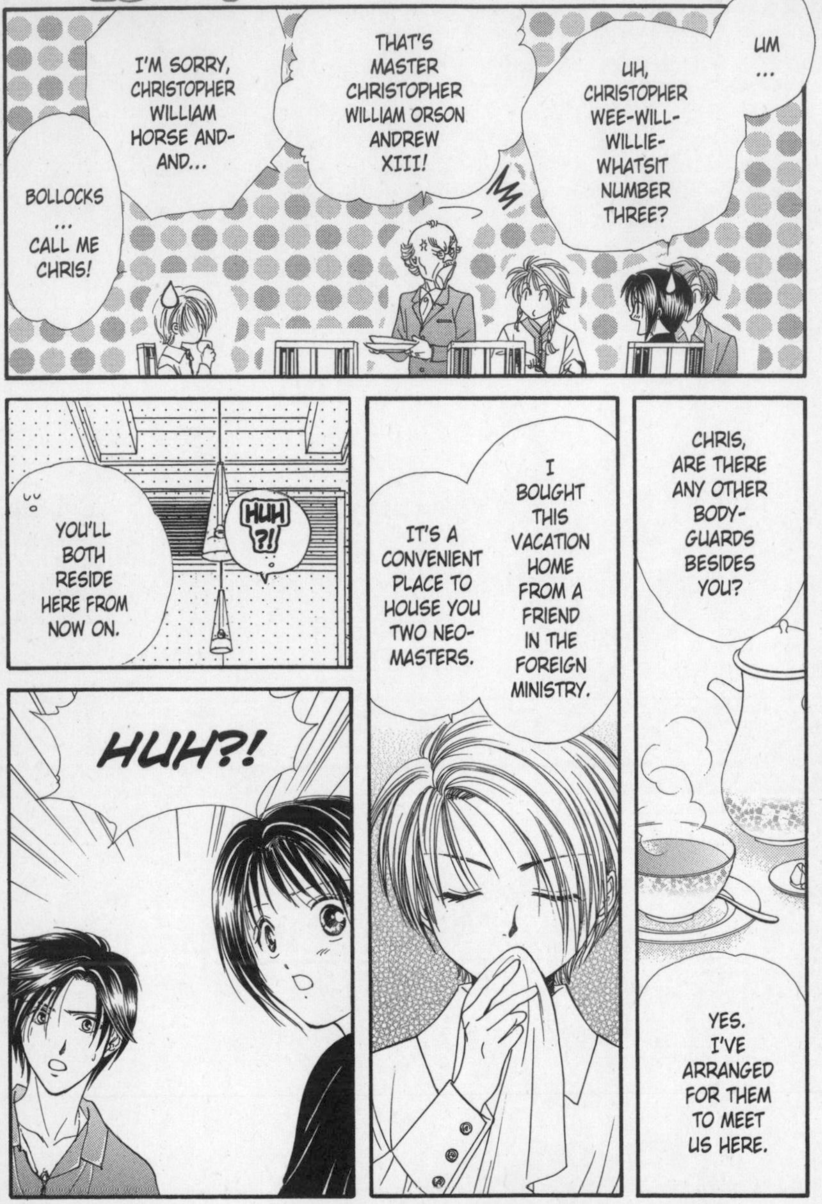
UM ...
UH, CHRISTOPHER WEE-WILL-WILLIE-WHATSIT NUMBER THREE?
THAT'S MASTER CHRISTOPHER WILLIAM ORSON ANDREW XIII!
I'M SORRY, CHRISTOPHER WILLIAM HORSE AND-AND...
BOLLOCKS ... CALL ME CHRIS!
CHRIS, ARE THERE ANY OTHER BODY-GUARDS BESIDES YOU?
YES. I'VE ARRANGED FOR THEM TO MEET US HERE.
I BOUGHT THIS VACATION HOME FROM A FRIEND IN THE FOREIGN MINISTRY.
IT'S A CONVENIENT PLACE TO HOUSE YOU TWO NEO-MASTERS.
YOU'LL BOTH RESIDE HERE FROM NOW ON.
HUH ?!
HUH?!

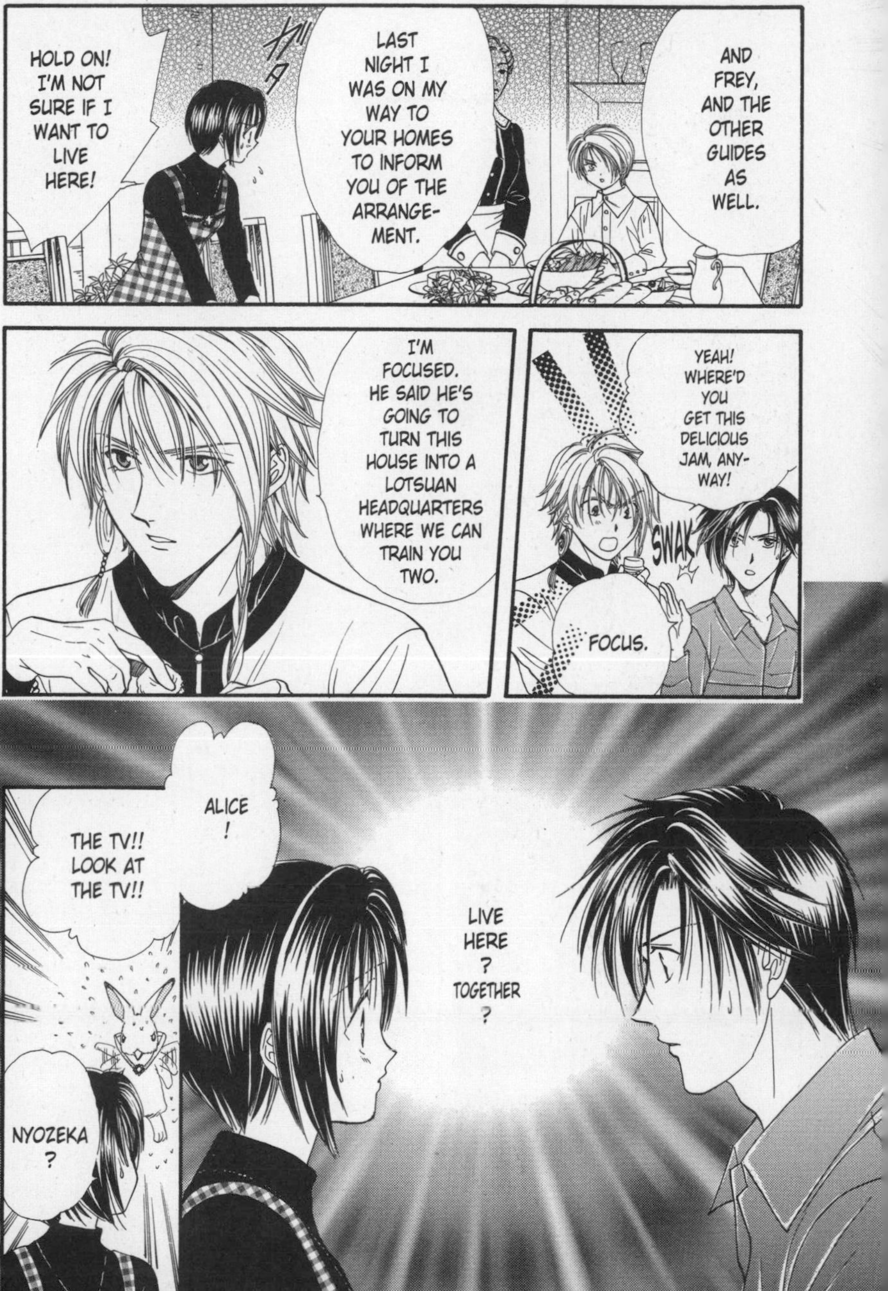
AND FREY, AND THE OTHER GUIDES AS WELL.
LAST NIGHT I WAS ON MY WAY TO YOUR HOMES TO INFORM YOU OF THE ARRANGE-MENT.
ガタ
HOLD ON! I'M NOT SURE IF I WANT TO LIVE HERE!
YEAH! WHERE'D YOU GET THIS DELICIOUS JAM, ANY-WAY!
SWAK
FOCUS.
I'M FOCUSED. HE SAID HE'S GOING TO TURN THIS HOUSE INTO A LOTSUAN HEADQUARTERS WHERE WE CAN TRAIN YOU TWO.
LIVE HERE? TOGETHER?
ALICE!
THE TV!! LOOK AT THE TV!!
NYOZEKA?

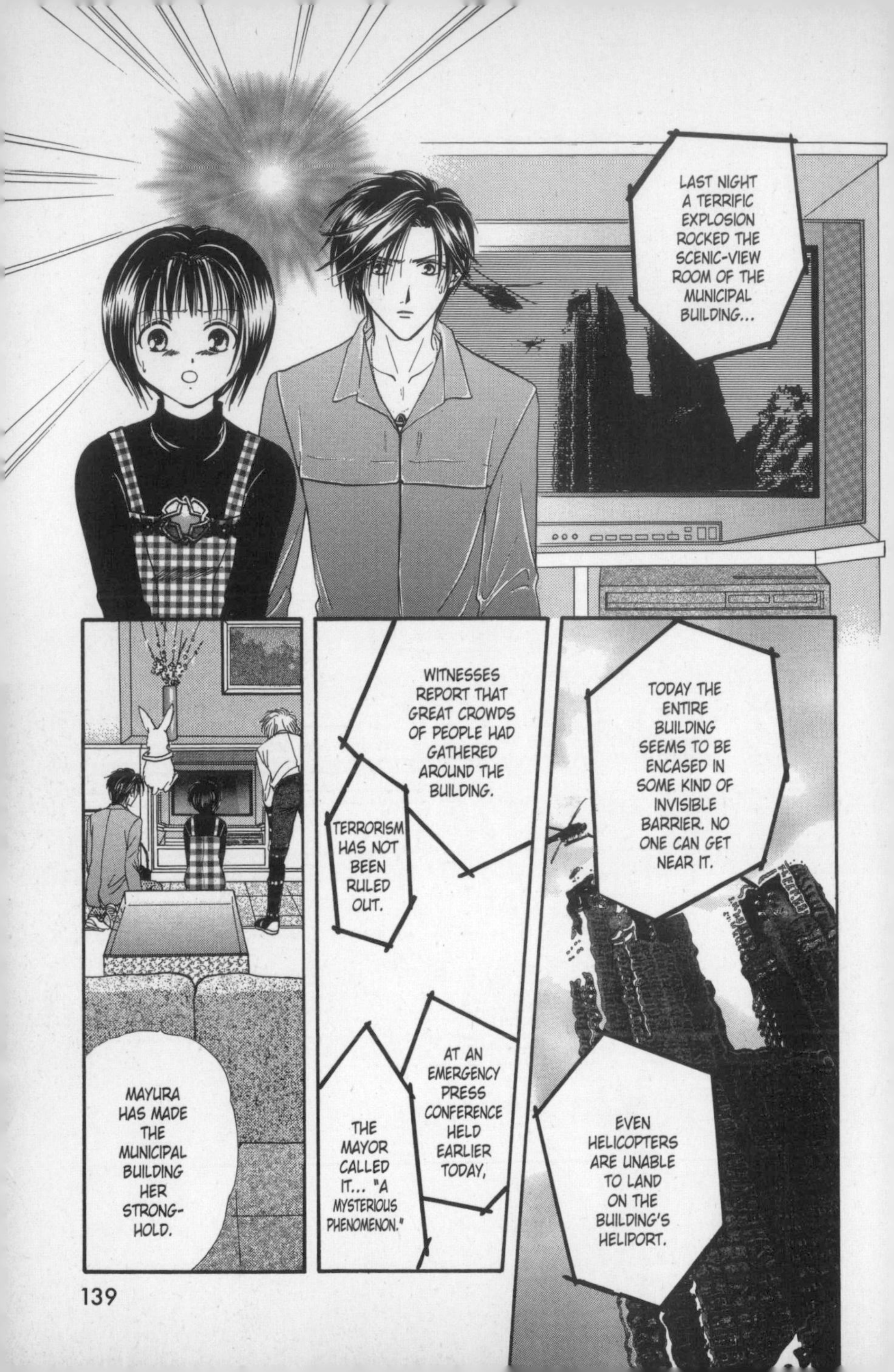
LAST NIGHT A TERRIFIC EXPLOSION ROCKED THE SCENIC-VIEW ROOM OF THE MUNICIPAL BUILDING...
TODAY THE ENTIRE BUILDING SEEMS TO BE ENCASED IN SOME KIND OF INVISIBLE BARRIER. NO ONE CAN GET NEAR IT.
EVEN HELICOPTERS ARE UNABLE TO LAND ON THE BUILDING'S HELIPORT.
WITNESSES REPORT THAT GREAT CROWDS OF PEOPLE HAD GATHERED AROUND THE BUILDING.
TERRORISM HAS NOT BEEN RULED OUT.
AT AN EMERGENCY PRESS CONFERENCE HELD EARLIER TODAY,
THE MAYOR CALLED IT... "A MYSTERIOUS PHENOMENON."
MAYURA HAS MADE THE MUNICIPAL BUILDING HER STRONG-HOLD.

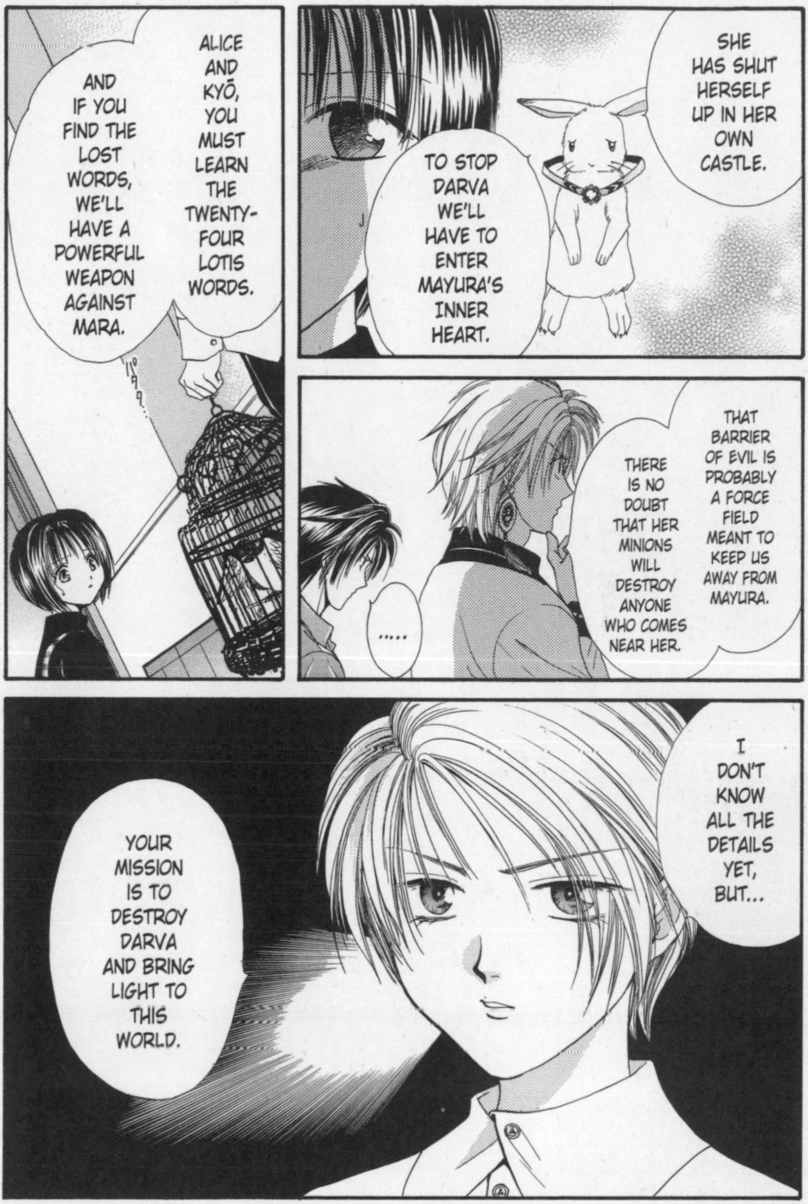
SHE HAS SHUT HERSELF UP IN HER OWN CASTLE.
TO STOP DARVA WE'LL HAVE TO ENTER MAYURA'S INNER HEART.
THAT BARRIER OF EVIL IS PROBABLY A FORCE FIELD MEANT TO KEEP US AWAY FROM MAYURA.
THERE IS NO DOUBT THAT HER MINIONS WILL DESTROY ANYONE WHO COMES NEAR HER.
.....
ALICE AND KYŌ, YOU MUST LEARN THE TWENTY-FOUR LOTIS WORDS.
AND IF YOU FIND THE LOST WORDS, WE'LL HAVE A POWERFUL WEAPON AGAINST MARA.
I DON'T KNOW ALL THE DETAILS YET, BUT...
YOUR MISSION IS TO DESTROY DARVA AND BRING LIGHT TO THIS WORLD.

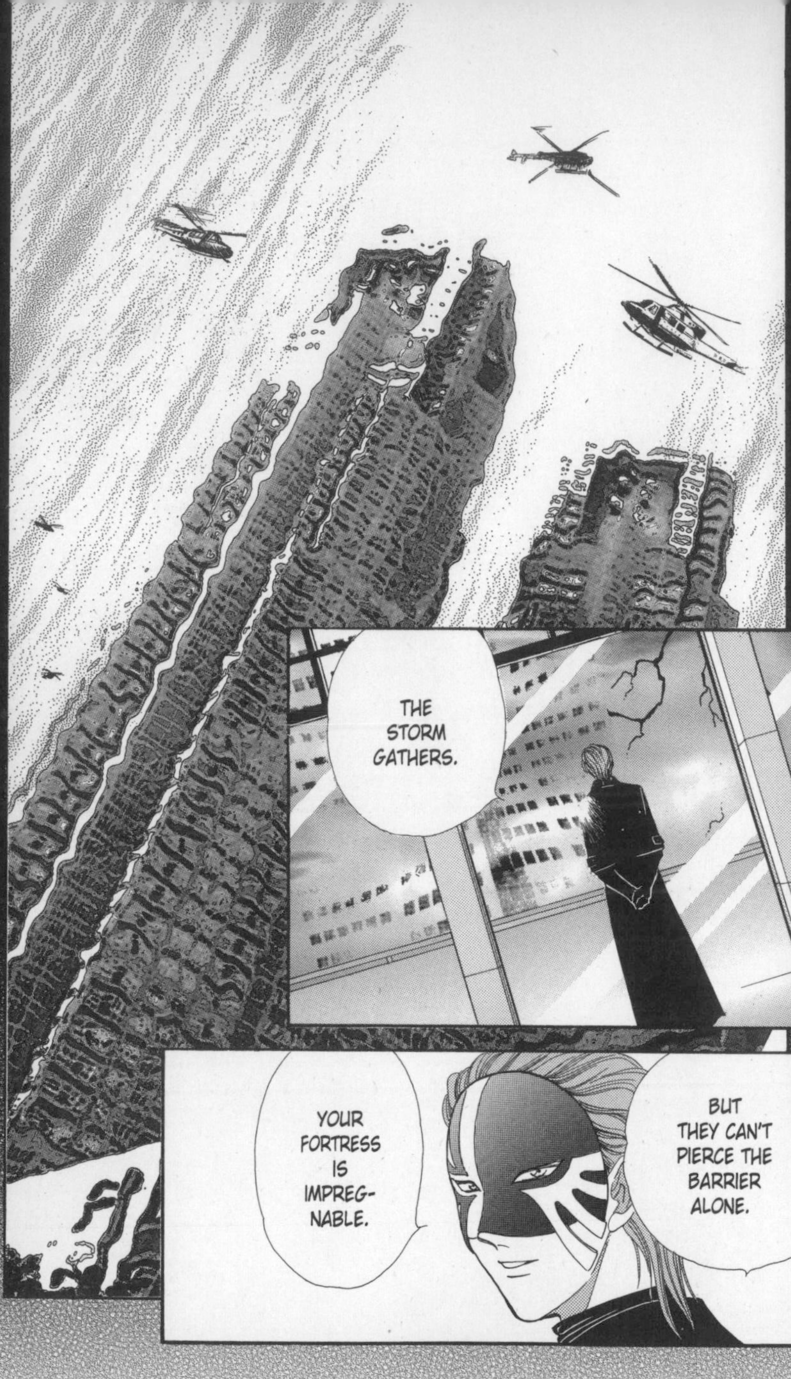
THE STORM GATHERS.
BUT THEY CAN'T PIERCE THE BARRIER ALONE.
YOUR FORTRESS IS IMPREG-NABLE.

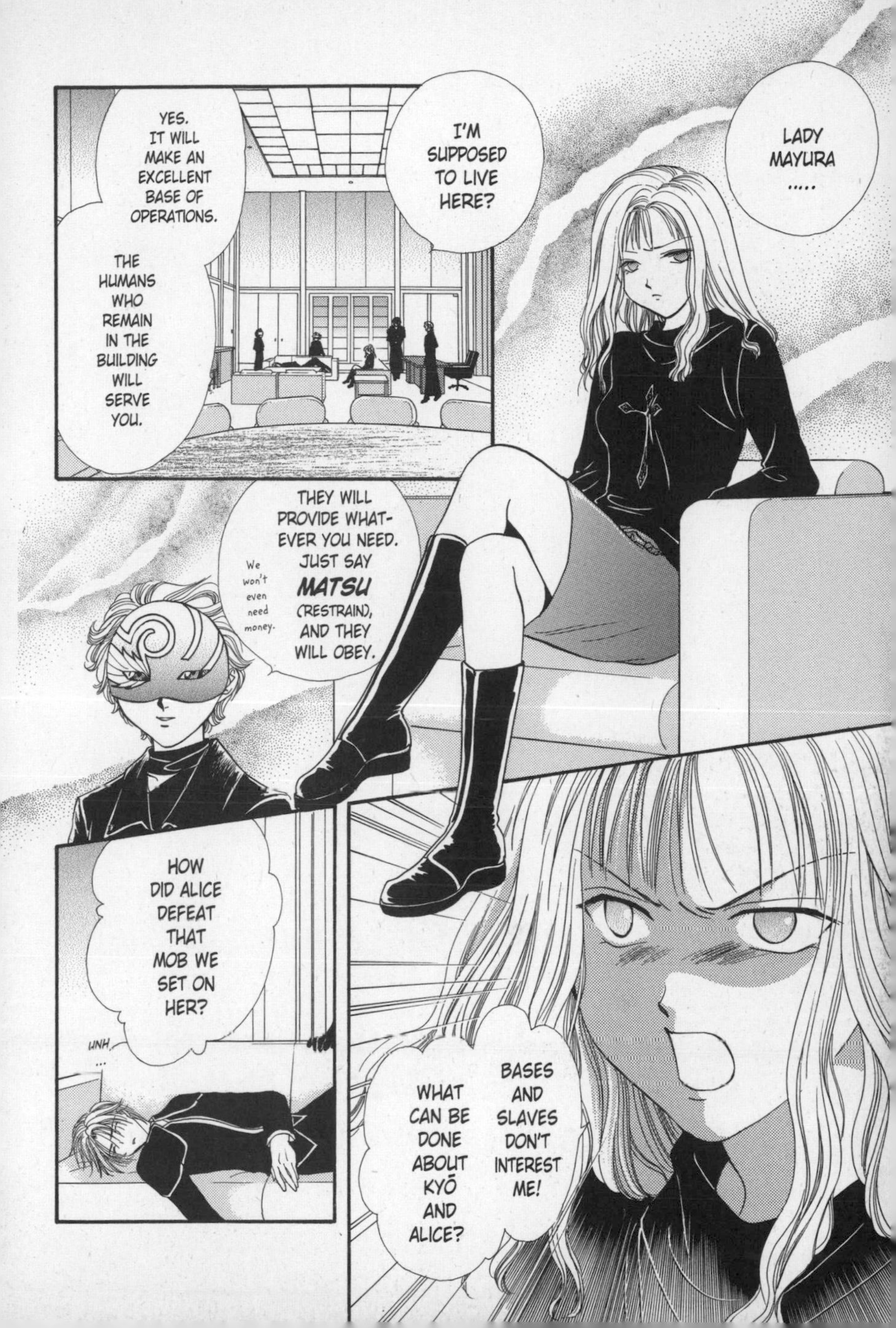
LADY MAYURA .....
I'M SUPPOSED TO LIVE HERE?
YES. IT WILL MAKE AN EXCELLENT BASE OF OPERATIONS.
THE HUMANS WHO REMAIN IN THE BUILDING WILL SERVE YOU.
THEY WILL PROVIDE WHAT-EVER YOU NEED. JUST SAY MATSU (RESTRAIN), AND THEY WILL OBEY.
We won't even need money.
BASES AND SLAVES DON'T INTEREST ME!
WHAT CAN BE DONE ABOUT KYŌ AND ALICE?
HOW DID ALICE DEFEAT THAT MOB WE SET ON HER?
UNH ...

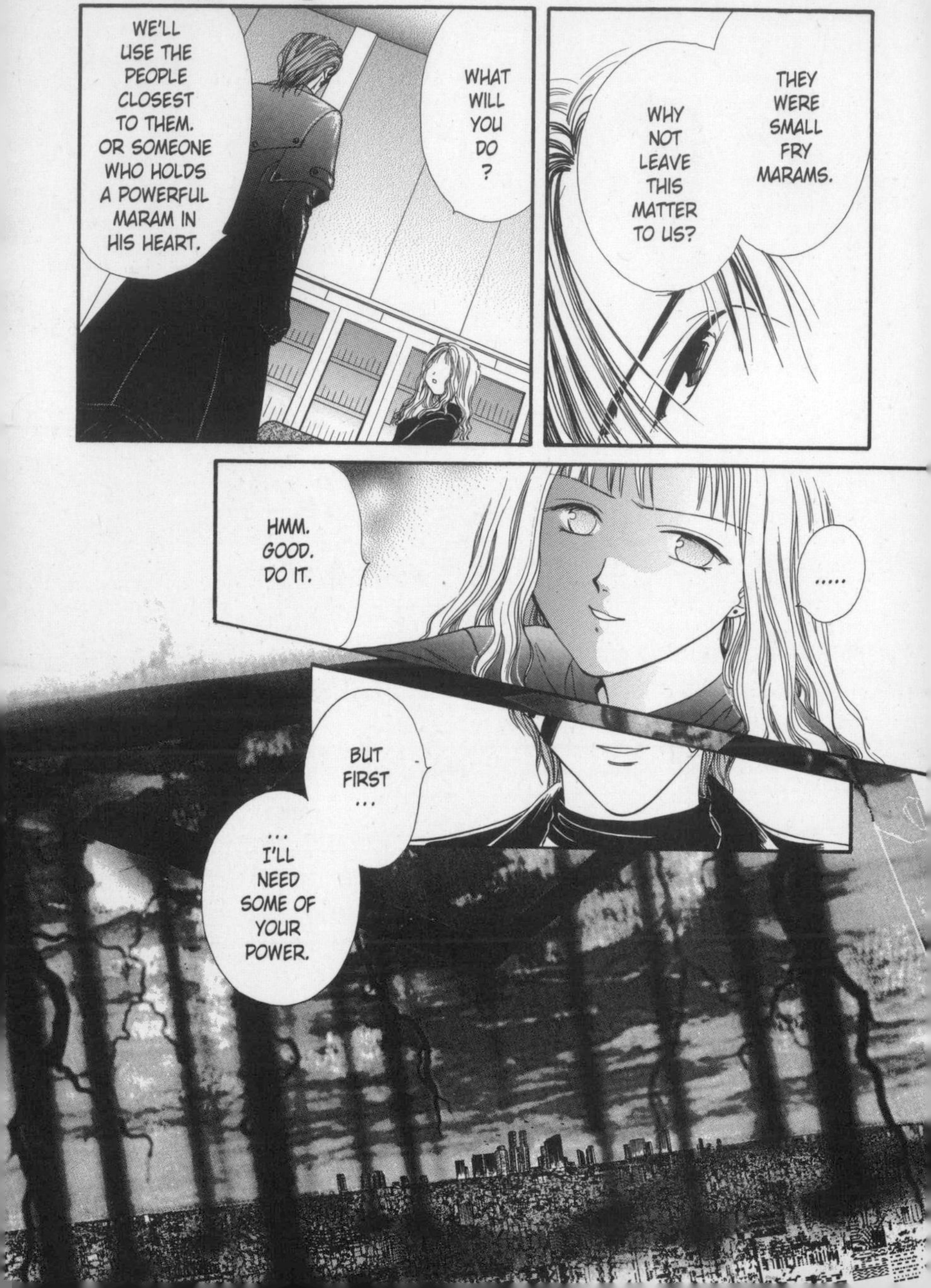
THEY WERE SMALL FRY MARAMS.
WHY NOT LEAVE THIS MATTER TO US?
WHAT WILL YOU DO ?
WE'LL USE THE PEOPLE CLOSEST TO THEM. OR SOMEONE WHO HOLDS A POWERFUL MARAM IN HIS HEART.
.....
HMM. GOOD. DO IT.
BUT FIRST ...
... I'LL NEED SOME OF YOUR POWER.

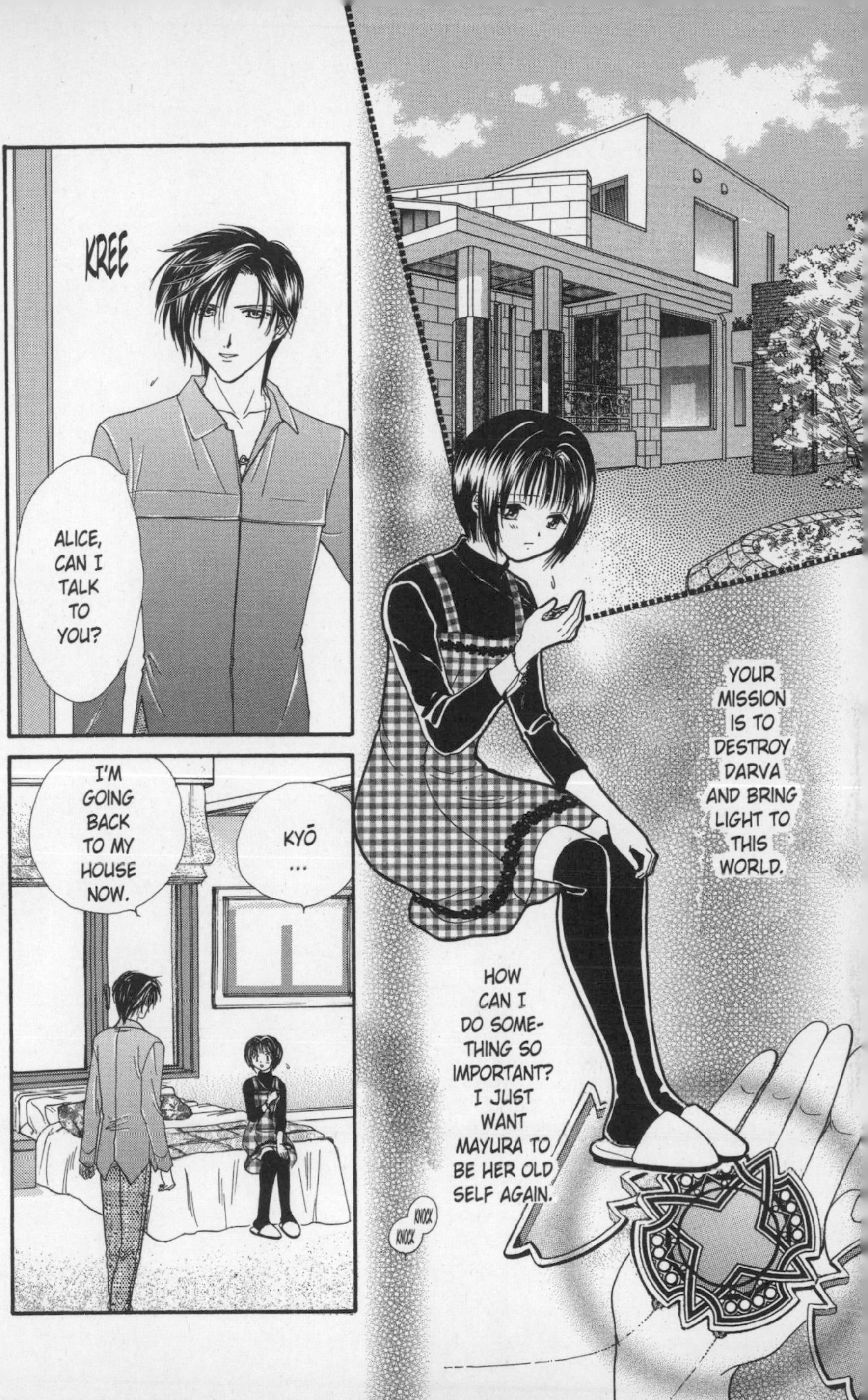
YOUR MISSION IS TO DESTROY DARVA AND BRING LIGHT TO THIS WORLD.
HOW CAN I DO SOME-THING SO IMPORTANT? I JUST WANT MAYURA TO BE HER OLD SELF AGAIN.
KNOCK KNOCK
KREE
ALICE, CAN I TALK TO YOU?
KYŌ ...
I'M GOING BACK TO MY HOUSE NOW.

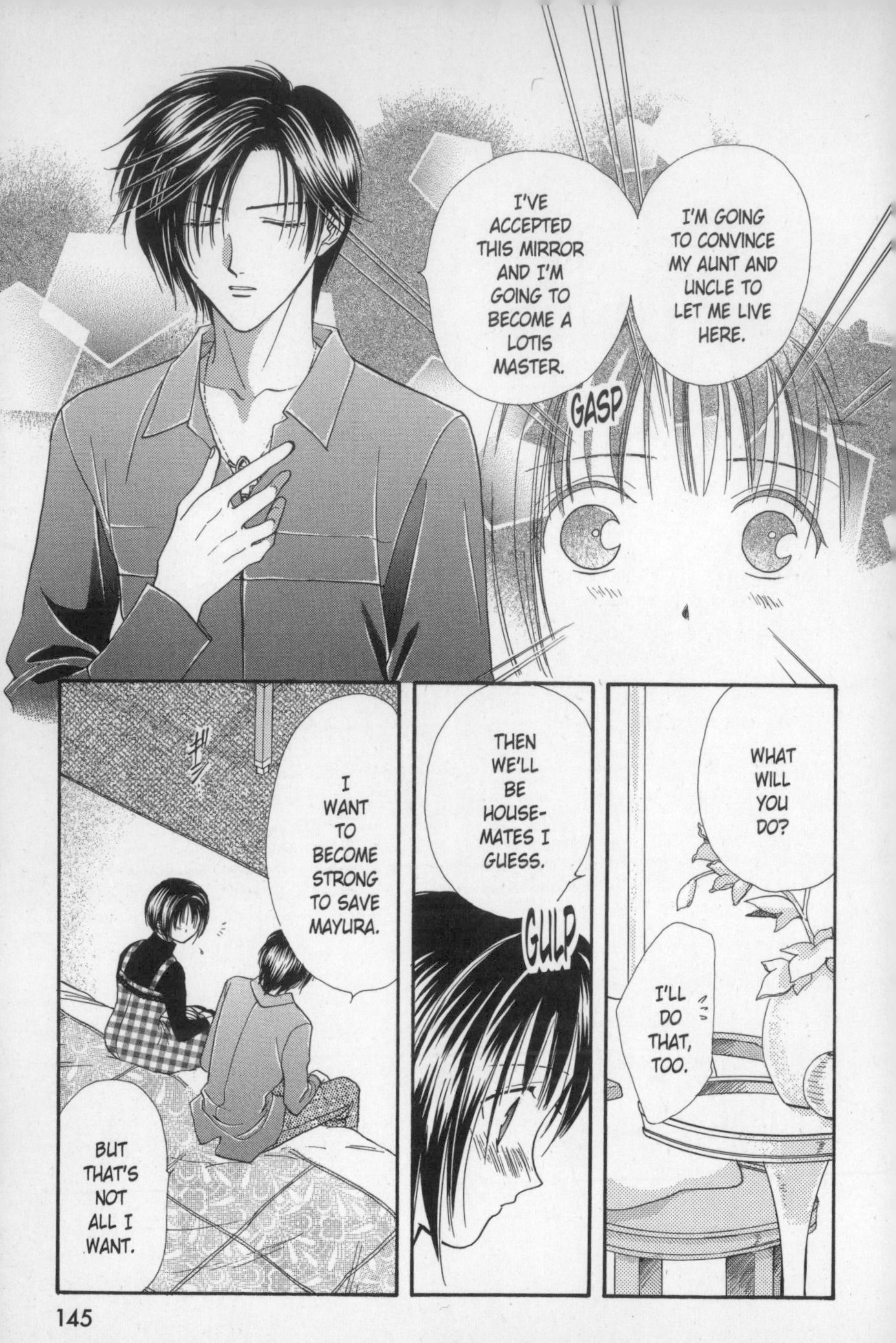
I'M GOING TO CONVINCE MY AUNT AND UNCLE TO LET ME LIVE HERE.
I'VE ACCEPTED THIS MIRROR AND I'M GOING TO BECOME A LOTIS MASTER.
GASP
WHAT WILL YOU DO?
I'LL DO THAT, TOO.
THEN WE'LL BE HOUSE-MATES I GUESS.
GULP
I WANT TO BECOME STRONG TO SAVE MAYURA.
BUT THAT'S NOT ALL I WANT.

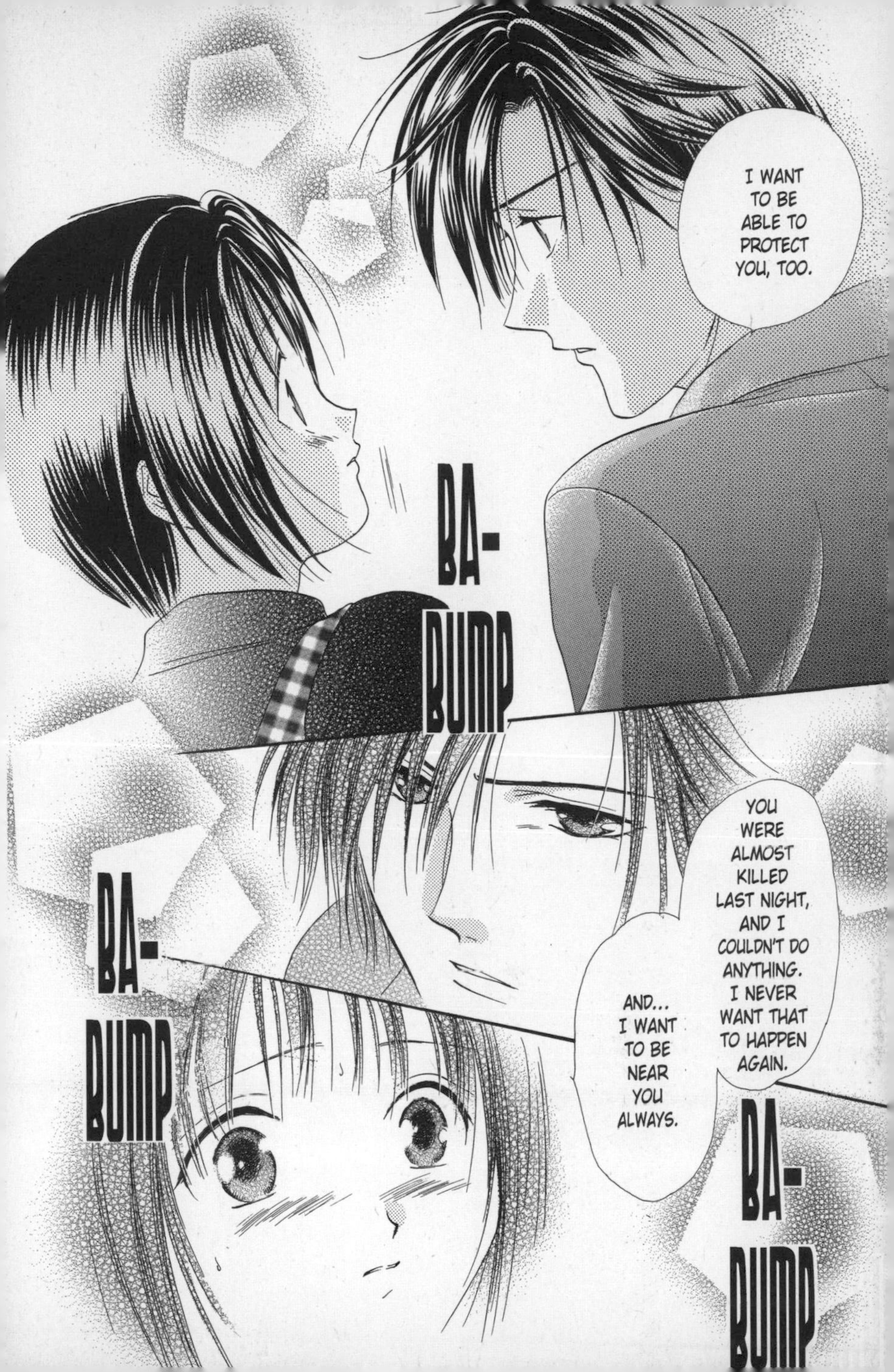
I WANT TO BE ABLE TO PROTECT YOU, TOO.
BA-BUMP
YOU WERE ALMOST KILLED LAST NIGHT, AND I COULDN'T DO ANYTHING. I NEVER WANT THAT TO HAPPEN AGAIN.
AND... I WANT TO BE NEAR YOU ALWAYS.
BA-BUMP
BA-BUMP

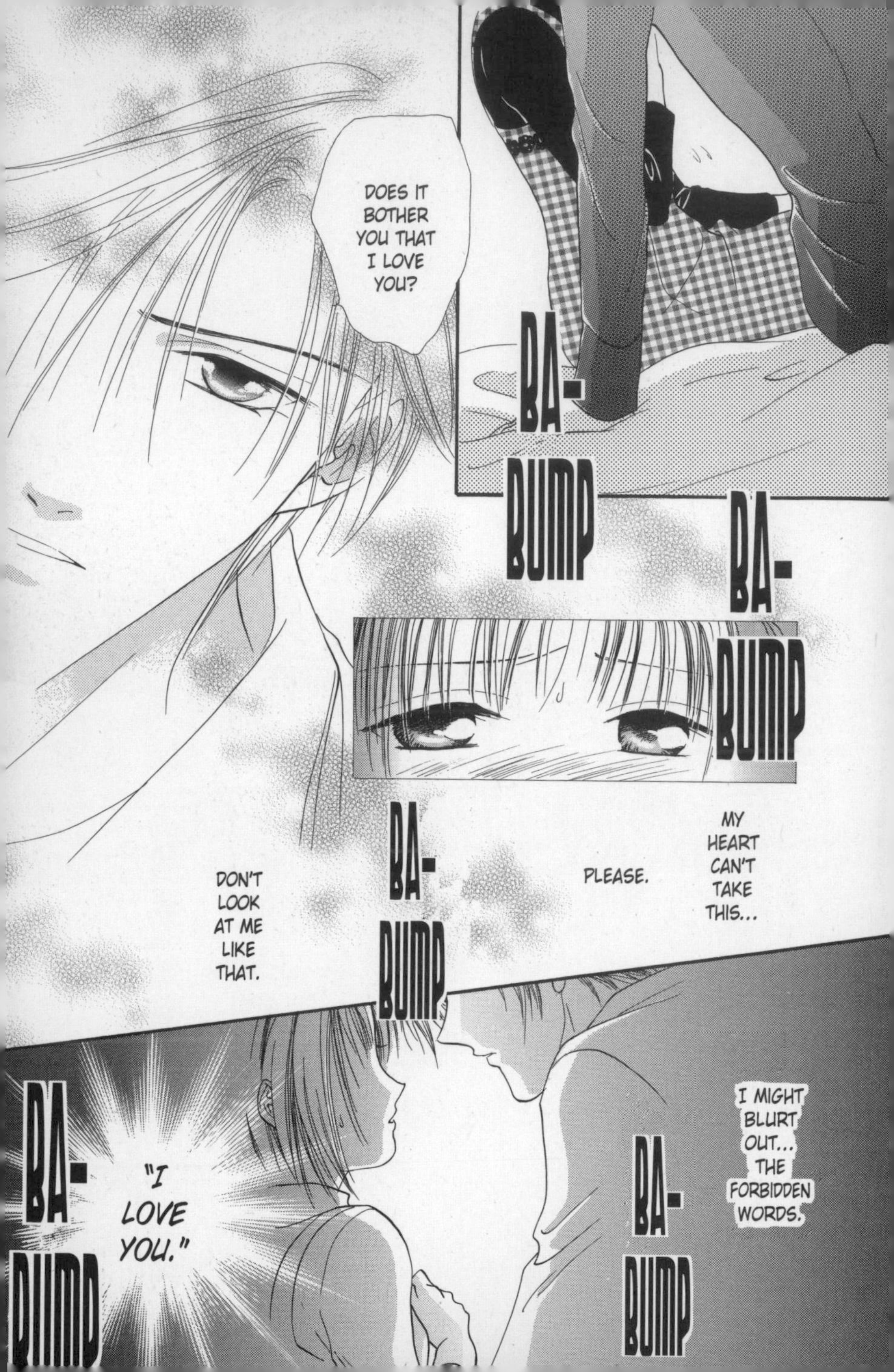

BA-BUMP
DOES IT BOTHER YOU THAT I LOVE YOU?
BA-BUMP
MY HEART CAN'T TAKE THIS...
PLEASE.
DON'T LOOK AT ME LIKE THAT.
BA-BUMP
I MIGHT BLURT OUT... THE FORBIDDEN WORDS.
BA-BUMP
"I LOVE YOU."
BA-BUMP

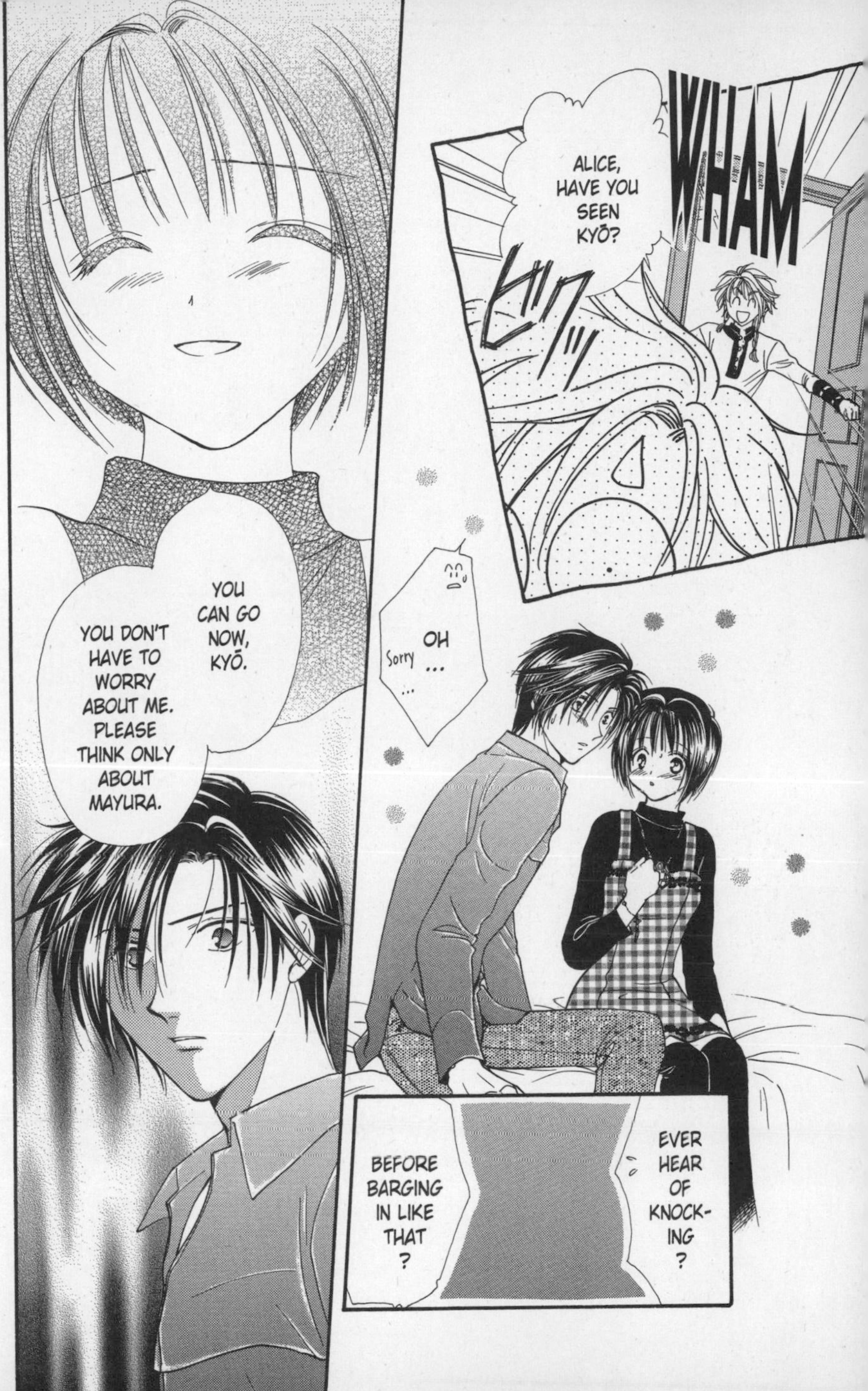
WHAM
ALICE, HAVE YOU SEEN KYŌ?
ビクッ
OH ...
Sorry ...
EVER HEAR OF KNOCK-ING?
BEFORE BARGING IN LIKE THAT?
YOU CAN GO NOW, KYŌ.
YOU DON'T HAVE TO WORRY ABOUT ME. PLEASE THINK ONLY ABOUT MAYURA.

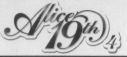

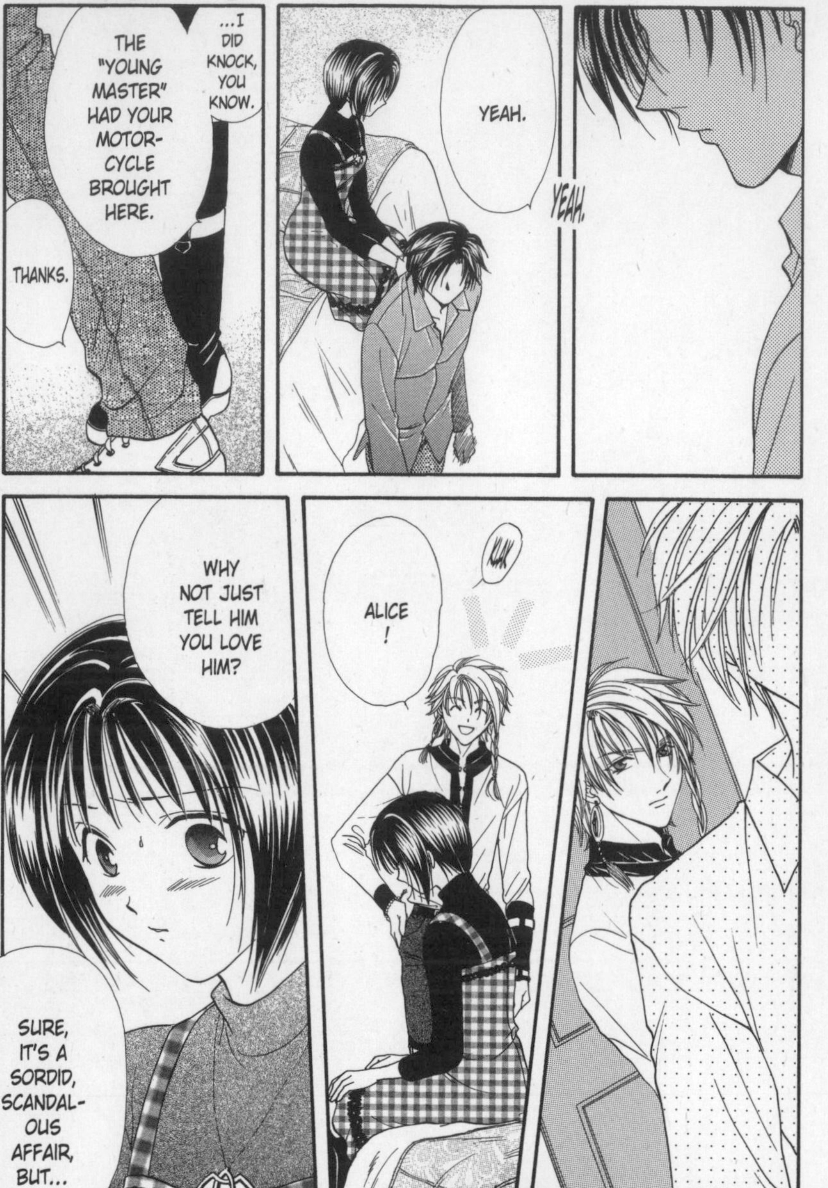
YEAH.
YEAH.
...I DID KNOCK, YOU KNOW.
THE "YOUNG MASTER" HAD YOUR MOTOR-CYCLE BROUGHT HERE.
THANKS.
KLAK
ALICE!
WHY NOT JUST TELL HIM YOU LOVE HIM?
SURE, IT'S A SORDID, SCANDAL-OUS AFFAIR, BUT...

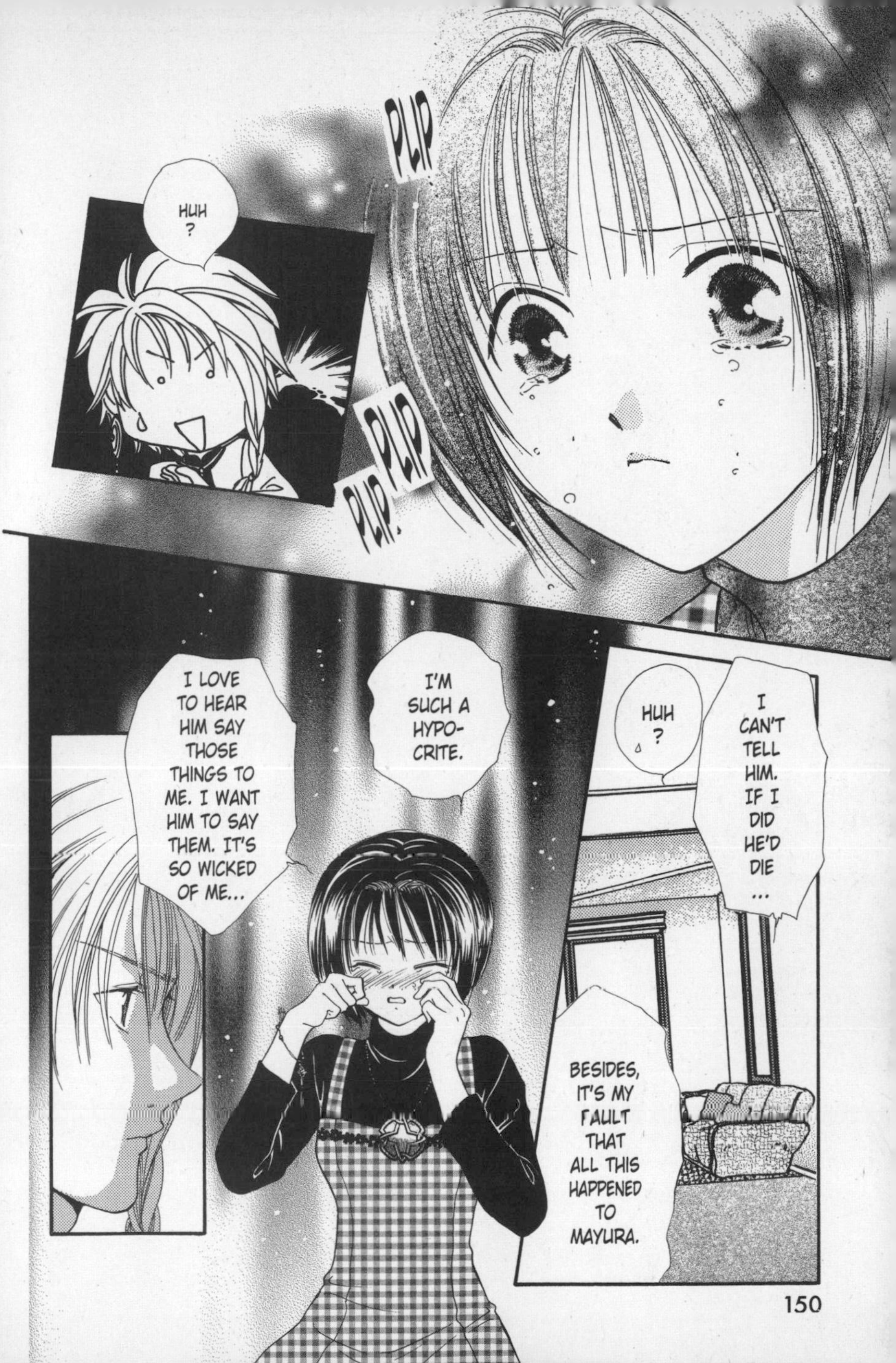
PLIP
PLIP
PLIP
PLIP
HUH ?
I CAN'T TELL HIM. IF I DID HE'D DIE ...
HUH ?
BESIDES, IT'S MY FAULT THAT ALL THIS HAPPENED TO MAYURA.
I'M SUCH A HYPOCRITE.
I LOVE TO HEAR HIM SAY THOSE THINGS TO ME. I WANT HIM TO SAY THEM. IT'S SO WICKED OF ME...

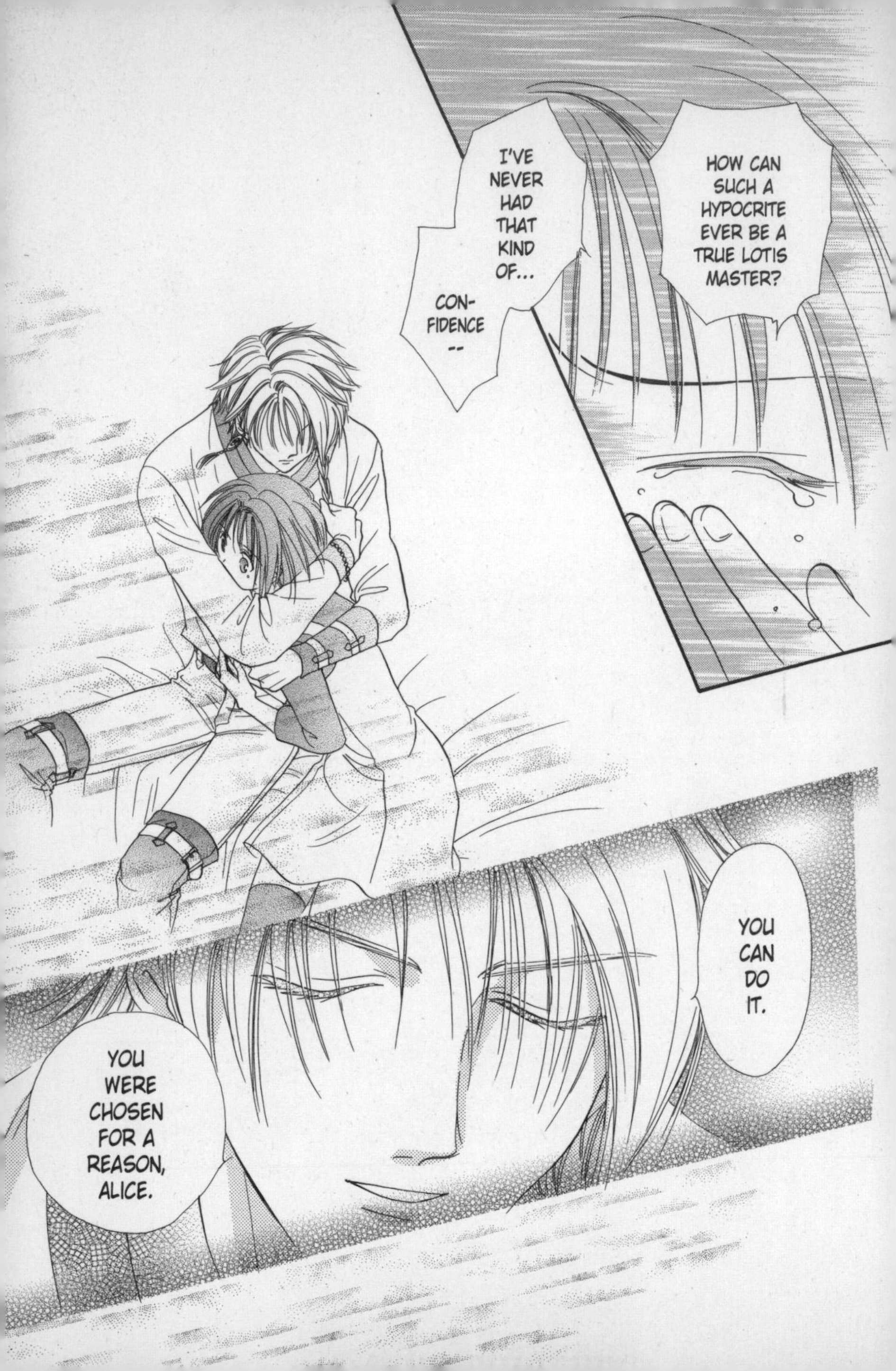
HOW CAN SUCH A HYPOCRITE EVER BE A TRUE LOTIS MASTER?
I'VE NEVER HAD THAT KIND OF...
CON-FIDENCE --
YOU CAN DO IT.
YOU WERE CHOSEN FOR A REASON, ALICE.

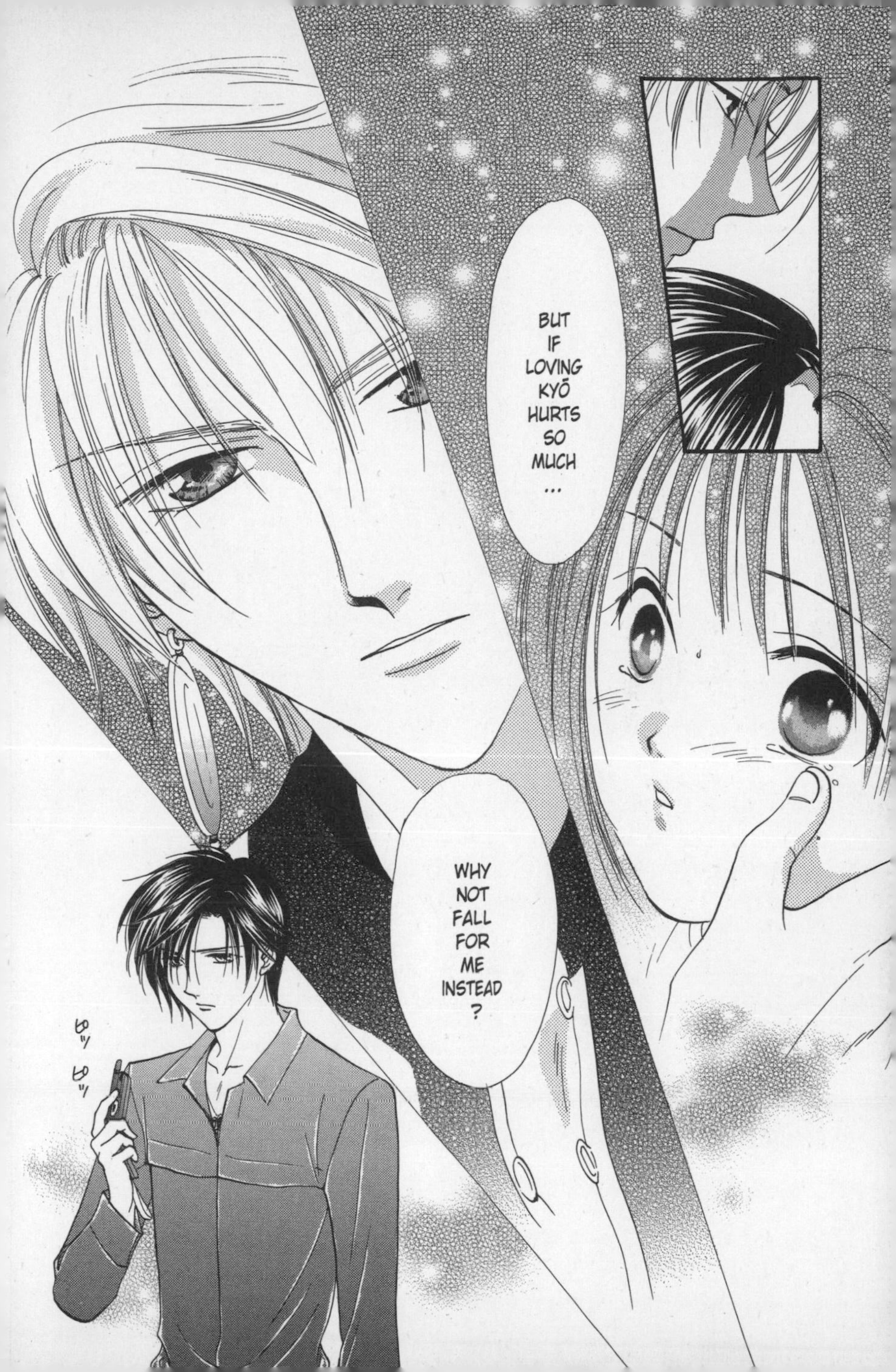
BUT IF LOVING KYŌ HURTS SO MUCH ...
WHY NOT FALL FOR ME INSTEAD ?
ピッ ピッ

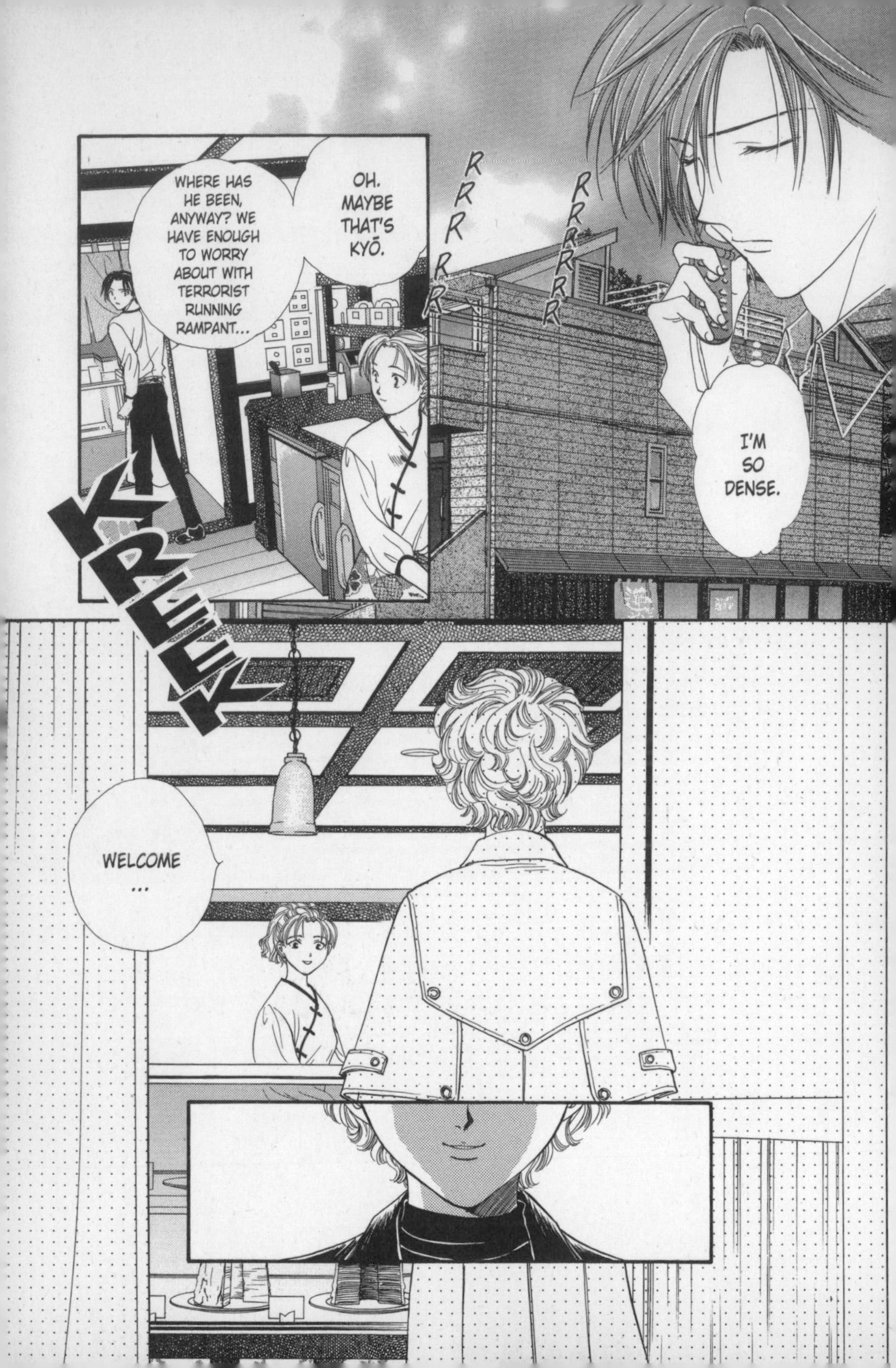
RRRRRRR
RRRRR
I'M SO DENSE.
OH. MAYBE THAT'S KYŌ.
WHERE HAS HE BEEN, ANYWAY? WE HAVE ENOUGH TO WORRY ABOUT WITH TERRORIST RUNNING RAMPANT...
KREEK
WELCOME ...

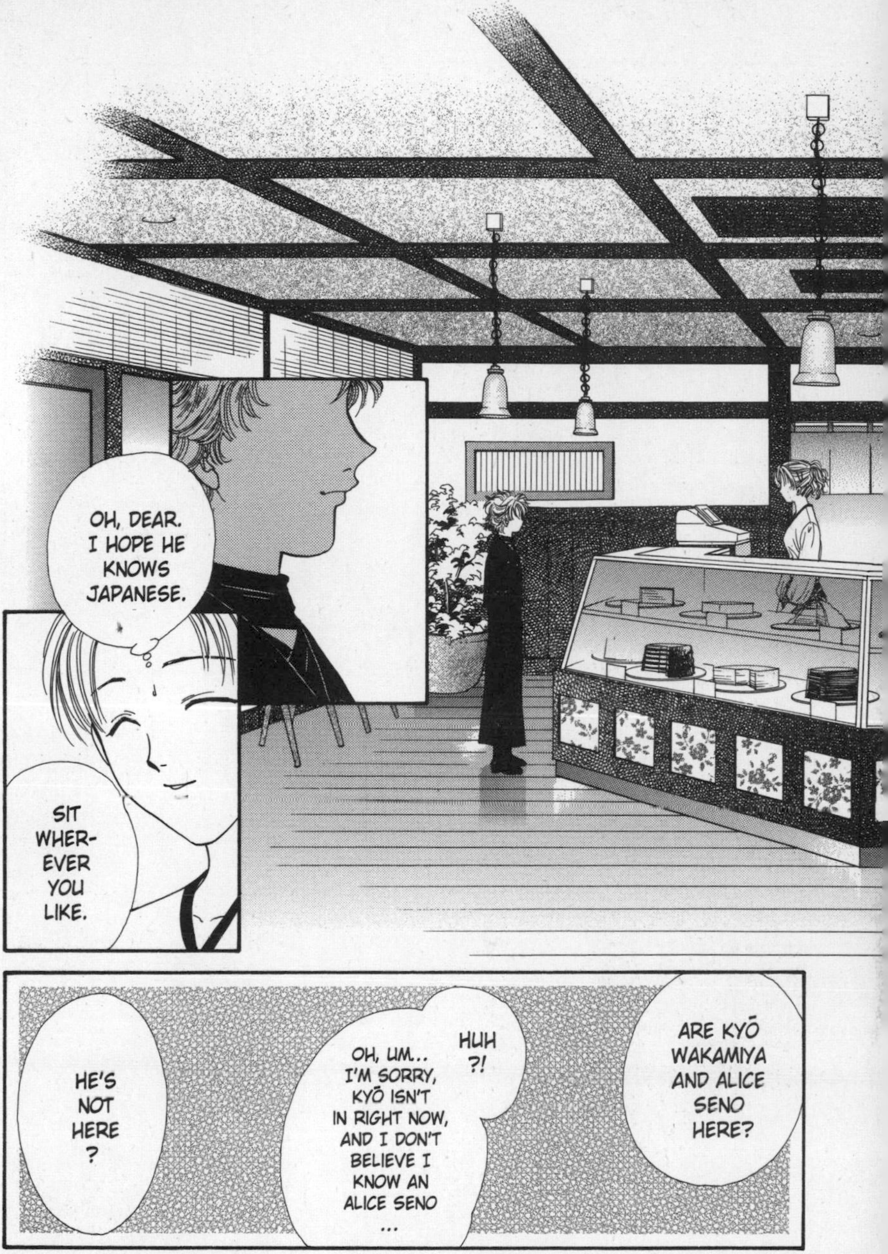
OH, DEAR. I HOPE HE KNOWS JAPANESE.
SIT WHER-EVER YOU LIKE.
ARE KYŌ WAKAMIYA AND ALICE SENO HERE?
HUH ?!
OH, UM... I'M SORRY, KYŌ ISN'T IN RIGHT NOW, AND I DON'T BELIEVE I KNOW AN ALICE SENO ...
HE'S NOT HERE ?

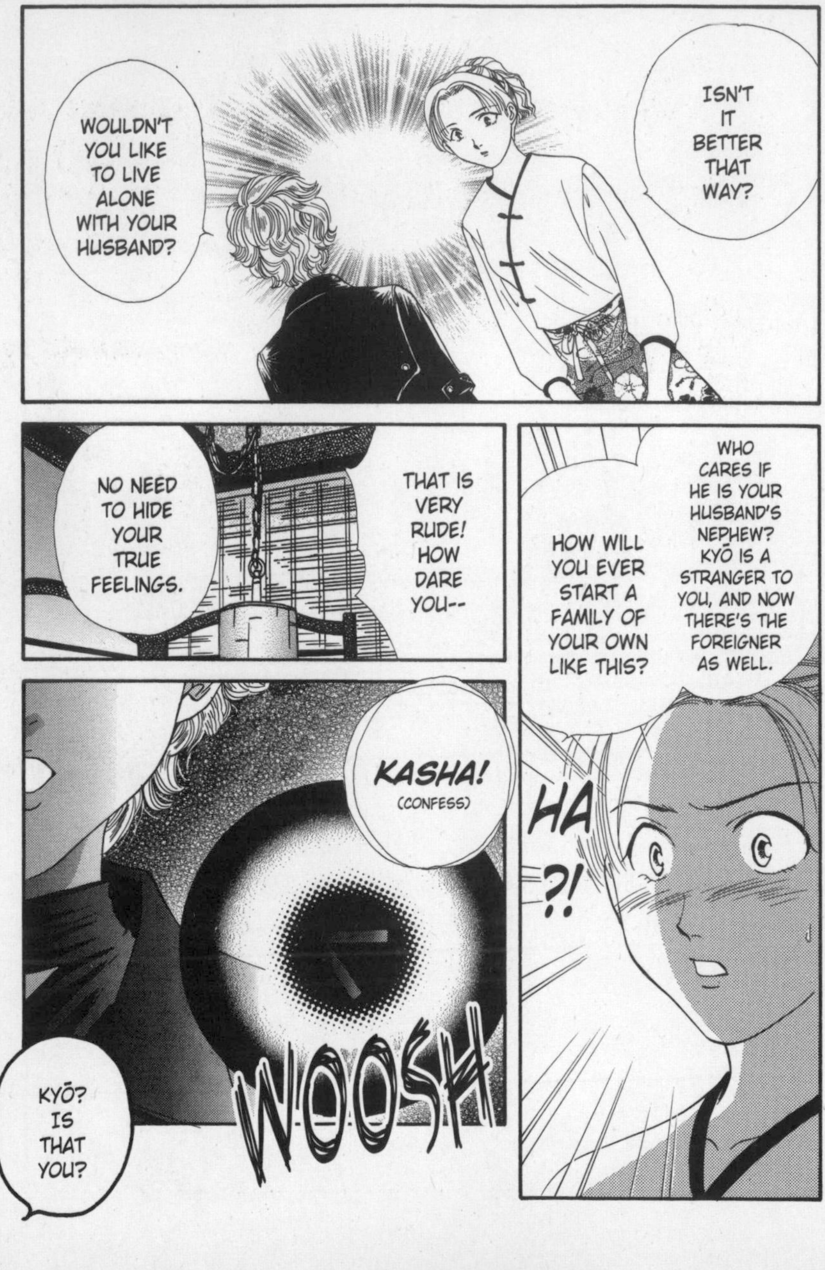
ISN'T IT BETTER THAT WAY?
WOULDN'T YOU LIKE TO LIVE ALONE WITH YOUR HUSBAND?
WHO CARES IF HE IS YOUR HUSBAND'S NEPHEW? KYŌ IS A STRANGER TO YOU, AND NOW THERE'S THE FOREIGNER AS WELL.
HOW WILL YOU EVER START A FAMILY OF YOUR OWN LIKE THIS?
HA?!
THAT IS VERY RUDE! HOW DARE YOU--
NO NEED TO HIDE YOUR TRUE FEELINGS.
KASHA!
(CONFESS)
WOOSH
KYŌ? IS THAT YOU?

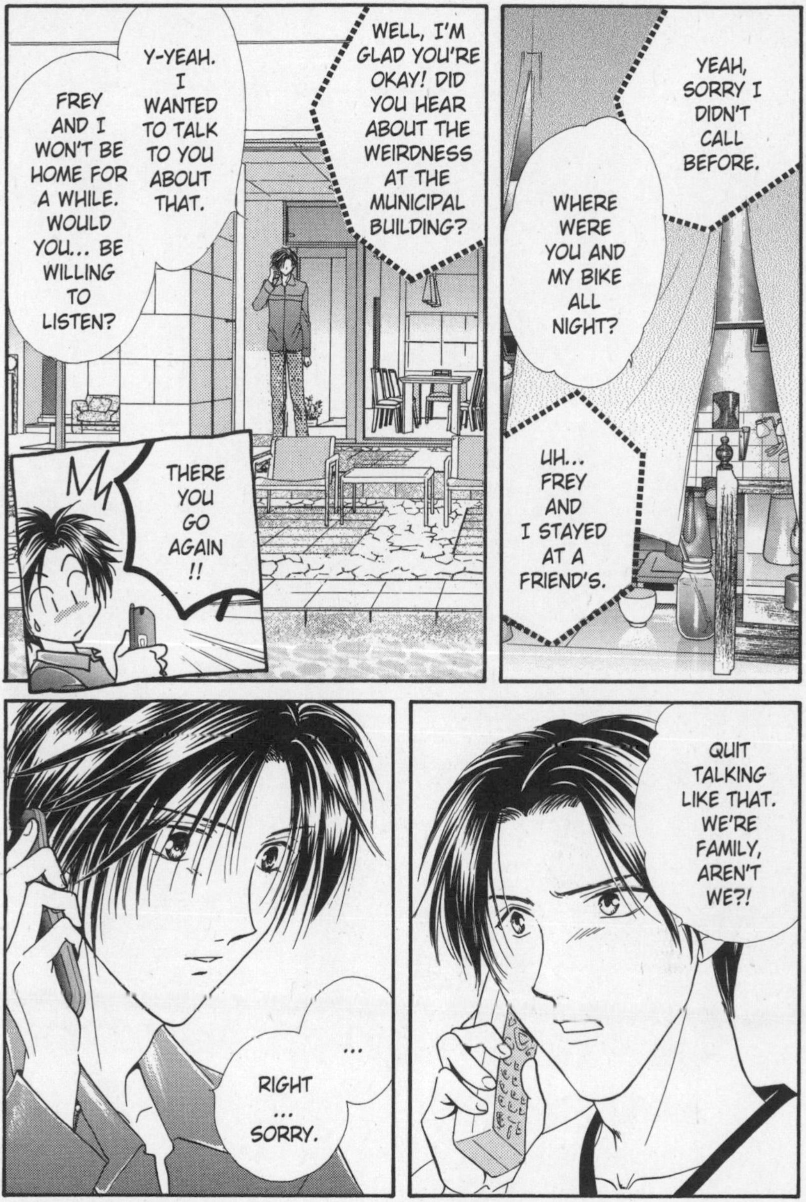
YEAH, SORRY I DIDN'T CALL BEFORE.
WHERE WERE YOU AND MY BIKE ALL NIGHT?
UH... FREY AND I STAYED AT A FRIEND'S.
WELL, I'M GLAD YOU'RE OKAY! DID YOU HEAR ABOUT THE WEIRDNESS AT THE MUNICIPAL BUILDING?
Y-YEAH. I WANTED TO TALK TO YOU ABOUT THAT.
FREY AND I WON'T BE HOME FOR A WHILE. WOULD YOU... BE WILLING TO LISTEN?
THERE YOU GO AGAIN!!
QUIT TALKING LIKE THAT. WE'RE FAMILY, AREN'T WE?!
...
RIGHT ... SORRY.

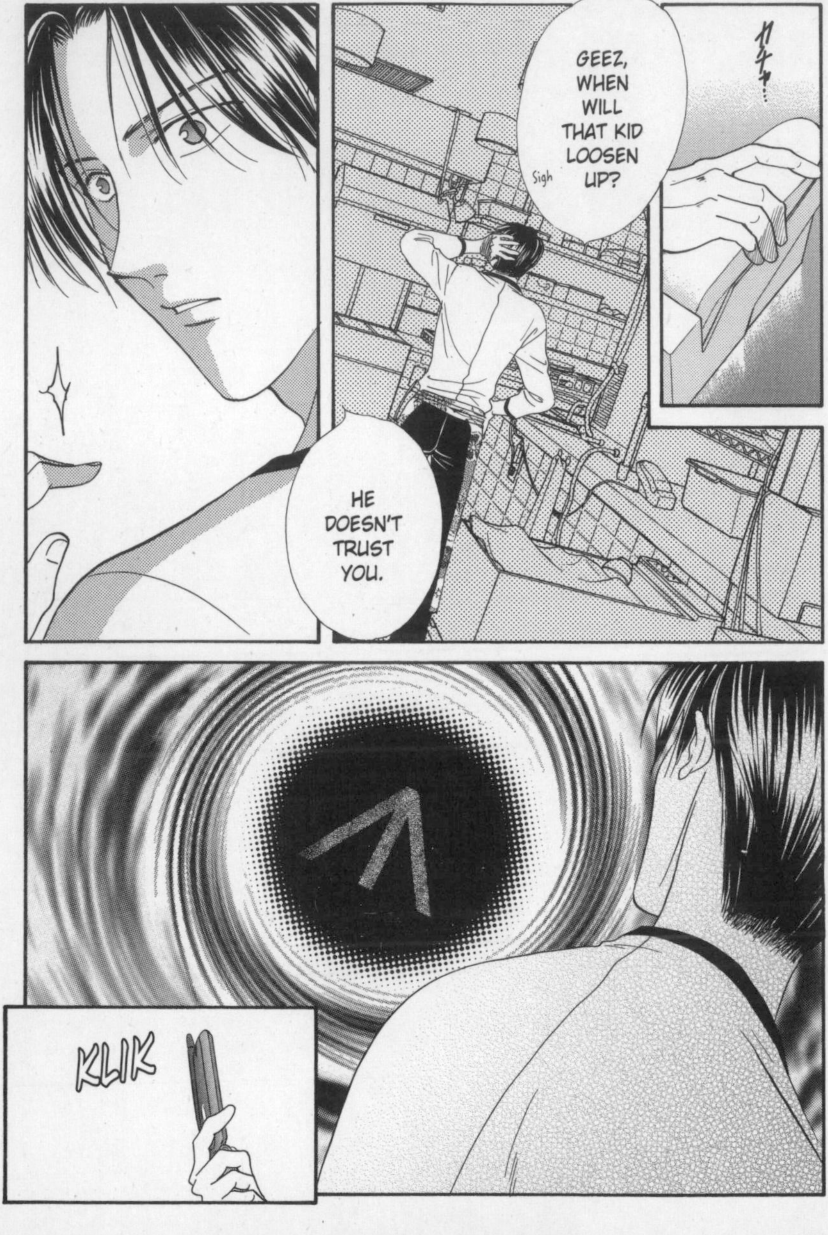
カチャ…
GEEZ, WHEN WILL THAT KID LOOSEN UP?
Sigh
HE DOESN'T TRUST YOU.
KLIK

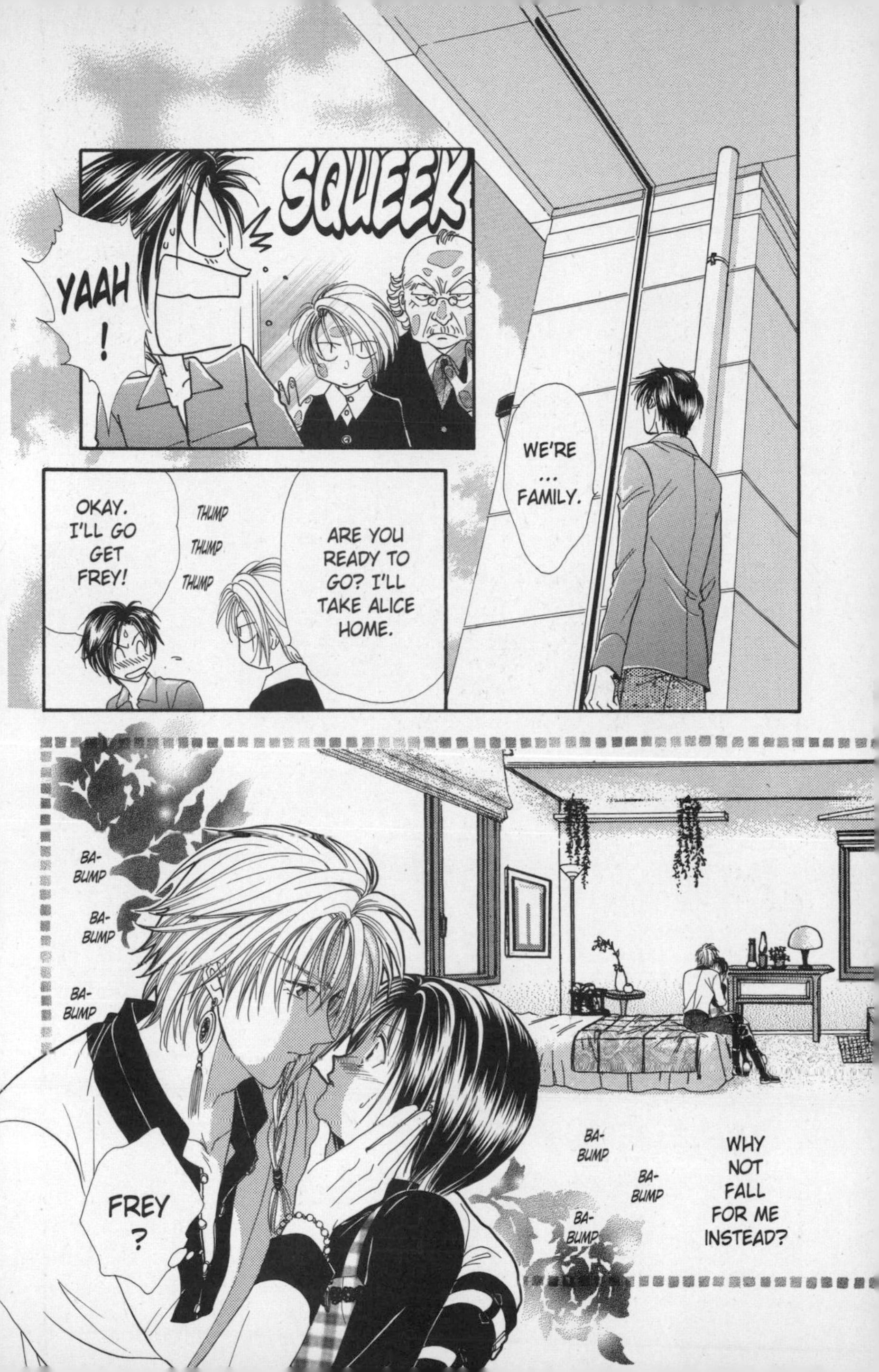

WE'RE ... FAMILY.
SQUEEK
YAAH !
ARE YOU READY TO GO? I'LL TAKE ALICE HOME.
THUMP
THUMP
THUMP
OKAY. I'LL GO GET FREY!
WHY NOT FALL FOR ME INSTEAD?
BA-BUMP
BA-BUMP
BA-BUMP
BA-BUMP
BA-BUMP
BA-BUMP
FREY ?

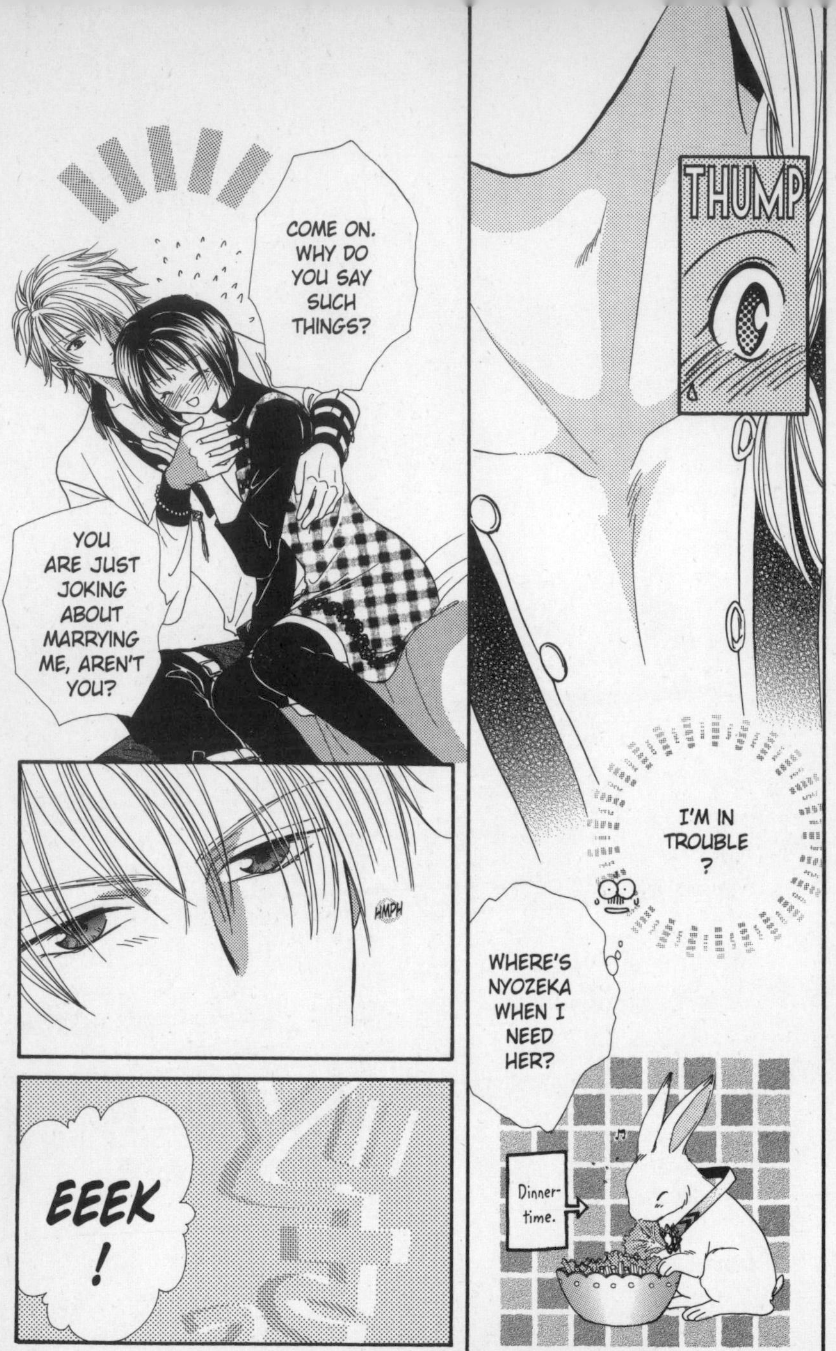
COME ON. WHY DO YOU SAY SUCH THINGS?
YOU ARE JUST JOKING ABOUT MARRYING ME, AREN'T YOU?
HMPH
EEEK !
THUMP
I'M IN TROUBLE ?
WHERE'S NYOZEKA WHEN I NEED HER?
Dinner-time.

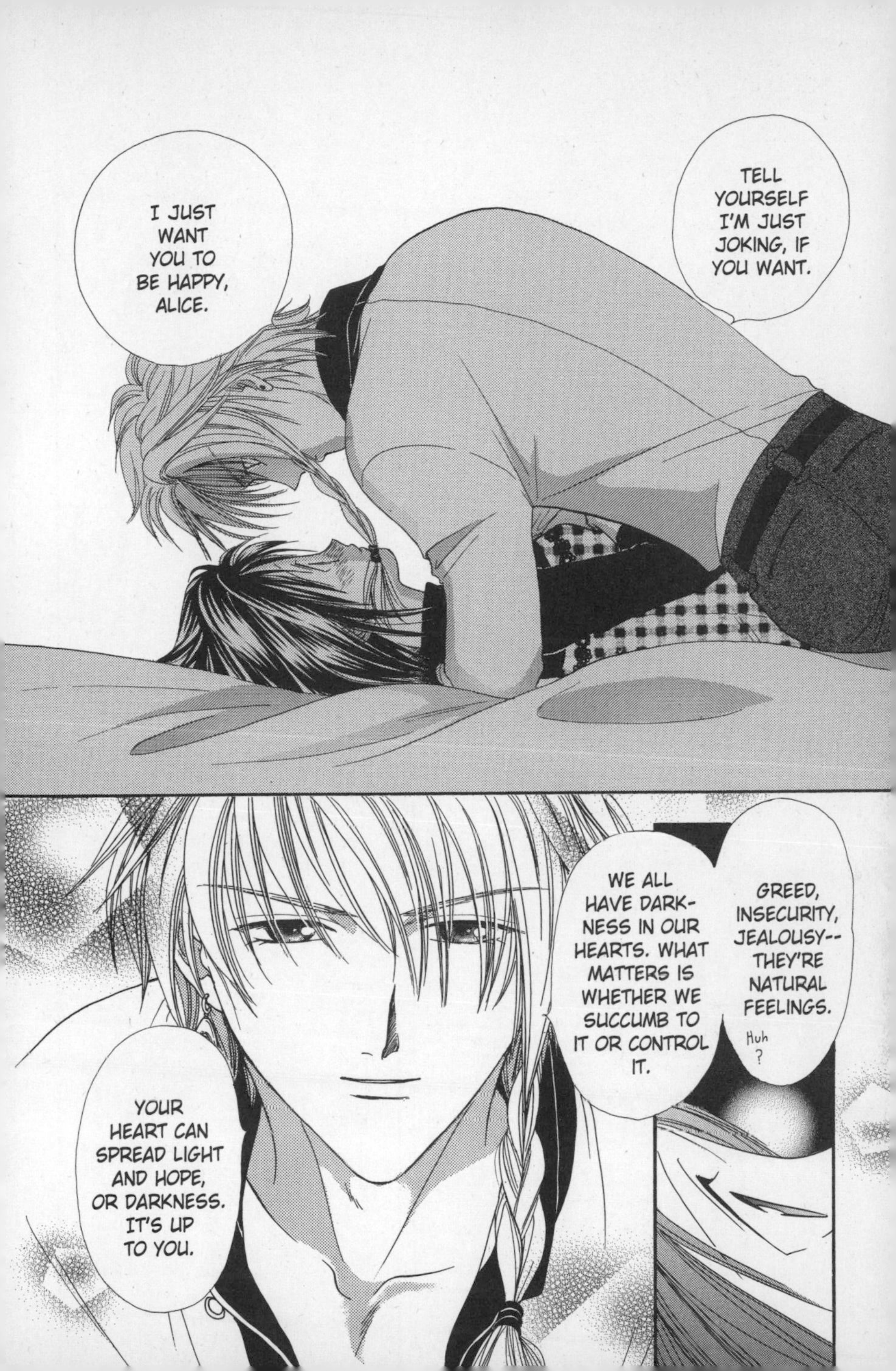
TELL YOURSELF I'M JUST JOKING, IF YOU WANT.
I JUST WANT YOU TO BE HAPPY, ALICE.
GREED, INSECURITY, JEALOUSY--THEY'RE NATURAL FEELINGS.
Huh ?
WE ALL HAVE DARKNESS IN OUR HEARTS. WHAT MATTERS IS WHETHER WE SUCCUMB TO IT OR CONTROL IT.
YOUR HEART CAN SPREAD LIGHT AND HOPE, OR DARKNESS. IT'S UP TO YOU.

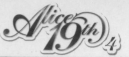

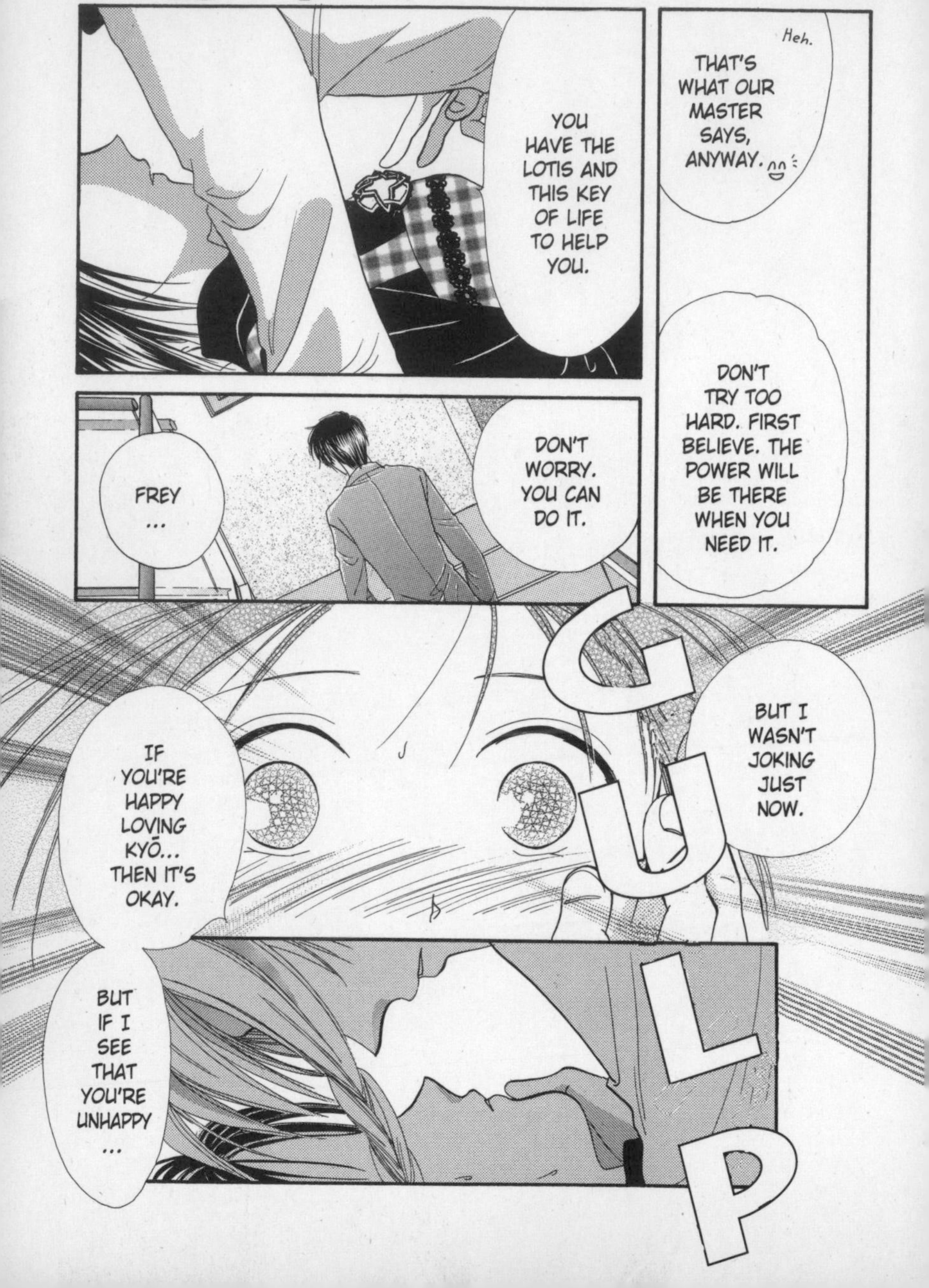
Heh.
THAT'S WHAT OUR MASTER SAYS, ANYWAY.
YOU HAVE THE LOTIS AND THIS KEY OF LIFE TO HELP YOU.
DON'T TRY TOO HARD. FIRST BELIEVE. THE POWER WILL BE THERE WHEN YOU NEED IT.
DON'T WORRY. YOU CAN DO IT.
FREY ...
GULP
BUT I WASN'T JOKING JUST NOW.
IF YOU'RE HAPPY LOVING KYŌ... THEN IT'S OKAY.
BUT IF I SEE THAT YOU'RE UNHAPPY ...

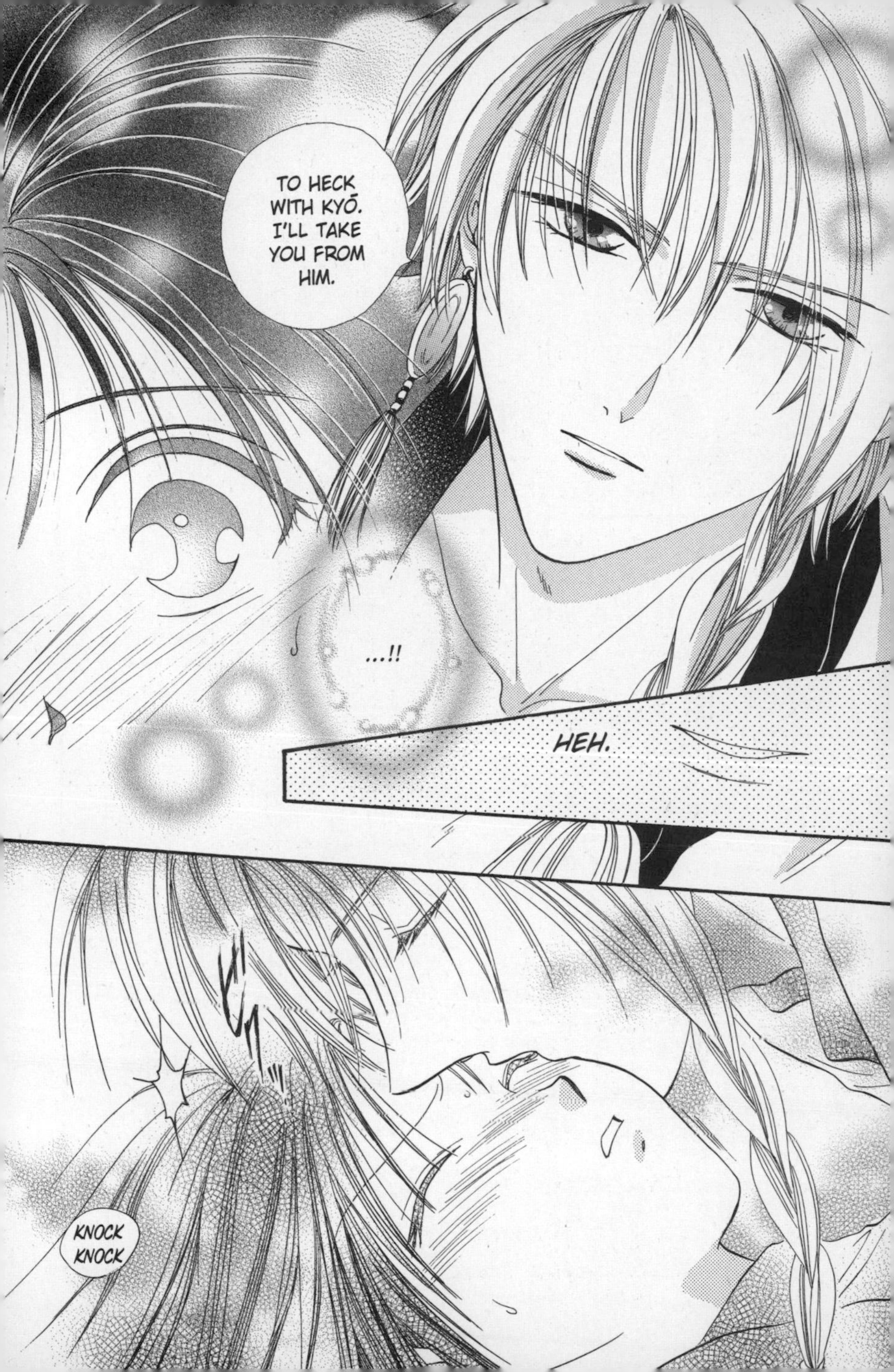
TO HECK WITH KYŌ. I'LL TAKE YOU FROM HIM.
...!!
HEH.
KNOCK KNOCK

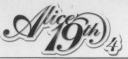

Maybe I'm working too hard lately, but I've been shocked to be suffering from severe headaches that come out of the blue.
My nerves must be shot. I'm sure. People need to rest, after all. I look healthy enough. I can't take the outdoors. When I go out, I start to get sick. First of all, I get motion-sickness, and the air where I live now doesn't agree with me. A few minutes after I step outside, my eyes start to water and my head starts to throb. By the time I get home I'm really sick.
It's just that the air is so bad here. My nose congestion started after I moved here, too.
The air was good in my hometown. Tokyo, after all, is pretty polluted. As soon as they landed at Haneda my friends said: "The air in Japan stinks!"
That's why. Along with the normal fatigue, Watase is known to be weak or sickly, not only in Japan, but at events abroad too.
My doctor says I'd be a prize-winning child in a health contest. ("Child," how do you like that?)
I could probably be healthy if I got rid of my stress and moved someplace with clean air and clear water like in the Southern Alps. I'd be more comfortable abroad...(As if I could really leave).
I believe people's working conditions and environment are very bad. Japan today is poisoned.
If this continues, we'll end up like Nausicaa of the Valley of Wind -- the original story, chapter four. Aren't people concerned? It bothers me quite a lot. I don't want to get used to poison! Maybe I'll have to learn English and live in the U.S.? I was kind of invited.
Just kidding. (I'd be like Milk-chan)

Anyway, see you next volume.

The most recent album I like is Rurutia's R. I'm looking forward to the second one.

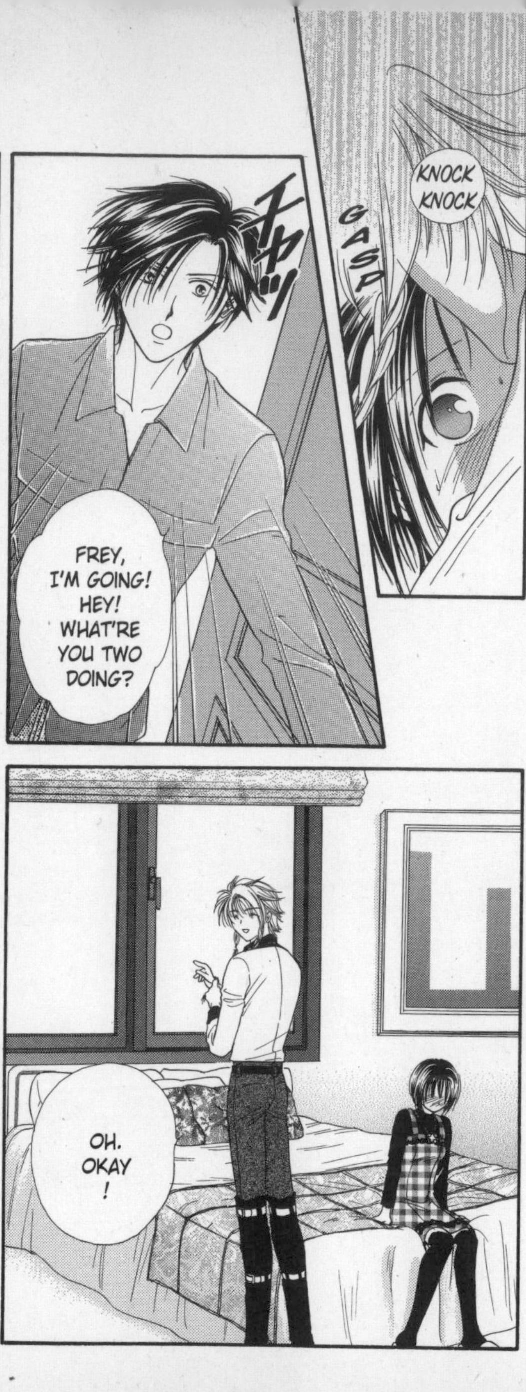
KNOCK KNOCK
GASP
FREY, I'M GOING! HEY! WHAT'RE YOU TWO DOING?
OH. OKAY!

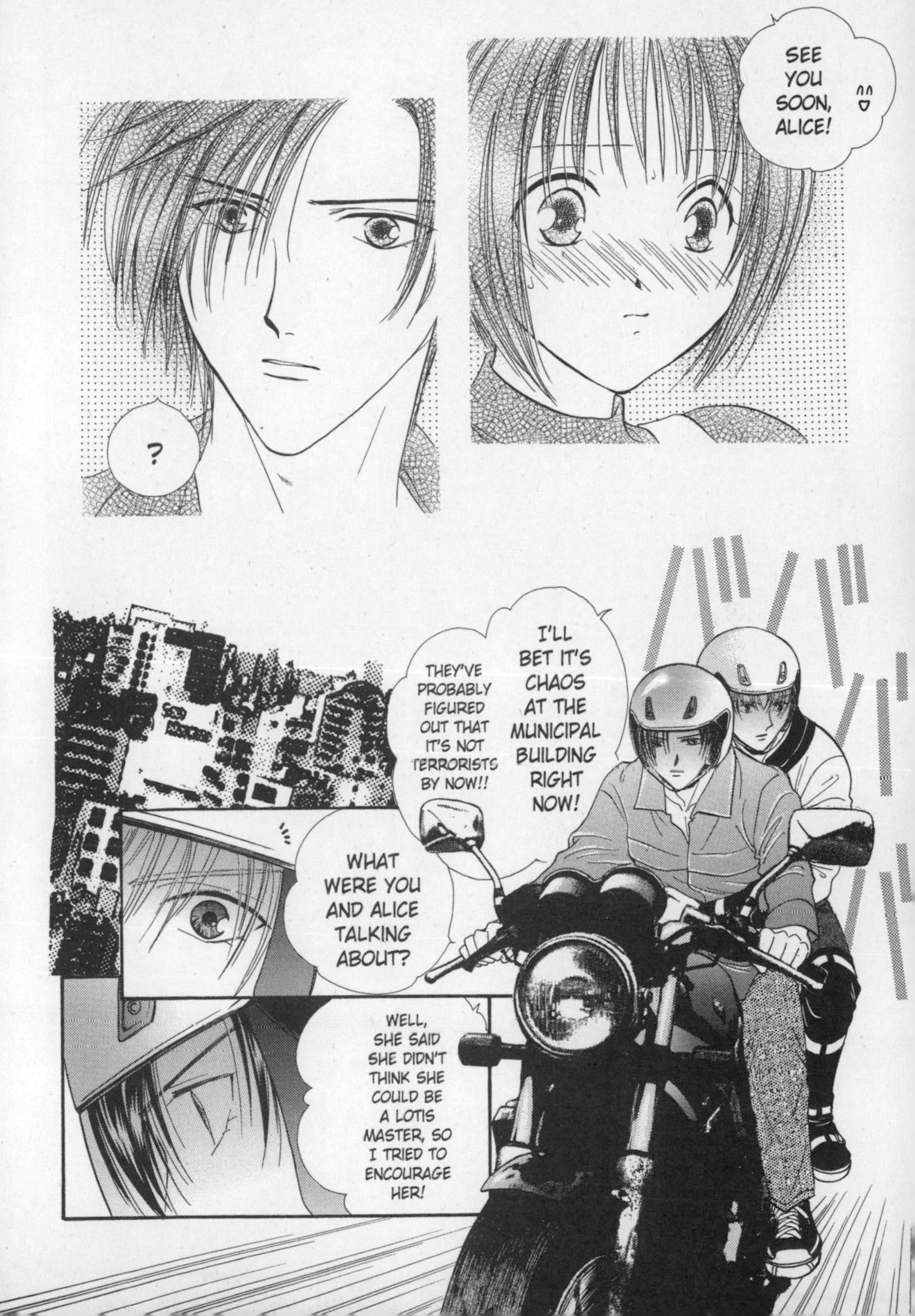
SEE YOU SOON, ALICE!
?
I'LL BET IT'S CHAOS AT THE MUNICIPAL BUILDING RIGHT NOW!
THEY'VE PROBABLY FIGURED OUT THAT IT'S NOT TERRORISTS BY NOW!!
WHAT WERE YOU AND ALICE TALKING ABOUT?
WELL, SHE SAID SHE DIDN'T THINK SHE COULD BE A LOTIS MASTER, SO I TRIED TO ENCOURAGE HER!

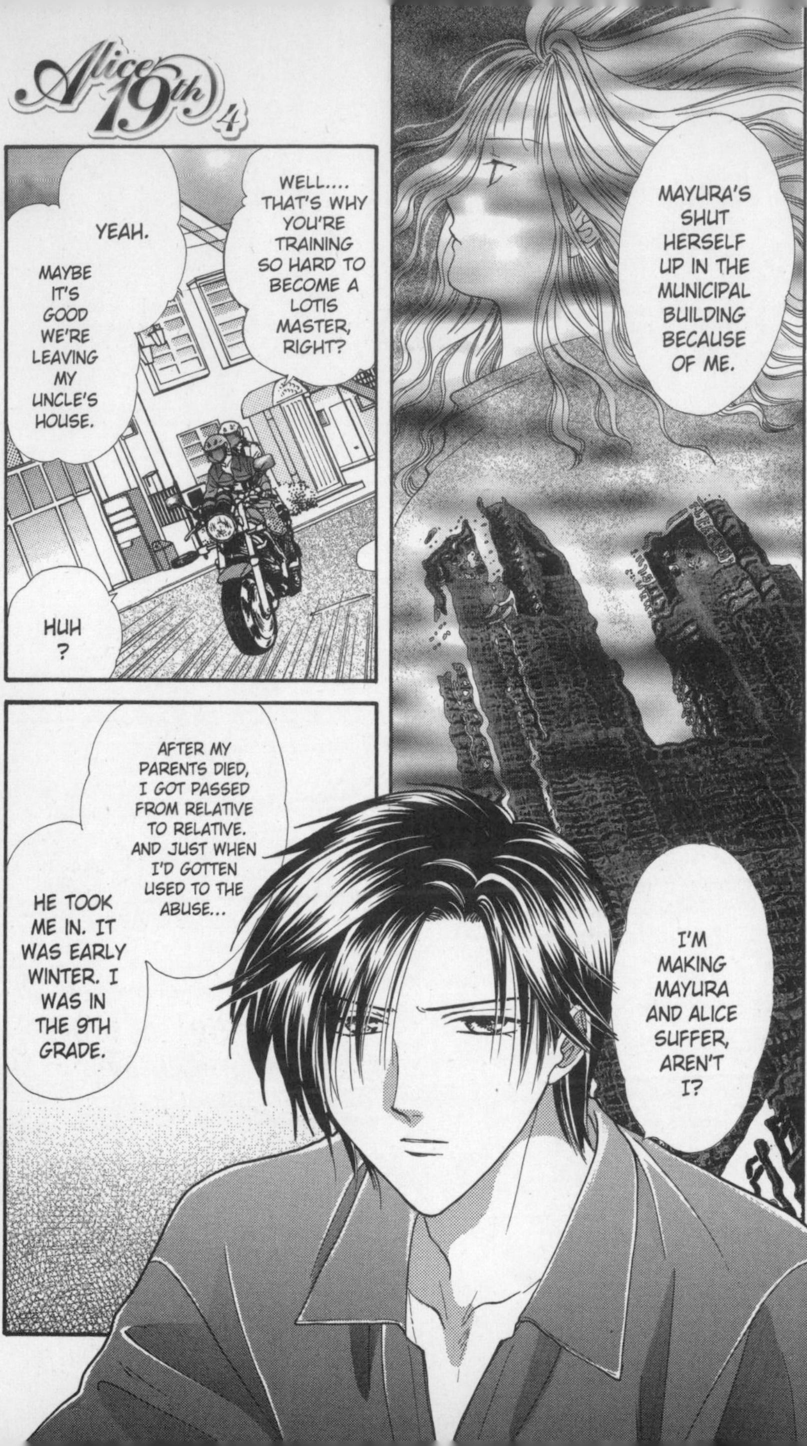
MAYURA'S SHUT HERSELF UP IN THE MUNICIPAL BUILDING BECAUSE OF ME.
I'M MAKING MAYURA AND ALICE SUFFER, AREN'T I?
WELL.... THAT'S WHY YOU'RE TRAINING SO HARD TO BECOME A LOTIS MASTER, RIGHT?
YEAH.
MAYBE IT'S GOOD WE'RE LEAVING MY UNCLE'S HOUSE.
HUH?
AFTER MY PARENTS DIED, I GOT PASSED FROM RELATIVE TO RELATIVE. AND JUST WHEN I'D GOTTEN USED TO THE ABUSE...
HE TOOK ME IN. IT WAS EARLY WINTER. I WAS IN THE 9TH GRADE.

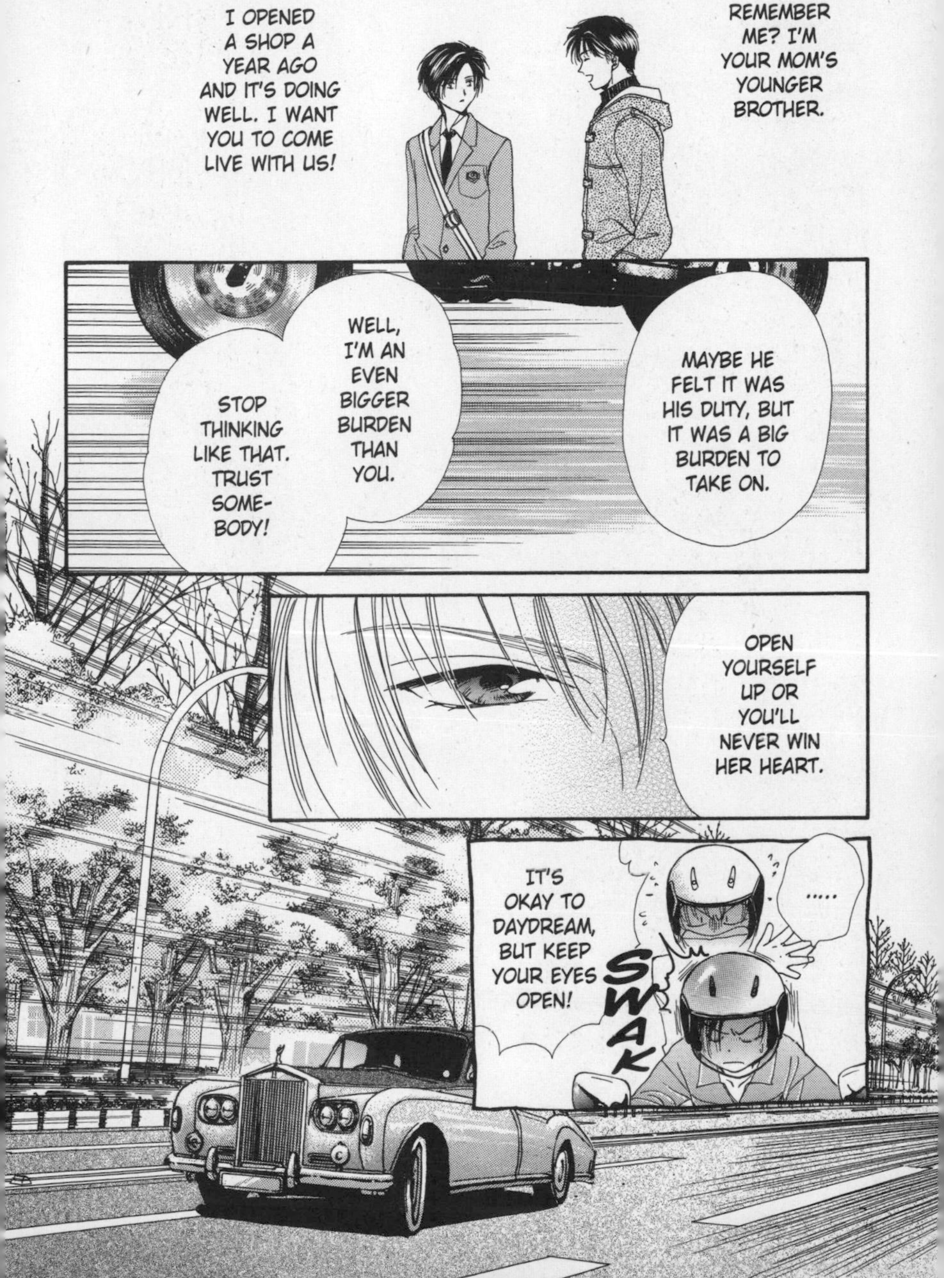
REMEMBER ME? I'M YOUR MOM'S YOUNGER BROTHER.
I OPENED A SHOP A YEAR AGO AND IT'S DOING WELL. I WANT YOU TO COME LIVE WITH US!
MAYBE HE FELT IT WAS HIS DUTY, BUT IT WAS A BIG BURDEN TO TAKE ON.
WELL, I'M AN EVEN BIGGER BURDEN THAN YOU.
STOP THINKING LIKE THAT. TRUST SOMEBODY!
OPEN YOURSELF UP OR YOU'LL NEVER WIN HER HEART.
.....
SWAK
IT'S OKAY TO DAYDREAM, BUT KEEP YOUR EYES OPEN!

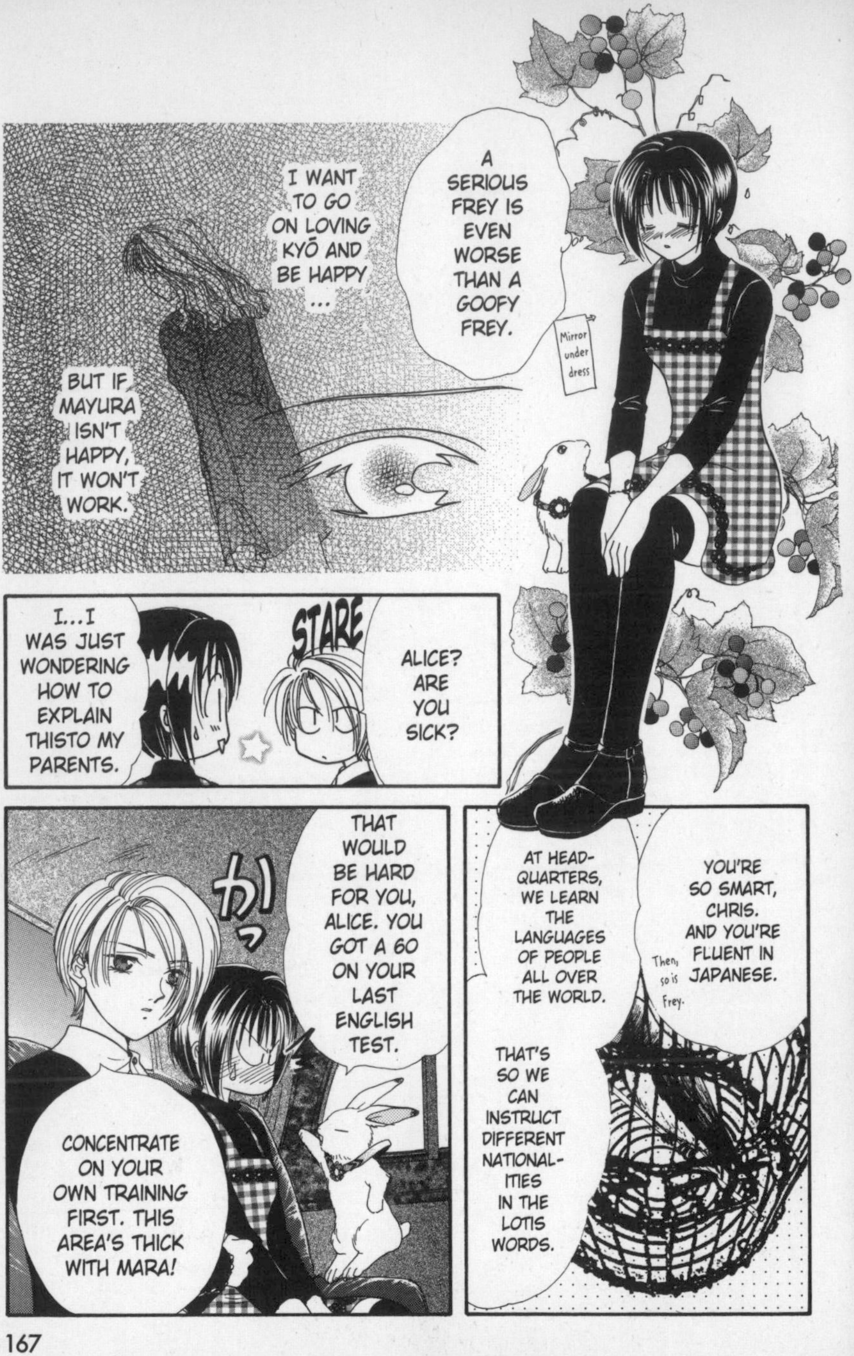
A SERIOUS FREY IS EVEN WORSE THAN A GOOFY FREY.
Mirror under dress
I WANT TO GO ON LOVING KYŌ AND BE HAPPY ...
BUT IF MAYURA ISN'T HAPPY, IT WON'T WORK.
STARE
ALICE? ARE YOU SICK?
I...I WAS JUST WONDERING HOW TO EXPLAIN THISTO MY PARENTS.
YOU'RE SO SMART, CHRIS. AND YOU'RE FLUENT IN JAPANESE.
Then, so is Frey.
AT HEAD-QUARTERS, WE LEARN THE LANGUAGES OF PEOPLE ALL OVER THE WORLD.
THAT'S SO WE CAN INSTRUCT DIFFERENT NATIONAL-ITIES IN THE LOTIS WORDS.
THAT WOULD BE HARD FOR YOU, ALICE. YOU GOT A 60 ON YOUR LAST ENGLISH TEST.
かっ
CONCENTRATE ON YOUR OWN TRAINING FIRST. THIS AREA'S THICK WITH MARA!

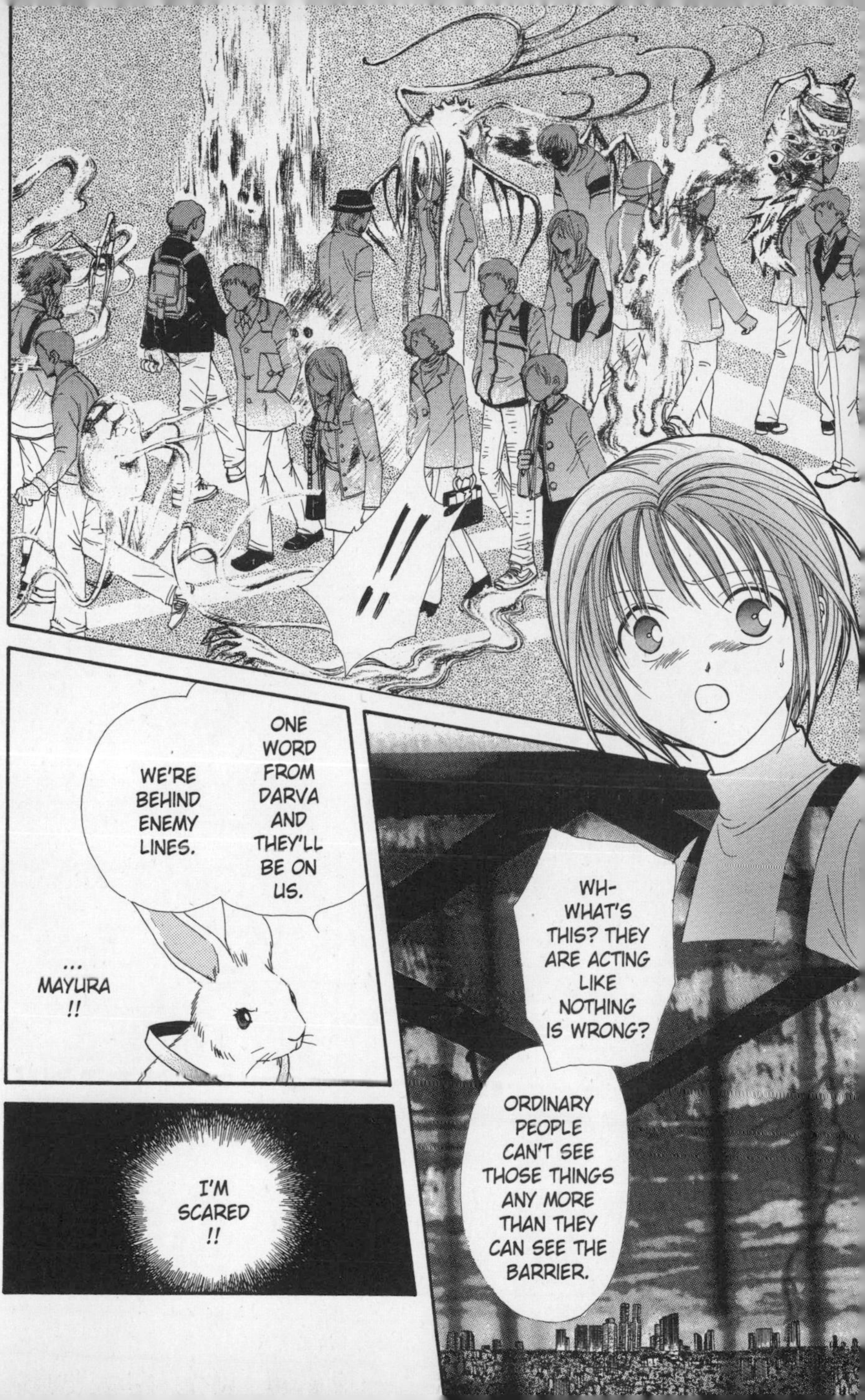

WH- WHAT'S THIS? THEY ARE ACTING LIKE NOTHING IS WRONG?
ORDINARY PEOPLE CAN'T SEE THOSE THINGS ANY MORE THAN THEY CAN SEE THE BARRIER.
ONE WORD FROM DARVA AND THEY'LL BE ON US.
WE'RE BEHIND ENEMY LINES.
... MAYURA !!
I'M SCARED !!

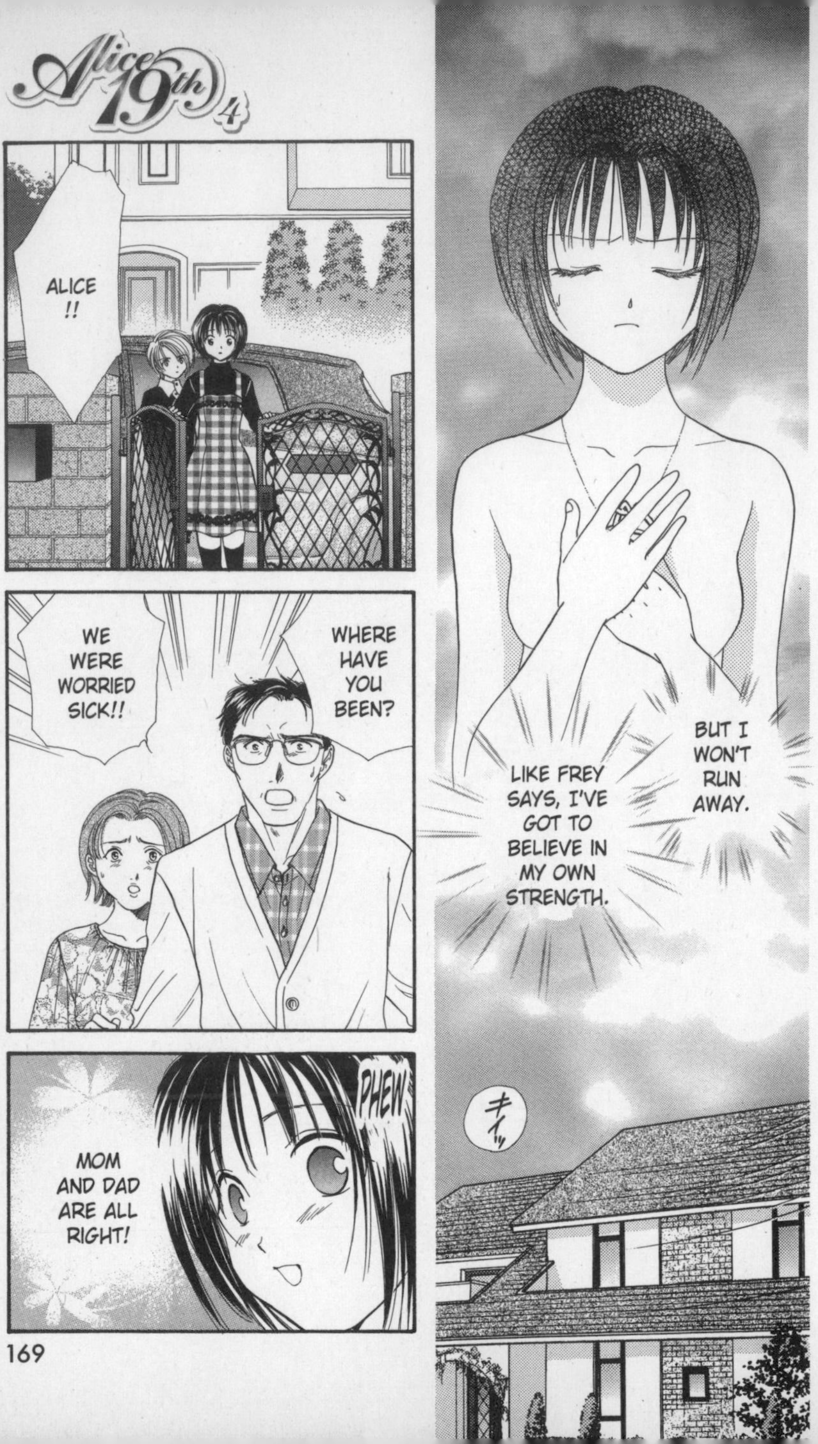
BUT I WON'T RUN AWAY.
LIKE FREY SAYS, I'VE GOT TO BELIEVE IN MY OWN STRENGTH.
キィッ
ALICE !!
WHERE HAVE YOU BEEN?
WE WERE WORRIED SICK!!
PHEW
MOM AND DAD ARE ALL RIGHT!

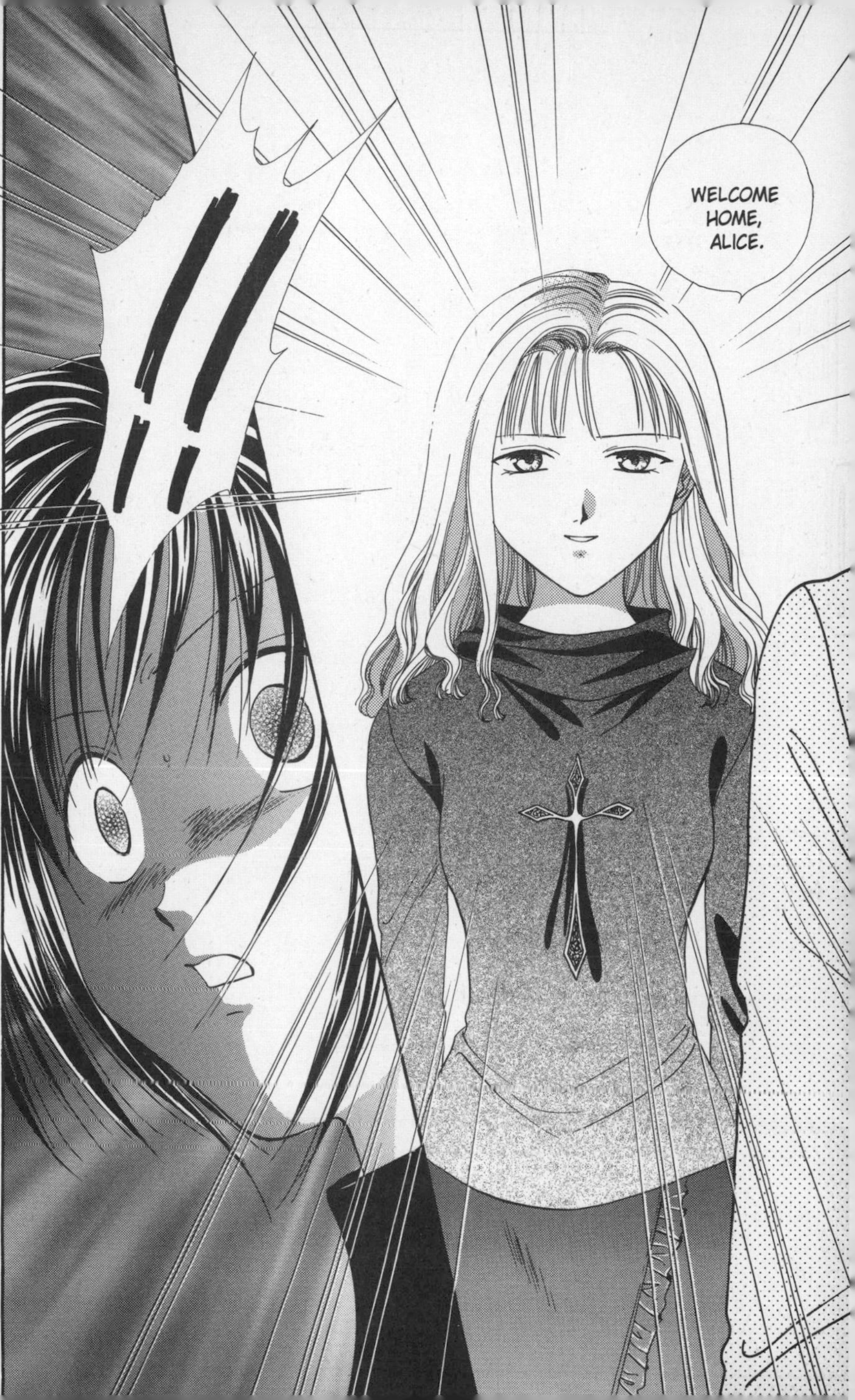
WELCOME HOME, ALICE.

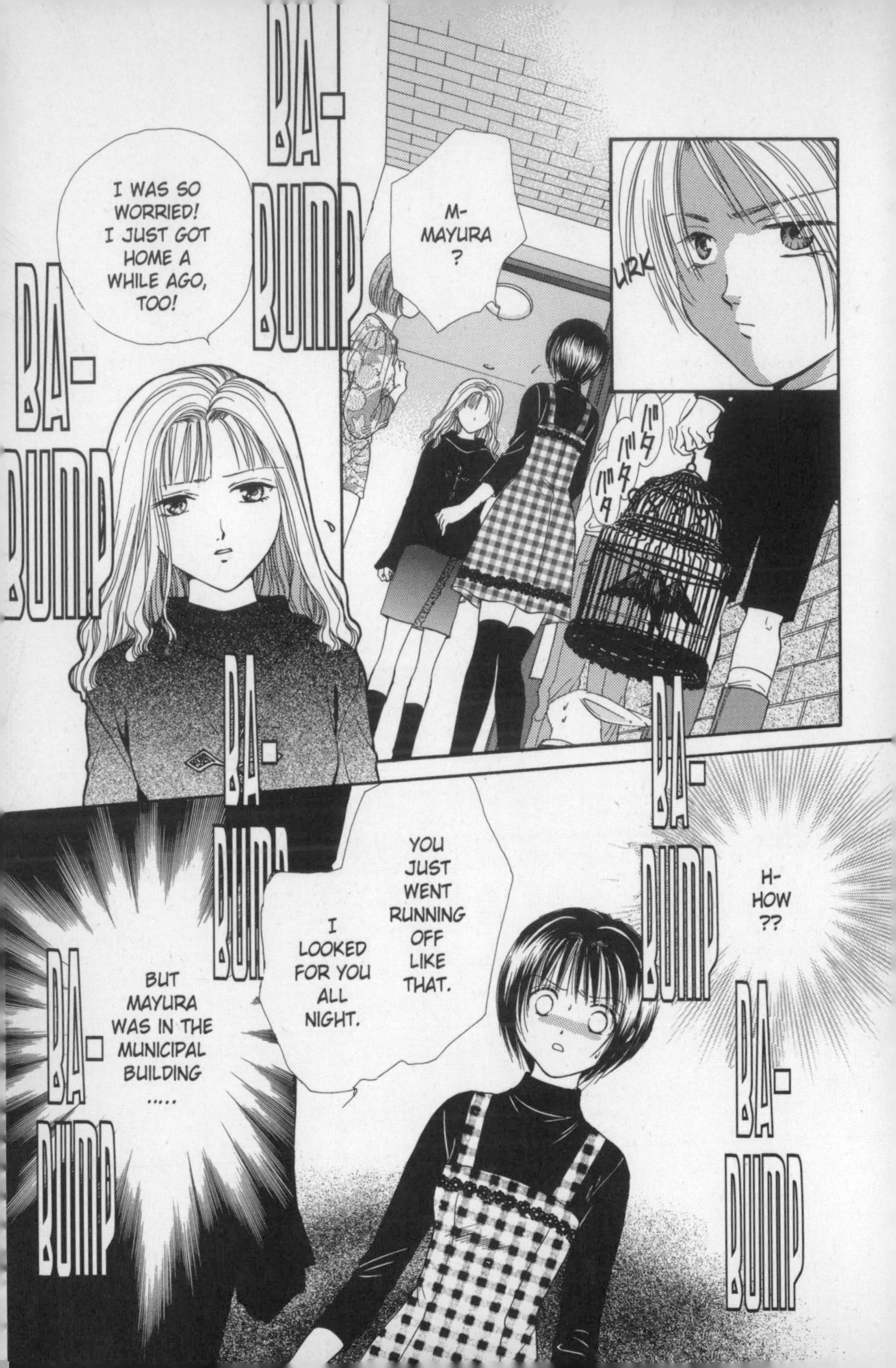
URK
M-MAYURA?
バタバタバタ
BA-BUMP
I WAS SO WORRIED! I JUST GOT HOME A WHILE AGO, TOO!
BA-BUMP
BA-BUMP
BA-BUMP
H-HOW??
BA-BUMP
YOU JUST WENT RUNNING OFF LIKE THAT.
I LOOKED FOR YOU ALL NIGHT.
BA-BUMP
BUT MAYURA WAS IN THE MUNICIPAL BUILDING .....
BA-BUMP

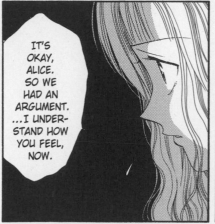

IT'S OKAY, ALICE. SO WE HAD AN ARGUMENT. ...I UNDERSTAND HOW YOU FEEL, NOW.

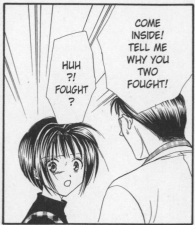

HUH?! FOUGHT?

COME INSIDE! TELL ME WHY YOU TWO FOUGHT!

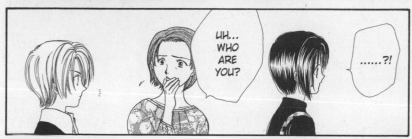

UH... WHO ARE YOU?

......?!

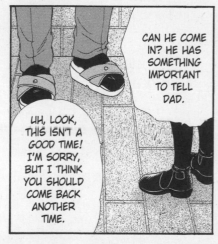

CAN HE COME IN? HE HAS SOMETHING IMPORTANT TO TELL DAD.

UH, LOOK, THIS ISN'T A GOOD TIME! I'M SORRY, BUT I THINK YOU SHOULD COME BACK ANOTHER TIME.

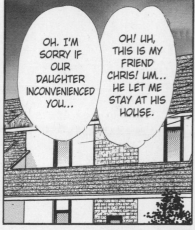

OH. I'M SORRY IF OUR DAUGHTER INCONVENIENCED YOU...

OH! UH, THIS IS MY FRIEND CHRIS! UM... HE LET ME STAY AT HIS HOUSE.

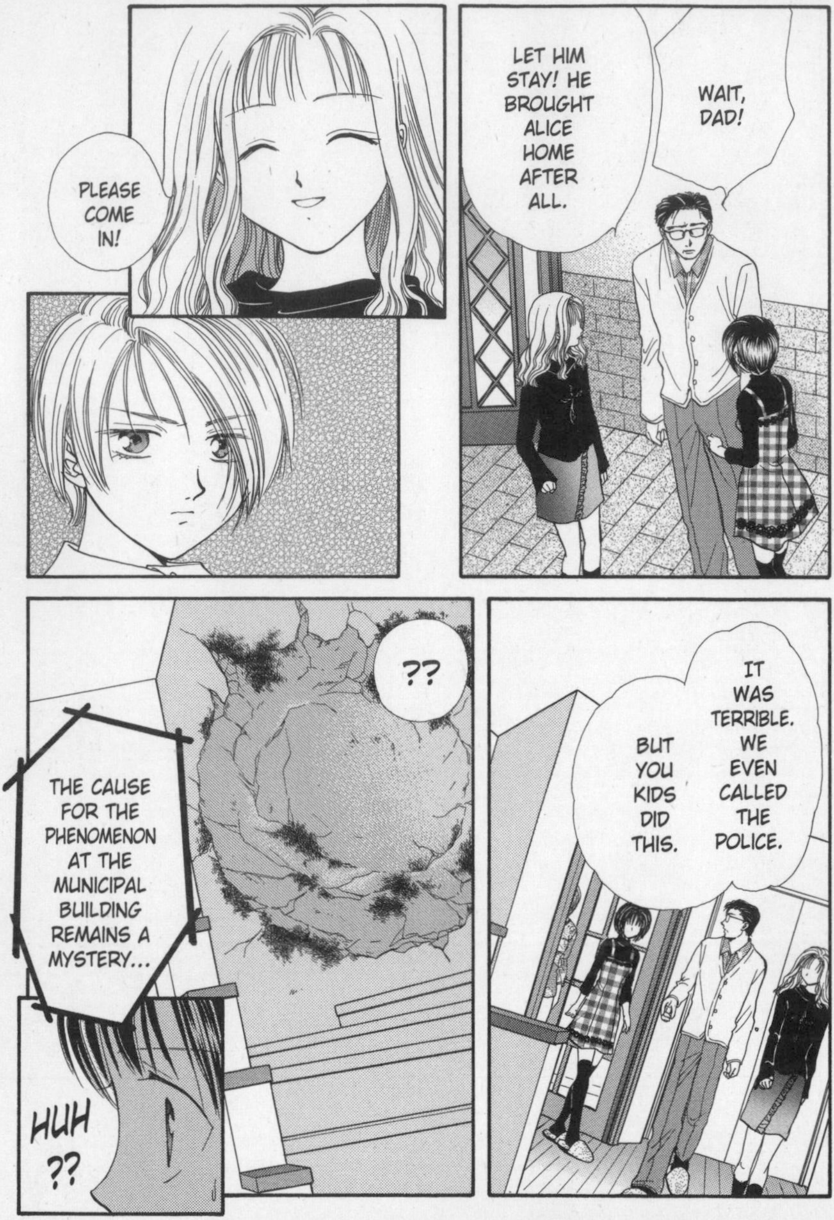
WAIT, DAD!
LET HIM STAY! HE BROUGHT ALICE HOME AFTER ALL.
PLEASE COME IN!
IT WAS TERRIBLE. WE EVEN CALLED THE POLICE.
BUT YOU KIDS DID THIS.
??
THE CAUSE FOR THE PHENOMENON AT THE MUNICIPAL BUILDING REMAINS A MYSTERY...
HUH ??

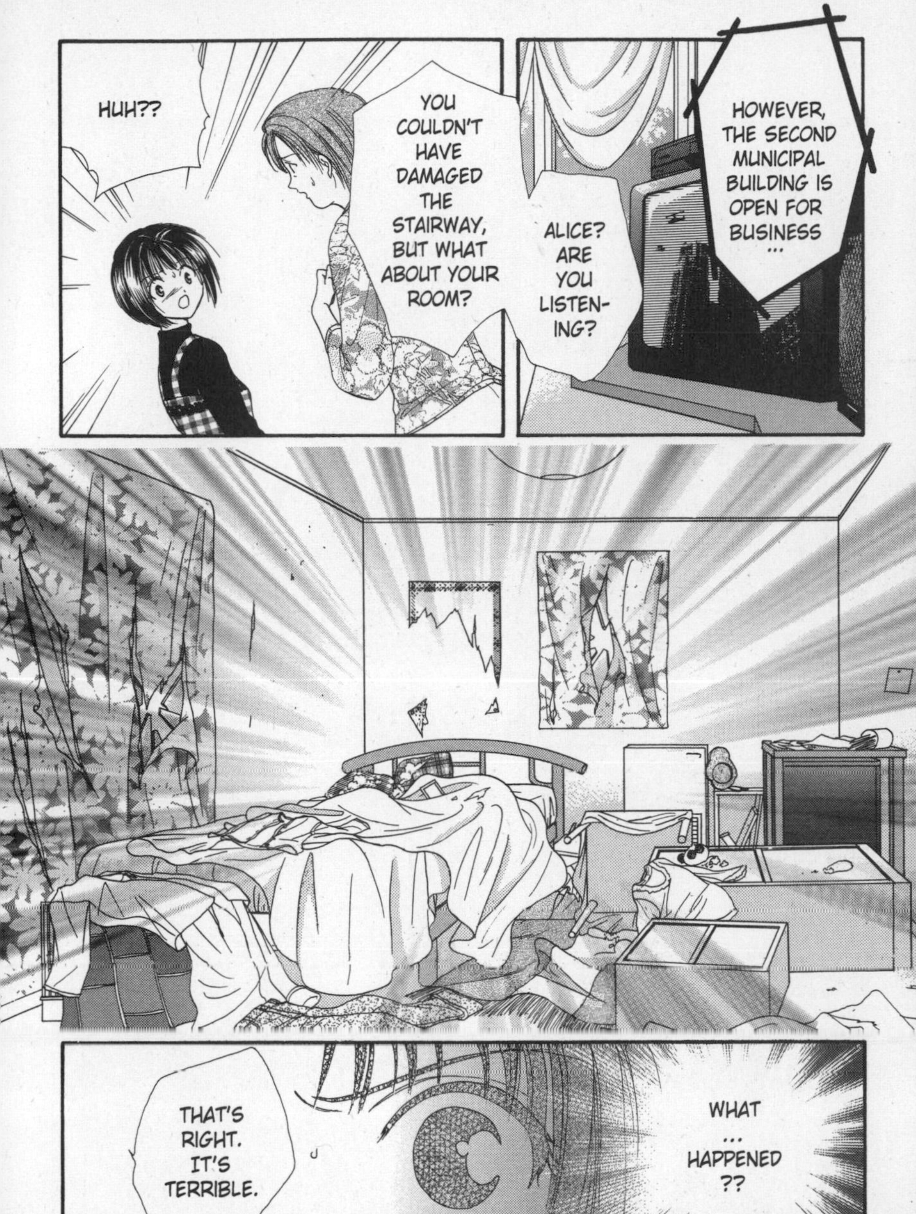
HOWEVER, THE SECOND MUNICIPAL BUILDING IS OPEN FOR BUSINESS ...
ALICE? ARE YOU LISTENING?
YOU COULDN'T HAVE DAMAGED THE STAIRWAY, BUT WHAT ABOUT YOUR ROOM?
HUH??
WHAT ... HAPPENED ??
THAT'S RIGHT. IT'S TERRIBLE.

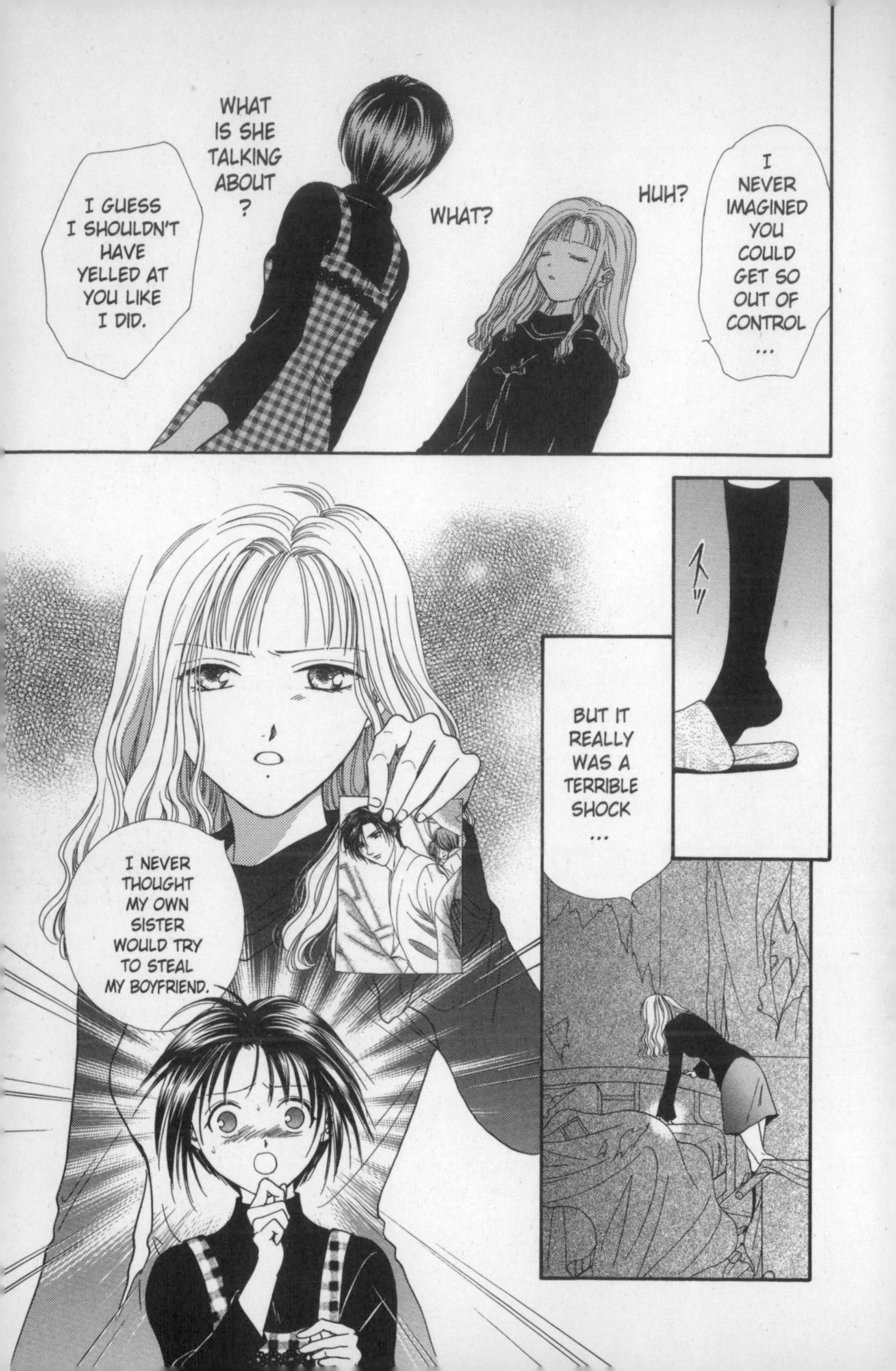

I NEVER IMAGINED YOU COULD GET SO OUT OF CONTROL ...
HUH?
WHAT?
WHAT IS SHE TALKING ABOUT ?
I GUESS I SHOULDN'T HAVE YELLED AT YOU LIKE I DID.
スッ
BUT IT REALLY WAS A TERRIBLE SHOCK ...
I NEVER THOUGHT MY OWN SISTER WOULD TRY TO STEAL MY BOYFRIEND.

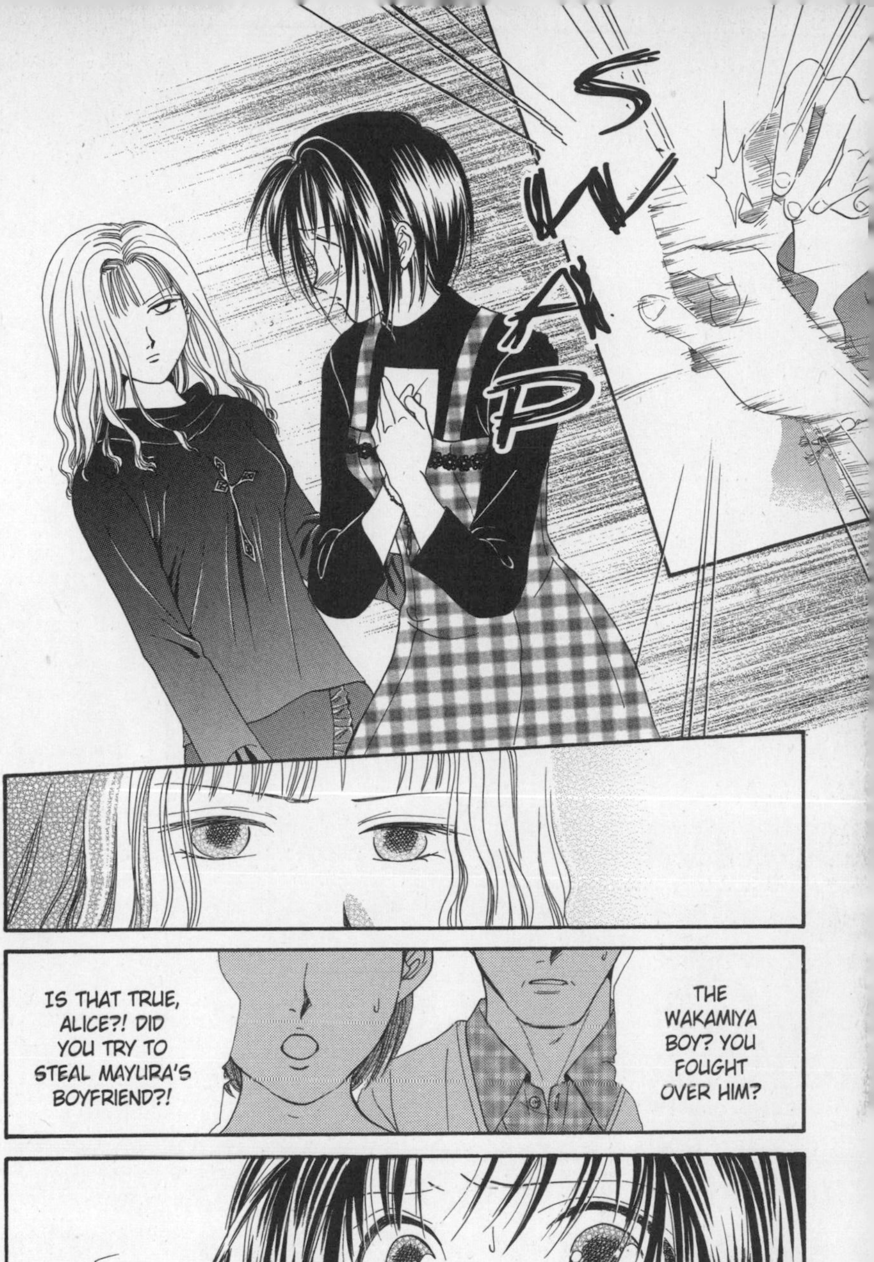
SWAP
THE WAKAMIYA BOY? YOU FOUGHT OVER HIM?
IS THAT TRUE, ALICE?! DID YOU TRY TO STEAL MAYURA'S BOYFRIEND?!

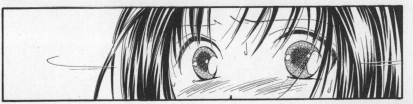

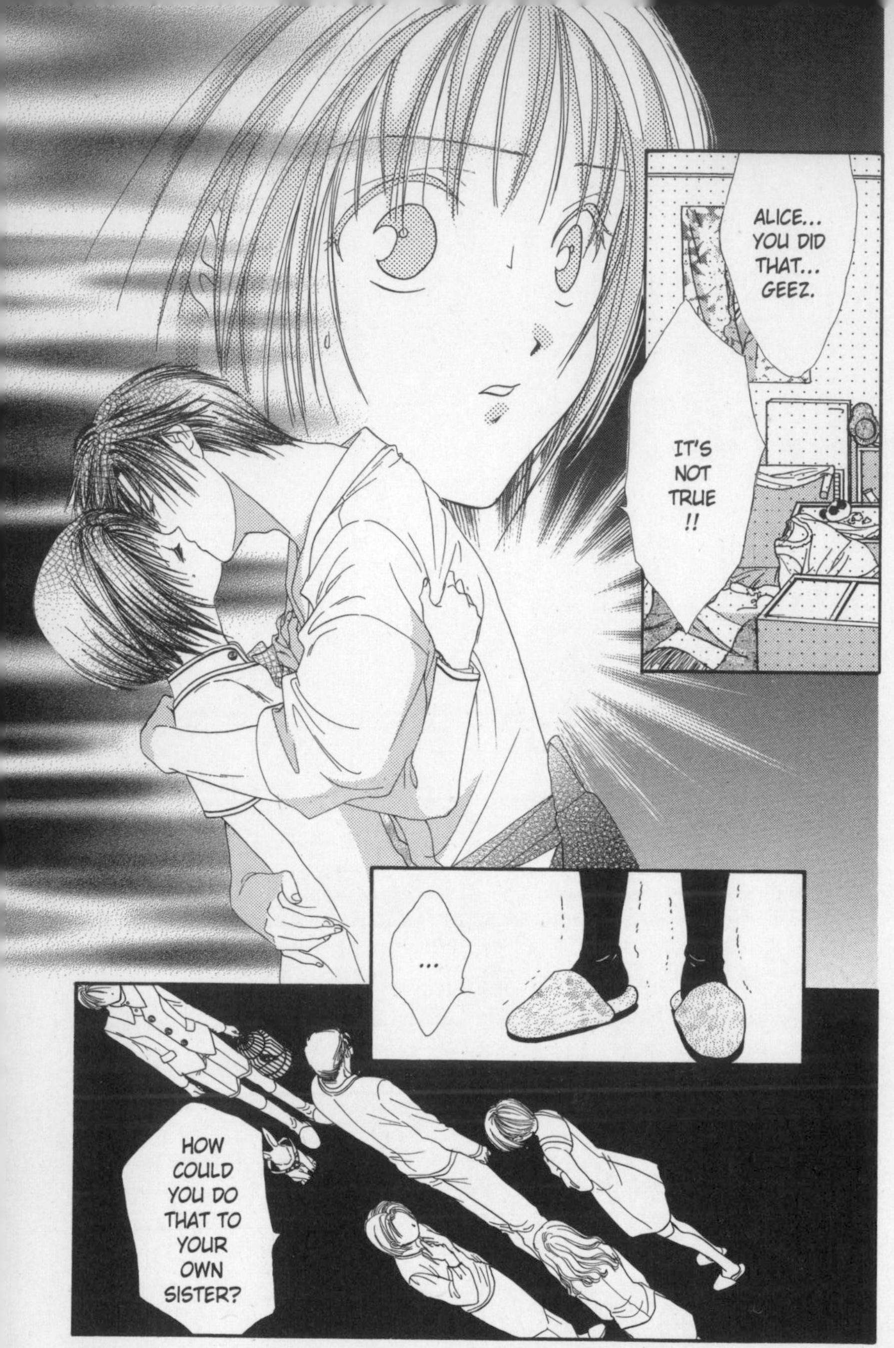
ALICE... YOU DID THAT... GEEZ.
IT'S NOT TRUE !!
...
HOW COULD YOU DO THAT TO YOUR OWN SISTER?

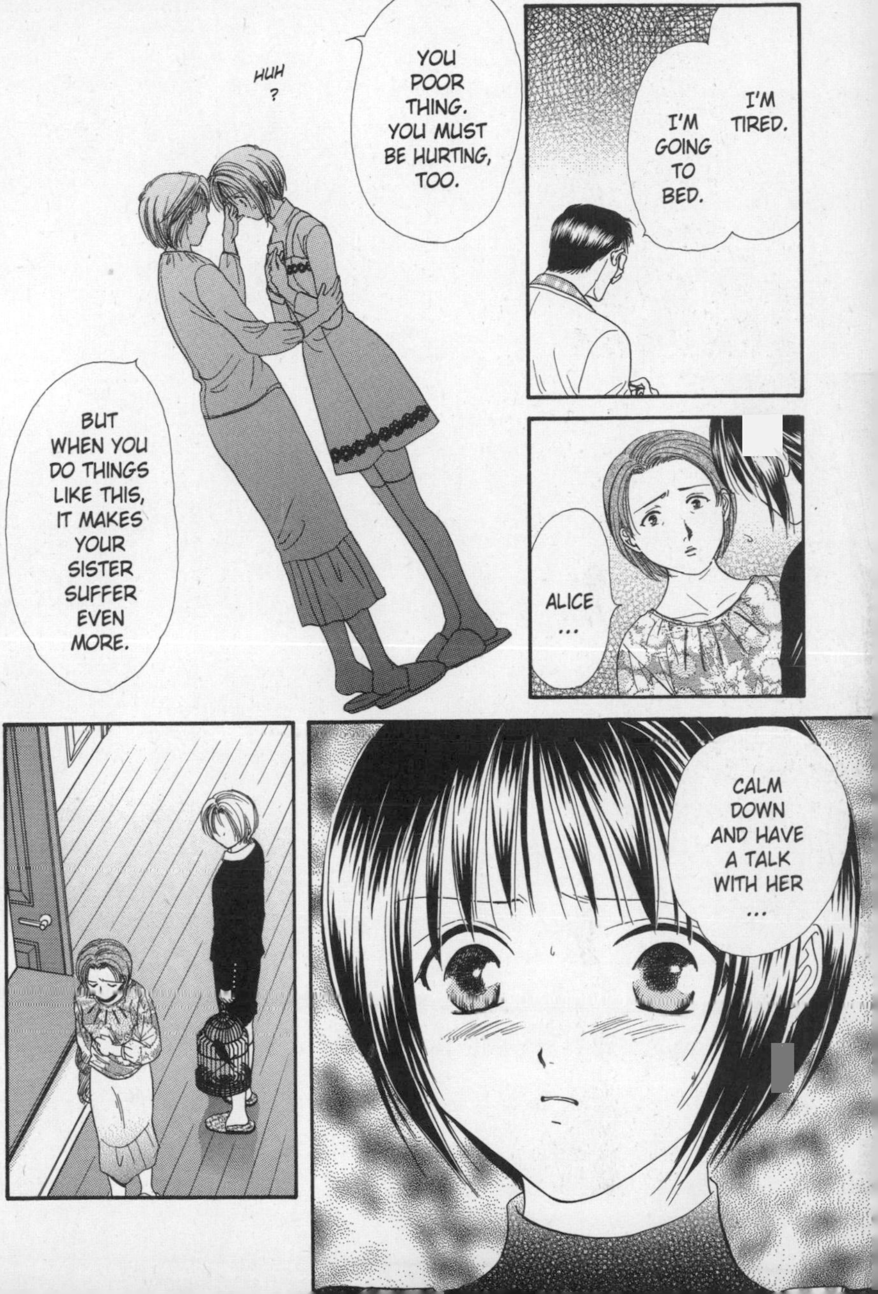
I'M TIRED.
I'M GOING TO BED.
ALICE ...
YOU POOR THING. YOU MUST BE HURTING, TOO.
HUH ?
BUT WHEN YOU DO THINGS LIKE THIS, IT MAKES YOUR SISTER SUFFER EVEN MORE.
CALM DOWN AND HAVE A TALK WITH HER ...

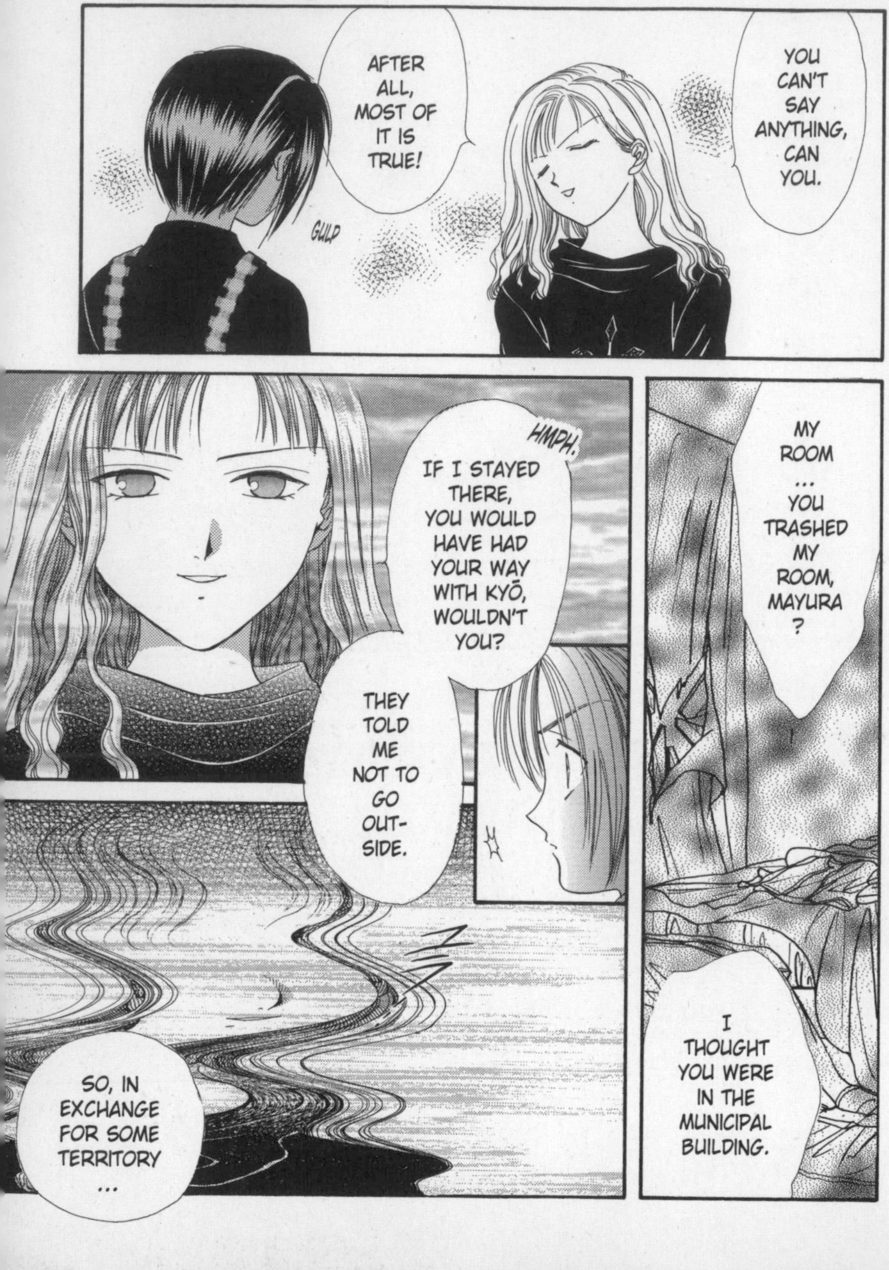
YOU CAN'T SAY ANYTHING, CAN YOU.
AFTER ALL, MOST OF IT IS TRUE!
GULP
MY ROOM ... YOU TRASHED MY ROOM, MAYURA?
I THOUGHT YOU WERE IN THE MUNICIPAL BUILDING.
HMPH.
IF I STAYED THERE, YOU WOULD HAVE HAD YOUR WAY WITH KYŌ, WOULDN'T YOU?
THEY TOLD ME NOT TO GO OUT-SIDE.
SO, IN EXCHANGE FOR SOME TERRITORY ...

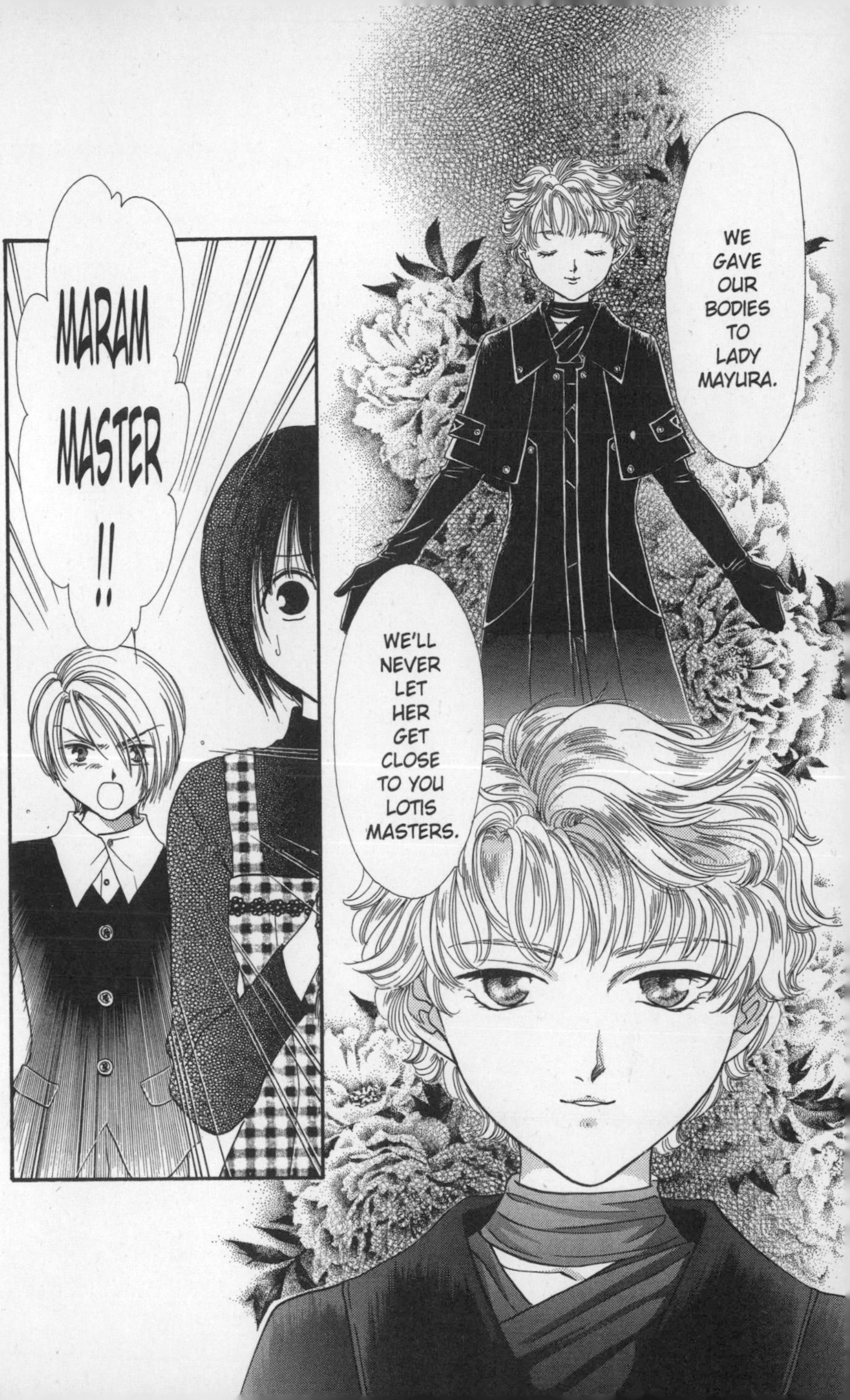
WE GAVE OUR BODIES TO LADY MAYURA.
WE'LL NEVER LET HER GET CLOSE TO YOU LOTIS MASTERS.
MARAM MASTER !!

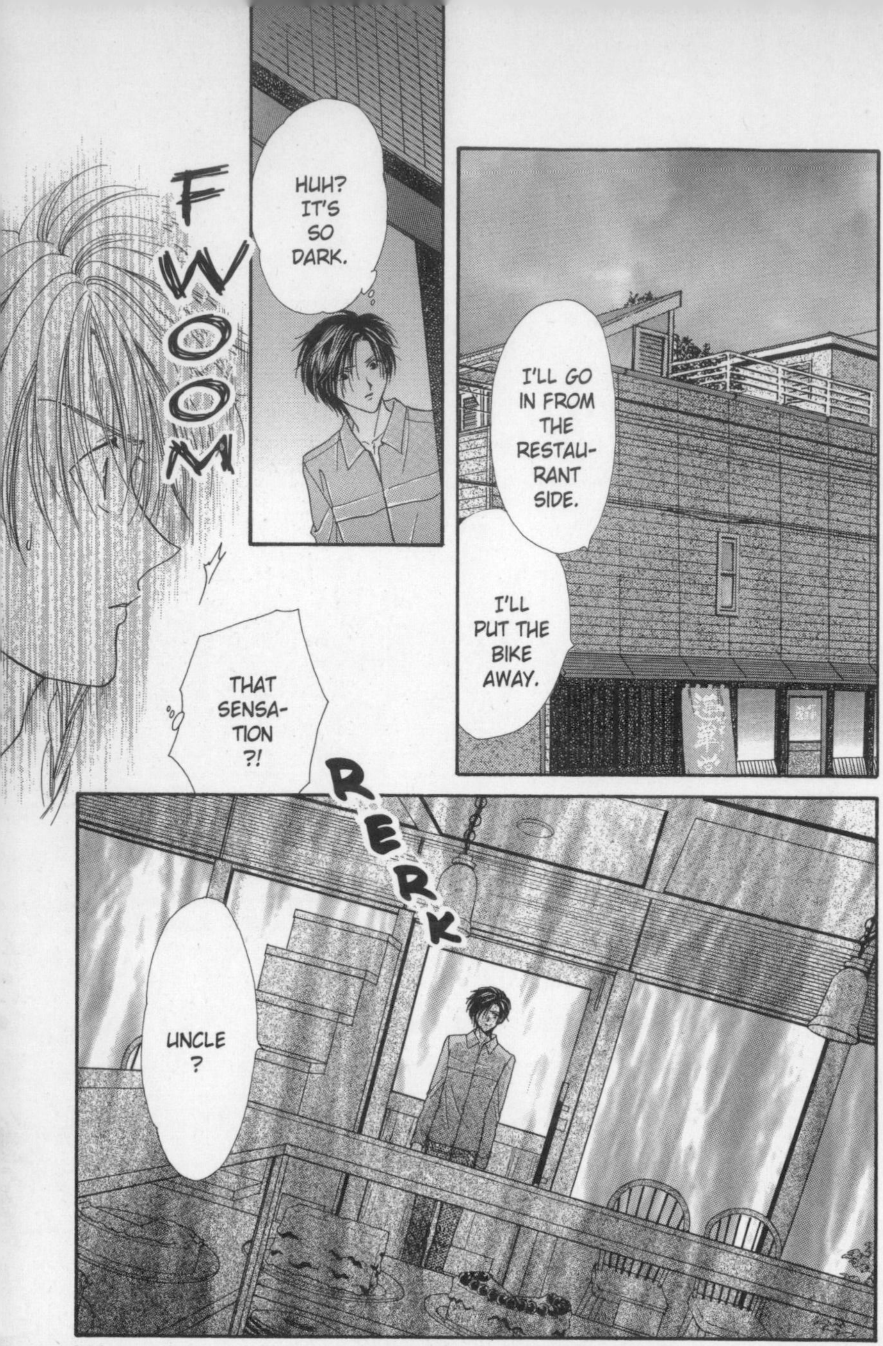
I'LL GO IN FROM THE RESTAU-RANT SIDE.
I'LL PUT THE BIKE AWAY.
HUH? IT'S SO DARK.
FWOOM
THAT SENSA-TION ?!
RERK
UNCLE ?

TO BE CONTINUED IN VOLUME 5

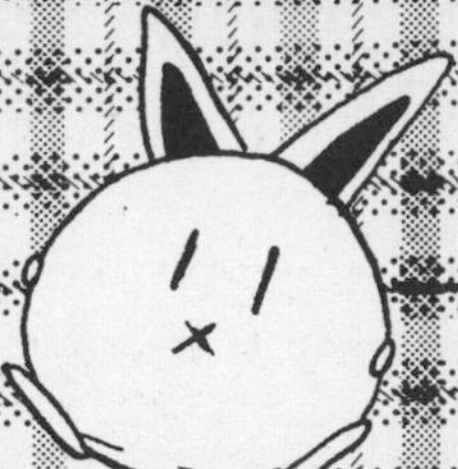

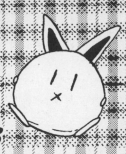

NYOZEKA'S MINI-MINI LOTIS CLASS

NYOZEKA EXPLAINS THE LOTIS USED BY ALICE AND THE OTHER LOTIS MASTERS!

NUMBER 1

RANGU

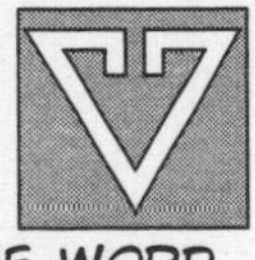

THIS IS THE WORD ALICE LEARNED BY SAVING NYOZEKA FROM BEING SQUISHED IN AN INTERSECTION. RANGU, THE 19TH LOTIS WORD, MEANS "COURAGE," AND "ACTION."

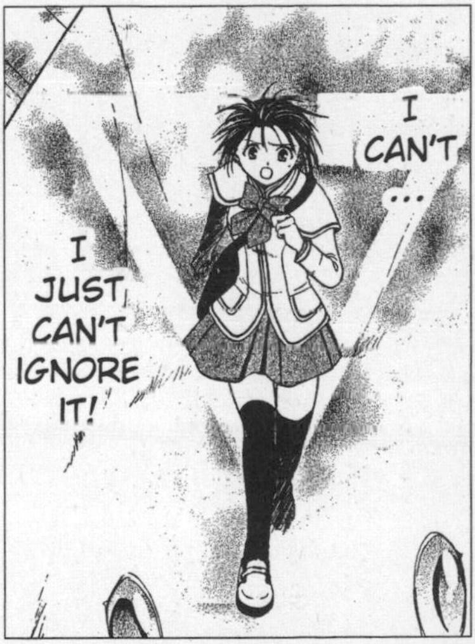
I CAN'T ...
I JUST CAN'T IGNORE IT!

KARA

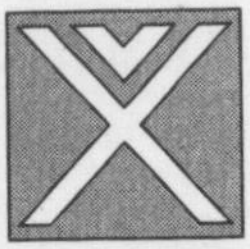

NUMBER 2

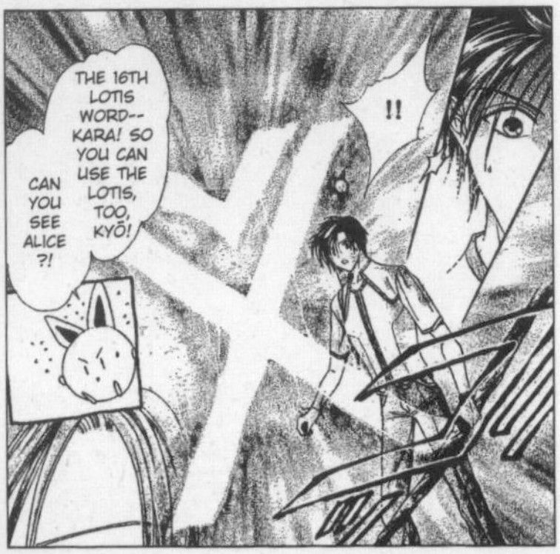
!!
THE 16TH LOTIS WORD-- KARA! SO YOU CAN USE THE LOTIS, TOO, KYŌ!
CAN YOU SEE ALICE ?!

THE FIRST LOTIS WORD KYŌ LEARNED WAS KARA WHICH MEANS "PROTECT," AND "COVER." IT'S USED TO PROTECT ONESELF FROM ENEMY ATTACKS. KYŌ MASTERED IT WHEN CHASING FREY, WHO HAD ABDUCTED ALICE.

NUMBER 3

VIMUKU

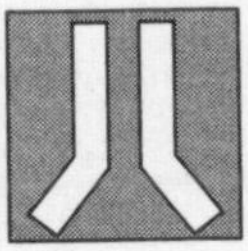

THE SECOND LOTIS KYŌ LEARNED. THE 23RD LOTIS, IT MEANS "RELEASE," AND "WIND." USED TO OPEN CLOSED DOORS. KYŌ USED IT TO OPEN THE DOOR TO OISHI'S HEART WHEN SHE WAS POSSESSED BY MARA.

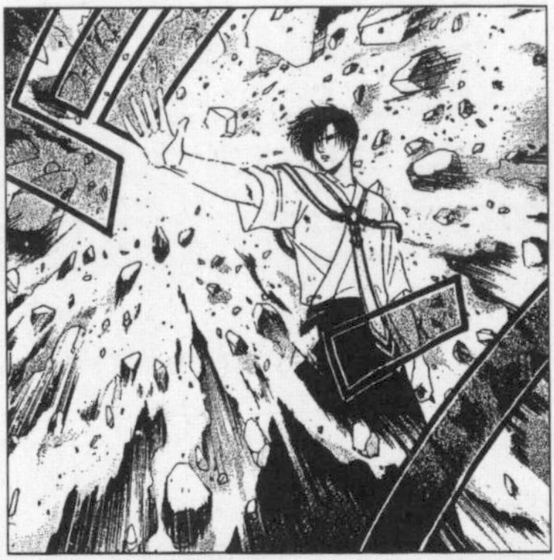

YUNA NUMBER 4

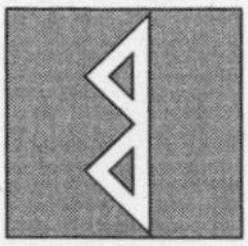

THE SECOND LOTIS WORD ALICE MASTERED WAS YUNA WHICH IS THE 1ST LOTIS AND MEANS "AFFECTION," "LOVE," ETC. USED IN OISHI'S INNER HEART TO RELEASE HER FROM MARA POSSESSION.

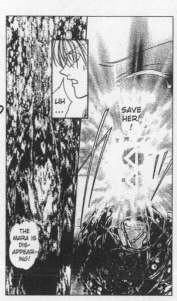

UH...

SAVE HER! !

THE MARA IS DISAPPEARING!

NUMBER 5

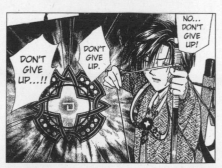

DON'T GIVE UP...!!

DON'T GIVE UP.

DON'T GIVE UP.

NO... DON'T GIVE UP!

RUTA

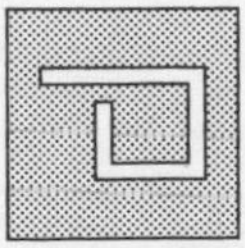

THE THIRD LOTIS WORD KYŌ MASTERED WAS THE 11TH LOTIS WORD THAT MEANS "PERSEVERE," "WILL," ETC. KYŌ LEARNED IT WHEN HE FOUGHT THE BYOMA, THE DEMON OF SICKNESS.

RIIYA

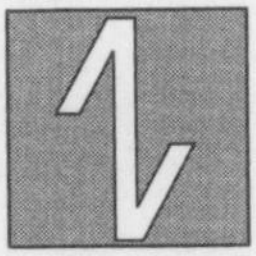

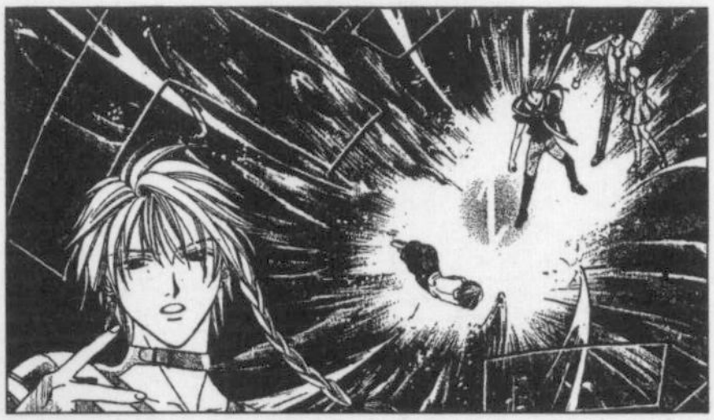

NUMBER 6

THE 7TH LOTIS MEANING "DEFENSE," "ELUDE," AND "SHIELD." NEITHER ALICE NOR KYŌ HAS MASTERED THIS LOTIS YET, BUT FREY USED IT IN INNER HEART TO PROTECT ALICE AND THE OTHERS FROM A MARA ATTACK.

NUMBER 7

JIVA

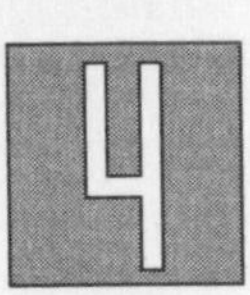

THE FOURTEENTH LOTIS MEANING "RECOVERY," "HEAL," FREY USED IT TO DESTROY THE BYOMA, AND CHRIS USED IT TO CURE ALICE.

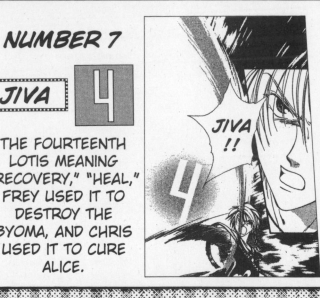

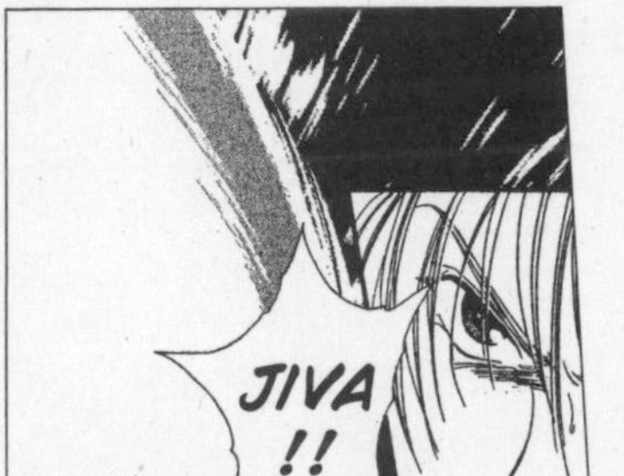
JIVA !!

Glossary of Sound Effects, Signs, and other Miscellaneous Notes

Each entry includes: the location, indicated by page number and panel number (so 3.1 means page 3, panel number 1); the phonetic romanization of the original Japanese; and our English "translation"—we offer as close an English equivalent as we can.

10.1 ——FX: bata, bata, bata, bata (tomp tomp tomp tomp)

10.2 ——FX: dosa (wump)

15.2 ——FX: ton, ton, ton (tmp, tmp, tmp)

18.1 ——FX: gatan! (bang!)

21.1 ——FX: gon, gon (bonng, bonng)

22.4 ——FX: tash (tmp)

22.5 ——FX: gyu (krk)

24.2 ——FX: para para (pit pit)

25.4 ——FX: saa (ksssh)

29.1 ——FX: zu (kii)

29.4 ——FX: ha! (Ooh!)

30.2 ——FX: zukun zukun (wobble wobble)

30.3 ——FX: kyu (krk)

32.2 ——FX: gaku (thunk)

32.3 ——FX: za (ksssh)

35.1 ——FX: za (ksssh)

35.2 ——FX: batan (wham)

36.2 ——FX: dobo dobo dobo (blub blub blub)

36.3 ——FX: zashi (kwussh)

38.2 ——FX: uro uro (tmp tmp)

38.4——FX: zun (zwoon)

39.2——FX: gacha gacha (rattle rattle)

39.3——FX: don don (bang bang)

40.5——FX: biku! (gasp!)

41.2——FX: basha (splash)

41.4——FX: sha (kwussh)

43.3——FX: sha (kwussh)

45.1——FX: za (ksssh)

45.2——FX: zuru (shmumm)

46.2——FX: za (ksssh)

47.6——FX: ton ton ton (bam bam bam)

48.1——FX: kacha (woosh)

49.2——FX: gashan (bam)

50.1——FX: kacha (woosh)

51.2——FX: su … (Heh …)

51.3——FX: fon! (Fwoom!)

53.5——FX: bata bata (wak wak)

56.3——FX: doki (blink)

56.4——FX: doki (blink)

56.5——FX: pari (swp)

57.1——FX: muga (smff)

57.3——FX: patan (klak)

60.4——FX: ga! (swup!)

61.2——FX: gu! (krusp!)

65.1——FX: pita (tmp)

67.4——FX: batan (wham)

67.5 ——FX: gyu (wssh)

68.4——FX: doki (blink)

71.3——FX: su... (tup ...)

76.5 ——FX: koso koso koso (fsh fsh fsh)

76.6 ——FX: don (wump)

77.5——FX: su (tmp)

85.4 ——FX: koto (klak)

87.2——FX: zuzu (thrrmmb)

94.1——FX: su (tmp)

94.4 ——FX: huh? (are?)

95.1——FX: furu furu (shake shake)

96.1 ——FX: dorun dorun dorun (vroom vroom vroom)

96.2 ——FX: dorun! (vroom!)

104.2——FX: bote (fwash)

108.4——FX: muku, muku (shuff, shuff)

111.3——FX: gyu...(tup...)

112.1——FX: gôn (Bong)

114.4 ——FX: ka (thoom)

115.1——FX: ka! (thoom!)

115.1——FX: hyu (fwoo)

115.3——FX: za za (ka-boom)

118.1——FX: fô (kreek)

120.3——FX: batsu (fwap)

122.1 ——FX: do (swomp)

131.4——FX: patan (klomp)

136.1 ——FX: zuka zuka zuka zuka (tomp tomp tomp tomp)

138.1 ——FX: gata (klak)

140.3 ——FX: patata (fwap)

145.1 ——FX: ha! (oh!)

148.1 ——FX: biku! (urk!)

149.1 ——FX: su (shhh)

152.4——FX: pi pi (beep beep)

157.1 ——FX: kach (klak)

159.6——FX: dochi (wump)

162.2——FX: fu (phew)

162.3——FX: biku (gasp)

163.2——FX:– cha (woosh)

164.3——FX: ba ba baaa (vreem vreem vreeeem)

167.5 ——FX: ka (hmph)

169.1 ——FX: kii (screech)

175.2 ——FX: su (suff)

179.5 ——FX: yura (wrerg)

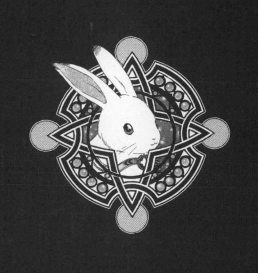

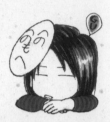

About the Author:

Yû Watase was born on March 5 in a town near Osaka, Japan, and she was raised there before moving to Tokyo to follow her dream of creating manga. In the decade since her debut short story, *PAJAMA DE OJAMA* ("An Intrusion in Pajamas"), she has produced more than 50 compiled volumes of short stories and continuing series. Her latest series, *ZETTAI KARESHI* ("He'll Be My Boyfriend"), is currently running in the anthology magazine *SHÔJO COMIC*. Watase's long-running horror/romance story *Ceres: Celestial Legend.* and her most recent completed series, *ALICE 19TH*, are now available in North America, published by VIZ. She loves science fiction, fantasy and comedy.

Editor Remarks:

Alice 19th has proved to be another successful hit from the talented manga-ka, Yû Watase in the States. The new novel has been topping charts since its first release back in November 2003. The combination of Watase's prevalent US fan base and the popularity of shôjo are some of the reasons why many people are rushing out to get the latest volume of ***Alice 19th***. Most importantly, Alice Seno's story of self-discovery, strength and love are all the reasons why ***Alice 19th*** has successfully captured the hearts of so many of us.

If you are enjoying this story and you are in the mood for more, here are three manga titles that you should check out:

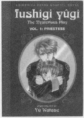

© 1992 Yuu Watase /
Shogakukan, Inc.

Fushigi Yûgi: An innocent girl named Miaka Yûki is magically transported to the Universe of the Four Gods by opening up an ancient book. Helpless and in danger in this ancient world she is rescued by the handsome Tamahome whom she will fall in love with. This magical world is based on an ancient Chinese legend, and is filled with action, romance and love triangles unimaginable. Another fantasy Shôjo brought to you by Yuu Watase!

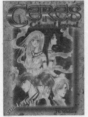

© 1997 Yuu Watase /
Shogakukan, Inc.

Ceres: Celestial Legend: Long ago, a young man fell in love with a heavenly goddess known as Ceres. He was struck so hard by love that he stole her *hagoramo*, a winged cloak, which bound her to Earth for eternity. Soon, they were married and began a family. But Ceres has grown weary of her human life and seeks to return to heaven. After many generations, Aya and Aki, twins who are distant descendants of Ceres, discover they are the guardians that hold the power over her fate.

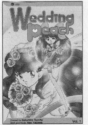

© 1994 Nao Yazawa /
Sukehiro Tomita /
Tenyu / Shogakukan,
Inc.

Wedding Peach: Momoko Hanasaki is a first-year Junior high school student with a major crush on upperclassman and soccer captain, Kazuya Yanagiba. So far, she seems to be an ordinary girl with an ordinary crush, until the day the angel of Limone gave her a compact that transforms her into the demon fighting love angel, Wedding Peach. She joins a troop of girls with special powers to stop evil demons from getting their hands on an ancient keepsake, which Momoko holds in her possession.

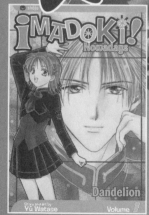

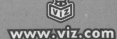

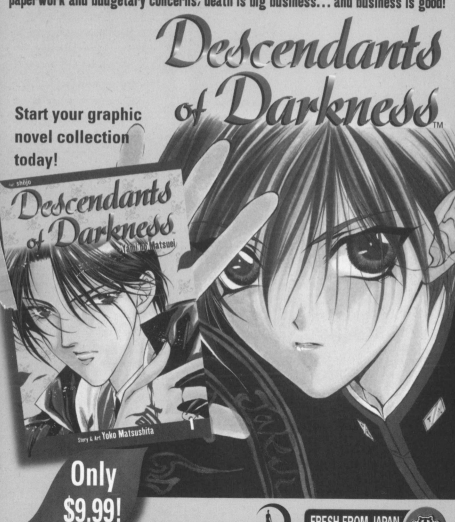

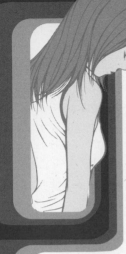
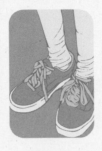
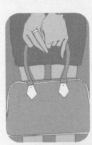

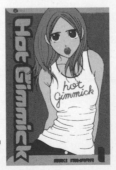
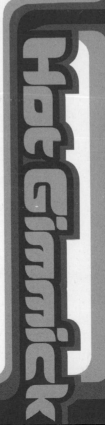

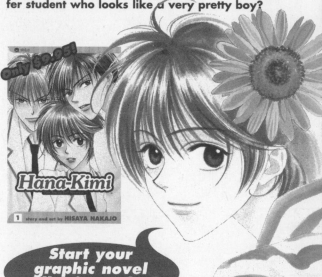

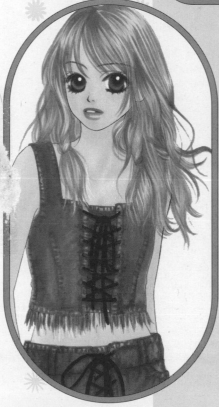
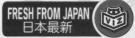

COMPLETE OUR SURVEY AND LET US KNOW WHAT YOU THINK!

☐ Please do NOT send me information about VIZ products, news and events, special offers, or other information.

☐ Please do NOT send me information from VIZ's trusted business partners.

Name: _____

Address: _____

City: _____ State: _____ Zip: _____

E-mail: _____

☐ Male ☐ Female Date of Birth (mm/dd/yyyy): ___/___/_____ (Under 13? Parental consent required)

What race/ethnicity do you consider yourself? (please check one)

☐ Asian/Pacific Islander ☐ Black/African American ☐ Hispanic/Latino

☐ Native American/Alaskan Native ☐ White/Caucasian ☐ Other: _____

What VIZ product did you purchase? (check all that apply and indicate title purchased)

☐ DVD/VHS _____

☐ Graphic Novel _____

☐ Magazines _____

☐ Merchandise _____

Reason for purchase: (check all that apply)

☐ Special offer ☐ Favorite title ☐ Gift

☐ Recommendation ☐ Other _____

Where did you make your purchase? (please check one)

☐ Comic store ☐ Bookstore ☐ Mass/Grocery Store

☐ Newsstand ☐ Video/Video Game Store ☐ Other: _____

☐ Online (site: _____)

What other VIZ properties have you purchased/own? _____

_____

How many anime and/or manga titles have you purchased in the last year? How many were VIZ titles? **(please check one from each column)**

ANIME	MANGA	VIZ
None	None	None
1-4	1-4	
5-10	5-10	
11+	11+	

I find the pricing of VIZ products to be: **(p**

Cheap
Reasonable
Expensive

What genre of manga and anime would you like to see from VIZ? **(please check two)**

Adventure
Comic Strip
Science Fiction
Fighting
Horror
Romance
Fantasy
Sports

What do you think of VIZ's new look?

Love It
It's OK
Hate It
Didn't Notice
No Opinion

Which do you prefer? **(please check one)**

Reading right-to-left
Reading left-to-right

Which do you prefer? **(please check one)**

Sound effects in English
Sound effects in Japanese with English captions
Sound effects in Japanese only with a glossary at the back

THANK YOU! Please send the completed form to:

VIZ

NJW Research
42 Catharine St.
Poughkeepsie, NY 12601

All information provided will be used for internal purposes only. We promise not to sell or otherwise divulge your information.